Miracles or Magic?

André Kole
and AL JANSSEN

HARVEST HOUSE PUBLISHERS
Eugene, Oregon 97402

Except where otherwise indicated, all Scripture quotations in this book are taken from the New American Standard Bible, © The Lockman Foundation 1960, 1962, 1963, 1968, 1971, 1972, 1973, 1975, 1977. Used by permission.

Verses marked KJV are taken from the King James Version of the Bible.

Verses marked TLB are taken from The Living Bible, Copyright © 1971 by Tyndale House Publishers, Wheaton, Illinois. Used by permission.

MIRACLES OR MAGIC?

Copyright © 1984, 1987 by André Kole and Al Janssen
Published by Harvest House Publishers
Eugene, Oregon 97402
(Original edition published by Here's Life Publishers under the title *From Illusion to Reality*.)

Library of Congress Catalog Card Number 86-062975
ISBN 0-89081-579-8

Printed in the United States of America.

Acknowledgments

I would like to acknowledge several sources and give special thanks to a number of people who have contributed significantly to this book.

I would like to thank Ray Hyman, expert on the paranormal and professor of psychology at the University of Oregon, for his input on Chapters 2, 5, and 7. Ray also introduced me to the Committee for the Scientific Investigation of Claims of the Paranormal and their quarterly publication *The Skeptical Inquirer* a number of years ago.

Larry Kusche shared his study of the Bermuda Triangle, and Bill Pitts provided valuable insights for the material on UFO's in Chapter 6.

Dr. William A. Nolen's book, *Healing: A Doctor in Search of a Miracle,* provided significant insight for Chapters 3 and 13.

My thanks also goes to the worldwide network of magicians. My many friends in this profession have kept me abreast of the latest in unusual happenings and their evaluation of the phenomena. I especially wish to thank James Randi for sharing information about his research on faith healing for Chapter 13.

A special thanks to the one who provides her own sparkling magic in my life—my wife, Kathy—and for the encouragement of our children, Robyn, Tim, and Stacey.

Finally, special thanks to my friend Bill Bright, President of Campus Crusade for Christ. His encouragement throughout the years has made for honest pursuit and evaluation of the illusion and reality in the world in which we live. He and the staff of Campus Crusade for Christ have provided many insights for Chapters 8-11 and 14.

Above all, it has been the request for truth from sincere inquirers and audiences throughout the world that has given me the desire to write about these subjects and make the book a reality.

Preface

Nearly every week, thousands of people enjoy "The World of Illusion." In this two-hour stage show I supposedly contact the spirit world, read with my fingers while I'm blindfolded, reveal the mystery of the Bermuda Triangle, and levitate high above the stage. But I am always careful to explain that what is seen is just a very well-done trick or illusion.

Such a performance inevitably leads to questions from the audience. Many wonder about the reality of psychic phenomena. They want to know how prophets like Jeane Dixon predict the future and how mind readers develop their powers of ESP. They inquire about hypnosis, the potential of the human mind, the chances of contacting the dead or the dead returning, faith healing, and the possibility of knowing God.

Today's thinking person demands to know the truth beyond the stark events that blitz his mind. For this reason I have made it both a profession and an avocation to investigate the paranormal and intrigues of the twentieth century. As an illusionist, I feel that my ability to recognize deception, plus my psychological training and magical techniques, qualify me to delve into and explain a number of perplexing phenomena.

In a sense this book is similar to the long-running TV show "You Asked for It" because it addresses the questions most frequently asked by my audiences. Al Janssen has provided valuable research and writing assistance, and we have tried to give insights into areas that affect most of our lives.

I should state right away that this is not intended to be an in-depth examination of the paranormal. Rather, my goal is to acquaint you with some of the many ways that people try to deceive us. Today there is an ever-increasing number of charlatans who would like us to believe they have supernatural powers and insights.

Contents

─────────────────────── **1**

How Do You Explain...?

The small room was crowded and warm. On three sides a fine screen allowed a slight breeze to drift among the observers. Pressed against one screen were the faces of several Filipino natives, each hoping for a glance at the miracle about to take place. On a narrow table lay a young woman draped with a white sheet. She looked up at an overweight, middle-aged man in a colorful native shirt. Surrounding this doctor were several assistants and two magazine reporters from the United States.

The surgeon quietly assured the young woman that she would feel little pain, and if she believed in God's power, she would walk out of that room healed. He opened a Bible to Psalm 23 and read, "Yea, though I walk through the valley of the shadow of death, I will fear no evil, for Thou art with me."[1]

Closing his eyes for a moment, he prayed silently. Then a nurse lifted the sheet and lowered the front of the woman's pants, exposing her abdomen. The doctor took a cotton ball, dipped it into a bowl of water, and began to swab a small area of the patient's skin. As he did this, a small amount of blood appeared. Suddenly he plunged his hand deep into the woman's abdomen, appearing to go almost through her body. A moment later his hand reappeared, holding what appeared to be a piece of diseased tissue. "This is your appendix," the doctor said triumphantly. "You should feel a lot better now."

He dropped the diseased organ and cotton ball in a bucket below the table, rapidly swabbed the area with a clean piece of cotton, and covered her again with the sheet. The observers could see no evidence of any incision. As he helped her to her feet, the doctor encouraged the woman to read the Bible every day and to continue to trust God. The whole operation had taken about five minutes.

• • •

More than 10,000 people had gathered for a Navajo tribal fair. During the festivities a half-dozen tribal leaders in full ceremonial dress spread a blanket on the ground. A medicine man threw a dozen feathers into the middle of the blanket, and the leaders sat in a half-circle around it, chanting and beating small drums.

After a few moments the feathers began to move. Gradually they stood erect on their quills. The Indians, seemingly in a trance, continued to chant and beat their drums while the feathers moved in intricate formations, as a precise military drill team.

• • •

In a typical church multipurpose room in Arizona, 50 high school and college youths gathered for a special program. The guest speaker planned to demonstrate the power that he said could be developed by anyone who trusted God completely with his life.

The demonstration began with two students placing a blindfold over the speaker's eyes and putting tape around the blindfold to ensure that no light entered. Then students produced various objects from their pockets and purses—a comb, pocketknife, wallet. While holding his fingers about 12 inches from the object, the man correctly identified each item.

The students were instructed to write questions on a piece of paper and pass them to the speaker. While still blindfolded, he held each paper in his hand and answered the questions. In some cases he revealed intimate details about that person, though he had never met anyone in the room. At the end of his demonstration he declared that by blindfolding himself he developed his other senses more keenly. He reemphasized that God gives each one of us special gifts, and we need to discover and use those gifts to help others.

• • •

With a loud yell the witch doctor, wearing only a grass skirt and numerous strings of beads, called the natives to the center of the village square. He shouted that the gods had cursed the village because of one man's guilt. Unless the culprit was punished, there would be a plague and many would die. Dramatically he grabbed his rifle and called the offender forward. The crowd withdrew toward their grass-thatched huts and watched in silence as the witch doctor raised his gun and shot once. Blood spurted out of the man's chest and he fell dead.

The dead man was placed inside a crude coffin.

Several men dug a grave outside the village, while the witch doctor uttered incantations to break the evil spell on the village. Then the box was buried.

Three days later the witch doctor made another dramatic announcement. The gods were satisfied with the retribution for the unnamed crime, so the dead man could return to the village. All the villagers quickly ran to the gravesite, and several young men dug down to the box while the witch doctor chanted. Then the coffin was raised up and set beside the grave. With a dramatic yell, the leader ordered the villagers to open the box. The young man who had been shot and buried for three days slowly began to move. With a dazed look, he sat up and was helped to his feet.

• • •

These four stories are just a sample of numerous interesting and unusual phenomena I have encountered throughout the world. Each of them had religious significance, and the feats performed supposedly were evidence of genuine spiritual power.

But were they really supernatural? Were these genuine miracles? Most casual observers would assume they were. They know what they saw with their eyes. They realize that these things they saw are not humanly possible according to the laws of nature. They conclude that they can only be explained in light of the supernatural. But could there possibly be other, purely natural explanations?

Since the late 1950s I have performed illusions in more than 70 countries of the world, baffling millions of people. Audiences have seen me "levitate" several feet above the stage, squeeze my daughter down to one-fifth her height, reenact a famous "seance," "read" with my fingers while blindfolded, and pull coins out of the air. Yet all my feats, though perhaps appearing supernatural, are accomplished by natural means. I often say that any eight-year-old can do what I do on stage—with 15 years of practice.

While artistically presenting illusion as reality, I also have studied numerous religions and so-called spiritual feats, attempting to discover if any paranormal phenomena are authentic—if any events could not have been caused by normal, natural causes. I have looked for evidence of genuine ESP, psychokinesis, prophecy, psychic healing, and levitation.

In talking with people around the world, I have discovered that most of them believe in God and/or a devil. They also believe that people are capable of displaying supernatural powers—what some people would call psychic phenomena. I have concluded from my research and studies as a magician and a psychologist that most of what I've seen is composed of clever tricks, magical effects trying to pass for supernatural phenomena.

Take for example the supposed resurrection from the dead performed by the witch doctor, which took place in Liberia. In my investigation I discovered what really happened. The doctor had prearranged the event with his victim, who had placed a balloon full of pig's blood under his shirt. The witch doctor fired a blank from his rifle, and the villager grabbed his chest, puncturing the balloon, and fell over, as if dead.

Once inside the coffin, the man slipped out through a trap-door in the back of the box, which then was buried empty. When the coffin was dug up, the victim, who had hid for three days, climbed back into it through the trap-door. Then he simply carried out his performance of being raised from the dead.

What appeared to be a dramatic miracle was only an illusion. But the native villagers were impressed, and were reminded again to follow the leadership of their witch doctor. Such tricks are handed down secretly from one generation to the next, and witch doctors in India and Africa actually have asked me to teach them some of my illusions, so they can increase their influence over their followers.

But villagers in Africa are not the only people being fooled today. Millions of supposedly well-educated Americans are being deceived by charlatans who pretend to have supernatural knowledge or skills. Some of them claim their power from God and draw many to their often-unorthodox theology. Others claim that their power is from Satan. Still others promote the possibility that individuals have latent power that can be developed, if they will learn the techniques, which are available to anyone . . . for a stiff price.

It is easy for Christians to assume that they can't possibly be deceived by such frauds. That is a dangerous assumption. We should be equipped to talk intelligently with those who are looking into the occult for purpose and answers in life. We need a healthy respect for the power that the kingdom of darkness holds over people. But we can also attribute more to Satan than he deserves. Satan would like us to believe that his earthly servants possess more power than they actually do. In fact, as we will soon see, he only presents a poor imitation of God. Christians should take courage; God has the real power! He doesn't need cheap imitations to impress us.

There is an even more subtle deception that has crept into some of our churches. A few men and women, posing as servants of God, have misled believers by displaying supposedly supernatural gifts when in reality they are using cheap tricks and deception. By doing so they make a mockery of Christianity before the world and draw attention away from the real work of God. We must be able to distinguish between the acts of God and the chicanery of men who are using God as a means to promote their own selfish ambitions. They may be few, but they are like a cancer in the body of Christ, drawing people away from the truth. Christ warned us to be careful:

> See to it that no one misleads you. For many will come in My name, saying, "I am the Christ," and will mislead many. . . . Then if any one says to you, "Behold, here is the Christ," or "There He is," do not believe him. For false Christs and false prophets will arise and will show great signs and wonders, so as to mislead, if possible, even the elect.[2]

In this book I will examine some of the most common phenomena that mislead people. Based on my research and personal observations, I will answer some of the questions I often am asked after my shows, such as "What do you think about astrology?" "Are there really UFO's?" "Can Uri Geller really bend spoons using only his mind?"

But first, I think it is important to ask why so many people are being deceived. Why do people attend seances, even though it is impossible to communicate with the dead? Why do they listen to seers like Jeane Dixon, whose percentage of correct predictions is no higher than chance? Why do so many spend money they can't afford to visit psychic healers in the Philippines, Mexico, or Brazil? Why do people attend exotic fire-walking seminars? Why do people who are crippled and confined to wheelchairs continue to flock to certain faith healers who have demonstrated no measurable track record for genuine miraculous healings?

I believe that we must understand how people are deceived, so we can discern accurately between what is true and what is false. If there is a God, and if He does give people genuine spiritual power, then it is important to know how to identify that power and separate it from fraudulence. I believe there are five basic reasons why people are mislead.

First, *the media blows many stories out of proportion.*

Tabloid publications such as the *National Enquirer* and *Globe* regularly print articles under sensational headlines such as "UFOs: At Last the Proof" and "Amazing Accuracy: Psychic Demonstrates 89% Accuracy." But even respected periodicals can print misleading stories. In May 1981, *Reader's Digest* published an article titled "New Evidence on Psychic Phenomena." The September/October 1980 *Science Digest* included "Physicists Explain ESP." In March 1980, *Instructor*, a magazine for teachers, ran the story "Your Kids Are Psychic!" with a subtitle "But they may never know it—without your help."

After seeing these articles, a casual reader would assume that ESP is an established scientific fact, even though that is not the case. Some articles reveal scientists' uncertainties, but the tone of the headlines and the first few paragraphs lead readers to believe that many people have genuine psychic abilities. Television documentaries can be even more deceiving because they seldom provide enough time to explain all the divergent facts and opinions.

Kendrick Frazier, editor of *The Skeptical Inquirer*, keeps a watchful eye on claims by various publications. In a story titled "Articles on the Paranormal: Where Are the Editors?" he explains:

> The problem is not of factual inaccuracy. Usually the *facts* are correct. The problem is with the selection process that determines which facts are included and which facts are omitted. Often the facts omitted are those that might weaken a seemingly good story. Hard, skeptical questions are not asked. The overall result is to drastically warp the article's perspective to give a dramatic, but not altogether accurate, view of the subject.[3]

For example, Frazier cites an article in *California Living,* a Sunday supplement magazine in newspapers such as *Examiner* and *Chronicle* in San Francisco and the *Los Angeles Herald Examiner.* The March 9, 1980, article, "The Psychic Body Finders," reports of cases where psychics supposedly helped police solve crimes. Frazier points out the story's shortcomings:

> The hard questions weren't asked: How often do these "psychic bodyfinders" fail? How many guesses do they make before they get one right? And how specific are they? Why do we hear only of the "successes"? And the article makes no mention of the only controlled study I know of that examines the claims of so-called psychic crime-fighters, the

one in which the Los Angeles police department found them to be of no use at all in criminal investigations.[4]

This leads directly into my second caution: *Determination of the facts is often difficult.*

One of the problems in evaluating reports of unusual phenomena is that only certain facts are selected; unfavorable ones are omitted. Other reports are exaggerated. In some cases, reports actually are fabricated.

I enjoy listening to people try to describe some of my illusions. Once when I was in Madras, India, I appeared to cause my daughter to float within the framework of a large pyramid. The next day, a waitress excitedly told me what some of her customers had said about my show. According to them, I not only had levitated my daughter, but I also had caused her to float out over the audience, turn in a large circle, and do several impossible gymnastic feats. Of course, when people exaggerate my illusions, it's hard to tell them that I really wasn't that good!

My good friend David Copperfield made a small Lear jet disappear on one of his television specials, but I've heard people say he made a 747 jet disappear while it was flying through the air. Such exaggerations are common and usually unintentional. People easily blow the facts out of proportion, so it is wise to be skeptical about eyewitness reports that deal with any supposed supernatural event.

People also can be deceived by the selection of facts. For example, stories about Bermuda Triangle disappearances sometimes can be explained easily by one piece of information that the writer neglected to mention.

I believe that most editors and writers attempt to be honest in their presentations, but occasionally stories are complete fabrications. Prominent on the cover of the bestseller *The Amityville Horror* was the label "A True Story." Lawyer William Weber, who defended Ronald DeFeo, convicted of the slayings of his family in that Amityville house that the Lutz family later bought, said in an Associated Press story, "We created this horror story over many bottles of wine that George Lutz was drinking. We were really playing with each other. We were creating something the public would want to hear about."[5]

Third, *science has difficulty discerning between the fake and real.*

Numerous scientific studies supposedly prove the existence of various paranormal phenomena. Most of these scientists probably sincerely believe in their experiments, and many want to believe that they have verified certain powers. But the facts do not bear them out. First, many experiments cannot be duplicated in other laboratories without widely divergent results. Second, tests that initially produce results significantly beyond the laws of probability produce very normal results when controls are tightened.

One reason scientists often fail to distinguish between illusion and reality is that they do not suspect that someone might try to deceive them. For example, two teenage magicians wrote to the McDonnell Laboratory for Psychical Research at Washington University in St. Louis, Missouri, claiming they had the power to bend metal with their minds. For two years the lab tested their powers, verifying their amazing talent. The boys finally admitted publicly that they had fooled the scientists.

Why are so many people fooled? Because *the average person can't detect deception.* The best person to detect a trick is an expert in trickery—not a scientist. In my opinion most people cannot distinguish between fraud and a genuine supernatural feat because they aren't trained in the field of deception.

As a magician, I take pride in my profession, and I resent those who misuse our methods, designed for entertainment, to lead others to believe they have supernatural powers, whether they claim it is from God, Satan, or some other source. In order to help reveal these frauds, a number of scientists and magicians founded the Committee for the Scientific Investigation of Claims of the Paranormal. The organization promotes careful, controlled testing of those who claim paranormal power, and publishes *The Skeptical Inquirer*, a quarterly journal reporting its investigations.

Fourth, *people deeply desire to see and believe supernatural phenomena.* There is excitement when we see or hear of someone miraculously healed, for that encourages us that we and our loved ones can also experience victory over illness. Likewise, there is an eagerness to know about the future, for that can help us cope with the uncertainties of daily life.

Is it wrong to desire healing or to wonder about the future? No, of course not. However, there is a danger when we desire these so much that we become vulnerable to those who would prey on our desires and mislead us for their own benefit. One well-known scientist talks about the emotional stakes involved in any examination of the paranormal:

> In many such cases we are not unbiased observers. We have an emotional stake in the

outcome—perhaps merely because the borderline belief-system, if true, makes the world a more interesting place; but perhaps because there is something there that strikes more deeply into the human psyche. If astral projection actually occurs, then it is possible for some thinking and perceiving part of me to leave my body and effortlessly travel to other places—an exhilarating prospect. If spiritualism is real, then my soul will survive the death of my body—possibly a comforting thought. If there is extrasensory perception, then many of us possess latent talents that need only be tapped to make us more powerful than we are. If astrology is right, then our personalities and destinies are intimately tied to the rest of the cosmos. . . . But the fact that these propositions charm or stir us does not guarantee their truth. Their truth depends only on whether the evidence is compelling; and my own, and sometimes reluctant, judgment is that compelling evidence for these and many similar propositions simply does not (at least as yet) exist.[6]

I have to agree on this point, for my research has led me to conclude this final point: *There are probably far fewer genuine supernatural phenomena than are generally supposed.*

But what about psychic healers? Aren't many patients healed? Yes, some are healed. Doctors have demonstrated, however, that as many as 50 percent of their cases are psychosomatic diseases or illnesses that will improve without any treatment, and many illnesses can be healed by suggestion. But when it comes to genuine psychic power, I have yet to investigate a demonstration that didn't prove to be the result of trickery.

That's only one example. Since 1966, magician James Randi has carried around a 10,000-dollar check that he will give to anyone who demonstrates one paranormal feat under controlled conditions. So far no one has collected the prize. "With all the claims of paranormal power that we see every day in the press," says Randi, "you'd think that I'd have many more people lined up to take the prize. As it stands, just fifty-two persons have passed the simple preliminaries, only to fail to support their claims to supernatural powers."[7]

During my years of investigation, I have discovered a real spiritual dimension to life, which I also will examine in this book. The evidence for this spiritual life, however, does not come from charlatans who pretend to have supernatural powers; on the contrary, their cleverly learned tricks draw millions of people and dollars *away* from the truth.

It is very easy to be sincere and yet be deceived. I saw this vividly when I was scheduled to do a series of shows in Mexico. A businessman offered to fly me and an interpreter to our various appointments. The pilot did not speak Spanish, and the interpreter did not know much about airplanes. One afternoon our pilot radioed through the interpreter to an airport tower, informing the controller that we had sighted the runway and were preparing to land. We received clearance and landed, only to be met by a dozen army trucks and soldiers with guns pointed at us. An officer demanded to know why we had landed at the military airport. We then realized that the public airport, with which we had communicated, was on the other side of the mountain. We had believed sincerely that we were landing at the right place, but we were wrong. Similarly, many people follow spiritual leaders because they are convinced they have supernatural powers, but in reality they have been misled.

Let me emphasize that supernatural power does exist. It is not my intention to dismiss all reports of miracles and say they are all simply magic. However, let's not go to the other extreme and assume that all reports of miracles are accurate. In fact, my investigations reveal that many reported miracles simply do not hold up under scrutiny. I have concluded that, rather than concentrate on trying to find and experience such miracles as mind-reading, healing, and foretelling the future, we can benefit far more if we focus on experiencing the supernatural power that God provides for all believers in Jesus Christ. The apostle Paul wrote about the incredible riches available to all the saints, and " . . . the surpassing greatness of His power toward us who believe."[8]

I have spent most of my life separating illusion from reality, and I would like to share with you some of my discoveries. Perhaps they will encourage you in your search for truth—and protect you from being deceived. You will see that many so-called paranormal phenomena have simple explanations. Then I want to look at the spiritual power that God promises to all believers. The Bible talks about miracles such as healing, but these are displayed according to God's discretion, not by the manipulations of men. The incredible power that God wants *all* of us to experience has to do with changed lives. Let's begin by examining some truths and myths about the power of our minds.

2

Limits of the Mind

In the early 1970's a handsome young man with a mop of dark, wavy hair burst into the public consciousness. On television shows and in laboratory experiments, the Israeli bent metal objects such as spoons and keys, fixed watches, recreated drawings without seeing them, predicted the roll of a die in a box, and altered the direction of a compass—all through only the use of his mind—or so he claimed. The perpetrator of those feats was Uri Geller, and many people still refer to him as a prime example of the human mind's potential power.

For years extrasensory perception, "ESP," has fascinated people. But what is ESP? Dr. Joseph Banks Rhine, for years head of the parapsychology laboratory at Duke University, originated the term, which is defined as the ability to perceive or act outside the realm of the five senses.

Generally this phenomenon is broken down into four manifestations. *Clairvoyance*, sometimes called second sight, is the ability to identify objects or events without using the five senses. Someone might demonstrate it by reading or driving while blindfolded, or describing an object or location he has never seen. The second, *telepathy*, or mind-reading, is communication between two minds by means other than normal sensory channels. *Precognition*, also called divination or premonition, is knowledge of a future event or state that cannot be inferred from present information. Finally, *psychokinesis* (often referred to as PK, or sometimes telekinesis) is the mind's ability to influence physical objects without using any physical energy or instrumentation.

The question is, do any or all of these elements of ESP (or psi, as it often is called) actually exist? Many people feel that most or all humans have latent ESP potential. They refer to numerous experiments, and particularly to a handful of well-publicized psychic superstars.

Perhaps the most commonly cited example is Uri Geller, who supposedly has demonstrated all four elements of ESP. Geller received much publicity after his powers were tested at the Stanford Research Institute (SRI) in Palo Alto by doctors Russell Targ and Harold Puthoff.

Targ and Puthoff published their findings in a very controversial article in *Nature* magazine, a highly respected scientific journal. They wrote that the results of their experiments suggest "the existence of one or more perceptual modalities through which individuals obtain information about their environment, although this information is not presented to any known sense."[1]

They reported on three experiments. First Geller was asked to reproduce simple line drawings, called targets, "while separated from both the target material and anyone knowledgeable of the material." Results of the 13 separate drawing experiments were mixed. Geller did duplicate one of the pictures, a cluster of 22 grapes. He also was reasonably close on four of the other 12 drawings. On three targets, he "got no clear impression"[2] and refused to submit drawings.

A second series of experiments involved 100 target pictures sealed in envelopes and randomly divided into groups of 20. Geller was asked to associate any envelope with a drawing he made. He expressed "dissatisfaction with the existence of such a large target pool" and refused to associate any of his drawings with specific envelopes. On each of the three days, two of his drawings "could reasonably be associated with two of the daily targets." But the authors concluded, "The drawings resulting from this experiment do not depart significantly from what would be expected by chance."[3]

The third experiment yielded the most spectacular results. After a die was shaken in an enclosed steel box, Geller was asked to identify its uppermost face. In ten tries, Geller passed twice and gave the correct response the other eight times. The authors concluded that the probability of this occurring by chance was approximately one in a million.

Regarding Geller's metal-bending ability, the authors declined comment, saying that they were not able to observe it under sufficiently controlled circumstances to support his claim of psychokinesis.

For all the publicity generated by the experiments, the results were not particularly impressive. In fact the editors of *Nature* expressed concern over the article:

> All the referees felt that the details given of various safeguards and precautions introduced against the possibility of conscious or unconscious fraud on the part of one or other of the subjects were "uncomfortably vague."

This in itself might be sufficient to raise doubt that the experiments have demonstrated the existence of a new channel of communication which does not involve the use of the senses.[4]

Author-researcher Martin Gardner examined Geller's most sensational experiment, where he correctly called the roll of a die in a steel box. He pointed out that Puthoff and Targ "describe the die test with a brevity that seems inappropriate for so extraordinary a claim. We are not told who shook the box, where or when the test was made, who observed the trials, how long Geller took to make each guess, whether he was allowed to touch the box, whether there were earlier or later die-box tests with Uri, or whether the experiment was visually recorded."[5]

Gardner correctly concluded that Geller could have cheated in many ways. The only way to rule out the possibility of trickery would have been to have a knowledgeable magician present, or to see a videotape of all the attempts. "In the absence of such controls for guarding against deception by a known charlatan, the die test was far too casual and slipshod to deserve being included in a technical paper for a journal as reputable as *Nature*,"[6] Gardner concluded.

I believe that Gardner and the editors of *Nature* were right to express concern. What most people do not realize about Uri Geller—what he has tried to suppress in his publicity—is that he studied and practiced magic as a youth in Israel. But he quickly realized that he attracted a far greater following by claiming paranormal powers than he did as a conjurer. In fact, most of what he does would be rather insignificant coming from a magician.

Geller also is a clever opportunist. Friends of mine who have observed him say he is a master at taking advantage of a situation. At a table full of silverware and keys, he may bend one, but he rarely announces what he will do, so people don't know what to expect. He has the audience under his control. In a controlled setting, when asked to bend one specific object without handling it, his powers mysteriously disappear.

Persi Diaconis, a professor of statistics at Stanford University, tells a story that demonstrates Geller's methods. Diaconis drove Geller to the airport after he had appeared at Stanford. While waiting for his flight, the psychic expressed disappointment that the professor remained a skeptic, and he offered to provide conclusive proof of his powers. He then asked Diaconis to reach into his coat pocket, grab his keys, and concentrate on a key that could be bent. The professor says, "I opened my hand and the key I was thinking of was bent. For about five minutes I was as badly fooled as I've ever been in my life."

Diaconis solved the mystery by reviewing the trip to the airport. Geller had insisted on sitting in the backseat, where Diaconis' coat lay. At the airport parking lot, Geller had insisted that he bring the coat "in case it gets too cool." The key ring contained four keys, only one of which could be bent easily. When he further examined his coat, he discovered an envelope turned inside out, and each of his pens' tops bent and twisted. Geller apparently had prepared several "proofs" of his powers.

A good friend of mine, Ray Hyman, professor of psychology at the University of Oregon, observed Geller firsthand during a portion of the SRI experiments. We talked about it one evening after I did a show on his campus. When I expressed my opinion that Geller seemed almost satanically cunning—that his cleverness seemed to come from another source—Dr. Hyman responded by characterizing Geller as a "pathological liar," a person who has "no twinge of conscience." He illustrated his point: "Geller spent the whole morning doing what I consider just blatant trickery. And now I was having lunch with him and I said, 'Look, Geller, I know you made your living in Israel working nightclubs and doing entertaining. Have you ever, in your career, used trickery at all?' He looked at me and put his hand over his heart. Tears welled up in his eyes. 'Ray, how could you even ask such a question of me? If I ever cheated even once, how could I live with myself?' At that moment I felt like a heel, even though I knew the guy was cheating right and left."

That's just another example of the charm and personality of Geller. When confronted by skeptics, rather than substantiate his claims, he often plays the role of a misunderstood genius and puts his opponents on the defensive.

Hyman also observed that Geller was very quick to pick up sensory clues from people. He learned what people expected from him as a psychic, and he didn't disappoint them. In a casual conversation, one SRI scientist said that psychics seemed to be very sensitive to electronic equipment. An hour later Geller balked at an experiment because a video machine was giving off "bad vibes." "Several times I would ask him a question," Hyman told me, "and before he could answer, one of the scientists would butt in and give the answer. Sure enough, when the subject came up again, Geller would rephrase what the scientist had said earlier."

All of this illustrates a point that I often make in my programs: Even the most intelligent people can be deceived when presented with a phenomenon—no matter how ridiculous—in a serious manner, in an atmosphere where honesty is taken for granted. The sad fact is that scientists may be the most ill-equipped to detect fraud. They will go to elaborate lengths to eliminate any possible form of sensory input in ESP experiments, but if they miss even one, then that avenue must be examined before their conclusions can be verified.

Hyman is in a unique position to verify this point because as a youth he became an accomplished magician and mentalist. The money he made from his mind-reading act helped put him through school. After earning a Ph.D. in psychology at Johns Hopkins University, he served as a professor at Harvard before moving to Oregon. He is one of the leading international experts in the investigation of the paranormal.

"It is fairly easy to fool a scientist," Hyman says, "because he thinks very logically. Scientists can cope with nature because nature doesn't change the rules. But an alleged psychic changes the rules. He takes advantage of the way you think and leads you down his path of deception. That's why children are much harder to fool—they aren't as well conditioned."

Project Alpha confirmed that statement. In 1979 Washington University in St. Louis, Missouri, was awarded a 500,000-dollar grant to form a laboratory for psychical research. James Randi arranged for two teenage magicians, Steve Shaw and Michael Edwards, to apply to the lab as candidates for a study on psycho-kinetic metal-bending by children. From among 300 applicants, they were the only two subjects chosen.

The scientists never suspected that they were set up, and the two boys performed all sorts of "amazing" feats in the lab. "There is no question that the lab personnel believed that Mike and Steve were actually psychic," wrote Randi after he and the two subjects exposed the project two years later. "It was this belief that made the deception exceedingly easy, and it was clear that, had the two entered the arena as conjurors, they could never have gotten away with all they did."[7]

This leads me to state two guidelines for anyone reading about or investigating paranormal powers. When investigating a potential case of ESP, assume every other possible explanation first. *The conclusion of ESP can be made only after every other possible natural explanation has been examined and eliminated.*

For most people, eliminating all the options is nearly impossible, since many methods are used to obtain information from a person without his knowledge. One is called cold reading, or unconscious sensory cueing. It is the ability to learn all sorts of information about a person from body language and facial expressions. It's great psychology, but a person using it may appear to read minds. (We will further discuss cold reading later in this book.)

Uri Geller often complains that he can't perform when a skeptic is in the room. (And especially if that skeptic is a magician!) He's using good showmanship, and protecting himself when controls become too tight. People usually are very sympathetic to that argument because they want to believe in Geller. But if someone really had psychic powers, we could reasonably expect him to demonstrate them under tightly controlled conditions. If nothing else, the monetary rewards would be fantastic. (Such a person could make a financial killing in a place like Las Vegas.)

A second guideline is: *Be wary of statistics.* Geller's chances of calling eight rolls of a die without a miss was one in a million. That seems most impressive, but all it tells you is that it didn't happen by accident. In and of itself, that doesn't prove the existence of ESP.

Persi Diaconis wrote about this in *Science* magazine. After reviewing several psi (parapsychology) experiments, he stated, "Most often these tests are 'highly statistically significant.' This only implies that the results are improbable under simple chance models. In complex, badly controlled experiments simple chance models cannot be seriously considered as tenable explanations; hence rejection of such models is not of particular interest."[8]

Diaconis went on to examine how statistical data can be drastically skewed if just one or two details of an experiment are altered—for example, if a subject receives unconscious sensory cues. "There always seem to be many loopholes and loose ends," he says in his conclusion. "The same mistakes are made again and again."[9]

Why are people so fascinated with ESP? I think author Dave Hunt (whose books include *The Seduction of Christianity, The Cult Explosion,* and *Peace, Prosperity, and the Coming Holocaust*) isolated the real issue when he said, "I believe that the ultimate purpose, the ultimate goal, of psychic power is to validate Satan's lie—the lie that man is God. Unless humanity can manifest these powers, they can't really validate what Satan has promised.... As to the various manifestations of psi, you could categorize them as attempts to mimic the attributes of God, because they try to appropriate the omnipotence, omniscience, and omnipresence of God. This is basically the *function* of psychic phenomena, theologically speaking."[10]

For several years, transcendental meditation was the rage among young people. But when participation dropped off, the movement, under the leadership of Maharishi Mahesh Yogi, came up with the idea of teaching students to levitate—for a substantial fee. This seems to be an ultimate dream of those who wish to use mind power. The Maharishi claimed that people could levitate through a purified, altered state of consciousness, plus lots of practice. Thousands of students enrolled, paying between 3000 and 5000 dollars each for the privilege of bouncing up and down. No one from the program, however, could publicly demonstrate the ability to levitate.

One of the highlights of my show is the self-levitation illusion in which I appear to rise and float about five feet above the stage. It is a most effective illusion: It baffles audiences even though it is accomplished entirely by natural methods. As I have said, I have no supernatural powers whatsoever.

Since I began practicing magic, I have performed 11 different forms of levitation. In my travels around the world, including five tours of India, I have attempted to find just one genuine demonstration of levitation. I have not succeeded. I feel confident that if someone had that ability, I would learn about it quickly through my worldwide network of magician friends.

Another "mind-over-matter" experience that has become quite popular in recent years is fire-walking. I witnessed my first demonstrations of fire-walking many years ago in India and Sri Lanka. The walk over a 20-foot-long bed of hot coals was attempted only after the participants put themselves into a trance, or following hours of religious ceremonies.

Fire-walking occurs in one form or another in cultures as diverse as Greece, Spain, Brazil, Trinidad, Tahiti, Japan, and China. Some of the ceremonies have religious trappings, others serve as a rite of passage, and still others are simply a form of tribal ritual or celebration.

It was first brought to popular attention in North America by a Pakistani magician named Kuda Bux. In recent years a number of people have developed seminars built around the fire-walking experience. Jim Parker went through one such workshop in Tucson, Arizona, which included the singing of spirituals, a message about coping with fear, the chanting of a Sanskrit mantra, a magic show, instruction in the basics of fire-walking, and hypnotic chanting before the big moment when participants walked on a 12-by-6-foot bed of coals sometime after midnight.

After the seminar Parker concluded, "When you look at the experience . . . closely, you realize that if you can will yourself to walk on a bed of scorching-hot coals, you can will yourself to do just about anything you can think of for the rest of your life—*if* you want to and *if* you're willing to take that first step."[11] So for some people fire-walking has become the ultimate self-improvement seminar, since those who can conquer the coals can control any kind of fear and pain.

But is fire-walking—actually taking two to four quick steps over hot coals in the period of a couple of seconds—really an evidence of mind over body? Can it really change a person's life, as some followers of fire-walker Anthony Robbins claim? It's hard to argue with a person's emotional experience in that setting, so no doubt some people find fire-walking meaningful. But as far as it being a demonstration of the power of the mind, it lacks credibility. If the mind is that powerful, why is it that we don't see people walking over beds of coals longer than 35 feet (supposedly the world record), or hot metal plates, without getting blisters? Writer Peter Garrison tried to get some answers for *OMNI* magazine.

Part of the research involved close examination of Robbins' "Fear into Power: The Firewalk Experience" seminar. UCLA plasma physicist Bernard Leikind and UCLA research psychologist Bill McCarthy enrolled in a seminar (cost is 100 dollars, with an average of 100 participants per seminar) in Southern California. They decided that McCarthy would participate in the seminar while Leikind remained outside to avoid the suggestions of the seminar. Then both walked over the coals. Leikind did so twice, the second time over a freshly laid bed of coals. Garrison observed the results:

> Psychologist McCarthy noted that the Robbins fire-walking techniques—turn your eyes upward, clench your fist, breath heavily, chant "Cool moss," and celebrate when you reach the end— involves a number of well-known stratagems for blocking pain. These include repeating a mantra-like phrase, looking away from the source of pain, and focusing attention on an internal cue, in this case a Lamaze-like breathing style.... McCarthy did get burned slightly, but he felt no pain, not even heat, at that time.
>
> Leikind fared better. "Once the coals had been spread out, they cooled rapidly," he says. "Incandescence is a simple gauge of temperature. I saw dark footprints where people's feet had been. Robbin's people claim to be blocking the heat somehow, but to me that meant much of the heat in the coals *was* being absorbed by the feet. But people apparently weren't getting burned, so I knew there just couldn't be that much heat energy present." In defiance of Robbin's prescription, Leikind looked down, breathed normally, and thought about the coals....

Kind's

> Leikind's walks were not a controlled experiment, and his success was not a scientific proof; it merely put his hypothesis on an equal footing with the mind-over-matter theory. But it is a preferable hypothesis, he says, because science does not seek farfetched reasons for things that can be accounted for by simple ones.[12]

It should be noted that not everyone emerges from the fire-walking experience unscathed. Some people do get blisters on their feet and many of them go through psychiatric counseling because of the depression brought on by their "weakness of spirit." But for those who do emerge unscathed, what is the explanation? One scientific explanation is "Leidenfrost effect," in which a liquid exposed suddenly to intense heat instantly forms an insulating layer of steam. It's the phenomenon which causes water droplets to dance on a hot skillet without dissolving immediately. The theory is that vaporized perspiration provides temporary insulation for the foot, much as a little saliva allows us to snuff out a candle with our fingertips.

Professor Leikind thinks there's an even better explanation:

> . . . he views the coals themselves as the principal factor. He thinks they are neither sufficiently dense and massive nor sufficiently good conductors of heat to burn the foot during brief contact.
>
> Laymen, Leikind argues, usually don't distinguish between temperature and heat. The motion of molecules is heat. Temperature is something else. It's analogous to "fullness." A small container can be filled by an amount of water that would barely wet a large one. Similarly, an object

having little mass can be raised to a high temperature by an amount of heat energy that would barely warm something more massive. . . .

Leikind cites the act of removing a cake from an oven as an example. You open the oven and thrust in your hand. The air in the oven is at the same *temperature* as the pan, but it does not burn you because it has little *mass*, and therefore contains very little heat energy. The pan, of course, has a large amount of heat energy. If you touch it without a potholder, which is a poor conductor of heat, you get burned.

Though the temperature of incandescent coals is at least 1200^0 F., they contain very little heat energy because they are not massive: They are a fluffy, spongy material, as light as balsa. . . . [Because] carbon is a poor conductor, the heat moves slowly, and the foot is gone before significant transfer has occurred.[13]

My conclusion is that fire-walking is not a dramatic demonstration of spiritual power or of mind over matter. In countries where people go barefooted and thus have thick-soled feet, it's really not very impressive. And as we've seen, there are logical scientific explanations to explain the successes.

One thing I haven't addressed in this discussion about mind power is the occasional unexplainable premonitions that many people have experienced. Almost all of us know a friend or relative who has had a dramatic premonition for no apparently logical reason. Is ESP, particularly precognition, a possible explanation?

I know of two such experiences in my family. One time my parents were in a movie theater when my mother sensed that my brother was in trouble and she began to cry. Later we found out that he was in an accident at that very moment, but he wasn't seriously hurt.

Another case involved my brother-in-law. He was driving a car when he suddenly had a tremendous impression that his father had died. He had to pull off the road because he was so emotionally upset. When he arrived home, a call informed him that his father had died at the exact moment the feeling had come over him.

Many cases like this are recorded. They are real and are difficult to explain. But I do not believe they prove the existence of ESP because they are only one-time, isolated events. No one has demonstrated such power in a regular, everyday manner.

Luis Alvarez of the University of California at Berkeley has one statistical explanation. Using a complex statistical analysis, he concludes that events such as I described should occur about ten times per day around the United States. "With such a large sample to draw from, it is not surprising that some exceedingly astonishing coincidences are reported in the parapsychological literature as proof of extrasensory perception in one form or another."[14]

Psychologists have an even better explanation. "My brother was killed in World War II and my mother had a dream about it the night before it happened," Ray Hyman says. "Both my mother and sister believe it was a prophetic dream, but I see nothing miraculous about it. All three of us had that dream many times. They just don't remember the others because nothing happened to make them come true.

"The current theory of memory is that you tend to remember those things that you can connect to something meaningful. Let's say you periodically have fleeting thoughts of Uncle Moe, but they come and go and you forget them. Then one day you happen to think of Uncle Moe and he calls that evening. You say to yourself, 'I haven't thought about Uncle Moe for years.' You probably thought of Uncle Moe many times, but nothing happened to make those thoughts memorable."

I enjoy performing an illusion in which my eyes are covered by two half-dollars, taped shut and covered with a blindfold. Then I invite members of the audience to test me. Without touching anything, I identify the colors of several scarves, identify objects such as wallets and combs, and read words they wrote on 3 x 5 cards.

Sound impressive? Would you believe I have the power of ESP? I want to assure you that I have no such power. Over the years, I practiced sometimes 12 to 16 hours a day with cards to master the art of finger manipulation. Often my fingertips were raw from the hours of practice; however, they never became so sensitive that I could identify objects, tell colors, or accomplish any of the other amazing feats I apparently do with my fingertips. I certainly do not have ESP, and I would strongly question anyone who claims that he does.

Another element of mind power that many people believe and experience has to do with physical healing. That is a subject which deserves a thorough examination. We will do that in two parts, beginning with some unusual men and women in Latin America and the Philippines.

Amazing Operations

The first reports were of wonderment. People in the Philippines were going to certain "doctors" and having major surgery without anesthesia in a matter of minutes, then walking out of the clinic without even a scar. It was a fact that many people had experienced healing. And the surgeons were using the Bible and urging their patients to pray and trust God.

"What should we make of this?" asked a prominent Christian leader in that country. "What these men are doing seems so good, yet we aren't sure if they're really gifted by God, or if they're tools of Satan meant to deceive us." He went on to tell how these surgeons could make a small incision in the body and reach through it to remove diseased tissue and organs. When they removed their hands, the skin closed, leaving no scar. I could not give my friend an explanation, but it sounded like some similar "operations" I had observed in Liberia and Latin America. I assured him that I would attempt an investigation when I visited his country in a few months.

The area of faith healing is one that has intrigued me for years. In the course of my travels around the world I have observed a wide variety of healers from various cultures and religions. My desire has been to try to determine which healings are truly miracles of divine healing, and which, if any, healers have genuine supernatural powers. My research has yielded some interesting insights into the methods of various faith healers as well as the healing properties of the human body. In this chapter I would like to concentrate on my research of psychic surgery. Later in the book I will deal more specifically with the subject of faith healing in general.

In almost every part of the world there are stories told of miraculous healers. One of the most unusual was Jose Pedro de Freitas, a Brazilian peasant known throughout the world as "Arigo," the surgeon with the rusty knife. For more than 20 years he saw 300 patients a day, five days a week. Each patient received a diagnosis, therapy, and/or written prescription. His normal method of treatment was to take a pocketknife, jab it into the body of the patient, twist it around, then reach in and pull out a growth or diseased tissue. Patients walked away without a scratch, and most of them claimed to be healed.

My first personal contact with psychic surgery was in Liberia, in 1968. Since then I have witnessed nearly 300 operations in Asia and Latin America. The best demonstrations by far were in the Philippines.

In the summer of 1973, a few months after my friend had asked me about the healings in the Philippines, David Aikman, a foreign correspondent for *Time* magazine, asked me to help him investigate several psychic surgeons in Banguio and Manila. During a tour of the island, I took some time between shows to observe seven different healers, five of whom were among the men most frequently mentioned in articles about spiritual healers. During this time I witnessed more than 50 operations by the seven healers. These men, thinking I was a news reporter, were very open and cooperative. They even asked me to assist in some operations, which gave me the best possible vantage point for studying their actions.

We first visited a plain, white, one-story building. Some 200 people were lined up from the door and down the street, waiting to see the surgeon. A photographer and I were invited into the operating room. I felt anxious, not knowing what to expect, but the doctor, dressed in a colorful native shirt, immediately put me at ease and asked me to assist him. He was operating on a woman's back, removing a small cyst just below her shoulders.

The doctor began by holding my right index finger in the air and moving it in a short line about 12 inches above the cyst. As he did, a small incision, about an inch long, appeared. A numb feeling came over me when I saw that cut and realized it was genuine. I knew that if the incision closed and the woman walked out of the clinic without any scar, I truly would have witnessed something supernatural.

Quickly the doctor reached into the cut and removed a small mass of material that looked like gristle. Then he took a piece of cotton on a stick, dipped it in coconut oil, lit it, and cauterized the cut; he did not heal the incision supernaturally. The whole operation took about three minutes.

It didn't take long to discover that the doctor used a very clever form of sleight of hand. The cut that my finger seemed to make actually was done with a small razor blade concealed in the healer's fingers. He concealed in his other hand the supposed diseased tissue, before apparently pulling it from the patient's body.

Strictly from the magician's point of view, apart from the moral and ethical issues, watching these healers was fascinating. They performed their fake operations using some of the most clever sleight of hand that I ever have seen. Their incredible dexterity immediately reminded me of the ability of Ben Chavez, a Philippine magician with nimble fingers and a quality of manual dexterity almost unequaled in the magic world. Before his death he trained some of today's best-known sleight-of-hand performers, and he taught me almost everything I know about prestidigitation. I never suspected how I would use this specialized knowledge in his country.

Most of these operations were performed on the abdominal area. Sometimes the surgeon made the operation more dramatic by making a small cut and covering it with a coin. Then he would take a cotton ball soaked in coconut oil, lay it on the coin, and light it. Next he would cover it with a small glass, creating a suction that drew blood out into the glass. While the people watched that procedure, the healer secured a piece of animal tissue in his fingers. When he removed the glass and coin, he rubbed his fingers in the blood and made it appear that tissue was being removed from the incision.

Most of the time the doctor did not actually cut the patient, yet his fingers appeared to reach through the skin and into the body, usually the stomach area. As I looked carefully, I saw that there was no opening in the skin—just a depressed area where the surgeon pushed, forming a small cup. By bending his fingers, he appeared to push them in much deeper than he actually did.

But when there was no incision, where did the blood come from? A little investigation revealed that the healers had put animal blood in a refrigerator to coagulate. Then they took some animal tissue, added a little of that blood, and wrapped cotton around it until it formed a ball. When it dried, it could be handled without getting messy. A bowl of water was always near the operating table. By quickly dipping this cotton in the water and gently massaging with it in the stomach area, blood appeared, and the tissue was available for quick removal. I later learned that some surgeons used a red dye made from betel nuts, rather than real blood, because it was less messy.

It was interesting to see the doctors' various procedures. Two men hid their loads (containing the tissue to be removed from the patient) underneath the table. Two others put theirs in the open side of the pillow slip on which the patient was lying. Another got his load in the cotton his nurse gave to him. One man wore a loose shirt and hid his loads under the bottom hem.

Another popular operation involved removing an individual's eye. The healer began by poking around the patient's eye, causing it to bulge from its socket. As he covered it with cotton, he appeared to take out the eye, but actually produced a cow or goat's eye. After washing it off and examining it, he supposedly replaced it. One doctor had used his animal eye so much that it had turned green.

While viewing all these operations, plus a couple of hundred more, in various parts of the world and on film, I never witnessed any evidence of supernatural healing ability. In every case, the surgeon used sleight of hand. Some people have said that the operations must be real because they have seen movies of them and could not see any tricks. Of course they could not see any tricks. If an average person—one not trained in sleight-of-hand techniques—could discover how the operations were done by watching the film, the healers would not have allowed the cameras. Several of my performances are on film and hundreds of copies are used around the world. People have slowed down the projector and even examined the film frame by frame, yet still could not tell how I did the tricks. I would not have put my effects on film if they could.

Some people see the accuracy of these doctors' diagnoses as evidence of their powers. Indeed they often do make correct diagnoses, which usually are educated guesses resulting from years of experience. They can "read" a person and size up a problem very quickly. When they aren't sure, they couch their guesses with general statements that sound impressive but have little substance. If you kept a record of their diagnoses, you would find that they miss at least as many as they hit.

Soon after my experience in the Philippines, I was asked to be an expert witness for the Federal Trade Commission in a case against several travel agencies in the Pacific Northwest. The agencies were promoting special tours to these healers in the Philippines. Unfortunately, some people never made it home, and others died soon after they returned, experiencing no benefits from their treatments.

That disturbed me the most about these men. I saw people who needed genuine medical attention come to these psychic surgeons. One young boy had burned his nose and it was swollen to the size of a tennis ball. Another patient had his appendix "removed" three times before a regular doctor finally removed it surgically.

Many of these healers appeared to be very sincere.

Some felt they were helping people believe in God; they prayed over the patients and read from the Bible. But they also told people that if they didn't have enough faith, they wouldn't be healed. That gave the doctors a good excuse when a person wasn't healed—it wasn't his fault but the patient's. He would have been healed if only he had had more faith.

After viewing the operations, I interviewed a number of the patients, asking them if they were helped. Many answered "I think so" or "I hope so." Yet, as I went down the line of people waiting to see the healer, I saw many returning with the same problems they had brought in previous weeks. Some had the same operation performed on them week after week.

Others were genuinely helped and even cured by these surgeries. The percentage of people cured, however, is much lower than articles written about the subject lead one to believe. And the healings do not result from the operations, which are fake, but from the operations' psychological effect on people who believe they are real.

One of the best studies on this phenomenon is by William A. Nolen, M.D. In his book *Healings: A Doctor in Search of a Miracle*, Nolen examined hundreds of volumes and visited several of the best-known faith healers, including several Filipino psychic surgeons, looking for "adequately documented examples of cures that could not reasonably be explained except in terms of miraculous powers." He could not find one such case.[1]

In the final chapters of his book, Nolen describes the healing process, which he concludes is a mystery: ". . . we doctors don't do the healing; the body does. And even though, by examining specimens of tissue in various stages of healing, we know something of how healing occurs, we don't as yet have any idea how to control it. We put things back together; the body—God, if you prefer—heals."[2]

So how are these people healed? Nolen writes: "It is possible that 'healers,' by their machinations, their rituals, their sheer charisma, stimulate patients so that they heal more rapidly than they otherwise might; charismatic doctors do the same. In all probability, this is why doctors who have warm rapport with their patients seem to get better results than doctors who treat their patients briskly and impersonally."[3]

The whole point of his book is that certain illnesses successfully lend themselves to treatment of this type. Others will naturally, over the course of time, heal without any outside help. At least half of all illnesses fall into these two categories, so any psychic healer automatically should have a success rate of at least 50 percent.

Nolan explains that the real problem is with organic diseases, such as heart attacks, infections, gallstones, hernias, slipped discs, cancers of all kinds, broken bones, congenital deformities, and many others. He writes:

> These are the diseases that healers, even the most charismatic, cannot cure. When they attempt to do so—and they all fall into this trap, since they know and care nothing of the differences between functional and organic diseases—they tread on very dangerous ground. When healers treat serious organic diseases they are responsible for untold anguish and unhappiness; this happens because they keep patients away from possibly

effective and lifesaving help. The healers become killers.

Search the literature, as I have, and you will find no documented cures by healers of gallstones, heart disease, cancer or any other serious organic disease. Certainly, you'll find patients temporarily relieved of their upset stomachs, their chest pains, their breathing problems; and you will find healers, and believers, who will interpret this interruption of symptoms as evidence that the disease is cured. But when you track the patient down and find out what happened later, you always find the "cure" to have been purely symptomatic and transient. The underlying disease remains.[4]

Several doctors actually have endorsed certain psychic healers while recognizing the absurdity of the operations. They are taken in because they are not trained in the field of deception. It would take too much time and space to describe all the variations and techniques these healers use, but the average person could never detect their trickery. Many people are deceived because they try to explain the operations in terms of science, psychology, theology, or medicine. That actually assists the healers by further drawing attention away from their sleight of hand.

Tony Agpaoa, probably the best-known Filipino surgeon, sometimes stretched a thin piece of goat intestine over the patient before making an incision. Cutting through it created the illusion of cutting the skin and caused a snapping sound. Then he reached down into the incision and pulled out what he claimed was a diseased organ, such as an appendix, tumor, or damaged vertebra. He disposed of the extra piece of skin in a bucket below the table, and left no trace of an incision on the patient, since no cut was made.

Because of my experience, I am very skeptical of reports about miraculous healing. People describe all sorts of spectacular feats that the healers could not possibly have done. Most operations are relatively minor, and exaggerated reports about cancer being cured, ruptured disks being repaired, and gallstones disappearing simply can't be substantiated.

For years during my show I cut my wife in half, then apparently divided the two parts of her body and walked through the center. I would have her move her head on one side of the stage, and move her feet on the other side of the stage. People were constantly baffled by the effect. They didn't know how I did it, but they knew that it must be a trick because I called myself a magician and I performed it on a stage.

But suppose I called myself a surgeon and performed the same procedure in an operating room, smearing some blood and using medical terms in a serious manner. If I claimed to correct an internal problem while she was divided, and even produced some tissue for effect, many people would think they were witnessing something supernatural. It certainly would be far more dramatic than anything these psychic healers produce—but it would be just as fraudulent.

A very important element in this study is the question of faith. The healers tell their patients that if they have enough faith, they will be healed. If the surgery was genuine, however, it wouldn't matter if the patient believed or not. A successful appendectomy depends on the surgeon's skill, not the patient's faith. (I will further examine faith healing and divine healing in Chapter 13.) Jesus warned of the consequences of falsely claiming supernatural power: "Not all who sound religious are really godly people. They may refer to me as 'Lord,' but they still won't get to heaven. For the decisive question is whether they obey my Father in heaven. At the Judgment many will tell me, 'Lord, Lord, we told others about you and used your name to cast out demons and to do many other great miracles.' But I will reply, 'You have never been mine. Go away, for your deeds are evil.' "[5]

Voices from the Past

What could be more fascinating than to communicate with a person who has died? This would be especially meaningful if you loved that person very much.

During the mid-1800's, dozens of spirit mediums traveled around the United States and England and demonstrated their powers, attracting large crowds. One of the most popular was a slender Irish blonde named Anna Eva Fay. She sat inside a large, custom-made cabinet, her wrists securely bound behind her with strips of cloth and tied to a harness ring attached to a post in the rear of the cabinet. When the curtains were closed and the spirits summoned, musical instruments were played, various objects were tossed, nails were hammered into a block of wood, and dolls were cut out of paper. These activities supposedly were evidence of spirits. The spectacular performance concluded when the "spirits" took a knife and cut Mrs. Fay's cords.

The effect was so astounding that thousands of people flocked to see her demonstrations. An eminent scientist, Sir William Crookes, tested Mrs. Fay, having her place her hands on brass handles that led to a galvanometer. While the galvanometer showed no break in the current, the mysterious manifestations were demonstrated. Later, various individuals exposed Mrs. Fay as a fraud, who performed her feats using clever trickery, yet people continued to flock into large theaters to see her amazing performances.

Before her death, Mrs. Fay's secret was passed on to a man from Ireland who later came to the United States, where he and his wife presented the seance. Before their death they taught it to their son Harry Willard, who presented the seance with his wife for nearly 50 years. They shared it with their daughter Frances, from whom I learned the secret of the Anna Eva Fay seance. I made arrangements for Frances to train my wife, Aljeana, to present the various kinds of "spirit" manifestations.

For several years we invited members of the audience to the stage to help tie my wife's hands to a post. Then, while she supposedly was in a trance, we closed the curtains on her. Immediately a tambourine played and a basket flew over the curtain. The curtain was closed for less than ten seconds before I reopened it, revealing my wife slumped in the same position, her hands still firmly tied. Then I invited a member of the audience to stand blindfolded inside the curtain. Soon after the curtain was closed, the participant came running out of the cubicle, a bucket over his head and his shoes removed.

We included this unique presentation in our performances throughout the world until Aljeana's death, in 1976. It was entertaining and got a lot of laughs, but it also showed how easily people can be deceived. My wife had no power to contact the spirits. Everything she did was an illusion, created exclusively by physical means.

Modern belief in communication with the dead, or spiritism, as it often is called, began in America in 1848 in the little town of Hydesville, New York. People began to hear mysterious knocking sounds in a farmhouse. Margaret Fox (age eight) and her younger sister, Catherine, began asking questions of the "spirit" inside the house, and answers came as distinct raps, apparently from inside the walls. For example, when one girl held up four fingers and asked, "How many fingers?" they heard four raps. Through their questioning, they revealed that the originator of the noises was the spirit of a man murdered in the house several years before. The story spread, and people from all over the country came to see this remarkable phenomenon.

For 40 years the Fox sisters traveled throughout the world and made a great deal of money demonstrating this spirit's communicative powers. The mysterious rappings followed them wherever they went, and though they were examined by leading doctors, scientists, and preachers, no trickery was discovered.

Then in 1888 the girls confessed that it was all a fraud. They had started by tying a string to an apple and bumping it on the floor at night to scare their superstitious mother. She did not suspect trickery, since her children were so young. When she called in her neighbors, the girls found a more effective method for producing the raps: They snapped the joints in their toes, in much the same way as one cracks the knuckles in his fingers. In the quiet darkness of a seance room, where a wooden floor served as a sounding board, those raps proved very effective.

A confession by Margaret Fox appeared on September 24, 1888, in the *New York Herald*. Among other things, it said, "As far as spirits were concerned, neither my sister nor I thought about it. I knew there was no such thing as the departed returning to this life. I have seen so much miserable deception that every morning of my life I have it before me. That is why I am willing to state that spiritualism is a fraud of the worst deception. I trust that this statement, coming solemnly from me, the first and most successful in this deception, will break the rapid growth of spiritualism and prove that it is all a fraud, hypocrisy, and delusion."

Unfortunately, the growth in spiritualism continued to mount, even in the face of evidence that these two leading mediums had used trickery.

The great magician Harry Houdini probably was most responsible for exposing fraudulent mediums. During the final years of his life he was consumed by an obsession to find a genuine medium to contact his mother. Shortly before her demise, the family had been rocked by scandal. His brother Nat's wife had left her husband to marry another brother, Leopold. Houdini could not forgive Leopold and told his mother that he looked to her for guidance on what he should do.

Houdini was in Europe when his mother died. During her final hours, she tried to give the family by her bedside a message for her son, but could not get the words out. Houdini wondered what his mother was trying to say. Did she want him to forgive his brother? He often visited his mother's grave, begging her to tell him her last words. Only spiritualists believed in communication with the dead, but Houdini believed that all the mediums he had met were frauds. He determined, however, that if a genuine medium existed anywhere in the world, he would find him.

During his remaining years Houdini attended some

5000 seances. In many of them, ghostly whispers claimed to be his mother, but there was one problem: The voices were always in English, while his mother spoke only Yiddish. As a result, he became very bitter against these charlatans who impersonated his dear mother, and he began an all-out campaign to expose fake mediums.

He also began making pacts with his friends, vowing that whoever died first would attempt to communicate with the other using a secret code. He lectured about spiritualism around the country, demonstrating common techniques used by mediums, such as table levitation, playing of musical instruments, and writing on blank slates. He also offered a 5000-dollar prize to any medium who could produce an effect that he could not duplicate. No one ever collected the prize.

Houdini wrote two books about his study, revealing the results of tests with the best-known mediums and disclosing techniques they used to gather information and perform various feats. In his book *A Magician among the Spirits* he concluded:

> To my knowledge I have never been baffled in the least by what I have seen at seances. Everything I have seen has been merely a form of mystification. The secret of all such performances is to catch the mind off guard and the moment after it has been surprised to follow up with something else that carries the intelligence along with the performer, even against the spectator's will. . . .
>
> I have said many times that I am willing to believe, want to believe, will believe, if the spiritualists can show any substantiated

proof, but until they do I shall have to live on, believing from all the evidence shown me and from what I have experienced that spiritualism has not been proven satisfactorily to the world at large and that none of the evidence offered has been able to stand up under the fierce rays of investigations.[1]

Shortly before his death, Houdini and his wife, Bess, made a pact that whoever died first would attempt to contact the other with these words: "Rosabelle, answer, tell, pray, answer, look, tell, answer, answer, tell." The words following "Rosabelle" were a code that spelled out the word "Believe." On Halloween of 1926, Houdini died of a ruptured appendix. Two-and-a-half years later a young medium named Arthur Ford sent to Houdini's widow a one-word message, "Forgive," supposedly from Houdini's mother. A message from her husband followed, with the pre-determined words in the correct sequence.

Two days later Bess met with Ford and heard her husband supposedly speak to her through the medium. News of the event spread quickly, and the next day newspapers blared headlines that Houdini had returned from the dead. The great magician's widow signed a declaration that read: "Regardless of all statements to the contrary, I wish to declare that the message, in its entirety and in the agreed-upon sequence, given to me by Arthur Ford, is the correct message pre-arranged between Mr. Houdini and myself." The statement was cosigned by three witnesses.

But was this genuine evidence of Houdini's return? Skeptics doubted it and found ample reason for their suspicions. Raymond Fitzsimons in his book *Death and the Magician* tells how a close friend of Houdini and his wife exposed the fraud to the widow:

> Joe Rinn heard the news and decided that
> the whole affair was a spook trick to end all
> spook tricks, a trick that must be exposed.
> Bess was convinced of the truth of Ford's
> seances, so Rinn and other friends of Hou-
> dini's reminded her of certain things which
> in her emotional state she had forgotten.
> Ford's message from Houdini's mother had
> included the evidential word FORGIVE, but
> the Brooklyn *Eagle* of March 13, 1927, a year
> before Ford's seance, had quoted Bess as say-
> ing that any authentic communication from
> Houdini's mother would have to include that
> word. Ford could have read this. She was
> also reminded that the code words used had
> been printed in Harold Kellock's biography
> of Houdini, published the previous year, on
> which she had collaborated. Bess admitted
> that she had not recalled these things. But
> at the time of the seance she had been sick
> with influenza and emotionally run-down.[2]

Later Bess retracted her statement about Ford, and
to her dying day maintained that she had not received
any communication from her late husband. Yet the
controversy over spiritualism still rages today. Millions
of people believe that contact with the dead is possible
and spend millions of dollars to communicate with
loved ones through mediums.

After numerous exposures of fraudulent tricks used
in seances early in the twentieth century, mediums
devised safer techniques. Mental mediums like Arthur
Ford became more prevalent. In his type of seance, the

medium usually goes into a trance and his or her body comes under the control of a spirit. (Ford supposedly became controlled by Fletcher, the son of a wealthy French-Canadian family. He had died suddenly in 1918 while attending college.) The spirit passes messages from other spirits, through the medium, to the sitter. In order to authenticate the communication, the spirit relates seemingly insignificant details that only the sitter could know or verify.

In his book *The Spiritual Frontier,* William V. Rauscher, an Episcopal priest, compares it to a phone conversation with a very poor connection, in which the operator serves as a go-between. The problem is to determine if your friend on the other end of the line really is who he says he is. To prove that the communication is genuine, the medium relates what appears to be trivial details. This information, which the client believes the medium could not possibly know, proves that contact with the deceased loved one or friend has been established. The argument sounds good on the surface, but ample evidence shows that many mediums keep extensive files about their clients.

In 1967, Ford conducted the most famous seance in recent history. The event was shown on network television in Canada and involved Episcopal bishop James Pike. During the seance Ford supposedly received communications from Pike's son, who had committed suicide in February 1966. Pike was convinced that Ford could not have obtained the facts he gave by any other means, thus supporting his belief that Ford was a genuine medium.

But in his book *Arthur Ford: The Man Who Talked with the Dead*, Allen Spraggett told about his shocking discovery after Ford's death.

William Rauscher and I, researching this biography, were sifting through Arthur Ford's private papers. Several boxes bulged with the medium's personalia—letters, diaries, books, newspaper and magazine clippings, scrapbooks, even his income-tax returns.... We knew that we had not inherited all Ford's papers; an unknown amount of personal material had been destroyed by a former secretary shortly after the medium's death, presumably on his instructions....

Bill Rauscher was holding a newspaper clipping and, as he scanned it, his face clouded over.

"What's wrong?" I asked.

Without a word, he handed me the clipping.

It was an obituary, undated, from the *New York Times.* The headline told me why Bill Rauscher was disturbed; it read: BISHOP BLOCK, 71, IS DEAD ON COAST.

In the Ford-Pike seance, one of the purported discarnates who communicated on television, in a manner that James Pike found peculiarly convincing, was his episcopal predecessor, the Right Rev. Karl Morgan Block, late Bishop of California.

As I read the obituary my disturbance increased.

The Block communicator had mentioned several small—even trivial—details which Pike considered especially evidential since their very triviality seemed to rule out the possibility of prior research by the medium. The details Pike found impressive appeared to be too obscure, too idiosyncratic, to be accessible to research. However, every one of these supposedly unresearchable items was mentioned in the *New York Times* obituary.[3]

Later the researchers discovered further evidence that most, if not all, of the information Ford gave in his TV seance was obtained through personal research, primarily newspaper accounts. While Spraggett and Rauscher say that this evidence does not discount the fact that Ford was a genuine medium, the truth is that Ford's two most famous seances, at the beginning and the end of his career, are shrouded in suspicion.

One of the most recent damaging revelations against spiritualism was made by a very successful medium, Lamar Keene. In his book *The Psychic Mafia* he details how he conned hundreds of people into believing that he had supernatural powers.

Lamar was raised in a Baptist family and for a time considered entering the ministry. In his twenties, however, he was introduced to spiritualism by a friend. Together they attended a large spiritualist church. After a little more than a year, the pair launched into their own work, half-believing they had genuine, though undeveloped, psychic power.

They quickly learned that to develop a following, they needed to give people tangible manifestations of the spirits. They soon discovered how to do that through a national information network. Mediums kept extensive files on their subjects and, using this network, they could obtain accurate information quickly about a visitor from any part of the country.

Many mediums add physical manifestations to their messages. Keene was adroit at dropping personal trinkets in the laps of sitters, but relied primarily on the quality of his information, which was culled from newspaper clippings and pilfered from the wallets and purses of unsuspecting clients.

James Randi in his book *Flim-Flam!* tells about an

interview with Keene shortly after his startling revelation:

> I interviewed him and discovered that he knew little about the more subtle methods of chicanery. He explained to me that he didn't *need* to know much. Anything he did would serve to convince the faithful, he said. They fell for the most transparent ruses, many of which were thought up on the spur of the moment, and he and his fellow charlatans laughed themselves silly, at the end of an easy day's work, as they recounted how simple it had been.[4]

It is interesting that Keene's book was named *The Psychic Mafia*. After his defection from spiritualism, his former friends threatened to kill him. One night several shots were fired at him from a passing car. He was wounded in the stomach and recovered only after a long hospitalization.

About a dozen companies in the United States specialize in building intricate props that spiritualists use in their performances. Several of these companies have extensive catalogs of items they stock or can build. Most of the catalogs also have a section listing books about spiritualistic tricks.

Recently I went to the shop of a man who was doing some work for me. He was building a spirit vase for one of his other clients, a witch doctor in Africa. A person could whisper a question into this apparently normal vase and a voice, supposedly from the spirit world, would answer in a mysterious whisper from within the vase.

At one time such items were very popular with spirit

mediums, but now most people in the United States know what can be accomplished through electronics. You can imagine, though, how such a "miraculous" demonstration of the witch doctor's powers would astound superstitious natives in Africa.

Despite such obvious frauds, people still ask, "Do the dead return?" After nearly 30 years of studying this question from the point of view of a magician, a psychologist, and a person deeply interested in spiritual truth, I have to conclude that willful communication with the dead is impossible. That is not to say that all mediums are insincere. Some may genuinely believe that they have the power to communicate with the dead.

When my daughter Robyn was a teenager, her boyfriend's mother became very involved with a spirit medium in Phoenix. My daughter attended one of her seances and was frightened by the experience. When she told me about it, I was angry and immediately wanted to confront this woman and expose her racket. On my way to meet her, I realized that my anger and hatred for what she was doing was not the right attitude. I asked God to forgive me and to give me a genuine concern and love for this person.

We ended up talking for several hours, and this woman started asking questions about reality, the meaning of life, and the person of Jesus Christ—many of the questions I had asked as a young man. She had turned to spiritualism while looking for answers. Like many mediums, she found that her clients demanded tangible demonstrations of communication with the dead. She had a sincere desire to help people, but felt trapped by her circumstances; she felt forced to cheat and produce spirit forms and other manifestations.

I think people look to mediums for two reasons.

First, they have lost loved ones and intensely desire to contact them and establish their existence. The other reason is curiosity, an interest in the unusual and supernatural.

The Bible makes it very clear that we are to avoid any dealings with mediums. In Deuteronomy, Moses told the Israelites:

> When you arrive in the Promised Land you must be very careful lest you be corrupted by the horrible customs of the nations now living there.... No Israeli may...call on the evil spirits for aid, or be a fortune teller, or be a serpent charmer, medium, or wizard, or call forth the spirits of the dead. Anyone doing these things is an object of horror and disgust to the Lord, and it is because the nations do these things that the Lord your God will displace them.[5]

Why doesn't God want His people to attempt to contact the spirits of the dead? First, such activities distract us from our faith in Him. They may even prevent us from learning about His plan of salvation. Second, most people will misinterpret what they see and hear. They so want to believe that they have contacted a loved one that they are easily deceived by fraud. Third, such attempts can place us in contact with demonic forces. Fourth, communication causes tremendous emotional feelings, with which God didn't intend for us to deal. Once a person believes he has contacted a loved one, he longs to continue the conversation. This can cause serious spiritual and psychological problems.

It is revealing to look at the lives of mediums after

many years in their profession. Awareness of their fates compelled Lamar Keene to give up his practice of spiritualism:

> Looking ahead, if I stayed in mediumship, I saw only deepening gloom. All the mediums I've known or known about have had tragic endings.
>
> The Fox sisters, who started it all, wound up as alcoholic derelicts. William Slade, famed for his slate-writing tricks, died insane in a Michigan sanitarium. Margery the Medium lay on her deathbed a hopeless drunk. The celebrated Arthur Ford fought the battle of the bottle to the very end and lost. And the inimitable Mable Riffle, boss of Camp Chesterfield—well, when she died it was winter and freezing cold, and her body had to be held until a thaw for burial; the service was in the Cathedral at Chesterfield. Very few attended.
>
> Whenever I looked it was the same: mediums, at the end of a tawdry life, dying a tawdry death.[6]

Some people cite the story in 1 Samuel 28, where King Saul visited the medium at Endor and called up the deceased prophet Samuel, as evidence of genuine contact with the dead. That is a dangerous conclusion. For one thing, the narrative never says that it actually was the ghost of Samuel. I don't believe that God would go against His specific command and do something He has condemned by bringing the spirit of Samuel back from the dead. In fact, if you study that passage carefully, you'll note that Saul never actually saw the form. The medium described what she saw, and everything "Samuel" spoke she easily could have known. Another possible explanation is that a demon appeared, impersonating Samuel. Since God had cut off communication with Saul, I doubt that Samuel returned. In any case, this unique example in Scripture should not be used as evidence that contact with the dead is possible.

The Bible warns us not to attempt to contact the dead. Desire to communicate with a loved one is a real feeling, but comfort doesn't come from a medium. The prophet Isaiah wrote, "Why are you trying to find out the future by consulting witches and mediums? Don't listen to their whisperings and mutterings. Can the living find out the future from the dead? Why not ask your God?"[7] As a Christian, I can say with the apostle Paul that to be absent from the body is to be present with the Lord.[8] That is where our focus should be. Our hope is that when our loved ones die, if they are in Christ, they will go to be with God and we will join them at the time of our death.

5

Exploring the Future

- New York City, Albany, and Boston soon will be destroyed.[1]
- The Civil War will be the start of a global conflict.[2]
- The moon is inhabited by a people of uniform size, about six feet in height.[3]
- In a few years, the people of the United States will be destroyed by pestilence, hail, famine, and earthquake.[4]

These prophecies were delivered between 1832 and 1837. They sound crazy now, yet the man who proclaimed them was a respected religious leader, whose followers now number in the millions. He is just one example of why we must be wary of modern-day prophets.

Millions of people spend their money in the belief or hope that they can satisfy their curiosity about the future. They use astrology, palm-reading, and modern-day seers like Jeane Dixon to help them plan their lives.

But are modern-day prognosticators legitimate? Can anyone predict the future?

I apply four basic tests whenever people claim to have psychic ability to predict future events: 1) How specific are their predictions? 2) What percentage of their forecasts are accurate? 3) Do their lives back up their claims? 4) What is the source (or claimed source) of their information?

Let's look at these questions in more detail. First: *How specific are their predictions?*

Psychic superstar Jeane Dixon is perhaps best known for predicting the assassination of President John F. Kennedy. *Parade* magazine (May 13, 1956) reported, "As to the 1960 election, Mrs. Dixon thinks it will be dominated by labor and won by a Democrat. But he will be assassinated or die in office, though not necessarily in his first term."

This is a classic example of vagueness that can, in retrospect, look like an accurate hit. Mrs. Dixon predicted that a Democrat would win—her chances of being right were 50-50. She didn't say who. And it wasn't a huge risk to predict that the president would die in office. Already three had done so in the twentieth century, and observers saw a cycle: The president elected every 20 years from the year 1840 either had been assassinated or had died while in office. Mrs. Dixon wasn't willing to state how the president would die, whether or not it would be an assassination, or even approximately when it would take place. If the president served two terms, she had eight years for her prophecy to be fulfilled. So her most spectacular forecast really wasn't that impressive.

But often that is how modern prophets work. Right now I can make some "prophecies" similar to that of many seers. I can tell you with a high degree of confidence that within the next 12 months:

- A major earthquake will take place, killing more than a hundred people.
- A major world figure will die in office.
- A major technological breakthrough will amaze the world and change our lives.

It doesn't take a prophet to make these kinds of predictions. It only takes a good observer, someone aware of what is happening around him in the world.

One of the most popular prophets over the last few centuries was the sixteenth-century seer Nostradamus. At age 50 he began composing vague quatrains (four-line verses) which he said were predictions. He divided the more than 900 verses into groups of 100, with each grouping representing a century. The prophecies contained elaborate symbolism and codes that Nostradamus admitted could not possibly be understood until after the events they predicted. That has led to several interesting interpretations over the years. For example, in World War II the Allied forces and the Germans used the same verse to prove opposite conclusions. A. Voldben in his book *After Nostradamus* writes about the prophet he praises:

> The quatrains are strewn about without any order in such a way that even if the beginning were found it would not be possible to continue them in the right order. They are usually vague, involved in the confused language of sybilline oracles, some literal and some symbolic. So much so that in the confusion between literal and symbolic, one is left hardly understanding anything at all! If some are easy to understand, others are

incomprehensible. He writes in the French of his day, mixed with Latin words with others made up by him and his own anagrams.[5]

It makes you wonder why people still diligently study his work. Yet Nostradamus is extremely popular, especially on university campuses.

My second question logically follows from the first: *What percentage of the prophet's predictions are accurate?*

In promoting their forecasts, today's prophets proudly recall their hits, while hoping that people will forget or ignore their misses. The public generally complies. When specific, verifiable predictions are made, it is relatively simple to go back and check the record. F.K. Donnelly, associate professor of history at the University of New Brunswick in Canada, reviewed the predictions that 21 psychics made in *The People's Almanac,* 1975 edition. The seers included Malcolm Bessent, David Bubar, Jeane Dixon, Irene Hughes, and many other well-known psychics. Donnelly evaluated their predictions from the time they were made through 1981:

> Out of the total of 72 predictions, 66 (or 92 percent) were dead wrong. Among the favorites in this category were those that China would go to war with the United States (predicted 4 times) and that New York City would soon be underwater (predicted 3 times). My favorite inept prognostication comes from the Berkeley Psychic Institute, which predicted a war between Greenland and the Soviet Union over fish. Since nuclear

weapons were to be used, this was to be very
sensibly fought in Labrador in May 1977.[6]

Of the six predictions that were not wrong, two were
only partially right or vague. Two others were not
exactly graphic evidence of psychic power: Russia and
the United States would "remain as leading world
powers," and there would be no world wars between
1975 and 1980. Donnelly concludes, "Even if we were
to accept that four (or 6 percent) of the 72 predictions
were correct . . . a further problem remains. Since we
do not know which of the 72 predictions will fall into
the six-percent category, then of what use is this? Who
among us would take the advice of a tipster with a track
record of being wrong more than nine times out of
ten?"[7]

It's easy to evaluate Jeane Dixon's track record. Here
are just a few of her prophecies that haven't come true:

1) Russia would be the first nation to put men on
the moon.

2) World War III would begin in 1954.

3) The Vietnam war would end in 1966. (It didn't
end until 1975.)

4) On October 19, 1968, she predicted that Jacque-
line Kennedy was not thinking of marriage. The next
day Mrs. Kennedy married Aristotle Onassis.

5) In 1970 she predicted that Castro would be over-
thrown from Cuba and would have to leave the island.[8]

These are just a handful of many examples. The
problem is that people remember only the successes.
When you compare Mrs. Dixon's hits with her misses,
you find that her percentage of accuracy is most unim-
pressive.

I opened this chapter with four prophecies made by
Joseph Smith, founder of the Mormon Church. Smith

claimed to be a prophet of God, and in the course of 18 years he made 64 specific prophecies. Only six of them were fulfilled. Many of his proclamations dealt with the future of his church. For example, in August of 1831 he stated that God had told him, "The faithful among you shall be preserved and rejoice together in the land of Missouri."[9] In September of 1832 he stated that the city of Independence would become the "New Jerusalem...even the place of the temple, which temple shall be reared in this generation."[10] Six years later the Mormons were driven out of Independence. No temple was built there. Eventually they were driven from Missouri and settled in Utah.

I could cite many other prophecies. Smith predicted the return of Jesus Christ to earth by the year 1890. He said Indians converted to Mormonism would turn white. He proclaimed that the United States would be utterly destroyed if there was not redress for the wrongs committed against Mormons in Missouri. None of these were fulfilled.

Third, I think it is important to *evaluate the lives of the persons making psychic claims*. The most revealing article I've found about Jeane Dixon was out of the *National Observer* (reprinted by *The Christian Reader*). The author, Daniel St. Albin Greene, spent weeks investigating her. "What gradually emerged," Greene wrote, "was a portrait of neither saint nor charlatan, but of a beguiling enigma whose real identity has been absorbed by the myth she herself created."[11]

Greene examined the chapters in Jeane Dixon's life that she has tried to suppress. It turns out that legend, not reality, made Mrs. Dixon's career. And it is a legend of her own making. "All the public knows about Jeane Dixon is what she has said."[12]

The article examined the claim that Mrs. Dixon has never used her "God-given gifts" for personal profit. In fact, her book royalties and revenue from her syndicated columns were paid to a company that Mrs. Dixon and her husband owned. Sponsors of her speeches donated money to a charitable foundation run by her. The foundation, Children to Children, actually had distributed less than 19 percent of its income.

Most of the information about Mrs. Dixon's background is found in *A Gift of Prophecy: The Phenomenal Jeane Dixon,* by Ruth Montgomery. A detailed check of records revealed that much of her earlier biographical material was fiction. A total of 14 years, including a former marriage, had disappeared from her past.

> If nothing else, the purged 14 years constitute a credibility gap that undermines the whole foundation of the Jeane Dixon story as told by Mrs. Dixon. Rereading the biography of her pre-Washington period in the new time frame, one must constantly choose among three possibilities: each incident that Mrs. Dixon says took place when she was a child prodigy in California either 1) actually occurred many years earlier in the Midwest; 2) happened when she was in her 20s or 30s; or 3) never happened at all.[13]

Such revelations severely limit her credibility. The same could be said about Joseph Smith. For the most part, the Mormons are very sincere people, but the Mormon Church stands or falls primarily on the reputation of this one man.

A careful examination of Smith's life reveals many

disturbing facts. Perhaps most damaging are the various versions of his first vision, in which he says that God the Father (and/or Jesus Christ, an angel, or a pillar of light, depending on the version) appeared to him when he was 16 years old (later amended to when he was 14 years old). In this version Smith was told that all churches were wrong, and that "all their creeds are an abomination in His sight."

Fawn Brodie states in the supplement of her meticulously researched book, *No Man Knows My History: The Life of Joseph Smith the Mormon Prophet:*

> One of the major original premises of this biography was that Joseph Smith's assumption of the role of a religious prophet was an evolutionary process, that he began. . .using the primitive techniques of the folklore of magic common to his area, most of which he discarded as he evolved into a preacher-prophet. There seemed to be good evidence that when he chose to write of this evolution in his *History of the Church* he distorted the past in the interest of promoting his public image as a gifted young prophet with a substantial and growing following. There was evidence even to stimulate doubt of the authenticity of the "first vision," which Joseph Smith declared in his official history had occurred in 1820 when he was fourteen.[14]

Numerous points darken this man's integrity. The 1835 edition of *Doctrine & Covenants* condemned fornication and polygamy and admonished, "One man should have one wife; and one woman but one husband; except that in the event of death when either is at liberty to marry again." Those words became a problem for Joseph Smith as he had affairs with more and more women. Finally he received a "new revelation" in 1843 giving God's blessing on plural marriages. The earlier command simply disappeared, without explanation, from later editions of *Doctrine & Covenants.* As best as Brodie can determine, Smith had 48 wives when he died in 1844.[15]

There are also many reasons to doubt *The Book of Mormon.* Joseph Smith said of this book, the keystone of his religion, that it "was the most correct of any book on earth."[16] Yet since its first printing in 1830 there have been 3913 changes! (These have been thoroughly documented by Jerald and Sandra Tanner, who marked all the changes on a photo reprint of the original edition.)

Besides that, archeology cannot verify *The Book of Mormon,* whereas the Bible is one of the best-documented books of history. Most of the mountains, rivers, cities, and regions named in the Bible have been identified by archeological scholars. But Josh McDowell and Don Stewart have summarized the problem with *The Book of Mormon:*

1. No *Book of Mormon* cities have been located.
2. No *Book of Mormon* names have been found in New World inscriptions.
3. No genuine inscriptions have been found in Hebrew in America.
4. No genuine inscriptions have been found in America in Egyptian (or anything similar to Egyptian) which could correspond to Joseph Smith's "reformed Egyptian."
5. No ancient copies of *Book of Mormon* scriptures have been found.

6. No ancient inscriptions of any kind in America which indicate that the ancient inhabitants had Hebrew or Christian beliefs have been found.

7. No mention of *Book of Mormon* persons, nations, or places have been found.[17]

Why be concerned with such details? Are they really that important? I believe that a person who claims to be a prophet creates for himself a high standard. By stating that he has divine revelations, he opens himself to scrutiny to see if his life supports his claims. J. Edward Decker, a former leader in the Mormon Church, writes, "A lie is a lie, is a lie, and when it comes out of the mouth of a man proclaimed to be a prophet of God, that man is sent not of God, neither has God commanded him."[18]

The final question is: *What is the source of the prophet's information?*

A favorite trick among magicians is to make a prediction of future news headlines—the winner of an election, the World Series champion, a winning lottery number—and seal it inside an envelope. Then the envelope is locked inside a safe. The more secure it appears, the better. It is best to have 24-hour security to verify that no one tampers with that safe. Of course, after the result is known, the envelope is opened amidst great fanfare to reveal that the magician had correctly predicted the event.

Many books explain various methods to accomplish this trick. Elaborate paraphernalia, some costing thousands of dollars, can help successfully create this illusion. Some inexpensive methods also do the trick, such as one I used one night during my show. I correctly predicted who would shoot J.R. of "Dallas" two hours before it was due to be aired on local television.

My audience was amazed, as this was one of television's best-kept secrets. CBS had filmed several versions, so even the cast didn't know who the culprit was. But my audience didn't know that backstage I had an open phone line to a friend on the East Coast. Of course, East Coast viewers would learn the answer three hours earlier than those in the West, where I was performing. Mystery solved!

One of the most blatant frauds was a tape of blonde psychic Tamara Rand predicting the attempted assassination of President Reagan nearly three months ahead of the event. The tape was shown on a Los Angeles station and then repeated on NBC's "Today Show" and ABC's "Good Morning America." Several newspapers published an Associated Press story about it before one of the cameramen who had filmed Ms. Rand revealed the truth. The tape actually had been made two days after the assassination attempt. Before she finally confessed, Ms. Rand tried to explain that she merely had been asked to "rearticulate" her prophecy in front of cameras because her words were not clear on the earlier tape.[19]

Some psychics claim that they have a God-given gift. Jeane Dixon has always made this claim. If indeed she has a gift from God, then God must make an awful lot of mistakes! The facts are conclusive that she has no gift of God. The Bible makes it clear that one evidence of a genuine prophet is that he *never* makes a wrong prediction. "You may say in your heart, 'How shall we know the word which the Lord has not spoken?' When a prophet speaks in the name of the Lord, if the thing does not come about or come true, that is the thing which the Lord has not spoken. The prophet has spoken it presumptuously; you shall not be afraid of him."[20]

Another primary tool of the fortune-telling trade is

called cold reading. It is used primarily by palm-readers and those who use a crystal ball, tarot cards, or tea leaves. Magicians also use it in stage shows to demonstrate "mind-reading" skills.

Cold reading is a combination of things, but essentially the reader gives back information that the client unknowingly has given him. He starts with a pre-prepared character assessment that is general enough to encompass approximately 85 percent of the population. The reader says things like, "You have many acquaintances but few close friends. . . . People frequently call on you for advice . . . . You have a tendency to worry at times . . . . You tend to put off jobs that must be done but that don't interest you . . . .

Ray Hyman, who helped pay for his college education with his nightclub mentalist act, explains the next step:

> The cold reader basically relies on a good memory and acute observation. The client is carefully studied. The clothing—for example, style, neatness, cost, age—provides a host of cues for helping the reader make shrewd guesses about socioeconomic level, conservatism or extroversion, and other characteristics. The client's physical features—weight, posture, looks, eyes, and hands provide further cues. The hands are especially revealing to the good reader. The manner of speech, use of grammar, gestures, and eye contact are also good sources. To the good reader the huge amount of information coming from an initial sizing-up of the client greatly narrows the possible categories into which he classifies clients.[21]

After his stock spiel, the cold reader begins to address

the client's problems and watches the reaction to determine whether or not he's on the right track. He is also a good listener and many times takes what he has heard and later rephrases it to make it sound like a fresh revelation. Fortune-tellers have learned that most clients already have decided what they want to do and simply want support to carry out their decision. General and ambiguous statements can be taken to mean whatever the client wants them to mean. Later the predictions seem more accurate than they really were.

Another area of prophecy is astrology. After my shows I am frequently asked my opinion of it. Three of my suggested questions again apply: How specific are the predictions? What percentage are accurate? What is the source of information?

Immediately we can discount the daily horoscopes in the newspapers. The statements are so general that true astrologers don't take them seriously. "Be careful on the highway . . . make sure you don't spend too much on pleasure and then later regret it . . . you may not like what a fellow worker is doing . . . one who has problems expects your aid . . . " and so on. These statements could apply to anyone and don't merit consideration.

But serious astrology has existed for thousands of years. H.J. Eysenck and D.K.B. Nias define it in their book *Astrology: Science or Superstition?*

> This [traditional astrology] deals with the connections believed to exist between the positions of the planets at the moment of someone's birth and that person's character, development, profession, marriage and general life history. This type of astrology can be descriptive (trying to help someone understand himself) or predictive (trying to

forecast what will happen to him) or post-dictive (trying to interpret and make sense of his past life). Predictive astrology can also concern itself with broader issues, such as the fate of nations, treaties and battles, arguing from the position of the planets at the time the treaties were signed, the battles were joined, kings or presidents inaugurated, and so forth.[22]

After studying the subject thoroughly, the authors concluded that, while astrology might provide meaningful insight into an individual's existence, the discipline as a whole has problems. "The major failure to which we have returned time after time is the lack of replication. It is not enough for a second researcher to set off on a similar trail of his own. If he is to validate the original research he must replicate it *in the same form*. . . . A hypothesis must survive repeated attempts to break it down. Only then can we place reliance on it."[23] We're back to the problem we've encountered in trying to test ESP—lack of repeatability.

A second problem is that "there is not one astrology but several—European, Indian, Chinese—and different astrologers therefore make different predictions from the same facts. In contrast, the laws of physics and astronomy are the same all over the world, and one would expect the same to be true of astrology if it did indeed have any factual basis. Science is international in its theories and findings, and astrology's failure to arrive at a set of universally agreed rules must speak heavily against it."[24]

Another problem is that people can interpret horoscopes to mean almost anything they want them to mean. One study of 38 college students demonstrates this. Each student was given two detailed horoscopes. One corresponded to his sign, the other was a "placebo"—a randomly selected horoscope from another sign. Of the 38 students, 22 rated their own horoscopes as accurate, 14 as inaccurate, and two said it was about even. As far as the placebo horoscopes, 19 rated them as accurate and 19 as not accurate. In comparing the two horoscopes, 19 rated their own as more accurate than the placebo, 18 rated the placebo more accurate than their own, and one said they were even.[25]

Evidently people feel a need to know something about their future. I believe that God understands this need. That is why it is important to understand one more principle: *We need to evaluate all prophecies in the light of Scripture.* The Bible clearly warns us about following after false prophets, sorcerers, diviners, mediums, etc. In the book of Isaiah God warned, "Let now the astrologers, those who prophesy by the stars, those who predict by the new moons, stand up and save you from what will come upon you. Behold, they have become like stubble, fire burns them; they cannot deliver themselves from the power of the flame."[26]

Jeremiah gave a similar warning: "Do not learn the way of the nations, and do not be terrified by the signs of the heavens, although the nations are terrified by them; for the customs of the peoples are delusion."[27]

God laid down strict regulations concerning prophets. First, genuine prophets were to point people to the one true God. Joseph Smith failed here because he declared that there were many gods.[28] Second, a genuine prophet cannot utter even one false prophecy. Prophets of the Bible told short-term and long-term prophecies. The fulfillment of their short-term predictions validated their long-range prophecies. Third, the purpose of prophecy is to cause people to obey God's commands and to believe in His Son, Jesus Christ.

The Bible contains numerous prophecies. Already many of these have been literally fulfilled. More than 300 of them concern the Messiah, and Jesus Christ fulfilled all of these. Other prophecies concern the end times, and we will examine these later in this book. But it is important to realize why God gave us these words: They are not intended to satisfy our curiosity, but rather to help prepare us for the future, and to encourage and comfort us.[29]

I believe Christians must be cautious of those who boldly claim to have inside information from God. As we have already seen, there are a few popular evangelists who give dramatic revelations of information about individuals in their audiences—addresses, names of their doctors, specific ailments—as a basis for making bold pronouncements concerning God's will for their lives. They are *not* speaking for God, yet some Christians cling to every word they say as if this was the word of God.

We must be careful. We do not want to miss the times when God does speak through His servants. Yet we must make sure that the one who claims to speak for God can indeed verify that claim in the manner God has prescribed in the Bible.

6

Solving Some Mysteries

Everyone likes a good mystery—just look at the sales of books by Von Daniken and Berlitz. There is always a substantial market for tabloids and paperback books with stories concerning the Bermuda Triangle, unidentified flying objects, the lost civilization of Atlantis, and other mysterious phenomena.

In the midseventies I started getting a number of questions about the Bermuda Triangle. Several movies and television shows had helped popularize it. I had discovered that attendance at my shows jumped dramatically when I dealt with popular mysteries, so I decided to research the subject. Unfortunately, it would be difficult for me to gain firsthand experience on this subject, as I had with other phenomena. I couldn't go out into the middle of the Triangle and wait for something to happen, so I had to look for other sources.

In his best-seller *The Bermuda Triangle*, Charles Berlitz defines the geographical area in question:

There is a section of the Western Atlantic, off the southeast coast of the United States, forming what has been termed a triangle, extending from Bermuda in the north to southern Florida, and then east to a point through the Bahamas past Puerto Rico to about 40 west longitude and then back again to Bermuda. This area occupies a disturbing and almost unbelievable place in the world's catalogue of unexplained mysteries. This is usually referred to as the Bermuda Triangle, where more than 100 planes and ships have literally vanished into thin air, most of them since 1945, and where more than 1,000 lives have been lost in the past twenty-six years, without a single body or even a piece of wreckage from the vanishing planes or ships having been found. Disappearances continue to occur with apparently increasing frequency, in spite of the fact that the seaways and airways are today more traveled, searches are more thorough, and records are more carefully kept.[1]

The author goes on to describe how planes have vanished while in radio contact with control towers, and how others had radioed "the most extraordinary messages, implying that they could not get their instruments to function, that their compasses were spinning, that the sky had turned yellow and hazy (on a clear day), and that the ocean. . .'didn't look right.' "[2] Boats, large and small, also have vanished without a trace. Others were found drifting, but with no survivors or bodies on board.

There have been numerous attempts to explain the mystery. Some of the explanations are extremely creative: sudden tidal waves, fireballs that explode the planes, a time-space warp, electromagnetic aberrations, and attacks by UFO's.

I found the best source of information on this subject in my own neighborhood. His name is Larry Kusche, and when I met him he was on the faculty of Arizona State University, just a few miles from my home. His book *The Bermuda Triangle Mystery—Solved* was a masterpiece of investigative reporting. From Kusche I learned enough information to draw several conclusions.

First, *15 to 20 percent of the incidents reported about the Bermuda Triangle never even happened.*

Berlitz reported that in October of 1978 three people on a 40-foot cabin cruiser disappeared in clear weather and calm seas during a short trip between Bimini and Miami. Author Michael Dennett did a detailed investigation of this and other recent Triangle incidents:

> This case is, as Berlitz might describe it, a classic Bermuda Triangle disappearance. It has all the hallmarks of such an occurrence; namely, an unidentified vessel, with three unnamed people on board, vanishes on an unspecified date. The local newspaper carried no report of this incident and the Coast Guard was unable to confirm that a vessel matching this description had been lost in October.[3]

Second, *25 to 30 percent of the mysterious disappearances did not even take place within the boundaries of the Bermuda Triangle.*

When it suited their purposes, mystery writers included air and sea disasters in the Gulf of Mexico and the far reaches of the Atlantic ocean hundreds of miles outside the Triangle borders. An American Globemaster that "disappeared north of the triangle in March 1950" actually exploded about 600 miles southwest of Ireland, at least 1000 miles outside the Triangle.

Third, *those who describe most of the cases try to convince readers that the disappearances took place on calm, clear days, when in reality they took place in very severe weather.*

In the epilogue to his book *The Bermuda Triangle Mystery—Solved,* Kusche wrote:

> After examining all the evidence I have reached the following conclusion: *There is no theory that solves the mystery.* It is no more logical to try to find a common cause for all the disappearances in the Triangle than, for example, to try to find one cause for all automobile accidents in Arizona. By abandoning the search for an overall theory and investigating each incident independently, the mystery began to unravel.
>
> The findings of my research were consistent. . . . Once sufficient information was found, logical explanations appeared for most of the incidents. It is difficult, for example, to consider the *Rubicon* a mystery when it is known that a hurricane struck the harbor where it had been moored. It is similarly difficult to be baffled by the loss of the *Marine Sulphur Queen* after learning of the ship's weakened structure and the weather conditions as described in the report of the Coast Guard investigation.[4]

My final conclusion was that *the number of disappearances within the boundaries of the Bermuda Triangle are actually no greater than the number of disappearances in almost any other comparable part of the world.*

In an exclusive interview in the *Globe*, a national tabloid, Berlitz claimed that 50 planes and more than 100 ships had vanished in two years, and that the government was conspiring to keep this information secret. Dennet found that only a dozen "unexplained" incidents occurred during a 25-month period ending in January of 1980. He systematically reviewed all 12 of the incidents mentioned by Berlitz and found that, with sufficient information, most of the "mysteries" were solved.

It's surprising that Berlitz hasn't tackled another mystery. On an average of nearly once a month, a small private airplane takes off from a United States airport and disappears. Despite searches, no debris is found. Everyone assumes that the lost plane crashed, but no one can find it. Occasionally it is found years later in some rugged mountains.

Bermuda Triangle writers make a big fuss over the fact that no debris is found. In fact, when flights are lost over water, debris is rarely found, especially if the crash is at night in rough seas. By the time morning light allows a search to begin, the seas have hidden all traces of a crash.

The popularity of the Bermuda Triangle mystery has spawned similar mysteries, such as the Devil's Sea near Japan and the Great Lakes Triangle. In my opinion, these mysteries exist only in the minds of those who make up and write the stories concerning them. These are further evidence that when anything, no matter how ridiculous, is presented in a serious manner, in an atmosphere where honesty is taken for granted, it can mislead even the most intelligent people if they do not investigate the facts.

To illustrate my point, I created an illusion for my show which I call "The Bermuda Triangle." After I seat myself inside a triangular box of lights, it is then closed. When the box is reopened, I have vanished. Most observers can't explain that illusion, but that doesn't make it any more authentic than these fabricated mysteries.

Probably the most famous mystery of the Bermuda Triangle was the disappearance of Flight 19. The legend makes for eerie reading. On December 5, 1945, five Avenger torpedo bombers took off from Fort Lauderdale Naval Air Station on a routine patrol. An hour-and-a-half later, when they should have been starting their return to base, the flight commander reported that he was lost over the Florida Keys, many miles from where he should have been. For the next few hours, frantic efforts were made to find the planes and guide them back home, but they were never located. In addition, a giant Mariner PBM search plane, called a flying boat, took off to try to find the Avengers, but never returned. A five-day massive air and sea search turned up no evidence of the six planes.

Over the years the story became a legend, to the point where it was almost impossible to separate fact from fiction. Larry Kusche meticulously studied all the available information, including the official Naval investigations, and interviewed most of the surviving people involved in the incident in order to reconstruct what actually happened. His book *The Disappearance of Flight 19* is exciting reading, but it is hardly the "Twilight Zone" type of mystery that Berlitz and others would have us believe.

Kusche concluded that the five Avengers almost certainly were over the Bahamas—their intended target—and not the Florida Keys. An accomplished pilot himself, Kusche flew the intended route of Flight 19 and observed several reasons why a pilot could become disoriented. He noticed that a haze, caused by the humid air, can cause the sky and ocean to blend so that there appears to be no horizon. On that fateful day in 1945, visibility was less than ten miles, and a slight error in navigation could cause the pilots to miss expected landmarks. Parts of the Bahamas and the Keys look remarkably alike. Thinking he was over the Keys, the leader, Chuck Taylor, apparently headed north in order to find the Florida mainland. But he never reached land. In the dark, with extremely rough seas, the planes ditched in the ocean approximately 200 miles east of the Florida coast.

The disappearance of the search plane also can be explained logically:

> The loss of the Mariner PBM search plane came to be considered mysterious after storytellers had it "vanish" at 4:25 in a clear, sunlit sky, as it was "approaching the zone where Flight 19 had strangely disappeared." The 7:50 explosion, the story went, was yet another mystery.

> Mariners were sometimes called "flying gas tanks" because they carried almost 2,000 gallons of fuel. Fumes were occasionally present inside the plane. The lighting of a cigarette, the flipping on of the PBM's unshielded electrical switches, the starting of the small auxiliary generator . . . any number of other activities could have provided the ignition. One officer I discussed this with told me that he had seen a Mariner explode while flying over an air base in Greece. . . .

Besides time warps and related so-called paranormal phenomena, other highly dramatic "theories" have been suggested to account for the
Mariner's loss. One is that one or more of the
Avengers had a midair collision with it. Another
is that when Taylor gave one of his students permission to drop his last bomb, it hit the Mariner.
Both guesses not only are extremely improbable,
but also they do not correlate with what is known
about the events of that day.[5]

Another mystery that has intrigued millions of
people is that of unidentified flying objects (UFO's).
A former president of the International Brotherhood
of Magicians, Bill Pitts, is one of the leading investigators of UFO's. He has told me that there are really
no authorities on the subject: "There are only authorities on reported sightings of UFO's. There are no
authorities because we have not had, to my knowledge,
one UFO that we could take pictures of and examine
every nut and bolt on it, and interview the beings on
the craft.

"I have been an investigator for many of the serious research organizations as well as for several
government agencies. I periodically receive calls from
law enforcement personnel and from radar control
tower operators who are trying to explain unusual
things." Pitts takes each case and tries to provide an
explanation—to turn a UFO into an IFO, an identified
flying object. "We can't do that in every case, but I
try to find out what it could have been. I don't say this
is definitely what they saw, because once it's gone, I
don't know. But I have ways of finding out what it
could have been. I carry with me phone numbers from

the FAA, control towers, various police departments, Norad, etc.''

The United States Air Force has conducted two exhaustive investigations and concluded that ''there is no evidence for the existence of UFO's with supernatural, extraterrestrial, or military origin.''[6] More than 90 percent of all UFO sightings can be attributed to purely natural causes.

Yet UFO's have become increasingly popular with movies such as *Close Encounters of the Third Kind* and *ET, the Extraterrestrial.* The number of UFO sightings increases markedly when movies like these are shown, or when the media report about a person who had a spectacular ''encounter.'' The sensational publicity garnered from cases such as the alleged abduction of Travis Walton in November of 1975 in Arizona result in further interest and in further distortion of the truth.

Jeff Wells, a reporter for the *National Enquirer*, was sent to Phoenix to interview Walton shortly after he claimed to have spent five days aboard an alien spacecraft. Wells reported that the most experienced polygraph examiner in Arizona gave Walton a lie detector test, but the results were not revealed in the *National Enquirer.* ''The kid had failed the test miserably,'' wrote Wells later. ''The polygraph man said it was the plainest case of lying he'd seen in 20 years.''[7]

Much of Walton's story developed during hypnosis sessions. ''It seemed that the kid's father, who had deserted him as a child, had been a spaceship fanatic, and all his life the kid had wanted to ride in a spacecraft. He had seen something out there in the woods, some kind of an eerie light that had triggered a powerful hallucination. . . . There was no question of any kidnap by mushroom men. The kid needed medical help.''[8]

Philip J. Klass has done extensive research in this area. In his book *UFOs Explained* he gives some very sensible explanations for the UFO phenomenon. The following is a sample of his "UFOlogical principles":

> Basically honest and intelligent persons who are suddenly exposed to a brief, unexpected event, especially one that involves an unfamiliar object, may be grossly inaccurate in trying to describe what they have seen.
>
> The problem facing the UFO investigator is to try to distinguish between those details that are accurate and those that are grossly inaccurate. This may be impossible until the true identity of the UFO can be determined, so that in some cases this poses an insoluble problem.
>
> News media that give great prominence to a UFO report when it is first received, subsequently devote little if any space or time to reporting a prosaic explanation for the case when all the facts are uncovered.
>
> Once news media coverage leads the public to believe that UFOs may be in the vicinity, there are numerous natural and man-made objects which, especially when seen at night, can take on unusual characteristics in the minds of hopeful viewers. . . . This situation feeds upon itself until such time as the news media lose interest in the subject. . . . .
>
> The inability of even experienced investigators to fully and positively explain a UFO report for lack of sufficient information, even after a rigorous effort, does not really provide evidence to support the hypothesis that spaceships from other worlds are visiting the Earth.

Many UFO cases seem puzzling and unexplainable simply because case investigators have failed to devote a sufficiently rigorous effort to the investigation.[9]

Robert Sheaffer is another student of UFO's. He has spoken at conferences such as the National UFO Conference and the Smithsonian Institution UFO Symposium. Sheaffer wrote a book, *The UFO Verdict: Examining the Evidence,* in which he applied rigid scientific methods to the UFO question. The following was his conclusion:

I maintain that we have found the answer to the question "What are UFOs?" through a rigorous application of the scientific method. As an unexpected dividend, we find that we have also obtained the answer to the same question that might be raised about ESP, Bigfoot, the Loch Ness monster, "psychic" spoon-bending, and other dubious . . . phenomena. Our answer must be that UFOs do not exist.

This answer is certain to disappoint many people who are eager to find that our galaxy . . . is populated by all manner of exotic and exciting creatures. No one would be happier than I should it actually be discovered that our earth is paying host to strange creatures from some unknown planet or universe. But wishing will not make it so. And so long as we wish to adhere to the scientific method (that is, to make factual statements about the real world, as opposed to seeking subjective mystical insight), we are forced to face up to the conclusion that UFOs as real and distinct entities simply do not exist. Those who continue to insist otherwise are openly proclaiming their allegiance to a different world-view, one which, although popular, is incompatible with the world-view of science.[10]

Sheaffer's negation of UFO's leads me to reiterate the point made in the past few chapters. Sensational stories of mysterious events usually lose their mystery under careful investigation. The absence of a possible explanation most often indicates the lack of sufficient information. It should not lead to rash conclusions about time warps, strange electromagnetic fields, and invasions from outer space.

Larry Kusche concluded that this was the problem with the disappearance of Flight 19. "The withholding of information and the failure to use reliable sources are standard procedures among sensationalists, since full disclosure of information destroys the false mystery they are trying to build."[11] This means that we should not jump to conclusions when we read some incredible "real-life" mystery. If a story seems too unbelievable to be true, it probably is not true.

Look into My Eyes

To the sound of music, my daughter Robyn walks on stage. Dramatically waving my fingers over her eyes, I appear to put her into a trance. Then she is assisted as she climbs into a box, and I proceed to saw her in half.

In another part of my show I seem to put myself into a trance as I sit in front of a circle of lights. Concentrating intently, I slowly begin to rise into the air. The levitation appears to result from my hypnotic state.

I'm going to let you in on a secret: When you see me hypnotized or hypnotizing someone else on stage, it's all for show. No one is actually in a trance. I dare say that this is true for most stage magicians. It's simply good showmanship—something expected of illusionists.

An aura of mystery surrounds hypnotism. Many books have been written on the subject, yet most people still misunderstand it. Many think it can do more than it actually can, while others think it is a tool of the devil. It has been used effectively in place of drugs for anesthesia in dentistry and minor surgery, and as a tool to help people break habits such as smoking.

The father of modern hypnotism was Anton Mesmer, an eighteenth-century German physician. Through controversial experiments, he tried to prove the existence of magnetic fluids in his patients. Using magnets, he attempted to cure physical illnesses. Later he set aside the magnets and used methods such as waving his hands over a patient until the patient went into a trance. Surprisingly, many of his patients found relief from their symptoms through his unorthodox practices. The term "animal magnetism" and the field of study called "mesmerism" resulted from his work.

In the 1800's, British surgeon James Braid coined the term "hypnotism" when he induced his patients into a sleeplike condition before performing minor operations. The word comes from the Greek word *hypnos*, meaning sleep. Later Dr. Braid realized that he had misnamed the phenomenon, for a hypnotized person definitely is not sleeping. But it was too late to change it, since the general public readily accepted the word.

The simplest way to understand hypnosis is to regard it as a state of mind characterized by increased suggestibility—the acceptance of an idea without being critical of the idea. It is a method for bypassing the conscious mind. Whatever is presented to the subconscious mind under certain conditions, such as hypnotism, may be automatically accepted and acted upon.

Psychologist Ray Hyman says that when it comes to clearly defining hypnotism, no one really knows what it is. "The only way we have of knowing someone was hypnotized is if that person says he was. There is no external way of measuring the hypnotic state—there is no physiological sign on which everyone can agree."

Hypnotism is used in a number of ways. Some entertainers hypnotize members of the audience and cause them to do unusual, humorous things that they normally would not do. Another widespread use of hypnotism is for medical purposes—to block pain and to help patients break bad habit patterns. Hypnotism is also used for interrogation, although we'll see later that there are serious questions about its effectiveness.

We've all seen or heard stories about hypnotists wielding tremendous powers over their subjects. Some movies and novels have portrayed hypnotists dominating weaker minds and using their power for evil purposes. This may be true in movies or books, but in this case real life does not match fiction.

To understand what hypnotism is, it helps to know what it *cannot* do. For instance, *you cannot be hypnotized against your will.* To be hypnotized, the patient must want to be hypnotized and must trust the hypnotist. Peter Blythe wrote in his book on hypnotism:

> If someone says, "Go ahead and see if you can hypnotize me," the answer is that you cannot. The person who makes the statement is challenging the hypnotist; and as he intends to resist, any chance of success is aborted from the outset.
>
> When one gentleman first started using hypnosis he tried out various induction methods on his wife, but without any result. She knew they

worked on other people, because she had seen them being applied, but she resisted because she felt no need to cooperate.

Then on a hot summer's day she fell asleep in the garden while sunbathing, and as a result was quite badly sunburned.

That same night she tried to sleep, but her skin was so tender that sleep eluded her.

After tossing and turning for more than an hour she asked her husband, "Could you hypnotize me, and take the pain away so that I can get some sleep?"

At that moment she discovered a need for hypnosis and quickly allowed her critical censor to be by-passed, and entered into the hypnotic state.[1]

Another misconception is that a person under hypnosis can be forced to do things that violate his moral values.

A person under hypnosis remains conscious of what the hypnotist says and does. He usually willingly submits to the hypnotist, doing what he instructs and accepting his suggestions. But *if the hypnotist inserts a command or suggestion against the patient's will, the patient will not respond.*

Blythe gives an interesting example of this:

Four people were on the stage in the hypnotic state and were carrying out the various suggestions of the hypnotist. Then, at a certain point, he suggested they were all concert pianists and were going to give a piano recital. Three of the subjects acted out this suggestion, one with greater aplomb than the other two; but the only lady on the stage just sat on her chair, deeply relaxed, and did nothing. . . .

I talked to the lady after the demonstration and asked her why she had chosen not to react to that piano-playing suggestion. Her answer was personal, but very logical. She told me that as a small child she had been made to take piano lessons against her will, but as soon as she was old enough to exert some pressure on her parents she stopped playing, and made a promise to herself that nothing would ever induce her to play again.[2]

Third, *information gained through hypnosis may not be any more accurate than other forms of interrogation.*

This area is controversial. Some states allow evidence gained through hypnosis to be used in court. Others do not. Dr. Martin Orne, editor of the *International Journal of Clinical and Experimental Hypnosis,* explains the problem: "You don't ever know whether you have testimony created by hypnosis or whether it was in fact refreshed by hypnosis. Until we have hard evidence of the differences between these two things, we can't distinguish between helping an eyewitness to remember what he saw versus creating an eyewitness who never was."[3]

The problem is evident particularly in UFO cases where evidence gained under hypnosis is displayed as conclusive proof. Orne states that under hypnotism the most accurate information comes from "free narrative recall," but this produces the lowest amount of detail. When questioned about details, accuracy decreases. "Hypnotic suggestions to relive a past event, particularly when accompanied by questions about specific details, put pressure on the subject to provide information for which few, if any, actual memories are available. This situation may jog the subject's memory and produce some increased recall, but it will also cause him to fill in details that are plausible but consist of memories or fantasies from other times . . . . It is extremely difficult to know which aspects of hypnotically aided recall are historically accurate and which aspects have been confabulated."[4]

Further difficulties arise if the hypnotist has specific beliefs about what actually occurred. It is easy for him to inadvertently guide the subject's recall to fit his own beliefs. Ernest R. Hilgard, professor emeritus of psychology at Stanford University and former president of the International Society of Hypnosis, claims that hypnotic recall, as evidence of UFO abduction, is an abuse of hypnosis. He explains how it is possible to fabricate stories:

> For example, under hypnosis I implanted in a subject a false memory of an experience connected with a bank robbery that never occurred, and the person found the experience so vivid that he was able to select from a series of photographs a picture of the man he thought had robbed the bank.
>
> Another time, I deliberately assigned two concurrent—though spatially very different—life experiences to the same person and regressed him at separate times to that date. He gave very accurate accounts of both experiences, so that a believer in reincarnation, reviewing the two accounts, would have suspected that the man had really lived the two assigned lives.[5]

When you submit to hypnosis, you actually give control of yourself and your mind to another individual.

So you should be extremely cautious about who you submit yourself to.

To be effective, hypnotism requires faith. A person can get similar effects through certain vitamin pills, a charismatic healer, exercise, etc. Hypnotism is not some magic formula; its effectiveness depends on the patient's faith.

I have seen this demonstrated in primitive cultures. For example, a witch doctor in Liberia put a curse on a person, and the victim took it so seriously that he went out of the village, lay down, and died. That same witch doctor became furious with me and cursed me, but it had no effect on me whatever because I did not believe him or his powers. Missionaries there have told me that they have had to talk people out of curses they believed were placed on them.

In a sense this validates some statements that Ray Hyman made to me in an interview at his home. He said that the same results obtained through hypnotism can be gained without hypnotism. Dr. Hyman explains, "There have been studies done on this, and they've found that with the right motivation, a patient can do the same things without hypnosis that he can with it. For example, take the area of pain tolerance. They'll take one group of subjects, hypnotize them and stick needles in them, and they won't wince. The second group is offered a sum of money and told that someone will stick needles in them and they are to act as if nothing is happening. Then they bring in trained hypnotists and they can't tell the difference."

Undoubtedly there is a hypnotic state, but experts have difficulty defining it. They can measure brain waves and tell when a person is asleep. They also can determine when a person is dreaming. But there is no comparable measurement of the hypnotic state.

"Some people will play the role," Hyman says, "In given circumstances, they will try to figure out 'what's expected of me' and behave that way. They will even do things they would never do under normal circumstances. Some psychologists argue that this is because they really wanted to do those things, and this just gave them an excuse. Most hypnotists will tell you that a person will not do something under hypnosis that he really doesn't want to do. He will resist or come out of the hypnotic state."

Technically hypnosis is not in the realm of the paranormal, but people claim to use it in that realm. They allegedly contact the dead, read minds, predict the future, and do other feats while in a hypnotic trance. In fact, though, the trance is usually a cover-up to justify their activities.

In spite of confusion in this area, people still look for answers from mediums, fortune-tellers, faith healers, and astrologers. They search for something to give them hope and direction, and they think they find it in the realm of psychic phenomena. But it is only an illusion. While some of these may be displays of genuine supernatural power, most of them are simply magic tricks that attempt to make us believe they are miracles. They are frauds that prevent us from recognizing the real thing.

I would now like to move out of the realm of magic to the world of reality. In the next few chapters we will focus on truth rather than illusion. Rather than examining the power, real or imagined, of Satan or his spiritual counterfeits, let's view the genuine, supernatural, miraculous power that God makes available to all who desire it. This is power that I first experienced in 1963. It totally changed my life, and I've never been the same since.

8

Magician or God?

My summer living quarters were simple—half of a double-car garage, rented from a family in Santa Monica, California. Most of my time out of class was spent in that garage, practicing sleight-of-hand exercises. At that moment, however, the cards and coins lay on the folding table as I rested on my bed. I could feel the blood throbbing at my fingertips, raw from hours of practice. But I ignored the pain as I mulled over an incredible idea.

At 18 years of age I was already an excellent magician. I felt that with consistent practice I could become one of the best in the world. It had all started when my mother gave me a "Peter Rabbit Magic Kit" for my seventh birthday. Shortly after that, my father got involved in a business transaction with a magician by the name of Mark Barker—professionally known as Moxo. He showed me a couple of tricks and encouraged me as I began to perform for my friends.

Over the next few years I performed in several states, Canada, and Central America during our extensive family vacations. My father, who was an attorney, a brilliant businessman, and civic leader, encouraged me in my hobby, until he realized that it was not just a hobby. Magic dominated most of my waking hours. At school I usually sat in the back row of class and practiced card and coin manipulations while the teacher spoke. The margins of my textbooks and notebooks were filled with illustrations and ideas for new tricks.

I spent hours dreaming of new magical effects and often would not allow myself to go to sleep until I had created at least three new tricks. I studied the great magicians of history, particularly Houdini, the master of escapes. For days I thought about how I might invent an escape more dangerous and daring than any Houdini had attempted. The result was my "Table of Death."

In this spectacular illusion, a committee from the audience shackled me to a platform underneath a table of 100 18-inch steel spikes. The table was suspended from a thin rope. After a small curtain was placed between me and the audience, a candle was lit underneath the rope. In 20 to 30 seconds the rope burned through, bringing the 400-pound table of nails crashing down. Then the curtain was pulled back and I was lying on top of the table, reading a magazine.

My first national television appearance—on the original "You Asked for It" show with Art Baker—resulted from this illusion. During this performance one of the spikes broke and flew through the curtain, hitting a cameraman in the head. Fortunately it struck him broadside, not point-first, and he wasn't hurt. On another occasion the spikes fell with such force that one of them was driven clear through a lock. Once I was a little slow to escape and two nails went through my left shoe, but missed my foot.

I prided myself on my creativity. In addition to the "Table of Death," I had invented "Helicopter Cups," which fooled some of the world's leading magicians, and "Spikes Through a Balloon," which became the best-selling magical trick in history. Now I felt those creative energies surging again as I lay on my bed, staring at the bare light bulb in the middle of the room. How impressive it would be if I concentrated hard on that bulb, and suddenly it exploded! I could do the trick fairly simply and claim that it was the power of my mind.

It would be so easy to deceive people. I could even form a religion of the mind. I could teach about the incredible potential of the human brain and do dazzling feats to demonstrate its power. I would make objects levitate, read and identify objects while blindfolded, and make incredible observations and prophecies concerning my followers. I could do it all through trickery.

My body was alert with excitement as I thought of the possibilities for such a religion. I could easily gain thousands, perhaps millions, of believers. I could become fabulously wealthy. The more I thought about it, the more I began to feel a supernatural high, as if spurred by some demonic force.

I pondered these thoughts for several weeks and came up with many ideas for this religion as I practiced manipulation skills. I even began to wonder if it were possible to do some mental feats without trickery. Then one Sunday morning I woke up early and felt a strange desire to go to church. I knew of a church of my family's denomination just six blocks away, so I decided to visit there. It was a warm, summer morning, and few people were on the streets, so I slowed my normal quick walking pace to enjoy the weather.

Again I started to think of my idea of forming a religion. All of a sudden I felt a warm, loving presence. It was so different from the thoughts that had captivated me for the past few weeks. I felt almost like a coat was being placed around my shoulders by a friendly, loving Person. In that moment I sensed the presence of God and that He had a plan for my life. In a flash I thought, "Someday you will be God's magician." That presence remained with me through the church service and was so overwhelming that I couldn't remember anything that was said or sung. It didn't depart until I returned to my temporary home.

From that time on, I had no further interest or desire to control the minds and lives of other people. I was determined to use magic solely as an art form, for entertainment purposes only.

Even to this day I am unable to find words that adequately describe my experience. People could interpret it in various ways, so I seldom share it. All I know is that what happened made a lasting impact on my life. It also showed me how easily my skills could be abused if they were not channeled in the right direction.

Today, some of the things I do in my shows create effects that might lead one to believe that I have supernatural powers. I constantly have to repeat that *everything I do on stage is accomplished entirely by natural means. I have no supernatural powers.*

That experience in Santa Monica heightened my spiritual desire, and for the next few years I embarked on a personal spiritual pilgrimage. I studied the major religions of the world, but I did not find reality in them. Nothing in Buddhism, Islam, Hinduism, or other religions led me to believe they were anything more than empty rituals like the ones I had seen in most

American churches I had attended.

In college I continued my search for truth. Though magic was my first love, I also desired to investigate how people think. Since universities did not offer a major in magic, psychology seemed a good choice. Perhaps I could learn some useful principles for my shows. So I enrolled in a basic psychology class.

The professor, whom I highly respected, presented answers to my most important questions: "Why am I here?" "Where am I going?" "What is the real purpose of life?" After I earned a degree in psychology, however, I learned that these answers were not really satisfactory. Only two years later, the professor whom I so highly respected committed suicide. What a devastating indictment against what I thought represented an almost holy search for truth!

While I was still in college, I married a beautiful young lady, and I started my own company for promoting and selling some of my magical inventions. I perfected and released a new magical effect each month. Then, for the first five years after graduation, I was very involved in the business world. At the age of 21 I was in charge of the statewide operation for Transamerica Corporation, co-owner of a ranch, and partner in a number of office buildings. In addition I did about 20 magic shows a month. By the world's standards I was extremely successful, but I was haunted by a feeling of emptiness. I couldn't understand how, with all my activities and achievements, I could be so tremendously bored.

I felt particularly restless when I walked out onto the stage after a performance, the heels of my shoes echoing through the empty theater. A few minutes earlier I had brought the crowd to their feet in applause. Now they were gone, and I felt loneliness, emptiness. Why had I worked so hard to be so successful? What had it brought me? What more could I possibly accomplish that would fill this emptiness?

I often thought of the true story I heard from a professor of one of my real estate business classes. In 1923, in a large hotel in Chicago, a very important meeting was held with nine of the world's most successful financiers: Charles Schwab, president of the largest independent steel company; Samuel Insull, president of the largest utility company; Howard Hopson, president of the largest gas company; Arthur Cotton, the greatest wheat speculator; Richard Whitney, president of the New York Stock Exchange; Albert Fall, a member of the President's Cabinet; Leon Fraser, president of the Bank of International Settlements; Jesse Livermore, the greatest "bear" on Wall Street; and Ivar Krueger, head of the greatest monopoly.

Twenty-five years later, Charles Schwab had died in bankruptcy; Samuel Insull had died a fugitive from justice, penniless in a foreign land; Howard Hopson was insane; Arthur Cotton had died abroad, insolvent; Richard Whitney had spent time in Sing Sing Penitentiary; Alvert Fall had been pardoned so that he could die at home; Jessie Livermore, Ivar Krueger, and Leon Fraser had all died by suicide. All of these men had learned the art of making a living, but none of them had learned how to live.

Neither psychology nor success provided the answers. I learned that psychiatrists had the highest suicide rate of any profession. One of my neighbors, a successful businessman, committed suicide. Another businessman whom I saw every day dived headfirst off the eleventh story of the building where I had my office. A world-famous magician, whom I had met and admired, literally drank himself to death. Yet, I reasoned, there had to be something that would give some hope, some reason for living.

Then one evening my wife and I visited a church and were invited to a meeting of young couples. Unlike other religious people I had met, they did not talk about religion or philosophy or a long list of do's and don'ts. I probably would not have listened if they had. Rather, they talked about how they had found a relationship with God that was changing their lives.

I was intrigued, but I had no intention of being deceived by a first-century trickster, if that was all that Jesus was. I took pride in the fact that I had never been fooled by another magician. So, accepting a friend's challenge, I spent several months investigating Christianity from a magician's point of view.

At this point I would like to relate some of the results of my investigation. We have already examined the feats of a number of people who claim to have supernatural or psychic powers. But what about the Person of Jesus Christ? How does He differ from all the charlatans and tricksters we have examined? Was He truly a miracle-worker, or was He only a clever magician? Jesus Christ claimed to be God. Does His life match His claim?

When I confronted those questions as a young man, I faced two options. If Jesus Christ was *not* God, and if what He said was not true, then Christianity makes little difference. But if He was and is God, and if what He said is true, then very little else makes any difference. The key for me was to examine His miracles to see if they backed up His claim to deity.

A clever magician easily can fool a scientist, professor, theologian, or almost anyone else. Most people do not think like magicians, and they do not understand all of the psychology and methods we use to fool our audiences. It is very difficult, however, for one experienced magician to fool another experienced magician. Because of my extensive knowledge concerning the art of magic, I concluded that I might be highly qualified to determine if the miraculous events attributed to Christ could have been accomplished by trickery, or if they were indeed genuine.

I will not attempt to ascertain if the Gospel events were accurately reported. Numerous studies already conclusively demonstrate the reliability of biblical documents.[1] So I will assume their validity and concentrate on the miracles of Christ. I analyzed these for several months before I became convinced of their authenticity.

The first thing that impressed me about the miracles of Jesus of Nazareth was their uniqueness. When we trace any subject's history from its origin, we usually find slow, gradual development over many centuries. Then it begins to accelerate at an ever-increasing rate. We start with the simple and move to the complex.

That certainly is true of magic. Magic done through misdirection and sleight of hand is one of the oldest forms of entertainment known to man. Various forms of magic also were associated with worship in many pagan temples. But it wasn't until the nineteenth century, primarily through the creativity of Robert Houdin, that large-scale stage illusions were developed. In the twentieth century we have seen an explosion of knowledge as magicians have constantly refined and developed the magical arts.

If Jesus Christ was a magician, then His illusions were totally different from anything any other magicians have done before or since, as you will see in examining five of His miracles.

Jesus' first recorded miracle was at the wedding in Cana of Galilee, when the host ran out of wine.[2] In the Gospel of John we read that six stone waterpots were set aside for the Jewish custom of purification. Jesus commanded that these 20- to 30-gallon pots be filled with water. After the pots were filled, Jesus commanded the servants to draw out some of the water and take it to the headwaiter. When he tasted the "water which had become wine," he told the bridegroom that normally hosts served the best wine first, but the bridegroom had saved the best until then.

Jesus might have fooled a few people with a simple trick, perhaps using a chemical to change the color and taste of the water, but there was no way He could have done that with 120 to 180 gallons of water. He could not have fooled all of those guests into thinking that it was some of the finest wine they had ever tasted.

On several occasions I have been asked to perform before magicians' conventions. One time a convention host asked me to perform on the beach before 700 magicians from around the world. He wanted me to create an illusion in which I would get out of a boat and walk on the water a short distance to land.

After spending many weeks trying to formulate all the methods we could use for such an illusion, it was finally scrapped. It was impossible to create any type of effect that would convince anyone I was really walking on water.

This experience showed me that, even with all our modern technology, we can't come close to duplicating many of the things Jesus did nearly 20 centuries ago. In Mark 6 we read about Jesus walking to the disciples on the Sea of Galilee, where they were straining at the oars because of the wind. The Sea of Galilee gets very rough under such conditions, yet in the midst of the waves Jesus walked to the boat. Filmmakers have used trick photography to portray this event in movies about Christ, but none of the films I've seen look at all realistic.

One miracle recorded in all four Gospels is the feeding of the 5000. The writers all record the presence of 5000 men, not counting women and children. It is reasonable to suppose that Christ actually fed 15,000 to 20,000 people with five loaves of bread and two small fish.

A few years ago I produced a show presenting some of the greatest events in the life of Christ. Presently I am working on a new version of the show, which will include a staged recreation of this miracle. The audience will see the bread visibly multiply in the hands of "Jesus," and then actors playing the disciples will pass out the bread. Every person in the auditorium will receive a good-sized piece of the bread either to eat or to take home as a reminder of that experience.

But you can do many things on a stage that you cannot do out in the open. Jesus was outdoors, with no stage protecting Him. He certainly could not have hid that much food up his sleeves! To do such a trick and fool so many people about the source of the bread would have required the disciples' involvement in the deception. And if indeed the disciples participated in that trick, then why do we never hear any more about it? None of them ever even hinted at collaboration to produce such a marvelous miracle.

All except one of the original apostles died a martyr's death for witnessing to the deity of Christ. Throughout history people have willingly died for a lie when they did not know it was a lie, but it is contrary to all human experience for a group of men to die as martyrs,

claiming that a lie was the truth when they knew differently. Jesus' feeding of the 5000 was obviously not a
trick.

If Jesus simply had been a magician, performing the
miracles He did would have required two or three
semitrucks full of equipment, plus numerous assistants.
When I do a major show, I require 20 to 30 assistants
backstage and two truckloads of equipment. Yet Jesus
had none of that.

The two other miracles I will mention involve
healing. Was Jesus any different from modern-day
psychic and faith healers, who cure mostly psychosomatic illnesses?

It is recorded that Jesus healed men who were blind
from birth, people who were born deaf and dumb,
lepers in advanced stages of decay, a woman who had
had a hemorrhage for a dozen years, and a man who
was lame from birth. These types of physical problems
cannot be classified as psychosomatic illnesses.

The writer of the Gospel of Luke was a physician,
and he carefully recorded many of the miraculous
healings. In Luke 6 we read about a man in the synagogue whose right hand was withered. While the
scribes and Pharisees watched him closely, Jesus told
the man to hold out his hand, and it "was completely
restored." How could that have been a feat of magic?
Everyone knew the man. Christ's enemies were watching every move. I have never seen or heard of any
documented case where a psychic healer performed
such a miracle.

One more miracle bears mentioning: Jesus raised
men from the dead. One such incident occurs in
John 11. Lazarus, a close friend of Jesus, died and was
buried in the typical Jewish manner of the day. After
washing the body with soap and water, they made a

final test to assure that he was not breathing. Then they wrapped the body in long strips of linen cloth, about six feet in length. They started at the feet, wrapping the legs, and between the wraps they put a very sticky, syruplike substance made of myrrh and aloes. This preserved the body. They wrapped each leg and arm separately, and then the trunk. Gradually the gummy paste, mixed in with the cloth, hardened. A man of Lazarus' stature in the community might have been encased in more than a hundred pounds of material and spices.

After the body was prepared it was laid in a cave, which was then sealed with a large rock so animals would not disturb it. No one doubted that the person was dead by the time he was laid in a cave.

Jesus arrived on the scene four days after Lazarus had died. Family and friends were still mourning. When Jesus asked them to roll the stone from the cave, Martha, one of Lazarus' sisters, protested that the body would stink from the decay. Nevertheless they removed the stone. Then Jesus, with a loud voice, called, "Lazarus, come forth!"

Then we read, "He who had died came forth, bound hand and foot with wrappings; and his face was wrapped around with a cloth. Jesus said to them, 'Unbind him, and let him go.' "[3] Many of the Jews who were with the sisters when Lazarus died believed in Jesus as a result of what He did.

We could examine many other examples of Jesus' miracles. Anyone honestly investigating His works would have to conclude from all the evidence that Jesus had supernatural ability.

Another factor that played a major role in my conclusions concerning Jesus Christ was His fulfillment of the more than 300 Old Testament references to the Messiah. These include: He would be born in Bethlehem, He would be in the direct line of King David, a special prophet would immediately precede His arrival (John the Baptist), He would heal the blind and deaf, He would be betrayed for 30 pieces of silver, His death would be by crucifixion among thieves, His executioners would cast lots for His clothing, He would be buried in a rich man's tomb, and He would rise from the dead three days after His burial.

I was impressed by the detail of these prophecies. One person conceivably might fulfill two or three of these, but not this many. Peter Stoner in his book *Science Speaks* shows statistically that it was virtually beyond the realm of chance that one man would fulfill even eight of the prophecies:

> . . . We find that the chance that any man might have lived down to the present time and fulfilled all eight prophecies is 1 in 10^{17} . . . . This is illustrated by taking 10^{17} silver dollars and laying them on the face of Texas. They will cover all of the state two feet deep. Now mark one of these silver dollars and stir the whole mass thoroughly, all over the state. Blindfold a man and tell him he can travel as far as he wishes, but he must pick up one silver dollar and say that this is the right one. What chance could he have of getting the right one? Just the same chance that the prophets would have had of writing these eight prophecies and having all come true in any one man. . . provided they wrote them in their own wisdom. Now these prophecies were either given by inspiration of God or the prophets just wrote them as they thought they should be. In such a case the

prophets had just one chance in 10^{17} of being absolute.[4]

The Bible prophecies concerning end times were another major factor in my conversion, because if they were accurate, they lent credibility to the rest of the Scripture. I spent many hours on this area of investigation.

Numerous prophecies in the Bible concern the return of Christ to this earth. The disciples specifically asked Him, "Tell us . . . what will be the sign of Your coming, and of the end of the age?"[5] The Bible contains so many references to the second coming of Christ that a major part of Scripture deals with this event. It is mentioned 380 times in the New Testament alone.

Before leaving the earth, Jesus told His disciples that He would physically return to earth at a future time in history when mankind was on the verge of destroying the entire human race. When His followers asked Him when this would occur, He said that it was not for them to know the day or the hour, but that He would give them a number of signs.

I found 27 specific signs relating to the end times and the physical return of Jesus Christ to the earth. They include such things as the regathering of the people of Israel in the Middle East, the rise of Russia and China, the European Common Market, an explosion of knowledge, extensive traveling, increased lawlessness, and many more.

To me, the most significant sign was the rebirth of the nation of Israel. When I first read about that I was shocked, because for 2600 years there was no nation of Israel. Yet Ezekiel, Daniel, Hosea, Zechariah, and Jeremiah all wrote that the final war would begin in and be centered around that nation. Jesus said that the city of Jerusalem "will be trampled underfoot by the Gentiles until the times of the Gentiles be fulfilled."[6] Jerusalem was controlled by Gentiles from 586 B.C. until June 1967. Then, in a six-day war, the Jews, outnumbered 80 to one, captured the city of Jerusalem, bringing the times of the Gentiles to an end.

If Christ's miracles, His fulfillment of Old Testament prophecy, and His accurate foretelling of twentieth-century life were not enough, His own resurrection—which He predicted several times—finally convinced me of His deity. In His death He suffered the ultimate in physical cruelty and torture. The Romans stripped Him, tied him down, then beat his back with a whip that had pieces of bone and metal tied in its leather thongs. The scourging literally tore the skin off His back and left Him near death.

Then He was crucified—the most hideous form of execution ever devised. Its purpose was not just to kill a person, but to prolong the suffering as long as possible. It often took three days for a person to die. Frederic W. Farrar described the suffering: "A death by crucifixion seems to include all that pain and death can have of horrible and ghastly—dizziness, cramp, thirst, starvation, sleeplessness, traumatic fever, tetanus, shame, publicity of shame, long continuance of torment, horror of anticipation, mortification of untended wounds—all intensified just up to the point at which they can be endured at all, but all stopping just short of the point which would give to the sufferer the relief of unconsciousness."[7]

Jesus was buried in the same manner as Lazarus was, and then a Roman guard was placed around the tomb at the insistence of the Jewish leaders, who feared that the disciples might steal the body.

Three days later the tomb was empty, and the entire

course of history was altered. Numerous theories have been proposed to explain away His resurrection—the disciples went to the wrong tomb, Jesus didn't really die, the body was stolen—but none of them stand up under scrutiny.

After carefully examining the evidence of the resurrection, many scholars have determined that it is one of the best-documented events of history. In his book *More than a Carpenter*, Josh McDowell writes: "A student at the University of Uruguay said to me, 'Professor McDowell, why can't you refute Christianity?' I answered, 'For a very simple reason. I'm unable to explain away an event in history—the resurrection of Jesus Christ.'

"After more than 700 hours of studying this subject and thoroughly investigating its foundation, I came to the conclusion that the resurrection of Jesus Christ is either one of the most wicked, vicious, heartless hoaxes ever foisted upon people, or it is the most important fact of history."[8]

Josh gives voluminous support to verify Christ's resurrection as a historical fact. Here is just one example: "While professor of law at Harvard, [Dr. Simon] Greenleaf wrote a volume in which he examined the legal value of the apostles' testimony to the resurrection of Christ. He observed that it was impossible that the apostles could have persisted in affirming the truths they had narrated, had not Jesus actually risen from the dead, and had they not known this fact as certainly as they knew any other fact. Greenleaf concluded that the resurrection of Christ was one of the best supported events in history, according to the laws of legal evidence administered in courts of justice."[9]

The conclusion from my study was inescapable: I

could not argue with Christ's miracles. To reenact them
as an illusionist would cost several million dollars, and
it would be very obvious that they were being accomplished through stage effects. I had to agree with
Nicodemus, who said to Jesus, "We know that You
have come from God. . .for no one can do these signs
[miracles] that you do unless God is with him."[10]

Likewise I was convinced that His prophecies were
not like those of Nostradamus, who told riddles that
people could interpret only after the fact, some hitting
and others missing. Jesus never missed. I can believe
those prophecies that haven't been fulfilled yet because
He's been right on every single one up until now. Only
God has that kind of accuracy.

Through the centuries since His resurrection, men
and women have studied this man to learn for themselves if He is indeed the Son of God. The exiled
emperor Napoleon, on the lonely isle of St. Helena,
said to his faithful General Bertrand, who did not
believe in the deity of Jesus:

> I know men, and I tell you that Jesus Christ
> is no mere man. Between Him and every
> other person in the world there is no possible
> term of comparison. Alexander, Caesar,
> Charlemagne, and I have founded empires.
> But on what did we rest the creations of our
> genius? Upon force. Jesus Christ founded His
> empire upon love; and at this hour millions
> of men would die for Him.[11]

There was one additional piece of evidence that
finally persuaded me that I had to personally surrender
my life to Jesus Christ. It was the lives of our new
friends at the church that my wife and I visited. These

people—students, businessmen, an athletic coach—had a different quality of life, which they attributed to their personal relationship with Jesus Christ. He was alive within their hearts. I started reading the Bible, trying to understand what made them different. I read again about Jesus Christ dying for our sins, which I had heard about for many years. It still sounded like a lot of hocus-pocus to me, until one night I heard a story about a man who worked on a railroad.

This man's job was to raise and lower a giant drawbridge over a river. One day he took his eight-year-old son with him to work. The bridge was up, as a ship had just gone through, but now a train was coming, so he started to lower the bridge. Suddenly he heard a horrible scream behind him. He turned around and saw that his son had slipped and fallen down among the giant gears of the bridge, and was being crushed.

The father knew that if he raised the bridge, he could save his little boy's life. But he also knew that this would cause the train to crash, killing hundreds of people. He had to make a decision. He chose to lower the bridge and watch his own son die, crushed among the gears. As the train went over the bridge a number of people waved to the father as they went merrily on their way, unaware of the sacrifice that he had made in order to save their lives.

Likewise, I realized that 2000 years ago God had watched the death of His only Son on the cross, when He could have stopped the whole thing at any moment. The Bible says, "For God so loved the world [so loved you and me] that He gave His only begotten Son, that whoever believes in Him should not perish but have eternal life."[12]

Finally it all made sense to me. One day, in the quiet of my own home, I simply prayed, "Dear Lord Jesus, thank You for dying for my sins. Right now I invite You to come into my life. Forgive my sins and make my life what You want it to be. Thank You, Lord Jesus, for coming into my life. Amen."

At that moment I knew that Jesus Christ had indeed come into my life. I was a new person! Shortly thereafter I read in Jeremiah, "You will seek Me and find Me when you search for Me with all your heart."[13] I knew that at last I had found truth; I had found God.

Ever since that momentous decision in 1963, I have spent much of my time learning how to experience more of the supernatural power and presence of God. As I've traveled the world and observed so many people trying to present imitations of true spiritual power, I've become increasingly convinced that we who are Christians have an incredible resource, for we are united with the powerful God who created the universe, and who has chosen to reside within those who have accepted His Son, Jesus Christ. I'd like now to take a brief look at some genuine, yes miraculous, supernatural power.

9

Called to Serve

The mail was piled several inches high on my desk when I returned from a long tour. I quickly sorted through it, setting aside a few business letters that required immediate attention. As I neared the bottom of the pile, one envelope caught my eye. It bore the insignia of the Magic Castle in Hollywood, one of the most successful nightclubs in Southern California. The old, mysterious-looking building, located on a hill right above the former Grauman's Chinese Theater on Hollywood Boulevard, had become world-famous for its creative and entertaining magical atmosphere.

The envelope contained a letter from the Magic Castle's president, William Larsen. Acting as a member of the board of directors for the Academy of Magical Arts, he informed me that I had been elected to receive a Performing Arts Fellowship—the highest award offered in my profession. It represents overall recognition for a lifetime of outstanding contributions to the field of magic. Larsen was inviting me to a gala dinner during which my award would be presented.

I leaned back in my chair, stunned by the news. Twenty years ago, when my goal was to become a world-renowned magician, this would have been a dream come true. Now the award brought satisfaction, but I felt no elation. That again proved to me that God had truly changed my motivations.

After becoming a Christian, I lost all desire to perform for fame or financial gain. I had seen enough of the show business world to know that some of the most disillusioned people were entertainers who had reached the top of their profession, expecting their success to bring them happiness. I had learned that this was not reality.

I thought back to the decision I made in 1963—to devote my life and talents to serving God. For months I had struggled to know what to do with my unique skills. Several well-meaning Christians advised me to give up magic and become a preacher. They said that God denounces all forms of magic. So I spent several weeks studying what the Bible says about various forms of magic. I learned that God specifically condemns:

Diviners: people who seek to obtain secret knowledge of past, present, and especially future events, supposedly through communication with demons.

Soothsayers: those who predict the future by observing the flight or actions of birds and omens.

Enchanters: men who subdue others through charms or spells.

Witches (also translated sorcerers): people who use supernatural means or the aid of evil spirits to accomplish unusual feats, or who make a pact with the devil or evil spirits.

Mediums: people who claim to be able to communicate with the dead.

Wizards: those adept in the black art, or the art of

accomplishing feats by supernatural means, often with the aid of evil spirits.

I realized that none of these described what I did. A magician is an artist who applies *natural* causes, whose operation is secret, to produce surprising effects. Everything I do as a magician is to entertain or instruct and is accomplished by natural means that usually involve much work and practice.

Still I struggled with how magic would fit into my life. One night, feeling completely miserable, I finally reached the point where I told God, "I will go anywhere You want me to go. I will do anything You want me to do." I really meant those words, even if they meant that I would never be involved in magic again. My heart felt strangely warm. I felt a wonderful peace—the same feeling I had had many years before while walking to church in Santa Monica, California. That night, at the age of 25, I knew I had found the answer to my frustrating, empty existence.

That struggle taught me a most important lesson: *All of us have to come to the point where we're willing to give up what we're afraid God might want us to give up. Only then can He begin to really use us.* I realized that God doesn't look for great ability; He looks for usability. Soon afterward, the doors opened for me to use my talent to help bring other people into a personal relationship with God. God seemed to tell me that He would rather I be a first-rate magician for Him than a second-rate preacher.

During this time I became involved in Campus Crusade for Christ (a nondenominational Christian movement) at Arizona State University. I figured that if any one group would resist spiritual matters, it was college students. Yet these were tomorrow's leaders, and therefore the most strategic group with which to share my discoveries.

Once while visiting my old fraternity, I heard a speaker get attention effectively through several excellent jokes. I wondered why I couldn't use magic for the same purpose. So I developed a program of magic and testimony to present to dormitories, fraternities, sororities, and other campus groups. Several people responded to the invitation to know Christ personally, and I soon realized that students *were* interested in spiritual truth. They were not interested in religion, but they were interested in Jesus Christ.

I began to see how I could use magic to present Christian truth, and I became captivated by a challenge far greater than that of entertaining. No business, adventure, or profession could begin to match the challenge of the Great Commission, Jesus Christ's final instructions to His disciples: "All authority has been given to Me in heaven and on earth. Go therefore and make disciples of all the nations, baptizing them in the name of the Father and the Son and the Holy Spirit, teaching them to observe all that I commanded you; and lo, I am with you always, even to the end of the age."[1]

Bill Bright, president of the Campus Crusade for Christ, has often said: "Only Christ offers a challenge worthy of total commitment. It is the one cause that demands the best that is in man, and which in turn accomplishes the most for the good of all men." That vision captivated me.

Many of our friends did not understand when my wife and I explained our decision to sell our businesses, leave the entertainment world, and spend time with college students and laymen who were seeking reality in a confusing world. I could only say that it was similar to the Coast Guardsmen who prepared for a rescue attempt of two fishermen lost in a storm off the coast of Maine. As they were about to set out into the storm, they heard someone say over the howling winds and the roaring waves, "Don't go out there. You may never get back." One of the guardsmen replied, "We don't have to get back. But we have got to go." Almost 2000 years ago, Jesus Christ gave the Great Commission to *go* into all the world and to share the gospel with every person. So I had to go. But I didn't have to "get back," for this would be my life's work.

In the nearly 20 years since that decision, nothing had diminished the conviction with which I held my call. Serving as an ambassador for Christ had taken me to all 50 states and to 76 countries. I had performed on national television in 40 countries and had audiences with monarchs and presidents, all for the purpose of presenting the Person of Jesus Christ through magic.

I thought about the opportunities I had had to return to show business. During my first year in ministry, a nightclub owner offered me a good deal of money—equal to two months' salary in my new work—to perform at his club on New Year's Eve. I couldn't help but think of the millions of people who would celebrate New Year's Eve in thousands of nightclubs across the country, only to return the following day to their lives of nightmare and frustration—a new year, but the same old lives. So I spent that New Year's Eve at a party for college students, presenting the reality of new life in Jesus Christ.

I had other opportunities as well, but they too were easy to turn down. I only had to look at the letters and notes from men and women whose lives were being changed—like the college student who wrote, "You saved my life. If I had not heard this message tonight, I would have committed suicide," or the coed in Portland, Oregon, who wrote this letter:

> . . . Last night my whole life changed. I heard Andre Kole speak in Portland, and for the first time in my life I accepted Jesus Christ as my personal Savior. Never before had I experienced anything like this. My life has been more like dying then living. I have used and abused drugs . . . was an honor student in high school . . . at 19 was arrested on three felony counts, for sale and possession of narcotics. When I turned 21 last month, I felt more like being buried than coming of age. But something deep inside drew me to the . . . meeting . . . Last night when I heard Andre speak, I truly believed for the first time and asked Christ to come into my life. This is a step I have tried to make for the last three years but failed to do alone.

I had so many memories. After a campus meeting in Sacramento, a Buddhist priest approached me and said, "I came today to see your magic, but after hearing your message I know I cannot continue with my present plans. My life will never be the same." A few months later I heard that he had returned home to Japan to work with a Protestant church.

I thought of the university professor who talked to me after a program. For many years he had been looking for meaning and purpose for his own life. He said he had moved from Philadelphia to Washington State "to try to get away from it all and have some time to think." Then he said, "I believe God brought me

3000 miles just to hear this message tonight. This is what I have been looking for all of these years."

A Midwestern doctor had written: "On October 30, 1971, I gave my heart to Christ on the campus of Northern Illinois University. An illusionist named Andre Kole presented a program touching the depths of my soul, a challenge to choose my eternal destiny. Jesus was and is the fulfillment of all my spiritual desires and thirsts. I want to thank you for introducing me to your best friend . . . . On my den wall I have my degree proudly framed. Next to it are the framed news clippings of Andre's visit—a kind of spiritual birth certificate!"

Another letter told me, "This December will be my tenth spiritual birthday . . . . When you told the story of the train coming down the mountainside as the drawbridge caretaker lowered the bridge, knowing it meant the death of his son. . . I felt as if I'd been slapped. Everything you said showed me that I'd been going through my life, simply waving merrily at God!"

I experienced numerous adventures in the course of seeing these results. Many unruly crowds were eager to heckle and disrupt my presentations, but each time God's Spirit produced a "holy hush" when the time came to present Christ. Before I spoke at Harvard, one person said that my message was too simple for those intellectual students. That night 350 students crammed into a small dining room. Fifty-seven made decisions for Christ; another 60 asked for more information. I was told that it made the greatest spiritual impact on that campus in 20 years.

Another time I spoke at Amherst College in Massachusetts. As I was about to walk on stage, a group of hooded Ku-Klux-Klan-type figures in long black robes entered the auditorium and sat down. I asked the people backstage who they were. They did not know, but they said the group had attended several meetings on campus and each time had succeeded in breaking up the meeting. The last time was earlier that week, when, after 15 minutes of their jeers and shouting, former Vice President Hubert Humphrey walked out in the middle of his speech.

News like this is great for relaxing you just before you perform! We prayed together that God would supernaturally stop the group from doing anything that would hinder His work that night. For the next two hours they sat there without saying a word or moving. At the end of the program they got up and quietly filed out. That night scores of students received Christ.

I also remembered various mishaps over the years, such as the time I spoke on the campus in Tampa, Florida. A student's cigarette dropped through the floor and started a fire in some curtain material below. Smoke began coming up around the stage. The aisles and doorways were jammed with an overflow crowd, and I knew people would be hurt or even killed if we announced the fire. Since the audience was not aware of the danger, I continued the program while the fire crew worked below. I explained that the smoke was part of the atmosphere for our presentation. Only after the danger was over did I tell them what had happened.

During another performance in Florida, as I reached the most important part of the program a horrible smell permeated the area. It was so bad I could hardly talk. A small group of radical students had entered the back of the auditorium and thrown a stink bomb into the middle of the audience to try to break up the meeting. However, because of their interest in the message, the audience endured the smell. Not one person left.

Some of the experiences overseas were even more

harrowing. In El Salvador I did a program for some top military men. Two generals were sitting in the front row. In one of my numbers I go into the audience and pull money out of the noses and ears of the people. At this program I picked up the hat of a soldier near the front and poured a number of coins out of it. He was surprised, but I was more surprised because. . . under the hat he was holding a loaded revolver in his hand! Afterward I learned that he was one of the men assigned to keep his eye—and revolver—on me since they didn't know much about me. With two generals in attendance, they weren't taking any chances.

In Liberia I had a performance before the President and about 50 government leaders he had invited. An attempt had been made on his life the week before, so secret service guards were stationed around the stage to watch my every move. One man kept a loaded gun pointed at me offstage—just in case I got too close to the President. Afterward the President commented over and over that this was the most inspiring talk he had ever heard, and he instructed his personal assistant to tape my presentation at the university the following evening so he could hear it again and refer to it later. We spent another hour talking about the spiritual needs of his country and the world.

Thinking back over all these experiences, I realized that though it was a great privilege to win the Performing Arts Fellowship, the equivalent of an Oscar in the movie profession, no honors could begin to equal the fact that people were resolving their eternal destinies. That was my greatest award. I wondered if I should even attend the banquet. It was scheduled while I was in the middle of another tour. One part of me felt that I should not be diverted. Yet this was a unique opportunity to give God the credit for what

He had accomplished in my life.

The award would be presented by Mark Wilson at a gala, black-tie event in the Beverly Wilshire Hotel. Many outstanding entertainers would attend—magicians such as Doug Henning, David Copperfield, and Blackstone; musicians and actors such as Cary Grant, Liberace, Bill Bixby, and Bob Barker. I wanted to share with them the significance of this award. I reached over to my desk and took a yellow pad.

"I am very grateful and deeply honored to receive this award," I wrote quickly. "The magicians here tonight who know me personally know that I very sincerely and very strongly believe that God is the One who gives each of us all the talent and abilities we have in this life.

"Through the years my greatest desire has been to honor Him and express my thanks to Him for all He has allowed me to do through the gift that He has given me. So in accepting this award, I not only want to express my thanks to you and to the Academy, but also to Him for who He is, and for allowing me to be involved with you in such an exciting and enjoyable profession."

Real Power

My missionary escorts had warned me that this campus was one of the most anti-American universities in Latin America. In recent weeks several speakers had been attacked and beaten. Two had nearly died.

We arrived at the university in Santiago, Chile, and immediately noticed that something was awry. Hundreds of students were milling around and the mood was tense, as if they anticipated a riot. "They're on strike," someone told us. I thought that this was a good reason to cancel the performance, but before I could suggest it, someone ran up to us. "They're waiting for you!" he shouted. "There are at least 2000 people!"

Several bodyguards surrounded me, and we were quickly escorted to an outdoor theater. The students were standing, surrounding the stage, and I immediately observed that I could not easily escape. Bodyguards would be virtually useless against such a mob.

I thought again of the words I had read in the book of Acts a few hours earlier. Paul had experienced severe resistance to his preaching, but God spoke to him one night: "Do not be afraid any longer, but go on speaking and do not be silent; for I am with you, and no man will attack you in order to harm you, for I have many people in this city."[1]

Those words were nearly 2000 years old, but they could not have been more relevant. I silently offered a prayer of thanksgiving for that encouragement, and with a surge of confidence I stepped out onto the stage. A chorus of whistles and shouts greeted me, drowning out the emcee's introduction. I reminded myself that this was only a sign of their great hunger and need for God. I silently prayed, "Lord, please draw them to Yourself through Your Holy Spirit."

I quickly noticed a group of young men near the front who appeared to be the ringleaders. I yelled for their leader to come forward to help me, explaining that he was surely the bravest man in the crowd. As he came forward, my Chinese cure for dandruff was rolled out. This contraption, which looks like an ancient guillotine, quieted the crowd slightly, yet the background music still could not be heard. My victim looked skeptically at the apparatus, but was too proud to back away. Kneeling, he inserted his head and hands. The blade descended and appeared to pass through the young man's neck without injuring him.

Without my usual patter between tricks, I got a bucket and began picking coins from the air. Reaching into the first row, I pulled coins from one student's nose, dumped some more from another's hat, and picked more from another's ear.

As I moved quickly through my tricks, the crowd became more quiet. I had been warned that students with rocks, eggs, and other objects were stationed in the crowd, waiting to break up the program on a given signal. But nothing happened.

After 30 minutes the bold, restless crowd had been supernaturally transformed into a quiet audience, spellbound as I began to share the message of Jesus Christ. At the conclusion of the 50-minute program, the students erupted into a long, sustained ovation. Many swarmed onto the stage, wanting to hear more. Others asked for appointments with local staff to talk more about Jesus Christ. It was another hour before we could begin to make our way off campus to another meeting.

As we left, a university administrator expressed amazement at the response and attention from the students. He had never seen any program so well received on the campus. I knew only one way to explain the crowd's transformation—the power of the Holy Spirit.

During my years of performing, God's power has protected me in all kinds of dangerous situations. I have never been injured by any audience. Even more incredible, I have never missed a performance, despite inclement weather, illness, and almost impossible travel schedules—as many as a hundred shows in a hundred days in a dozen different countries.

I did not always understand the power of the Holy Spirit. The first three years of my Christian experience were perhaps the toughest years I ever lived through. I was convinced of the reality of Jesus Christ, and that He had accepted my prayer of invitation and had come into my life, but I fell into the trap for which I had criticized others: I became busy in church and religious activities while finding it almost impossible to live a consistent Christian life each day.

Probably the greatest lesson I have ever learned is that God does not want us to work for Him. He simply wants us to allow Him to do His work in and through us.

During those three years of trying to live a good religious life, I experienced little real joy or happiness. Life was a constant struggle. Then I began to hear about the Holy Spirit. I learned that Jesus Christ, as He finished His ministry on this earth, said He had to go away: "I tell you the truth, it is to your advantage that I go away; for if I do not go away, the Helper [another word for the Holy Spirit] shall not come to you; but if I go, I will send Him to you."[2] In other words, Jesus Christ physically left the earth so that He could be present spiritually within the lives of everyone willing to receive Him. At the very moment a person receives Christ, the Holy Spirit enters into the life of that person.

Regarding the Holy Spirit, the testimony of one Bible character particularly impressed me. This man, Simon the Sorcerer, was exceptionally qualified to recognize whether or not Christianity was just a trick. Simon was one of the greatest, if not *the* greatest, magician of his time. We read in Acts 8 that he was practicing magic in the city of Samaria, claiming to be someone exceptional. Everyone was giving him attention until Philip began preaching the gospel. As Philip preached, a number of miracles happened, including the healing of several people who were lame and paralyzed. Simon was so impressed that he also believed and was baptized.

As I have said, it is easy for an experienced magician to fool scientists, theologians, ministers, and priests, because they do not think like magicians, but it is extremely difficult to fool another magician. Simon would not have been easily fooled. Apparently the miracles he saw were greater than anything he had ever observed.

Then the apostles Peter and John came to town, and as they laid their hands on the believers, the Holy Spirit was manifested. Simon offered money to buy the secret of the apostles' power, but they rebuked him for thinking that he could buy the gift of God with money. He was terrified by the power he saw.

Just what does it mean to be filled with the Holy Spirit? It is something like a picture I saw many years ago of a single piece of straw that was driven through a telephone pole during a tornado. How in the world could a flimsy blade of grass go clear through a pole? It could not in its own strength, but the power of the tornado drove it through the pole. Likewise, we are weak until we are willing to surrender to the power of the Holy Spirit. Only then can we experience supernatural power.

In John 15, Jesus used the analogy of the vine and branches to explain what it means to be filled with the Spirit. Today He might use an illustration of electricity and the light bulb. No matter how hard a light bulb tries to shine in its own power, it cannot succeed. The only way it can shine is to surrender itself to the power of the electric current. Perhaps Jesus would say something like this:

"I am the electricity, you are the light bulbs, and my Father is the electrician. Abide in me as I abide in you. Just as the light bulb cannot produce light unless it abides in the electricity, so neither can you unless you abide in me. I am the electricity, you are the light bulbs. He who abides in me and I in him sheds much light. Apart from me you can do absolutely nothing. If you abide in me and my words abide in you, ask whatever you wish and it shall be done for you. By this is my Father glorified and illuminated, that you shed much light and in so doing prove to be my disciples."

We experience the power of the Holy Spirit by surrendering to the Lord by faith. The Bible commands Christians to be filled with the Holy Spirit. It also promises that if we ask anything according to God's will, He hears us and grants our requests.[3] So we can be filled with the Holy Spirit through prayer—an expression of our faith. We can invite God to take control of our lives through the power of the Holy Spirit.

I do a number of illusions with light bulbs to illustrate how the Holy Spirit works. One illustration incorporates three bulbs of different sizes: One is 200 watts, another is 50, and the third is only 2½ watts. I use these to illustrate how God gives each of us different talents. Becoming jealous of another person who may have more talent is a great danger. So is feeling superior to someone with less talent. Just as each light bulb was created for a different purpose, so are we. The 200-watt bulb does not make a good night light, but the 2½-watt bulb does. They have different functions. And no light bulb will work without the power of electricity flowing through it. If the 200-watt bulb thinks that because it is so much brighter it doesn't need electricity, it will become useless.

I found out how true this is in my life when I did four programs in one day on a Midwest campus. I had performed and given my Christian testimony for several years and had always seen people respond by giving their lives to Jesus Christ. On this day, however, I had a tremendous audience at the first program, but no spiritual response. At the second performance the same thing happened. I couldn't understand what was wrong. At the third program the audience was again very warm and receptive, but not a single person indicated that he had received Christ.

I spent an hour alone before the final program, searching my heart to see what was wrong. As I grew silent before God, I realized that a certain thought had crept into my thinking. It was the idea that if a person just learned to do what I did and to say what I said, he would automatically see the same type of spiritual response. The outcome did not really depend on God; it was just a matter of doing the tricks and saying the words.

God used those three shows to demonstrate that without the power of the Holy Spirit, I could do nothing. I confessed my wrong attitude and thanked Him for showing me this truth. I asked Him to again do His work through me. That night I gave the same program, but saw different results. Sixteen students indicated that they received Christ. To my knowledge, from that day onward every single program I have done has had a spiritual response from the audience. Sometimes the response has been in the hundreds, but I cannot take credit for that. The Holy Spirit, working through me, is responsible for every conversion.

I also use light bulbs to illustrate the problem Christians have with sin. That battle confuses many people; they can't understand why they continue to want to sin. When we receive Christ, however, we do not lose the old sin nature with which we all are born. Instead, we receive a new nature.

I illustrate this with two light bulbs mounted on a Y-shaped socket. The little, dark, ugly bulb represents the old nature; the bright light bulb represents the new nature. I tie ropes to each bulb, symbolizing the fact that our old nature is tied to Satan and our new nature to God. Satan constantly tries to tempt us, while God tries to communicate His life to us through the Holy Spirit.

Thousands of Christians throughout the world live in defeat because they listen to the wrong voice. They listen to Satan instead of God. Whichever voice we give our attention to will dominate our lives. It's like the story of the Indian who said two dogs were fighting inside him—a black dog and a white dog. When he was asked which dog was winning, he answered, "The one I feed the most." *The secret to growing in the Christian life is to feed our new nature while starving the old.* We can do this through day-by-day studying the Scriptures, spending time with other believers, witnessing for our faith, and praying.

I have seen the power of the Holy Spirit at work in innumerable ways. One is the fact that I speak before thousands of people each year, and millions on television. It certainly is not my nature to be a speaker. I am very shy and quiet, and content to be alone for long periods of time. But God has given me a tremendous desire to share what I have discovered, and to explain to others how they can experience the same joy and excitement in their lives.

The Holy Spirit was the only reason I could go out before dangerous, unruly crowds in Latin America, knowing that I could easily be killed. The reality of Christ overcomes my fear of death, and I am confident that I am safest while in God's will. Many times I have stood before antagonistic crowds which had been whipped to a fervor by Marxist students, and each time I have seen God's Spirit change that crowd so that by the time I started sharing the message of Christ, they were completely silent and attentive.

The only way I can explain this is with the words of the apostle Paul: "I was with you in weakness and in fear and in much trembling. And my message and my preaching were not in persuasive words of wisdom, but in demonstration of the Spirit and of power."⁴ I am convinced that, as Christians, we have tremendous potential. We can accomplish anything God wants us to if we're empowered by the Holy Spirit. God has given each one of us unique talents, but we can utilize them only through His power. With His Spirit, our lives reflect a dramatically different lifestyle that is evident to those around us—a difference that is even worth dying for.

As Bill Bright has said, "The dedicated, Spirit-filled Christian life is not an easy life, but it is a life filled with adventure and thrills, the likes of which one cannot possibly experience in any other way. Whether or not we're Christians, we are going to have problems in this life. Christians or not, we will one day die. If I am going to be a Christian at all, I want all that God has for me, and I want to be all that He wants me to be. If I am to suffer at all and one day die, why not suffer and die for the highest and best, for the Lord Jesus Christ and His gospel?"

The potential of the Spirit-filled Christian life is dramatically illustrated in the story of the 40 singing wrestlers. In the days when the ruling passion of the Roman Emperor Nero was the extermination of the Christians, he had a band of soldiers known as the "Emperor's Wrestlers." These men were the best and bravest of the land. In the great amphitheater they upheld the arms of the emperor against all challengers. Before each contest they stood before the emperor's throne and cried, "We, the wrestlers, wrestling for thee, O Emperor, to win for thee the victory and from thee the victor's crown."

When the great Roman army was sent to fight in faraway Gaul, no soldiers were braver or more loyal than this band of wrestlers led by their centurion,

Vespasian. But news reached Nero that many of the wrestlers had accepted the Christian faith.

To be a Christian meant death, even to those who served Nero best. Therefore this decree was immediately dispatched to Vespasian: "If there be any among the soldiers who cling to the faith of the Christian, they must die." He received the decree in the dead of winter, while the soldiers were camped on the shore of a frozen inland lake. The winter had been hard, but enduring the many hardships together united them more closely.

Vespasian's heart sank as he read the emperor's message. He called the soldiers together and asked, "Are there any among you who cling to the faith of the Christian? If so, let him step forward."

Forty wrestlers instantly stepped forward two paces, respectfully saluted, and stood at attention. Vespasian paused. He had not expected so many. "The decree has come from your emperor," he said, "that any who cling to the faith of the Christian must die. For the sake of your country, your comrades, your loved ones, renounce this false faith." Not one of the 40 moved.

Vespasian pleaded with them long and earnestly without prevailing upon a single man to deny his Lord. Finally he said, "The decree of the emperor must be obeyed, but I am not willing that your blood be on your comrades. I am going to order that you march out upon the lake of ice and I shall leave you there to the mercy of the elements. Fires, however, will be waiting here on the shore to welcome any willing to renounce this false faith."

At sundown, the 40 wrestlers were stripped of all their clothing. Without a word they turned and, falling into columns of four, marched onto the lake of ice. As they marched, they broke into a chorus with the old chant of the arena: "Forty wrestlers, wrestling for Thee, O Christ, to win for Thee the victory, and from Thee the Victor's crown."

Through the long hours of the night, Vespasian stood by his campfire and waited. The words of the wrestlers' song became fainter and fainter. As morning drew near, one figure, overcome by exposure, crept quietly toward the fire. In the extremity of his suffering he had renounced his Lord. Then faintly but clearly from out of the darkness came the song, "Thirty-nine wrestlers, wrestling for Thee, O Christ, to win for Thee the victory, and from Thee the Victor's crown."

Vespasian looked at the figure drawing close to the fire, then out toward the frozen lake. Who can say, but perhaps he saw the greater light shining there in the darkness. Off came his helmet, down went his shield, and he sprang onto the ice crying, "Forty wrestlers, wrestling for Thee, O Christ, to win for Thee the victory, and from Thee the Victor's crown."

The number of God's 40 singing wrestlers was complete.

11

Is Prayer Magic?

Is prayer magic? That question was asked recently in a magazine article. It's a fair question, for many people repeat certain prayers as a religious ritual, hoping for some magical benefit. Some try prayer only when all else fails.

One reason that people find prayer unfulfilling is that they don't understand what it really is. When my children were small, it occurred to me that I could hypnotize Robyn and Tim and make them do almost anything I wanted to. I could tell them to stand up, sit down, or eat their spinach, and they would do those things. I could tell them, "I want you to tell me 'I love you,'" and they would say, "I love you." But it would mean nothing to me because they would only be doing what I had commanded them to do.

One afternoon I was working in my office and Robyn was running around the room, making a lot of noise. I asked her to leave so I could concentrate. "I don't want to leave, Daddy," she said. "I'll just sit here and be quiet." She sat down near me, but I figured she couldn't keep quiet for long. "Why don't you go out and play with Timothy?" "No, Daddy," she answered, "I just want to be with you."

When she said that, I gave her a big hug. She responded and said, "I love my daddy." And I said, "I love my Robyn."

In that moment I learned by experience more about prayer and God's love than I could by reading a dozen books on theology and religion. God desires our fellowship, but He doesn't force us to communicate with Him. He gives us a free will to express our love to Him, or else to reject His love. Robyn helped me see that prayer is a voluntary relationship with our heavenly Father.

A few years ago I heard about a big, rugged construction worker named Joe. Joe was very quiet, but all the men liked him, and they knew he had a very strong faith in God. Every day during lunch break he went into the chapel to pray. One day one of the men asked him, "What do you say to God when you go and pray?" Joe answered, "I just say, 'Jesus, this is Joe.' "

Sometime later, Joe was hospitalized from an accident. His fellow workers visited him, but he couldn't talk and part of his face was bandaged because of the injuries. They all noticed, however, a tremendous expression of peace on his face despite the pain. Later, after Joe recovered, one of the men asked him, "How could you endure such pain and still have such a peaceful look while you were in the hospital?" Joe answered, "During the time I was lying there, I kept hearing the words, 'Joe, this is Jesus.' "

That story explains prayer as well as any I've heard. Often we think prayer consists of long sentences and many words. In reality, it may just be the awareness of God—sitting in His presence and enjoying Him. I especially like the following definition: *Prayer is simply a conversation between two people who love each other.* So often people feel they need to do all the talking in prayer, but genuine prayer also allows God time to speak to us through His Holy Spirit.

The author of the article I referred to at the start of this chapter summarized this concept well:

> Prayer is not magic. It is a relationship with God in an intimate, ongoing relationship of love, where we may express our adoration of Him as a person and our God. It is where we can safely express ourselves in the depth of whom we are, confessing our sins and accepting His forgiveness. Prayer is where we seek God's support in our vulnerability and needs, and lastly, where we ask for His help and encouragement in our lives, relationships, and work, by His will and His love for us. To engage in prayer as magic is to reject the autonomous holy person, God. To engage in prayer as relationship is to be vulnerable, and to trust God's goodness and wisdom.[1]

The beauty of such a relationship is that we can pray anytime, anywhere, about anything. The apostle Paul wrote that we should "pray without ceasing."[2] To me, that means we should enjoy God's presence at all times, not just go to Him when we are in need.

But I find that I also need some time each day to be totally alone with God, so in solitude I kneel and pray. (Kneeling is not necessary for prayer; it simply helps me reflect my heart attitude toward God.) During these times I can concentrate solely on Him and bring Him my concerns.

A young man who was desperately seeking God sought out a wise old man who lived in a nearby beach house. He asked him, "Old man, how can I see God?"

The old man obviously knew God and had a depth which few of us ever experience. He pondered for what seemed to be a very long time, then finally responded quietly, "Young man, I am not sure that I can really help you. You see, I have a very different problem from yours. I cannot *not* see Him." Prayer means involving God and seeing His hand in anything and everything.

Perhaps the part of prayer most important to me is praise. That's when I tell God how wonderful He is and reflect on His attributes. Reading through the Psalms and even praying some of them back to God helps me do this.

Praise is important because it increases our confidence in God, which is the key to answered prayer. The more we pray and believe God, the more we see Him answer our prayers, and the more confidence we have in Him. This is illustrated in a story about a church in a Kansas farming community that was concerned about a severe drought. The problem was so serious that one Sunday the members agreed to return to the church after lunch to pray for rain.

As one man walked to church that afternoon, he met a little boy carrying an umbrella. "Where are you going with the umbrella?" he asked.

"Haven't you heard?" the boy answered. "We're going to pray for rain today."

The man smiled as they walked to church together. After the prayer meeting, the man enjoyed sharing the little boy's umbrella as they walked home in the rain.

So many times we pray without really believing that God hears us and will answer. Yet He is the God who created the heavens and the earth; He controls the wind and the waves and the rain. A God that powerful is a God I can believe will hear and respond.

This doesn't mean that God always answers my prayers the way I intended. I mentioned that I have never missed a scheduled performance in all my years of traveling, but I did almost miss one. I was in Sri Lanka (when it used to be called Ceylon) and had a program scheduled the next day in Singapore. There were only three flights a week to Singapore, and the one I was scheduled to take was running 24 hours behind schedule. So I phoned ahead to tell the university staff that I would not make the show. They rescheduled the program for the next day.

They had built a special outdoor stage for my show and prayed that it would not rain. The weather was fine on the day it originally was scheduled, but as I arrived in Singapore, the storm clouds were moving in. By show time it was raining too hard to hold the program outside, so hundreds of people crowded into a small auditorium. As we saw people being turned away, we wondered why this was the first program I had missed, and why God had prevented us from having that program outside where more people could enjoy it. After the show we learned that the outdoor stage had collapsed. If we had used that stage, several people would have been seriously injured and perhaps even killed.

I have found that God is just as concerned about the little things as He is the large things. No circumstance is too small for Him. Once while I was in California, I was scheduled to meet with Bill Bright at Campus Crusade for Christ's international headquarters. As I entered his office, I heard him ask his secretary, "Have you prayed about this?" Embarrassed, she said, "No, I haven't." He responded, "Why don't we pray that God will help us find this tape?"

A minute later the secretary returned and explained to me that she was having a hard time finding a tape by a certain speaker. I told her, "Arlis Priest in Arizona has that tape." I was probably the only one out of hundreds of people at the headquarters who knew where the tape was. A coincidence? Because I have seen many such prayers answered over the years, I prefer to believe that God brought me into the office at that precise moment to serve as the answer to that prayer.

During the early years of my ministry, I needed a trailer to use on our tours, as we were traveling with small children. But we didn't have the money, and trailers were expensive. We prayed about it as a family, and then I visited a dealer.

When I told the man what I needed, he showed me a trailer that fit our needs perfectly. "This trailer has been on the lot for months and I haven't been able to sell it. I don't know why it hasn't moved. Maybe God was reserving it for you." He thought for a moment, then said, "Why don't you take this trailer and use it as long as you need? I won't charge you for it. Just bring it back when you're finished."

That was another experience that strengthened my confidence in God. Over and over again I have seen that faith is like a muscle, and prayer is the exercise that helps it grow. Bill Bright told me that when he started his ministry in 1951, he prayed that one person would come to Christ. When God answered that prayer, Dr. Bright prayed for a dozen converts. As God answered that, his vision grew. He prayed for hundreds of conversions through the ministry of Campus Crusade for Christ, then thousands, then millions. All of those prayers have been answered, and now he is believing God for more than a billion people throughout the world to come to Christ.

My faith began to grow when, as a young boy, I was in an orange grove one day. The fruit wasn't ripe yet, but I was thirsty and craved an orange. My friend suggested that I pray. I did not know Christ yet, but I prayed. Then I walked over two rows, looked up into a tree, and saw a beautiful ripe orange. I believe that God answered that prayer to show me that He is real.

In the early sixties I prayed for an opportunity to perform and speak at university fraternities and sororities to present Jesus Christ. When I saw the response at those meetings, I began praying for larger, campus-wide meetings. Soon I was speaking before groups of more than a thousand students. Then I began praying for a way to further expand my ministry. God provided the opportunity to make two films, which have been shown to millions of people throughout the world.

As I have observed God's faithfulness, my faith has increased. For several years I've prayed about producing the world's largest stage show, during which I would recreate some of the great miracles of the Bible. God has started to answer that prayer through special Christmas and Easter shows, and I anticipate the day when the full dream will be realized.

I find it exciting to be in situations where my only hope is to trust God, such as my most recent trip through India, which was during the monsoon season. Because of the anticipated size of the audiences, all except one of the programs were scheduled to be outdoors. I was to visit seven cities in seven days, but it seemed impossible to avoid being rained out of several shows.

Together with the national staff, we prayed that God would allow all seven of the programs to go as scheduled. In every city the weather cleared as we arrived. At all our outdoor performances, we had overflow crowds and no rain. And as we left the city, the rains returned. The one exception was the show we scheduled indoors. A group of Marxist students protested outside, trying to break up the program. They disturbed us to the point that we were afraid the confusion might disperse the crowd. On stage I silently prayed that God would supernaturally intervene so we could continue. As soon as I had prayed, I heard a crash of thunder and a torrential downpour. The radicals quickly fled, allowing us to proceed without further interruption.

As I've traveled throughout the world, I have had opportunities to speak to people of many different religions. Sometimes, in situations where crowds were almost 100 percent non-Christian, I have been tempted to dilute my message. But God always has demonstrated His power in answer to prayer.

On my first tour in Asia, I performed for a Hindu and Muslim audience in Madras, India's fourth-largest city. Invitations had been sent to the city leaders for this special appearance, in which the mayor had agreed to preside. Despite the temptation to water down the message, I proceeded with my normal program. At the end, the mayor—a very devout Muslim—came on stage and took the microphone. For a moment I thought he was going to denounce what I said. But to my amazement and that of many others, he talked about the problems of India and said that he felt the message he had just heard was the answer to that country's problems.

Another time I appeared at a college in Pakistan. Nearly a thousand students squeezed into the auditorium, and of those 95 percent of them were Muslim. My custom in every show is to tell the audience that after a break I will explain how a person can come into a personal relationship with Jesus Christ. I encourage those who are not interested to leave. The Christians responsible for arranging this meeting advised me not to do this, as they feared that everyone would leave. But we took the ten-minute break, and only three people left. I later found out that the three who left were Christians, and they later returned. All the Muslim students stayed, and their interest and attention was phenomenal. That further proved to me that if God is knowable, people want to know Him.

If you doubt that God hears or answers prayer, I challenge you to put God to the test. I think God may answer some prayers of a nonbeliever, but it's like asking a neighbor to do something for you in an emergency, as opposed to asking a close member of your own family. You can be certain, however, that He will hear one prayer—your cry for forgiveness, and the receiving of God's Son, Jesus Christ, into your life. Once you become a Christian, God becomes your Father—a loving Father who wants to provide for His children.

If you are a Christian but don't see God answering your prayers, I encourage you to keep a small notebook and record your requests and God's answers. He may not respond in the way you ask, but He will answer. Keeping a journal of His answers is one of the best ways to develop confidence in God.

Most important, remember that prayer is not *asking for things*, but a *relationship*. God loves us, and He wants us to enjoy His presence through prayer.

12

The Ultimate Test

In a time when many marriages are disintegrating, I have been privileged to experience not one, but two wonderful marriages. My first wife, of 20 years, went to be with the Lord in 1976. One year later God brought Kathy into my life, and later we were married. She was not a replacement of Aljeana, but God's perfect provision for both of our needs.

In this book we have talked about reality as opposed to illusion. In my presentations I always try to dispel the illusion that becoming a Christian eliminates all problems. In fact, only when we are confronted with pain, suffering, and death is the reality of our faith tested.

According to the latest statistics, the death rate for every hundred people is still 100 percent. The Bible says, "It is appointed for men to die once."[1] Everyone has an appointment. For some people it is a few years earlier than for others. For Aljeana it was November 28, 1976, at the age of 38.

I first met Aljeana in grade school, when she started

to assist me in some of my shows. The main purpose of an assistant is to make the magician look good. Aljeana was perfect in that respect—very attractive, with good stage presence. Also, she was small and agile and just right for some of our unusual illusions. Over the years we developed a oneness of feeling and timing so that we knew what each other was thinking on stage without speaking. She could anticipate any problems and help me out of a jam.

We married while I was in college. Aljeana, with her sweet spirit, was committed to my career in magic to the extent that she was willing to sacrifice her own desires in order to help acquire some of the very expensive equipment we needed. We labored together toward the same goals, intent on making our lives count for eternity.

In December 1974 Aljeana was Christmas shopping with our two children, Robyn and Tim, when suddenly she experienced a strange dizziness and had to be helped to a chair. The feeling passed in a few minutes, but during the holidays it occurred several more times.

After consulting several doctors, we learned that she had an incurable brain tumor. In layman's language, the doctors said she had a time bomb in her head that could go off at any moment. Eventually they would have to operate, but that would only prolong her life for a short time; it would not cure the problem. They advised us that if we wanted to do anything or take any trip, we had better do it soon.

Aljeana and I talked and prayed about what we should do. For more than a decade we had traveled throughout the world, sharing our discovery about the reality of Christ with millions of people through our TV shows, films, and personal appearances. We both concluded that we would continue working together as long as possible.

We shared the news of Aljeana's condition with our children and explained that their mother might go to heaven soon. Then we talked about the fact that everyone in the world is infected with a sickness far worse than Aljeana's—the disease that the Bible calls sin. This disease would not only kill a person physically, but could also cause a person to be separated from God forever. We explained that even though there was no known medical cure for Aljeana's problem, there is a cure for the disease of sin. So as long as we could, we wanted to keep telling people how they could know this cure, Jesus Christ, in a personal way.

During the two years leading up to Aljeana's departure, God taught us many great lessons about life and the exciting adventure of death. He gave each of us supernatural peace and joy beyond our human understanding or ability to express. The prayers of many friends from around the world strengthened us, and our trust in God freed us of any worry, anxiety, or fear.

While Aljeana still could do some speaking, she always shared a poem that ended with these lines: "We would not long for heaven, if earth held our only joy." In the last weeks of Aljeana's suffering, she experienced a great longing and anticipation of heaven. The Bible says, "Let heaven fill your thoughts; don't spend your time worrying about things down here."[2] We found that the more we know about heaven, the less important this life seems to be, including its suffering.

Another source of power and victory during this ordeal came from our times of praising the Lord. As long as Aljeana could read the Bible, she spent about 90 percent of her time in the Psalms. There she gained comfort and strength for every phase of her experience.

As the illness progressed, her suffering increased. Gradually she began to lose the ability to do anything for herself. She lost the use of her arms and legs. She could not move her head or body. She became totally blind. Other people had to move her, bathe her, feed her (when she could eat), and care for her every need. After her brain surgery and radiation treatments, she lost her hair. Day after day she could do nothing but lie in bed.

Yet not once did I hear her complain. On the contrary, many times she said, "Thank You, Lord, for the pain." One day while a friend was sitting quietly with her, she noticed a smile on Aljeana's face. "Aljeana, what are you smiling about?" she asked. "Oh, God is so good to me," my wife replied.

God heals all of His children, sometimes in this life, sometimes in the life to come. Some people did not understand why God did not heal Aljeana in this life. I believe that God chose her for a very special and important task: to demonstrate His ability to impart supernatural strength in the midst of pain, suffering, and death.

I too experienced this sustenance. In my eyes, Aljeana was the most attractive and lovely person I had ever known, but as her illness progressed, her physical beauty diminished. Yet my love for her did not. Instead, it grew and deepened. The inner beauty that radiated through her far surpassed any physical beauty she ever had. I experienced a God-given, supernatural love far beyond the deep, wonderful love I had known for her when she was in good health.

The time came when it looked as though Aljeana would die soon. For several days she was in a coma, and the doctor said she could expire at any moment. With my permission, he tried one last bit of surgery. As a result, she made a remarkable recovery for a few days.

When she came out of the coma, one of the first things Aljeana said was, "Who was the man who was with me all the time?" She explained that a young man stood by her bed and never left her during the critical days through which she had just come.

In her words, "He seemed to have a special feeling for me, and when the pain was very bad, he held my hand and comforted me. I don't think I could have made it without him." When I asked if he was still there, she said, "No, he left yesterday morning"—the time when she began to recover. That day we received in the mail a card with the Bible verse, "The Lord stood with me, and strengthened me."[3]

I hesitate to jump to any conclusions concerning this experience, but I have often wondered if God allowed Aljeana to return to us so we could know the extent of His care for us when we come to our final hours. The Bible says, "His loved ones are very precious to him, and he does not lightly let them die."[4] The Bible also teaches that, when we die, the angels will carry us into the presence of God.[5]

Aljeana didn't want to talk more about her experience. A few weeks later, however, her life once again began to fade. I had mixed emotions when she quietly said to us one night, "That young man has come back and I am glad he is here." Shortly thereafter she lost consciousness and never recovered.

One of the greatest lessons God taught me through my wife's death concerns our transition from earth to heaven. I illustrated this at her memorial service through the use of two large light bulbs. One represents our present, earthly bodies; the other our heavenly bodies.

The Bible tells us, "We know that when this tent we live in now is taken down—when we die and leave these bodies—we will have wonderful new bodies in heaven, homes that will be ours forevermore, made for us by God himself, and not by human hands."[6] A few verses later it says, "Every moment we spend in these earthly bodies is time spent away from our eternal home in heaven with Jesus."[7] As long as we are on earth, the light is on in our earthly bodies. "This precious treasure—this light and power that now shines within us—is held in a perishable container, that is, in our weak bodies."[8]

In the last weeks before Aljeana left her earthly body, she seemed to be in a twilight zone between earth and heaven. A couple of times she seemed to be getting better, and I saw her grow brighter here again. Then as her life began to fade and grow dimmer here, I pictured her growing brighter and brighter in heaven.

On the final night of Aljeana's earthly life, my brother, his wife, and I entered her hospital room together. She had not responded to anything that day. We noticed the long pauses between each breath, and my brother started counting the seconds between breaths. We counted 20 seconds. Then 30 seconds. Then 40 seconds. Then there was no more. We had just witnessed her last breath. After 38 years, Aljeana's light here had gone out. She was released into total healing, free to begin her new life in heaven.

The visual illustration of lights was a tremendous comfort to me because when the night came for her light to go out completely here, I was already thinking of her as being more in heaven. This made the transition easier for me. It is tragic that many people think of their loved ones who have died as being in a coffin. Not once have I thought of Aljeana as being anywhere but in heaven with Jesus. All that remains in that fancy box is what the Bible calls "the perishable container." It also says that to be absent from the body is to be present with the Lord.[9] Today Aljeana is alive in heaven, and her light is shining brighter than ever.

A Christian's death is a time of sorrow for loved ones because of the temporary separation. But it is also a time of joy and celebration as we rejoice with the believer in his new life and home in heaven. Because of this, my family and I planned a very special service of thanksgiving and praise for Aljeana's life here and her new life in heaven.

Aljeana and I had agreed that we did not want the slow, depressing organ music usually associated with a funeral. This was her heavenly coronation, and we thought the music should be in keeping with the celebration. By waiting a week, we had time to arrange an unusual service, which included a singing group and orchestra.

The memorial service was important, but even more important to me was the time I took to be alone with my thoughts and memories. I prayed alone, wept alone, and allowed God to minister to me alone in my grief. This was the greatest and most precious religious experience of my life.

Some people wanted to do me a favor by not giving me time to think, but that would have cheated me out of an important experience. I was very jealous of this time and guarded it carefully. Probably at very few times in my life will God's Word and presence mean as much to me. I soaked up His presence, allowing Him to love and comfort me.

Another source of blessing was the cards and letters

that so many people sent. I took the time to read and meditate on each one. One of the most comforting and meaningful thoughts I received was: "If Aljeana is with Jesus, and Jesus is with me, then Aljeana cannot be far away."

During my three intensive days alone with God, I confronted and dealt with the sorrow of losing my wife. Then I realized that life had to go on. I would face times of sadness from our separation. Various memories would remind me of my loneliness. Yet I did not want to dwell in the past. I had work to do. I had new dreams for a major stage show that would recreate some of the miracles of the Bible. I wanted to dramatize the story of Shadrach, Meshach, and Abednego in the fiery furnace, Moses leading the Israelites through the Red Sea, Ezekiel's dream in which the valley of dry bones becomes a nation, Jesus walking on the water, and the resurrection of Christ. I wanted people to experience in a small way the greatness of my God.

Early in 1977 God brought Kathy into my life. Some mutual friends arranged our meeting at the Tucson airport on my way home from Los Angeles. It was hard to imagine that I could fall in love again, yet that night I almost missed my flight to Phoenix, and driving home I got lost twice in an area where I had lived for years.

Until I met Kathy, I had given little thought to the possibility of remarriage. For one thing, I figured it would be almost impossible to find someone who would fit into my unusual lifestyle. I had at least seven prerequisites: She would have to be a Christian. She would have to be interested in my work. She would have to endure my extensive traveling. Because of the pace of my life, she probably would have to be younger than I. She would have to love my two teenage children. She would have to be satisfied to not have any more children. Finally, I did not want her to fall in love with Andre Kole, the showman, but with the real me. The chances of one woman meeting all seven requirements seemed remote.

It was not my normal character to move quickly into a romantic relationship. In fact, I had avoided every situation where someone had tried to match me with a girl. Yet soon after we met, Kathy and I felt God's leading so strongly that we didn't want to waste any time. I have often told her that if I did not believe in God for any other reason, I would have to believe in Him because of her.

We were married on August 10, 1977, and God has continued His perfect plan for our lives. Without her, I am convinced that I would have had to greatly reduce my workload for the sake of my children. Instead, the ministry has flourished. Together, we look forward to many years of service to God.

13
God's Healing Business

The service was under way as I slipped into the back of the packed auditorium and glanced around, looking for a seat. Finding none, I moved toward a group of people in wheelchairs and stood among them to observe.

The audience eagerly listened to the 200-voice choir which was accompanied by a five-piece band. Some patients tried to keep time with their feet or hands. One child was attached to an intravenous tube that hung from a pole on his chair. A quadriplegic had a motor-driven chair he controlled with a lever in the palm of his right hand. Another patient, in the advanced stages of multiple sclerosis, leaned over far to one side. All of them had a look of expectation that this night would mark their return to health.

After enthusiastic singing by the congregation, an offertory, and a rousing solo by a young gospel singer, the evangelist/faith healer came on stage. "God wants to do a miracle in *your* life tonight," he said. The more than 3000 people present applauded. "God is in the miracle-working business. If you're here tonight and you have problems with your finances, God wants to heal your finances. If you're here because of problems in your marriage, God wants to heal your marriage. And if you're here tonight because you are sick physically, I am here to tell you that *God wants to heal you.*"

The crowd was ecstatic with those words. Some raised their hands and shouted "Praise God!" and "Hallelujah!" Others leaned forward in their seats to catch every word. The evangelist held a well-worn Bible in his hands and spoke confidently about miracles that it recorded. He said that across the country today, whenever he spoke, he saw God perform miracles just as He had in the time of Christ. And tonight some people with cancer were going to be healed. Others who suffered chronic back pain were going to be cured. "I do not heal anyone," he emphasized. "It is the Holy Spirit who heals."

When he finished preaching, the evangelist invited all who desired healing to go into the aisles that surrounded the auditorium. Workers would pray for them there and anoint them with oil. For nearly an hour the auditorium hummed with prayer and counseling.

Finally the crowd began to thin. Many left rejoicing in the great work that God had done in their lives. Others left with tears in their eyes as they pushed away their crippled children. The faces that only an hour ago had shone with anticipation now betrayed a deep and bitter dejection. They had come hoping for a miracle, but God had let them down.

Why can some people give dramatic testimonies about God's healing, while others are left wondering if God even heard their prayers? Many friends fervently prayed that my first wife would be healed, yet despite our faith, she died. Is God playing a lottery game in which only those with the lucky combinations win?

I have purposely saved this subject for now because I wanted us to first examine the supernatural work of God as displayed in Scripture and demonstrated in the lives of believers who are filled with the Holy Spirit. The service I just described illustrates the conflict which many Christians feel concerning the subject of healing. We hear much about the exciting testimonies of God's healing, but there are also many silent tragedies—people who are hurting because for some reason God didn't choose to heal them physically. Many suffer deep guilt because they believe that if only they had enough faith, they would be healed.

I believe that the preacher in the service I described was probably sincere. He didn't intend for any in attendance to leave depressed and disheartened. But that isn't true of all preachers. Today there are a number of popular television evangelist/faith healers who prey on the hopes of people who are suffering. They have developed theatrical shows complete with detailed "revelations from God" about individuals in the audience and "miraculous cures" on stage for a wide variety of ailments. How do we deal with these difficult questions?

I can't begin in this space to deal with all of the theological questions involved in this issue. There are many books devoted to what the Bible has to say about the gifts of the Spirit and about healing. I do believe in God's healing power and that He provides various spiritual gifts to individuals in the church. However, I am deeply concerned about the overwhelming evidence that some of these television evangelists are not demonstrating God's power. Rather, they have used trickery and deception to produce cheap imitations of the supernatural. As a result they have attracted thousands of followers and millions of dollars. They have also left many people confused about how God works.

It is likely that many of the followers of these evangelists have benefited from their ministry despite the deception. Unfortunately, there are many more who have been hurt and disillusioned because God didn't operate in the way the preacher promised He would. Still others have a false impression of Christianity because of these few preachers, and they are hindered from seeing the truth. That's why I believe it is necessary to openly examine the claims and actions of these men to see how they measure up to the standards of Scripture.

The man who has most thoroughly researched this area is a professional colleague, James Randi. Although Randi and I disagree about the Christian faith, his investigations confirmed some facts of which I was aware and revealed much more that I had suspected but hoped was not true.

Randi's investigation focused on three popular preachers—W.V. Grant, Peter Popoff, and David Paul. Each of them conducts rallies and healing services around the United States, and each tapes his services for viewing on television stations across the country. (Grant alone appears on at least 93 stations.) The investigation centered on two areas: the practice of "calling out" members of the audience to demonstrate the preacher's gift of knowledge, and the methods and results of healing.

First, let's briefly examine the gift of knowledge as practiced by these three men. Each of these preachers either wanders through the audience and talks to individuals or calls people to the stage—supposedly as he is led by the Spirit. The evangelist usually identifies the person by name and then proceeds to identify that person's street address and other information, such as an account of that person's affliction and the doctor who is treating it. Usually the evangelist makes it a point to in some way assure his audience that he has never spoken to or questioned this person before. Of course people find this amazing, and it gives credibility to subsequent pronouncements that God wants to heal that person.

Has the Holy Spirit actually supernaturally given these preachers inside information about certain people in the audience? If He has, it's purely through natural means, for the three television preachers that Randi investigated all gained their information by thorough research. Randi and his team of observers always arrived for the services at least two hours early, the moment the doors of the auditorium opened. They found that all three of the evangelists have their wives or other "front men" walk through the auditorium and strike up casual conversations during which they gather names, addresses, and other information, including a brief description of the person interviewed and the location of his seat. In addition, cards were often passed out so individuals could write out prayer requests, along with their names and addresses. This was another rich source of information.

Each of the evangelists used a different method for recalling that information. For a long time David Paul had his information on small slips of paper inserted into his Bible (apparently as bookmarks to mark passages he would refer to during the service). On the slips were first and last name, a disease, a doctor's name, and sometimes an address. Former employees of Paul said that he would burn those slips following each service.

Randi showed how such information can be used by the preacher:

> Suppose you have on the slip "William Parsons," "Dr. Brown" and "heart attack." Those six words can be expanded into a minor melodrama. To wit (the following is taken from an actual recording of David Paul in action): "I have an impression of you clutching at your chest. The pain is more than you can bear. It's enough to make you cry out in agony. You fall to your knees. 'Dear God!' you are saying, 'Take this burden from me! Let this travail pass!' The doctors are working over you, doing what they can for you. But they can't do anything except get you to bed, and Dr. Brown tells you, 'Take it easy, Bill. You're a sick man. But doctors are only human. Only *Dr. Jesus* can do what you need, Bill. I want you to go home— because I see an angel of the Lord standing at your front gate right now, Bill—and tell all the folks there that Dr. Jesus has put a whole new heart into your body! It's done! Hallelujah!'"[1]

Peter Popoff has made use of modern technology to gain his information during a service. One of Randi's associates discovered a small radio receiver in his left ear. At a service in San Francisco, he arranged for an expert to set up a radio scanner to intercept the transmissions. They discovered that Popoff's wife was feeding information about individuals in the audience. A recording of the service plus the transmissions revealed that every single one of Popoff's miraculous revelations was fed to him by his wife from a sealed-off section of their mobile television studio trailer. She and an assistant had gathered that information before the service and also gleaned information from some of the more spectacular prayer cards.

Initially after Randi played an excerpt from the recordings on the "Tonight Show," representatives from Popoff's evangelistic organization denied the charge, claiming that the electronic receiver in Popoff's ear was used only to stay in touch with the television crew. Later, Popoff said his wife supplied him with about half of the names and said he intended to start putting a disclaimer at the beginning of his television shows. His "disclaimer" consisted of an attack against magicians who were a tool of Satan to try to destroy his ministry.

As far as the explanations by Popoff and his staff, Randi says, "In all the hours we have of Mrs. Popoff speaking to you, *not once* is the television operation referred to. As for the 'occasional' name given you . . . we found that *all* of the people you 'called out' were given to you by the secret transmitter, and that *no* names were given to you that you did *not* call out."[2] Incidently, after the revelations on the "Tonight Show" and a subsequent report on the television news program "West 57th Street," Randi received several threats on his life.

But what about the healing ministry of these men? Despite the obvious natural means being used to gain information from the audience, is God still working through them to miraculously heal people? I am not about to say that God can't or isn't working in spite of these men, but the evidence is overwhelming that much, if not all, of the "healing" isn't at all miraculous.

One of the most popular tools which all of these men

use is the rented wheelchair. People who are slightly unsteady in their walk as they enter the arena are invited by an usher to sit in a wheelchair and are pushed to the front of the auditorium. They are the ones usually invited to the stage, where they are dramatically ordered, in the name of Jesus, to stand up and walk. Sometimes the evangelist will dramatically declare, "You don't need that wheelchair anymore, do you?" Of course the person says no because he didn't need it in the first place. W.V. Grant occasionally made the display even more dramatic by having the former wheelchair victim push him across the stage or up the aisle. That always brought a rousing ovation from the crowd.

The tragedy of this scam is portrayed by Randi in this description of a revival meeting by W.V. Grant in St. Louis:

> Before we entered the auditorium...we encountered many invalids in wheelchairs. They included children in advanced stages of cerebral palsy. Two chair-bound children, suffering from conditions I would not presume to diagnose, were strapped into their chairs. They made loud noises from time to time and thrashed about uncontrollably while their parents attempted to quiet them.... It was a depressing sight and I wondered what Grant would do when confronted with these cases.
>
> ...People in wheelchairs lined the front and sides of the seating area. Several of these people were subsequently commanded by Grant to get up and walk. But not one of those I'd seen earlier was even approached for healing. They were all placed at the back of the auditorium, and when

one of the noisy chair-bound children approached the stage, Grant turned to an aide and told him, out of the range of the microphone, to "get him to the back." Later the child cried out from the side of the auditorium, where he'd again been placed by his parents. Grant, busy with a miracle on the other side, was forced to acknowledge the shriek and said, "I'm gonna git to that in just a minute." But he never did.[3]

In an earlier chapter, we talked about the difference between functional versus organic diseases. Functional illnesses often respond to suggestion, and in this area we would expect a faith healer to have success. It's in the area of *organic* diseases that we have problems. If these men are truly God's representatives in His healing business, it's reasonable to expect that we would see some successful healing in the organic as well as the functional diseases.

Unfortunately, it's hard to verify the results that these men claim. Randi decided to follow up on several of the people supposedly healed at some of Grant's services. From a tape of a service in Atlanta, Randi gained the name of a patient who was planning to have a coronary operation on a certain date, in a specific hospital, and even heard Grant give the names of the patient's six doctors. Grant had proclaimed that "Dr. Jesus" had put a new heart in the man's body and that he therefore didn't need the operation. Because of the number of specific facts, this seemed like an ideal case to check out.

Four weeks after that service, Randi visited Atlanta and discovered that not one of the six doctors was listed under the Medical Association of Georgia, which keeps a directory of all of the state's more than 8000 physicians, whether members of the association or not. Neither were the doctors listed as chiropractors. The hospital mentioned had no record of the patient and no such operation planned for the date given. In fact, cardiac surgery had never been performed at this particular hospital. "We had apparently discovered an absolute 'ringer,' " Randi concluded. "The man, for one reason or another, had fabricated the whole story. And he made W.V. Grant and Dr. Jesus look pretty good in that videotape."[4]

From the St. Louis revival, Randi was able to follow up several participants. One was a Mr. Clark who was blind in one eye. Grant had led the audience to believe that Clark's vision was restored. But Clark was still blind in one eye, and very angry.

Randi also followed up some of the testimonies of healing written up in Grant's publication *New Day*. One man from Erie, Pennsylvania, claimed he was healed of sugar diabetes. A phone conversation with the man revealed that, although his doctor still said he had the disease, he believed he was healed because he was taking smaller doses of insulin.

Following Randi's public accusations, Peter Popoff broadcast an appeal to television viewers to send him healing testimonials. He claims he received 200,000 replies. Randi immediately wrote to Popoff and suggested that he choose any five of those testimonials and submit them to an independent, neutral board for evaluation. Popoff ignored the invitation.

All of this is just the tip of the incredible findings of this investigation. Even when I first learned of the results, I wanted to continue to believe what I've thought for years—that these faith healers were sincere but simply naive and misguided. I can no longer think that. An example will illustrate what I mean.

W. V. Grant had encouraged people to write letters expressing their prayer needs. "I will take each letter and anoint it with this holy oil from Israel, and I will pray over your letters back in my church in Dallas," he promised.

> But the most callous fact we uncovered was that some letters, some several pages long and filled with heart-rending pleas for the minister's prayers and intercession of God, had been torn up, crumbled, and tossed into the garbage. They never even reached Grant's hands. Only by piecing together the scraps of the congregation's hopes, bit by bit, were we able to finally see the true attitude of this pastor toward his flock.
>
> Grant says in no uncertain terms that it is as a result of his anointed status that he possesses the Gifts of the Spirit and that he is thus able to call out members of his audience.... Grant even has the gall to tell them—in several different ways—that he is not doing an "ESP act" or a "magic show." He attributes it all to divine gifts.[5]

What are we to make of this information? How do we evaluate what is of God and what is of man? I'm convinced that much of the confusion in this realm of healing stems from a misunderstanding of faith healing as opposed to divine healing. Let me define the two as I understand them.

Faith healing means that a person is relieved of symptoms or healed because of his faith. The object of a person's faith may be God, a doctor, a faith healer, a psychic surgeon, or even a witch doctor. Miraculous faith cures certainly are not confined to Christianity; they occur in various cultural and religious settings throughout the world. Putting faith in someone—no matter who—can have positive effects on certain diseases, because that is how God has created us. But even the most charismatic healers can never cure some injuries and diseases. Dr. William Nolen explains:

> Patients that go to a . . . service, paralyzed from the waist down as the result of injury to the spinal cord, never have been and never will be cured through the ministrations of [the faith-healer/evangelist]. . . . The patient who suddenly discovers . . . that he can now move an arm or a leg that was previously paralyzed had that paralysis as a result of an emotional, not a physical disturbance. Neurotics and hysterics will frequently be relieved of their symptoms by the suggestions and ministrations of charismatic healers. It is in treating patients of this sort that healers claim their most dramatic triumphs.
>
> There is nothing miraculous about these cures. Psychiatrists, internists, G.P.'s, any M.D. who does psychiatric therapy, relieve thousands of such patients of their symptoms every year. Psychotherapy, in which suggestion plays a significant role, is just one of the many tools with which physicians work.[6]

A doctor sometimes uses the principles of faith (sometimes called the placebo effect) to his advantage. He may prescribe sugar pills to help a patient believe he is getting helpful medicine. He may use suggestions like "You should start feeling better in two days." Sometimes this really helps a person recover.

Nolen states that half of the patients who go to a general practitioner will improve even if they do nothing. Another 20 percent can often be helped through suggestion. This means a cure rate of 70 percent, which helps explain the successes of faith healing. After his investigation of faith healing, Nolen also arrived at an explanation for its popularity:

> I've gotten a better understanding of why intelligent, rational people go to healers. They go to healers because, for one reason or another, the medical profession has let them down.
>
> Sometimes we doctors let our patients down because, quite simply, we have nothing curative to offer. For example, we don't as yet know how to cure multiple sclerosis, widespread cancer or congenital brain disorders. We explain to patients with these diseases that we are truly sorry but we can't help them. No matter how nicely we do this, no matter how logically we explain that no one else, to our knowledge, can help them either, patients sometimes refuse to accept this bad news.
>
> A second reason people go to healers . . . is that some healers offer patients more warmth and compassion than physicians do. Sure, we pass our pills and perform operations, but do we really care about the people we treat? . . .
>
> A third reason why patients go to healers is that healers do, in fact, help them. . . . We doctors have in the past made the mistake of "putting down" the healers as though they, and those who patronized them, were idiots beneath our contempt. This has been a serious error.[7]

The danger is that most faith healers don't know when to stop. They cannot recognize those disorders that have no psychosomatic cause and will not respond without proper medical attention. For these people a visit to a faith healer can be tragic.

How does divine healing differ from faith healing? *Divine healing is God supernaturally reaching down and miraculously healing a person.* His healing is timely and complete.

An example of divine healing comes from a Mid-western pastor who told me about how he was severely burned in an accident when he was a boy. As he was rushed to the hospital, his parents prayed for him. When nurses unwrapped him at the hospital, the burns were gone. As a result, he received Christ and later entered full-time ministry.

Many others have experienced divine healing, but as far as I can determine, this represents only about 5 percent of what people claim are miraculous healings.

How can we distinguish God's hand in healing? And why are some people healed while others, who are equally sincere in their belief, have their prayers for healing go unanswered? Confusion in this area causes many people to doubt the reality of God, so it is important to understand a few principles.

First, *God is not required to perform in a theatrical setting.* He will work in His own manner, for His own purposes, free from anyone's manipulations.

One respected leader of a charismatic denomination told me that the greatest problem in his churches is "the temptations of pastors to manipulate the emotions of the crowd. People want to see sensational things, so pastors feel they have to cause sensational things to happen in each service."

Often faith or positive thinking may relieve some

symptoms for a few days, but frequently the problems recur. God's healing, however, is total and complete, and He can touch a person anytime—He doesn't require the crowd psychology of a healing service to do his work.

Faith healers like to use the excuse "You lack faith" when a person is not healed. That takes the healer off the hook. But God doesn't need excuses. Our lack of faith never negates His power. He can heal us even if we do not believe. Does that mean we don't need faith? No, the Bible clearly teaches that we need to exercise faith. But our faith or lack of it doesn't change God's power.

We also need to realize that God rarely supersedes His laws of nature. Many people get sick because they ignore God's laws of good health, then run to Him for healing. If two people, one a Christian and the other not, jump off a 30-story building, no matter how much the Christian prays on the way down, both will be devastated when they hit the ground. Likewise, we cannot violate God's laws of good health and expect God to keep healing us.

Second, *we need to be cautious of dramatic testimonies.* People are often eager to share about healings, but their experiences do not necessarily prove that God was at work. Often the problem is selection of facts. This is especially true when hearing about a healing through a letter or a secondhand source. The teller often exaggerates his story or leaves out essential information.

When people share dramatic testimonies, they often imply that they were healed because they had exceptional faith. This can cause those who aren't healed to doubt God.

Joni Eareckson Tada graphically illustrates this

struggle. She worked up her faith to believe God would allow her to walk again. At a special prayer meeting, church elders, pastors, and family laid hands on her, anointed her with oil, and prayed for her. She described what happened in the following days:

> A week went by . . . then another . . . then another. My body still hadn't gotten the message that I was healed. Fingers and toes still didn't respond to the mental command, "Move!" *Perhaps it's going to be a gradual thing*, I reasoned, *a slow process of steady recovery*. I continued to wait. But three weeks became a month, and one month became two. . . .
>
> Then came to my mind the ten-thousand-dollar question, the question that is in the mind of so many I've met over the years who have not been healed in response to their prayers—*Did I have enough faith?*
>
> What a flood of guilt that question brings. It constantly leaves the door open for the despairing thought: *God didn't heal me because there is something wrong with me. I must not have believed hard enough.*[8]

After reviewing her doubts, Joni concluded that her problem was not a lack of faith. She realized that God sometimes does heal people in miraculous ways, but it was His decision—His sovereign choice.

This leads to my final principle. *We need to understand that God sometimes chooses not to heal.* When my wife Aljeana was sick, I wanted to see her healed. My friends prayed for that healing with us. As we waited, I began to understand why people look to unusual techniques outside the medical profession in hope of finding relief.

Looking back, I now believe that divine healing would not have been nearly as great a demonstration of God's power. He used Aljeana's victory over pain, suffering, and eventually death as a testimony to thousands of people.

Certainly God can and does heal today, but He does not heal everyone who comes to Him, even when they come in faith. Jesus Christ, when He lived on this earth, healed many people, but He did not heal all. Many wanted to be healed but never had the chance. God still loved them, and He loves us too. We may never understand His workings, but we can rest assured that His individual plan for each one of us is best. Joni explains it well:

> I sometimes shudder to think where I would be today if I had not broken my neck. I couldn't see at first why God would possibly allow it, but I sure do now. He has gotten so much more glory through my paralysis than through my health! And believe me, you'll never know how rich that makes me feel. If God chooses to heal you in answer to your prayers, that's great. Thank Him for it. But if He chooses not to, thank Him anyway. You can be sure He has His reasons.[9]

Charles Swindoll states that God follows a consistent pattern when He chooses to perform a miracle. First, God alone is glorified. Second, there is no showmanship. Third, the unsaved are impressed and brought to the Lord. And fourth, biblical principles and statements are upheld, *not* contradicted.

In summary, I again will say that God does heal today. If He has healed you, rejoice and thank Him. But many people are being misled by dynamic personalities who claim to have a gift from God. They may have a gift, but it definitely is not healing. They simply have learned, accidentally or intentionally, some good psychological principles and some theatrics. People need to understand that fact when they go to healing services.

Ultimately, we must realize that God does not serve at our bidding. We see that in the book of Job. After Job lost everything and endured his friends' rebukes, God answered Job, not by explaining His actions, but by giving him a glimpse of Himself. God asked Job question after question: "Have you ever caused the sun to rise in the morning?... Can you lift up your voice and command the clouds to release their rain?... Can you satisfy the appetite of a lion and the raven?" On and on He went, graphically showing Job that God is God.[10]

That is what we need—a glimpse of God. When we see Him, the proper perspective on healing will follow naturally.

Ultimate Reality

In Latin America, peasants walk for miles on their knees to prove their repentance. South Sea Island natives stick hundreds of needles into their bodies. In the Philippines, people have their backs beaten raw and sometimes even crucify themselves. African witch doctors drive "magic" pegs into the ground at each corner of a village or hut.

These are just some of the religious rituals that I've observed over the years. Each is designed to help people find inner peace with themselves and God. There are 11 major religions in the world today, but almost every week someone invents a new religion or cult. Among the thousands of options, how does anyone know which one is right? And how does Christianity differ from all the other religions?

It is interesting to hear what some of the world's most prominent religious leaders have said. Buddha made this statement to his closest followers shortly before he died: "I have given you all the truth I have known. I have shared with you all the life that I have been given. But there cometh one after me who is a fulfillment of all truth and who is the light of the world.''[1] Five hundred years later Jesus Christ said, "I am the light of the world.''[2] No other person in history has made such a fantastic claim, and backed it up with his life.

Shortly before Mahatma Gandhi's death, the great Indian guru reportedly said, "It is a constant torture to me that I am still so far from the one whom I know to be my very life and being. I know it is my own wretchedness and wickedness that keeps me from Him.''[3] Jesus said, "I am the way and the truth and the life; no one comes to the Father but through Me.''[4]

Of course, not everyone follows the great religions and religious leaders of the world. Some people are atheists. Many have dedicated their lives to political causes, particularly Communism. In Latin America the audiences for my university performances are frequently 50 to 80 percent Communists or Marxists. One former Communist professor said, "Students are Communists not because of conviction, but because of frustration."

I find that most people are frustrated by the emptiness in their lives. Some try to fill that void by pursuing material pleasure. Others seek political power. Some look for popular recognition. Still others pursue sensual pleasures. People then look to religion as an answer to the emptiness they find in such pursuits.

To some people Christianity appears to be little different from other religions. They may view it as a sober lifestyle that takes all the fun out of life. Or they may see it as a long list of rules and regulations. Some see it as a series of steps to heaven, or classes in which the believer hopes to make a passing grade before he dies. Still others see it as a ritual of prayers and ceremonies.

But none of these things is Christianity. Genuine Christianity centers around the gospel, which means "good news." In fact, Christianity is the greatest news ever announced. There are thousands of religions, denominations, and philosophies, but only one gospel.

Religion is a process of reasoning by the human mind. The gospel is revelation of the divine mind.

Religion originates on earth. The gospel originated in heaven.

Religion is the story of what sinful man tries to do for a holy God. The gospel is a wonderful story of what a holy God has done for sinful man.

Religion is good views, the opinions of mere men. The gospel is good news, the declaration of a righteous and loving God.

Religion commences by trying to create an outward reformation. The gospel begins by creating an inner reformation.

Religion is based on the teachings of man. The gospel is not based merely on the teachings of Jesus, but on His death, burial, and resurrection. Jesus did not come to earth merely to preach the gospel, but rather that there might be a gospel to be preached.

As we study the various religions and philosophies of the world, this is where we find the difference. Apart from the gospel, there is no provision for man's sin.

God originally created man to have fellowship with Him, so He gave man a body, soul, and spirit. But man chose to go his own independent way, and therefore fellowship with God was broken. This is what the Bible means by the word "sin." In essence, man said to God, "You go Your way, I'll go mine. I can run my own life."

The results of that decision were disastrous. God said that in the day man sinned, he would surely die. But man did not die physically—he died spiritually. I demonstrate this in my shows with a lamp in which the light represents a person's spirit. As a result of man's sin, he is born physically alive but spiritually dead. He has no light in his life—just a great void or emptiness.

Everywhere I go in the world, people tell me that this describes their lives. They feel the emptiness, but most people try to cover it up. As a result they are laughing on the outside but crying on the inside. They try to fill the vacuum with things like sex, drugs, alcohol, education, materialism, and religion, but none of these things can fill it. We can take an empty bottle, put a label on it, and say it contains anything we want it to, but until something is put into it, the bottle is still empty. Our label may say Protestant, Catholic, Muslim, Hindu, or Jew, but that does not change the emptiness inside. Without God, man is incomplete.

Everyone shares this common problem, but there is a solution. In John 3 we read about a great religious leader, Nicodemus, who came to Jesus one night. This man was extremely religious. He probably knew the entire Old Testament by heart and prayed seven times each day. He worshiped God in the temple three times daily. Yet despite his devotion to religion, he knew that something was missing in his life.

Nicodemus acknowledged that Jesus had come from God. Jesus answered him, "Unless one is born again, he cannot see the kingdom of God."[5] Those words baffled Nicodemus. Then Jesus explained that to experience physical life, you must be born physically. Likewise, to have spiritual life, you must be born spiritually. That turns on the spiritual light in your life.

Those who are "born again" become members of the family of God.

John Wesley was once asked, "Why do you spend so much time speaking on the subject 'You must be born again'?" He answered, "Because you must be born again." If we miss this point, we miss the most important point of the entire Bible. Being born again is the difference between Christianity and religion.

The following illustration helped me understand what it means to be born again and to have a relationship with God through His Son Jesus Christ. It's about a man who many years ago was discovered pacing back and forth in front of the gate to the White House. Occasionally he'd stop and ask the guard if there was any way he could see the President to give him a most urgent message. But the guard just shook his head and turned away.

A little boy was sitting on a bench by the gate, watching this take place. As the man continued to pace, the boy finally walked up to him and asked, "Mister, are you worried about something? Are you in trouble?" The man stopped in surprise, then put his hand on the child's head and said, "Yes, Sonny, I am. I must see the President, but there is no way that I can get to him."

The boy said to the man, "Take my hand." While he was tempted to ignore the boy, he decided to humor him by following his suggestion. With the boy's hand in that of the man, the guard bowed and the great gate swung open. The young boy led the amazed man into the inner sanctum of the President's study. Through that boy—the President's son—the man gained access to the President.

I learned that this is exactly how we gain access to God—through His Son. When we establish a personal relationship with Jesus Christ, He takes each of us by the hand and personally leads us into the presence of His Father.

Becoming a Christian is not a process but an event. A story of two law students helps to illustrate this point. These students were best of friends in law school. After they graduated, one went on to become a prominent attorney and later a judge. The other took to a life of drinking and gambling, and got into trouble with the law.

One day the second man was arrested and brought before his onetime friend. Naturally everyone wondered what the judge would do. They were all surprised when he levied the stiffest fine the law would allow. If the man didn't pay it, he would be forced to go to jail. Then the judge surprised the people even more. He stepped down from the bench, took out his own checkbook, paid the fine, and allowed his friend to go free.

That is what God has done for each one of us. Everyone on earth is born spiritually dead. By nature we are sinners, which means that we live our lives independent of God. The only way the light of our spirit can be illuminated is by being born again. And that is possible only because God, in His love, stepped out of eternity into time and visited earth. For 33 years He walked this planet, and at the end of that time He allowed the people He created to spit upon Him, beat Him, and nail Him to a cross. He came to die on a cross of wood, yet He made the hill on which it stood.

But it didn't end there. Three days later Jesus was raised from the dead, so that we who were dead in sin could be raised to new life in Him.[6]

The Bible says, "He who has the Son has life; he who does not have the Son of God does not have life."[7] A

Christian is a person in whom Christ dwells, through the Holy Spirit. People without Christ may be very religious, but they are not Christians.

Perhaps for the first time you understand that Christianity is not a long list of do's and don'ts, but rather a spiritual relationship with the Son of God. You know that if you died tonight, you would not enter the kingdom of God because you never have been born again. The solution is to invite Jesus Christ to come into your life.

Jesus is a gentleman. He will not force His way into your life; He enters only by invitation. If you are ready to receive Him, I invite you to pray a prayer similar to the one I prayed many years ago. God is not so concerned about your words, but about the attitude of your heart. He knows if you are sincere in wanting to turn from your sin and to accept the payment He made for you. Here is a suggested prayer:

> Lord Jesus, thank You for dying for my sins. Right now, I invite You to come into my life. Forgive my sins and make my life what You want it to be. Thank You, Lord Jesus, for coming into my life because I asked You to and because You promised that You would. Amen.

If you prayed that prayer, I encourage you to begin reading the Gospel of John, the fourth book of the New Testament. As you read, ask God to make Himself real to you. You will find, as I have, that ultimate reality is found in the Person of Jesus Christ.

NOTES

Chapter 1

1. Psalm 23:4 KJV.
2. Matthew 24:4b, 5, 23, 24.
3. Kendrick Frazier, "Articles on the Paranormal: Where Are the Editors?" in *The Skeptical Inquirer*, Winter 1980-81, p. 2.
4. Ibid., p. 4.
5. "Amityville Hokum: The Hoax and the Hype," in *The Skeptical Inquirer*, Winter 1979-80, p. 3.
6. Carl Sagan, "Night Walkers and Mystery Mongers: Sense and Nonsense at the Edge of Science," in *The Skeptical Inquirer*, Spring 1986, pp. 223-24.
7. "Paranormal Powers Are So Much Hocus-Pocus," in *Science*, Jan. 25, 1980, p. 389.
8. Ephesians 1:19 NASB.

Chapter 2

1. Russell Targ and Harold Puthoff, "Information Transmission Under Conditions of Sensory Shielding," in *Nature*, vol. 251, Oct. 18, 1974, pp. 602-07.
2. Ibid.
3. Ibid.
4. "Investigating the Paranormal," in *Nature*, vol. 251, Oct. 18, 1974, p. 559.
5. Martin Gardner, "How Not to Test a Psychic: The Great SRI Die Mystery," in *The Skeptical Inquirer*, Winter 1982-83, p. 34.
6. Ibid., pp. 38-39.
7. James Randi, "The Project Alpha Experiment: Part 1. The First Two Years," in *The Skeptical Inquirer*, Summer 1983, p. 31.
8. Persi Diaconis, "Statistical Problems in ESP Research," in *Science*, vol. 201, July 14, 1978, pp. 131-36.
9. Ibid.
10. "Interview with Dave Hunt," in *SCP Journal*, vol. 4/2, Winter 1980-81, p. 4.
11. Jim Parker, "Firewalking," in *Arizona*, July 8, 1984, p. 7.
12. Peter Garrison, "Kindling Courage," in *OMNI*, 1985, pp. 84-85.
13. Ibid., p. 84.
14. Luis W. Alvarez, "A Pseudo Experience in Parapsychology," in *The Skeptical Inquirer*, Summer 1982, pp. 72-73.

Chapter 3

1. William A. Nolen, M.D., *Healing: A Doctor in Search of a Miracle* (New York: Random House, Inc., 1974), p. 265.
2. Ibid., p. 272.
3. Ibid., p. 274.
4. Ibid., pp. 292-93.
5. Matthew 7:21-23 TLB.

Chapter 4

1. Harry Houdini, *A Magician Among the Spirits* (New York: Harper and Brothers, 1927), pp. 266, 270.
2. Raymond Fitzsimons, "Death and the Magician: The Mystery of Houdini," in *Reader's Digest*, July 1981, p. 205.
3. Allen Spraggett and William V. Rauscher, *Arthur Ford: The Man Who Talked with the Dead* (New York: New American Library, 1973), pp. 245-46.
4. James Randi, *Flim-Flam!* (Buffalo, New York: Prometheus Books, 1982), p. 246.
5. Deuteronomy 18:9-12 TLB.
6. M. Lamar Keene, *The Psychic Mafia* (New York: St. Martin's Press, 1976), pp. 147-48.
7. Isaiah 8:19 TLB.
8. See 2 Corinthians 5:8.

Chapter 5

1. *Doctrine & Covenants* (Salt Lake City: Church of Jesus Christ of the Latter Day Saints, 1949), section 84:114, Sept. 22 and 23, 1832.
2. *Doctrine & Covenants*, Dec. 25, 1832, section 87:1-8.
3. Oliver H. Huntington Journal, Book 14, 1837 (original in Huntington Library, San Marino, California).
4. Joseph Smith, *History of the Church*, Jan. 4, 1833, vol. 1, pp. 315-16.
5. A. Voldben, *After Nostradamus* (Secaucus, NJ: Citadel Press, 1974), p. 54.
6. F.K. Donnelly, "People's Almanac Predictions: Retrospective Check of Accuracy," in *The Skeptical Inquirer*, Spring 1983, p. 49.
7. Ibid., p. 50.
8. Josh McDowell and Don Stewart, *Understanding the Occult* (San Bernardino, CA: Here's Life Publishers, 1982), pp. 58-59.
9. *Doctrine & Covenants* (Salt Lake City: Church of Jesus Christ of the Latter Day Saints, 1949), section 62:1, 6, 7.

10. Ibid., section 84:4.
11. Daniel St. Albin Greene, "The Real Story of Jeane Dixon," in *The Christian Reader*, April-May 1974, p. 70.
12. Ibid., p. 71.
13. Ibid., p. 74.
14. Fawn M. Brodie, *No Man Knows My History: The Life of Joseph Smith the Mormon Prophet* (New York: Alfred A. Knopf, 1975), p. 405.
15. Ibid., pp. 457-88.
16. Joseph Smith, *History of the Church* (Salt Lake City: Deseret Book Company, 1957), vol. 4, p. 461.
17. Josh McDowell and Don Stewart, *Understanding the Cults* (San Bernardino, CA: Here's Life Publishers, 1982), p. 96.
18. J. Edward Decker, *To Moroni with Love* (Seattle: Life Messengers), p. 43.
19. "A Psychic Watergate," in *Discover*, June 1981, p. 8.
20. Deuteronomy 18:21, 22.
21. Ray Hyman, "Cold Reading: How to Convince Strangers that You Know All About Them," in *The Zetetic*, Spring/Summer 1977, p. 21.
22. H. J. Eysenck and D.K.B. Nias, *Astrology: Science or Superstition?* (New York: St. Martins, 1982), pp. 12-13.
23. Ibid., p. 214.
24. Ibid., pp. 215-16.
25. "A Controlled Test of Perceived Horoscope Accuracy," in *The Skeptical Inquirer*, Fall 1981, pp. 29-31.
26. Isaiah 47:13, 14.
27. Jeremiah 10:2, 3.
28. See Marvin W. Cowan, *Mormon Claims Answered* (Salt Lake City: Marvin Cowan, 1975), pp. 19-20.
29. See Matthew 24:42-44; 1 Thessalonians 4:13-18.

Chapter 6
1. Charles Berlitz, *The Bermuda Triangle* (New York: Doubleday, 1974), p. 11.
2. Ibid., p. 12.
3. Michael R. Dennett, "Bermuda Triangle, 1981 Model," in *The Skeptical Inquirer*, Fall 1981, p. 48.
4. Lawrence David Kusche, *The Bermuda Triangle Mystery —Solved* (New York: Harper and Row, 1975), p. 275.
5. Larry Kusche, *The Disappearance of Flight 19* (New York: Harper and Row, 1980), pp. 175-76.

6. Gerald Jones, "UFOs," in *The Dial*, Oct. 1982, p. 10.
7. Jeff Wells, "Profitable Nightmare of a Very Unreal Kind," in *The Skeptical Inquirer*, Summer 1981, p. 51.
8. Ibid.
9. Philip J. Klass, *UFOs Explained*, New York: Random House, 1974, pp. 14, 22, 30, 89, 174, 233.
10. Robert Sheaffer, *The UFO Verdict: Examining the Evidence* (Buffalo, New York: Prometheus Books, 1981), pp. 212-13.
11. *The Disappearance of Flight 19*, p. 172.

Chapter 7
1. Peter Blythe, *Hypnotism: Its Power and Practice* (New York: Taplinger, 1971), pp. 6-7.
2. Ibid., p. 11.
3. Larry Bodine and Douglas Lavine, "Hypnosis in Courts: Still on Trial," in *American Way*, April 1981, p. 24.
4. Philip J. Klass, "Hypnosis and UFO Abductions," in *The Skeptical Inquirer*, Spring 1981, p. 21.
5. Ernest R. Hilgard, "Hypnosis Gives Rise to Fantasy and Is Not a Truth Serum," in *The Skeptical Inquirer*, Spring 1981, p. 25.

Chapter 8
1. See Josh McDowell, *Evidence That Demands a Verdict* (San Bernardino, CA: Here's Life Publishers, 1979), pp. 15-79.
2. John 2:1-11.
3. John 11:44.
4. Peter W. Stoner and Robert C. Newman, *Science Speaks* (Chicago: Moody Press, 1976), pp. 106-12.
5. Matthew 24:3.
6. Luke 21:24.
7. Frederic W. Farrar, *The Life of Christ* (Dutton, Dovar, Cassell and Co., 1897), p. 440.
8. Josh McDowell, *More Than a Carpenter* (Wheaton, IL: Tyndale, 1977), p. 89.
9. Ibid., p. 97.
10. John 3:2.
11. Frank Mead, ed., *The Encyclopedia of Religious Quotations* (Westwood, NJ: Fleming H. Revell, 1965), p. 56.
12. John 3:16
13. Jeremiah 29:13

Chapter 9
1. Matthew 28:18-20.

Chapter 10
1. Acts 18:9, 10.
2. John 16:7.
3. Ephesians 5:18; 1 John 5:14, 15.
4. 1 Corinthians 2:3, 4.

Chapter 11
1. Karen C. Hoyt, "Is Prayer Magic?" in *SCP Newsletter*, Jan.-Feb. 1984, p. 3.
2. 1 Thessalonians 5:17.

Chapter 12
1. Hebrews 9:27.
2. Colossians 3:2 TLB.
3. 2 Timothy 4:17.
4. Psalm 116:15 TLB.
5. Luke 16:22.
6. 2 Corinthians 5:1 TLB.
7. 2 Corinthians 5:6 TLB.
8. 2 Corinthians 4:7 TLB.
9. 2 Corinthians 5:8.

Chapter 13
1. Taken from as-yet-unpublished article by James Randi titled "In the Name of God! Be Healed. . ." Used by permission.
2. Ibid.
3. James Randi, "Be Healed in the Name of God!" in *Free Inquiry*, Spring 1986, pp. 12-13.
4. Ibid., p. 11.
5. *Free Inquiry*, p. 17.
6. William A. Nolen, M.D., *Healing: A Doctor in Search of a Miracle* (New York: Random House, 1974), pp. 286-87.
7. Ibid., pp. 305-06.
8. Joni Eareckson and Steve Estes, *A Step Further* (Grand Rapids: Zondervan, 1978), pp. 124-25.
9. Ibid., p. 155.
10. See Job 38.

Chapter 14
1. Source unobtainable.
2. John 8:12.

3. Source unobtainable.
4. John 14:6.
5. John 3:3.
6. See Ephesians 2:5, 6.
7. 1 John 5:12.

LOVE &
OTHER CRIMES

ALSO BY SARA PARETSKY

Dead Land

Shell Game

Fallout

Brush Back

Critical Mass

Breakdown

Body Work

Hardball

Bleeding Kansas

Fire Sale

Blacklist

Total Recall

Hard Time

Ghost Country

Windy City Blues

Tunnel Vision

Guardian Angel

Burn Marks

Blood Shot

Bitter Medicine

Killing Orders

Deadlock

Indemnity Only

LOVE & OTHER CRIMES

STORIES

SARA PARETSKY

wm

WILLIAM MORROW

An Imprint of HarperCollinsPublishers

This is a work of fiction. Names, characters, places, and incidents are products of the author's imagination or are used fictitiously and are not to be construed as real. Any resemblance to actual events, locales, organizations, or persons, living or dead, is entirely coincidental.

These stories first appeared in the following publications: "Miss Bianca," *Ice Cold: Tales of Intrigue from the Cold War,* eds. Jeffery Deaver and Raymond Benson (2014); "Is It Justice?" *Suspense Magazine* (2013); "Flash Point," first published as "A Family Affair" in *Fifty Shades of Grey Fedora,* ed. Bob Randisi (2015); "Acid Test," *Deadly Housewives,* ed. Christine Matthews (2006); "Safety First," *It Occurs to Me That I Am America,* ed. Jonathan Santlofer (2018); "Trial by Fire," *From Sea to Stormy Sea,* ed. Lawrence Block (2019); "Murder at the Century of Progress," *Mary Higgins Clark Mystery Magazine* (1999); "The Curious Affair of the Italian Art Dealer," *In the Company of Sherlock Holmes,* eds. Laurie R. King and Leslie S. Klinger (2014); "Wildcat," first published as "A Family Sunday in the Park," *Sisters on the Case,* ed. Sara Paretsky (2007); "Death on the Edge" was first published as an e-book original by William Morrow (2018); "Photo Finish," *Mary Higgins Clark Mystery Magazine* (2001); "Publicity Stunts," *Women on the Case,* ed. Sara Paretsky (1996); "Heartbreak House," *Murder for Love,* ed. Otto Penzler (1996); "Love & Other Crimes" is original to this collection.

HarperCollins books may be purchased for educational, business, or sales promotional use. For information, please email the Special Markets Department at SPsales@harpercollins.com.

FIRST EDITION

Designed by Diahann Sturge

Library of Congress Cataloging-in-Publication Data has been applied for.

ISBN 978-0-06-291554-2

20 21 22 23 24 LSC 10 9 8 7 6 5 4 3 2 1

For Margaret Kinsman

CONTENTS

LOVE &
OTHER CRIMES

INTRODUCTION

I grew up in a time and place and milieu where a lot was expected of women inside the home, but not much outside it. I was supposed to get married, raise a family, but work as a secretary until that happy day arrived. I finished university, but was not married nor on my way to that estate, and so I worked as a secretary. At the same time, I began a graduate degree in history, without much focus or direction.

The one thing I did with concentrated pleasure was read crime fiction. I went to the used bookstores in my neighborhood and picked up paperbacks for a dime—those were the days. I read the small collection in the University of Chicago library; they chiefly collected writers from the so-called English Golden Age: I read Christie, Sayers, Allingham, Marsh. In a break from Tudor Puritanism and Victorian science, I took an elective on popular fiction by one of the early giants in popular culture studies, John Cawelti. I read Carroll John Daly and Dashiell Hammett.

The Golden Age writers had a lot of love, conducted in elegant repartee, but not much sex; the American noir writers had a lot of sex but not much love. The love in the books came from the readers, namely the passion we brought to what we were reading.

At one point, the women in the small office where I worked simultaneously came under the spell of Lord Peter Wimsey. He was sensitive, elegant, witty, accomplished. He drove a cool car. We swooned as we compared notes during our coffee breaks. One day we agreed to ask the people we were dating why they didn't make love to us in the French language. I can't remember what anyone else reported, but when I put the question to Courtenay, whom I was dating (and some years later married), he gave me a Groucho leer and said, *"Voulez-vous fuckez?"* Definitely the American hard-boiled school.

In *Strong Poison,* Wimsey asks Miss Climpson, who runs an inquiry agency for him, why people kill each other.

"'There is—passion,' said Miss Climpson, with a slight hesitation at the word, 'for I should not like to call it *love,* when it is so unregulated.'"

We kill out of passion, we kill out of love—love of money, but also love of family, a desire to protect those for whom we feel responsible. We kill to protect our reputations, to protect property; we kill out of a narcissistic wound when we've been betrayed or abandoned. We kill for revenge.

I wrote the stories in this collection over a period of about twenty years. Some predate the Internet and smartphones, some are on the cusp of changes in the publishing industry, but almost all of them feature people who kill for love. Family love crops up over and over in this collection: in the title story, where the big kids protect the baby brother; in "Wildcat," where V.I. tries to protect her father; in "Is It Justice?" where another sister looks after another brother. In "Acid Test," a highly disciplined young engineer goes to bat to save the aging hippie mother she can't help loving. "Miss Bianca" features a ten-year-old girl who loves a laboratory mouse.

Two of the stories are my homage to my own first love, the

crime fiction of the late Victorian and early twentieth-century eras. "Murder at the Century of Progress" features the progenitor of noir detectives, Race Williams, side by side with the kind of elderly spinster beloved of Anna Katharine Green and Agatha Christie.

"The Curious Affair of the Italian Art Dealer" plays games with the master of all investigators, Sherlock Holmes. I tweak him a little: Anna Katharine Green's *Leavenworth Case* preceded *A Study in Scarlet* by a good ten years. Her sleuths, Ebenezer Gryce and Amelia Butterworth, practiced many of the deductive and observational arts that Holmes is known for. Her books topped bestseller lists in England and the States; Conan Doyle is known to have studied Green's marketing practices and even wrote to her, hoping for a personal meeting with her when he first came to America. (She lived in Buffalo, New York.) It's not known if the meeting ever took place, but I wanted to bring Green and her female sleuth back into people's minds, and this story was my chance to do so.

Another story in the collection that I loved writing is the final one, "Heartbreak House." I wrote it for the collection *Murder for Love*; we were supposed to write love stories, and so I created a romance writer and a cornucopia of love stories.

As for me, I love—not necessarily in this order—my husband, my dog, chocolate, my 1995 Jaguar convertible, my friends, the United States Constitution, early music, the Bill of Rights, peace, singing, cortados, justice, walking Chicago's lakefront, reading fiction, clean water. I might even kill to protect and defend them.

Sara Paretsky
Chicago, November 2019

LOVE & OTHER CRIMES

I

"They're trying to frame Gregory," she announced baldly.

"Who are 'they,' who is Gregory, and what are 'they' saying he did?" I asked.

"Fucking Warshawski snob," she said. "I might have known. Like your mother, too good to walk around the planet with the ordinary mortals."

"Anyone who compares me to my mother is paying me the highest possible compliment. But I still don't—oh, Gregory? Baby Gregory? Are you Sonia Litvak?" She'd given her name as Sonia Geary when she made the appointment.

"I got married. Did you think that was impossible?" she jeered.

She saw my inadvertent glance at her bare left hand. "It didn't last. Neither did yours, what I heard, but you had to keep your own name, didn't you? No one else could be as good as a Warshawski."

"Do you want to tell me who framed Gregory for what?" I asked. "Or just needle me about my family?"

"I want you to understand I don't need any Warshawski pity or handouts. I came here for help and I plan to pay your bill."

"That assumes I agree to help you," I snapped.

"But—you have to!" She was astonished. "You're from South Houston, same as me. And I need a private cop to go up against the city, although come to think of it, your father was a Chicago cop and—"

"If you insult my father on top of my mother, you'll have to leave."

"Oh, don't get your undies in a bundle," she grumbled. "I never went to finishing school."

It was as close as she would come to an apology. I turned away to type Gregory Litvak's name into a legal database, and he popped right up: charged with second-degree homicide along with criminal destruction of property. Ten days ago, someone—allegedly Gregory Litvak—had gone through the Roccamena warehouse and smashed about twenty-five million dollars' worth of wine and booze.

Sonia was reading over my shoulder. "See, I told you—they framed him for this."

"Sonia—this doesn't prove anything about anyone."

I scrolled down the screen. Roccamena had fired Gregory a week or so before the destruction. The state—and the liquor distributor—claimed he sought revenge by rampaging through the warehouse.

He might still have made bail, but the crime held a second, more serious offense: when the cleanup crew started hauling out the debris, they'd found the body of Eugene Horvath mixed in with the broken bottles in aisle ninety-seven. Horvath was Roccamena's accountant; the state's theory was that Gregory blamed him for losing his job.

"They fired Gregory for no reason," Sonia burst out. "And then, because they feel guilty, they have to frame him for destroying the warehouse and killing Horvath. The Roccamenas probably did it themselves to collect insurance."

"What made the police pick up Gregory?" I asked.

"His prints were on the forklift. Well, of course his prints were on the forklift. He drove it for them, loading and unloading crap for them all day. Eighteen years he worked there, and then, bingo, he's getting close to being a hundred percent vested, out the door with him. I need you to prove he didn't do it."

She glared fiercely. When she'd been young, carting baby Gregory around, her hair grew in lopsided clumps around her head, as though she got her brother Donny to cut it for her. Today the thick curls, dyed bright orange, were symmetrically shaped. Her face was covered with the armor of heavy makeup, but beneath that, she was still the ungainly, needy girl of fifteen.

Sonia didn't want Warshawski pity, and I didn't want to give her any, so it annoyed me to find myself stirred by it.

"He has a lawyer, right? Or is he in the system?"

"The public defender. We're trying to put the money together for a real lawyer, but we can't even make bail right now. They set it for two million. Who can come up with that kind of money? Reggie could help, but he won't. Taking his brats to Disney World instead of taking care of his own flesh and blood."

I didn't think suggesting that his children were also Reggie's flesh and blood would help. Instead, I laboriously pried details from her. Reggie had moved to Elgin, with his own little company. Sonia was vague about what they did, but it had something to do with computers. She seemed to think Reggie had become another Gates or Jobs, and that he wouldn't help Gregory out of spite.

Donny worked for Klondike insurance. This was an agency that had the inside track on a lot of city and county business, which somehow, inevitably, also seemed to mean some of their clients were Mob fronts. It sounded as though he was the agency's handyman, repairing broken machines, changing lightbulbs, ordering supplies. I could picture him siphoning off supplies and selling them on craigslist, but not engineering the big deals that make a successful mobster.

"So it's not like Donny's got a lot of money," Sonia was continuing to whine, "and then his ex is sucking the marrow out of his bones. He doesn't even get to see the kid except weekends and then the kid doesn't want to hang around Donny because Donny doesn't have a PlayStation or any of that crap."

"Stanley can't help?" I asked.

"He dropped all the way out." Sonia snorted. "First he was in business with Reggie, but he said late-stage capitalism was draining his lifeblood, whatever the fuck that means. He lives in a cabin in the hills somewhere in Arizona and thinks great thoughts. Or maybe it's no thoughts."

That left baby Gregory.

"Gregory is super smart," Sonia said. "Like, he had really high ACT scores, so Daddy wanted him to go to college. He even got a scholarship to go to the University of Illinois, but then he never went. So Daddy threw him out of the house, which was when I was married, and he lived with me, then Ken threw him out, which led to me beating Ken up and him getting an order of protection and then a divorce. Anyway, that's when Donny found Gregory a job at Roccamena's, and he's been there ever since. Until they fired him for no reason at all."

"They must have told him something."

She tossed her head, but the orange curls didn't move. She must have sprayed some kind of epoxy on them.

"Ask him yourself. Maybe you can turn on some Warshawski charm and he'll tell you stuff he won't talk to me about."

The chin beneath the thick makeup wobbled; she fished in her handbag and blew her nose, a good loud honk. "You going to help me or not?"

Not, I chanted silently. Not, not, not.

So why did I find myself printing out a copy of my standard contract for Sonia? I thought when she saw my fees and the nonrefundable deposit she'd walk out, but she signed it with every appearance of nonchalance, counted out five hundred dollars in twenties, and swept from the office. Sort of. She was wearing a sweatshirt that proclaimed her attachment to Liggett Bar and Grill's Slow Pitch team; the sleeve snagged on the lock tongue on her way out and she had to stop to pull it free.

2

Even the cockiest gang members look wilted after a week at County, and Gregory Litvak hadn't been cocky to begin with. Like all the Litvaks, he was short, with wide shoulders and a mass of wiry curls. Unlike his siblings, he sat hunched on his side of the table, looking at the floor.

I hadn't seen him since he was a baby, seemingly glued to his sister's hip, but when the guard brought him into the room for lawyers and clients, I recognized him at once.

"I used to live up the street from your family," I said, to break a growing silence. "I sold my house when my dad died. Are you still in South Chicago?"

"I, uh, moved," he mumbled, without looking up. "After Karen and Arthur died. Over to Fernwood. Sonia and Donny, they found me a place."

It took a minute for me to realize Karen and Arthur were his parents. "Did Sonia tell you she's hired me to find evidence to exonerate you?"

His thick neck bobbed fractionally. He'd been shifting boxes of liquor at the Roccamena warehouse for the best part of twenty years; his broad shoulders were also heavily muscled. I could see him easily bashing—but I was on his team. Put those thoughts firmly away. Anyway, he wasn't a fighter: the bruises all over his face and arms showed that he was easy prey in the halls and exercise yard.

"Sonia says you didn't do it."

"I didn't." His voice, even in protest, remained a monotone. "It sounds awful, what happened, but I didn't see it. I didn't do it."

"You didn't see it?" I was puzzled.

He looked up for a second. "They showed me pictures. But I didn't see it happen. I don't know who did it."

"Do you have an alibi for the night?"

"I live alone. I guess you could ask Gattara." He gave a bark of unhappy laughter. "That's my cat. It's the name of a wine we—they sell. It has a cat on the label."

"Donny says you do have an alibi."

"He told me," Gregory said, listless. "I don't know what he's talking about. I guess he thinks he can rescue me. Him and Sonia, like they've always done." His voice trailed away.

3

My dad used to say that Donny Litvak would end up in prison, but only after taking over the Chicago Mob. "Kid's constantly skating close to the edge, except on the wrong side," he grunted, "but he's got brains and the Outfit could use a few."

Gabriella would respond, "The one who should be in prison is the mother. She pays no attention to her children, so they run around like—like *teppisti*. The girl, she is even worse than the brothers. I thought maybe I could help, but—!"

There were five Litvak children—Sonia, who was a couple of years older than me, and four younger brothers. Donny was in my year, but I never saw him in school, only on the streets. He ran with the sports kids, so my cousin Boom-Boom was part of his life, but he also hung out with the guys who boosted booze from delivery trucks to help out the local bars. In exchange they got a few bucks and free cigarettes.

The cops picked Donny up a couple of times, until he got more skilled at avoiding capture. On at least one occasion, Sonia stomped to the station and stared down the desk sergeant.

"Donny was with me. Baby Gregory has croup, it takes two of us to look after him when he's feverish and coughing like that."

Except when Sonia was at school herself, baby Gregory was part of her wardrobe. When he grew too heavy for her to carry, he held on to the belt loops on her jeans. He was an unhappy baby who cried easily; the howls in the police station brought out the watch commander, who let Donny go, even though he knew as well as Sonia that her brother was guilty as charged.

Reggie and Stanley, identical twins two years younger than Donny, flew below the radar. Boom-Boom used to say they were running a gambling game that moved around in the dark, but no one ever proved anything. However, when they graduated from high school, they had saved enough pocket money to pay for college.

Mrs. Litvak was a massively fat woman who spent her days in front of the television with a cup that she refilled frequently from an unplugged coffeepot in the corner of the kitchen. It infuriated my mother that she never seemed to stir whenever any of the boys got into trouble.

Mr. Litvak was an engineer at the Ford Assembly Plant on 130th. He had a ferocious temper, and in a neighborhood of small houses divided by narrow passageways, we all knew all the fights.

Mr. Litvak claimed his wife slept around: *You're lucky I let those damned kids live in my house when not one of them is mine. That's why Donny keeps getting C's. Your children have the IQs of monkeys. No, wait, monkeys are smart. Your children have the IQs of hamsters.*

Mrs. Litvak wasn't intimidated, or at least she fought back: her husband was a mama's boy who couldn't wipe his own ass if his mother wasn't there to do it. And so on.

The children dressed in odd mismatched clothes. A rich aunt in New York sent Sonia her daughter's castoffs, but they were two or three sizes too small, and so the girl went to school in her mother's clothes, clumsily cut down to fit her. Once a year, for the Jewish New Year, Mr. Litvak marched the children to services, the older boys looking like clowns in their father's sports jackets, Sonia looking like a middle-aged woman in her mother's ill-fitting dress.

Kids like the Litvaks would normally be the butt of taunts and assaults, but Donny and Sonia seemed to have some kind of force field around them—it repelled attack, but it also repelled any overture of friendship. Sonia's basilisk stare dried up words in the biggest bully's mouth.

My mother either didn't sense the force field, or figured she could penetrate it. She knew what it was like to be an outsider and an outcast; she thought all Sonia needed was an adult to show her some kindness.

Each fall, when school started, Gabriella commissioned a new dress for me from Signora Rapellini, who made the few elegant outfits Gabriella herself owned. My mother had a good eye for color and fit; one September, she asked Signora Rapellini to make something for the Litvak girl at the same time.

When we picked up the clothes, I didn't want to go with Gabriella to the Litvak house. I had a nasty feeling in the pit of my stomach about what could go wrong. Sonia answered the door, Gregory on her hip. We could hear the TV in the background and Mrs. Litvak's hoarse demand to know who was at the door. The twins were fighting over something. All the noise drowned out Gabriella's little speech, offering Sonia something to bring luck in the new school year.

Sonia looked at Gabriella in astonishment, but when she saw the dress inside the parcel and fingered the fine material, her face softened and she muttered a startled thanks. However, while we were at dinner, Mr. Litvak barged into the house. He flung the dress—which he'd cut into strips—at my mother.

"How dare you come into my house and act as if I can't look after my own children? We don't need your pity, your charity, your saintly good deeds. Come near my family again and I'll have the law on you."

My father, the most peaceable man on earth, was on his feet, moving Litvak back to the door. "If you ever threaten my wife again, I will arrest you myself. You don't deserve a family. You're the only man in the neighborhood who isn't at your son's baseball games, isn't listening to your daughter's piano recitals. Not that she has any, because she's looking after your children and your home. Go away and don't come back until you've taken on adult responsibility for your family."

It was as if someone had stuck a pin into Mr. Litvak. All the air oozed out of him. He left without another word.

That was the last time I actually saw a member of the family up close: after that, Sonia and her brothers would cross the street when they saw me, making ostentatious retching noises. And then the day came when Sonia showed up in my office.

4

Before visiting Gregory at County, I had gone to see Sergeant Pizzello. She'd been transferred to the Eighth District, which included the section of south Pulaski where the Roccamena warehouse stood. She'd handled Gregory's interrogation when they picked him up.

"Was he on the run? How did you find him?"

"Solid police work, Warshawski. We knocked on the door of the crappy little hellhole he lives in. He was drinking bourbon and eating chicken wings. In his underwear. At five in the morning."

"I missed the latest set of new felonies out of the legislature. Is it the hour, the underwear, or wings with bourbon that made him a suspect?"

"You trying for Second City? Your act needs polish. When a guy with a grudge is awake at five A.M., and his place of employment was turned into a shambles an hour earlier, it raises questions. The shortest way to point B is from—"

"The right starting place," I interrupted. "Did he have glass on him? From what I read about the damage, there must have been glass dust in his hair and face—you couldn't keep it off you."

"The humble police sergeant thanks the superior intellect of the private investigator. Litvak was naked except for his Y-fronts. Any clothes that would have carried glass into the apartment he'd ditched before he came home."

"You find them?"

She shook her head regretfully. "Still, doesn't mean anything. It's a big city, and there are a lot of places you can get rid of incriminating evidence."

"Any witnesses report a heavy-set white man wandering around naked at five A.M.?"

She pressed her lips together and looked away.

"Eugene Horvath," I said. "It sounds like a hideous death, buried under a mound of broken bottles."

"It was." She clicked on her keyboard and turned the screen around to show me the crime scene photos.

I sucked in a breath when I saw the destruction at the warehouse: twenty-foot-high shelves had been toppled on top of each other. Thousands of bottles had crashed as the shelves went down. Broken glass lay hip deep in some places.

Pizzello also showed me copies of half a dozen stills from the internal security cameras. They showed the forklift at the head of an aisle. The teeth were under a set of shelves in one frame. In the next the shelves had jackknifed at a crazy angle, as if a tank had crashed into them. The other stills showed piles of broken glass and pools of alcohol. The forklift had clearly been driven by an experienced handler.

"Why we picked up Litvak. Someone knew that warehouse inside and out. They were skilled with a forklift. Litvak's prints were all over the forklift."

"Anyone else's?" I asked.

She bit her lower lip, a kind of "tell" with her that she was on thin ice. "Some of the other operators."

I made a show of entering her answer into my tablet. "How long did this mayhem go on? Don't they have an alarm system?"

"Disabled. Which also points to Litvak. He *says* he never knew the codes on the door or on the internal alarms, but after eighteen years—you'd have to be a total zombie not to pick up that stuff."

If it had been Donny, yes, but Gregory seemed too listless and depressed to spy on someone typing in an alarm code.

"Who called the cops?" I asked.

"Litvak lost his head—left through the loading bays. They have bar locks that you can slide open from the inside, but if you do, that triggers the alarm system. We had a patrol there in fifteen minutes, but he'd taken off."

I made another note.

"What about the dead man? How did he end up in the warehouse during the rampage?"

"That's a mystery." Pizzello bared her teeth in a hideous parody of a grin. "Something for the suave sleuth. We don't know. His wife says he had a dinner meeting, but she doesn't know who with. His phone has disappeared and his desktop calendar was wiped clean. We don't know if he was lured to the warehouse, or if he went in to check on something—the wife says he worked odd hours sometimes, especially at tax season—or if he drove past and saw lights blazing and went in to investigate."

"The suave sleuth thinks time of death could narrow that down."

Pizzello brought up photos of Horvath's body. He looked as though he'd been through a cattle stampede, the skin flailed from most of his body, left ear dangling from the skull.

"I get it," I said, my voice thick with nausea. "Hard to pin down. I assume that applies to the cause of death, too."

"What do you mean?" She stared. "You imagining some kind of superhero able to withstand a ton of glass coming down on your head?"

"I'm wondering if the murder was the sideshow or the main attraction. Maybe he was killed by the ton of glass, but maybe it was an altercation that got out of hand and was covered by a ton of glass. Or a bullet, covered ditto, or if he was even alive when he came into the warehouse."

She digested those possibilities in silence, but said, "Whether it was a sideshow or main attraction, Litvak is still in the frame."

"Then it will be my job to paint a new canvas." I left on that grandiose line and went to County, where I met with Gregory.

By the time I'd finished interviewing him, I was sure of two things: he wouldn't survive a month in the jail, and he hadn't killed Horvath or even destroyed the Roccamena warehouse.

5

Nick Vishnikov, Cook County's deputy chief medical examiner, was a fracquaintance: somewhere between friend and business contact. He'd personally conducted Eugene Horvath's autopsy. They'd x-rayed the body: it didn't hold any extraneous metal; he had a plate in his left elbow and quite a few dental crowns, but no bullets.

"He ate his last meal about two hours before he died. Find out what time he ate and you'll know what time he was killed. Beyond that—was he dead before being mangled by glass and a warehouse tractor? No way of knowing. Not even Abby Sciuto or Ducky could tell you."

I had already exchanged emails with Gregory's harried public defender, getting his permission to be signed on as part of Gregory's legal team. That had allowed me access to him in prison, as well as to the state's case. Now I told the PD I thought we could raise significant doubts about the murder, along with the warehouse destruction; I thought it worthwhile to apply for a new bail hearing.

The PD, an anxious young man named Colin Vilot, was reluctant, mostly because he was juggling 123 cases, but he finally agreed to set up a hearing if I promised to put everything he should say into writing, complete with bullet points.

The new hearing was set for a week away. In the meantime, it could be worthwhile to look at Roccamena's finances. Sonia had said maybe the Roccamenas had destroyed the warehouse themselves to collect the insurance—a not uncommon strategy for a business with cash flow problems, but one that usually involves arson.

Colin Vilot refused to subpoena the Roccamena financial records. He had about three minutes for me to explain why that would help: if we could show dubious finances, we could raise additional doubts about Gregory's involvement.

"You want to take over his defense? Be my guest. I can't handle the cases I've got, anyway," he finally exploded.

I hastily demurred, mended my fences. I hadn't been a litigator for two decades—even a harassed PD could outmaneuver me. Anyway, Roccamena would fight a subpoena, we'd be in court a dozen times or more, and the clock would keep ticking on Gregory.

Instead, I went to Roccamena's offices. They were a big outfit— besides the central warehouse where Gregory had worked, they had satellites around the city perimeter, and had recently expanded to Milwaukee and Peoria. Their offices were inside their main depot, in the maze of half streets and warehouses south of Midway Airport. I often get lost there. This time I drove in circles around a multiplex and a few big-box outlets before realizing that Roccamena occupied all of a spur of Eighty-Seventh Place.

A foreman blocked my passage at the main entrance. When I explained I was a lawyer working for Gregory Litvak, he unbent slightly: Gregory had been an odd duck, a loner, but he wouldn't hurt a fly. If he had killed Horvath, it was an accident, no way should he be arrested for murder. The foreman called inside, and in a few minutes a man in coveralls and a hard hat came out to escort me to the office.

My escort took me around the side of the building to an exterior iron staircase that led to the offices. The door at the top opened from the inside only. My escort kept a finger on a buzzer until someone let us in. Once inside, I saw there was a camera and a monitor that overlooked the stairwell.

The offices occupied space built above the truck bays. They'd been pretty well soundproofed, but they still shook as the semis pulled in and dropped their loads.

As Harry Truman sort of said, if a detective wants a friend, she should get a dog. Fortunately I had two at home, because my welcome was somewhere between glacial and frigid. The HR director wouldn't tell me why Gregory had been fired.

"State secret?" I suggested. "Altering wine labels to send coded messages to Putin? Or was he spending too much time playing games on his phone?"

The HR director said that she couldn't talk to Gregory's lawyer, since his dismissal was a legal matter.

"Is he suing for wrongful dismissal?" I was startled—neither Gregory nor Sonia had told me this.

"No, no." She was impatient. "You must know—he's being tried for murder."

"No, we don't know that, Ms."—I squinted at the name plate buried behind some computer manuals—"Forde. He's a long way from being tried. There are a lot of holes in the state's case, and I am finding out more every half hour I'm on the job. So let's go back to why he was fired. Was he fiddling with the company's finances?"

Unless Gregory was the best actor since Humphrey Bogart, I couldn't picture him doing something that active. I only said it to try to force Ms. Forde into blurting out an indiscretion, so I was surprised when she looked frightened. Eyes wide, looking nervously to her office door, she said, "Of course not. What a ridiculous idea, a loser who moved boxes around knowing how to break into our computers."

The words were scornful, but the tone was quavery.

"Had Eugene Horvath discovered something wrong with the company's books?" I asked.

"I'm just the HR secretary. You need to talk to Mr. Roccamena." She tapped a couple of digits on her phone. "Ellie? It's Carmen in HR. One of Gregory Litvak's lawyers is here, and she's asking about the pension fund. Can Harvey talk to her?"

A few minutes later, a tall man with thick gray hair and a deeply lined face joined us. "Harvey Roccamena. You the lawyer? We aren't discussing why we terminated Litvak. Just be assured it was for cause."

"The pension fund?" I said. "How did he have access to that?"

The crags between the creases in his cheeks turned burgundy. He waited a fraction of a second too long before saying, "Who knows what a punk can figure out."

"So there is something wrong with the pension fund?"

The burgundy deepened to cabernet. "We run a liquor business, not a fishing company. Off you go, counselor."

Off I went. On my way back to my car, I passed the loading dock where trucks hauling California wines, Europeans, South Americans, liquors, liqueurs, mixers, beers, were lined up to water the Roccamena empire.

Every bay at the loading dock had a semi backed up to it. I hoisted myself up onto the lip of the dock. Forklifts were beetling from the semis into the warehouse, stacked with high loads of crates. So much booze made me feel unwell. Made me wonder what it meant for the son of a determined alcoholic like Karen Litvak to work in the liquor business. Pizzello had said they'd found Gregory in his Y-fronts drinking bourbon. Maybe he'd been fired for siphoning off the inventory.

At each bay, a couple stood with a clipboard, ticking off the load. One from the truck, one from the warehouse. When they'd agreed on the delivery, the Roccamena employee signed the bill of lading and the trucker took off. The insurers must have come through quickly for the restocking to be happening at this pace.

I went back to my car for the hard hat I keep in the trunk and wandered into the interior of the building. In the press of activity, no one had time to notice me.

New floor-to-ceiling shelves had been bolted into place, new signage hung above the ends of the aisles. Men were on catwalks high above the aisles, shifting crates from the lifts to the shelves. It was like watching a futuristic horror movie, maybe *Metropolis*, where people are enslaved to machines and the machines know the human addictions.

I slipped among the tractors, wondering which one had done last week's damage, looking for someone taking a break. I came to a side door, propped open, and found what I needed—a trio of smokers. When I joined them, they moved closer together, solidarity against an outsider.

"That's a zoo." I jerked my head toward the open door.

One of them stubbed out his cigarette against his boot heel. The other two took that as a signal that the break was over. Before they disappeared into the building, I said, "I'm Gregory Litvak's lawyer. One of the team, anyway."

"Don't know a Litvak," the stubber said.

I spoke to the parking lot on his left. "If Gregory didn't do all that damage and didn't kill Horvath, who did? He seems depressed and lethargic to me. Maybe that's just from being at County, but it's hard to picture him doing all the planning it took to destroy the inventory here."

The stubber paused.

"He needed to figure out the door code, needed to make sure his face didn't show up on the security cameras. Needed to get Horvath into the warehouse in the middle of the night."

"You saying he's not guilty?"

"I'm saying the proof isn't there. It's sketchy, it's circumstantial. I'd love to know why they fired Gregory. Was he stealing? Drinking on the job? I'd also love to know how Eugene Horvath happened to be in the warehouse that night. And I'd like to know if there's a problem with the pension fund. Harvey Roccamena didn't want to talk about it."

The three men exchanged glances, nodded to one another.

"Litvak. You're right about him. He did a hard day's work most of his damned life here. Not a sociable guy. Never went out for a beer or whatever at the end of his shift. You think when you first meet him he's a snob, then you realize he's scared twenty-four seven, afraid we'll pick on him, whatever. Two years ago they brought in a new floor manager, couldn't leave the guy alone. Twenty years, your pension is fully vested. They went after vulnerable targets, forced 'em to quit, and most of them did, but Litvak, what was he going to do? He didn't have a life, far as I could tell. But it got to him. He started missing shifts. Not a lot, but every month, there'd be a day, sometimes two. So they sort of had cause.

"Horvath, who knows why he ever did anything he did. He was

tight with Walker. Clarence Walker, the new floor manager. Speaking of which, I need a full paycheck this week. We were off for four days while they cleaned out the mess and put up new shelves."

I handed them my business card and trailed after them into the warehouse. At the far end of the floor, an interior staircase also led to the offices I'd just visited. A few plate glass windows were cut into the wall so that management could look down on the operation, but security cameras were also plentiful: they were mounted at every aisle as well as in the corners. Roccamena had an inventory that people wanted. A determined filcher could lift a few bottles along the way, but it would be hard to lift a whole case.

I stood in the Nebbiolo aisle. After studying the cartons for a few minutes, I pulled one toward me and started to undo the staples holding it shut. It took about ninety seconds for a forty-something man in a hard hat and shirtsleeves to appear, shouting at me.

"Get the fuck away from that shelf. Who the fuck are you and what are you doing in a restricted zone?"

"You Clarence Walker?" I said. "I'm checking your security system. Do you know how easy it was for me to get into this warehouse? Is anyone monitoring your cameras, or are they only for decoration? Your insurance carrier is going to have a bucket of questions about whether you were negligent, and whether they should force you to return your claim check. You say the perpetrator of the damage hid from the cameras, but someone should have seen a feed of what he was doing."

Walker opened and shut his mouth a few times, like a beached carp. Finally he said, "Litvak knew the security code to get into the building. If he'd broken in, the alarm would have gone off on my phone, but people come in in the night sometimes. Horvath did, to catch up on his paperwork. Mr. Roccamena likes to call his Italian suppliers at three A.M. when no one's around. If someone's here on legitimate business, the alarms don't go off."

"You were tight with Horvath, right? Did he come here that night to catch up on his paperwork? Were your security cameras even functioning so that we can see whether he arrived or not?"

"Are you with the police?" Walker demanded, recovering his balance. "Let me see some ID."

"I'm not with the police. I'm an investigator who works with insurance companies. When people wreak havoc at their businesses to collect insurance, the companies I represent become very cranky. They unleash their massive array of lawyers and do ugly things to companies. If you can't let me see the full security footage for that night, then that will affect the report I write."

"Klondike was satisfied. Which makes me think you're a scam artist yourself. Let me see some ID."

"Klondike." I rolled the name on my tongue like a bad vintage. "They're your insurance agency, they're not the company that underwrote the policy."

I walked away, out past the loading bays, where the forklifts were still racing back and forth. The cigarette stubber gave me a half wave.

6

Don't try spinning me a line, Donny. I've been watching you cheat at marbles since we were six."

I had called Sonia, demanding to talk to Donny. She'd arrived forty minutes later, her brother in tow. Donny claimed to know nothing about Klondike's client list, especially Roccamena Liquor Wholesalers, Inc. And no way had he gotten Gregory his job there.

"Besides, that was eighteen years ago. Even if someone did put a little pressure on Roccamena, they'd have fired Gregory if he wasn't up to the job. Just like they fired him two weeks ago."

"The damage to the warehouse was what—ten days ago? Two weeks? Roccamena is back up and running. Did Klondike get the carrier to cut a check, or did they advance money to Roccamena? No way would suppliers provide as much inventory as I saw unloaded today because they love Harvey Roccamena."

That's when Donny said he was just the Klondike handyman; he didn't know anything about their client base or who paid claims to whom. When I said I couldn't keep working for Sonia if he didn't tell me a few truths, he said that Klondike had gotten Ajax Insurance, who underwrote the Roccamena policies, to give them a bridge loan until the claim was settled.

This is common in the industry: an important account could get a favorable interest rate on a short-term loan to tide them over a bad patch. In this case, since the claim was almost certain to be paid, Ajax had demanded the most nominal possible interest.

"Gregory says you've promised him an alibi," I said to Donny. "We're trying to get his bail reduced, so letting the judge know he's got a believable alibi will make a big difference."

Donny cracked his knuckles. "You come up with evidence showing someone else had a bigger interest in offing Horvath. If you can't, I'll see about the alibi."

"You'll 'see' about it? Crap, Donny. Does that mean you don't have one but you'll manufacture it?"

"It means the alibi would embarrass some people, so I'd rather not have to use it."

"You'd let Gregory rot?" Sonia exclaimed.

"Sonny, Sonny." Donny patted her broad shoulders. "You know I wouldn't. Remember the time the cops arrested me but Stan told the cops it was him and Reggie said it couldn't be because Stan was with you; it was really him? We all look after each other, even Stanley, down there in Sedona communing with interplanetary forces. Even Reggie, snotty little capitalist that he is. We won't let Gregory down."

Sonia gave a reluctant smile. "Then Reggie will come up with the bail money?"

"Probably not," Donny said, "but I'm working on him."

"Tell me about Eugene Horvath," I said. "Why was he so despicable?"

Donny spread his hands. "I didn't know the guy. He's the one who—oh. You think if Gregory didn't murder him, I did? I did not kill him. He was a jerk and I'm not crying over him, but he has ten thousand clones on the South Side. I know Roccamena will find just as big an asshole, if not bigger, to take his place. Gregory didn't kill him, either. Nor did Sonia or Reggie or even Saint Stanley."

"I want to see the security tapes for that night. Not just the stills that the cops have, the whole footage for the whole evening."

"Can't help you," Donny said.

"Give me the code to the warehouse and I'll find them myself."

"How would I know the code?"

I shook my head. "Maybe Klondike has it in their client database. Or you have a friend at the alarm company. They've probably changed it since the bust-up, but I have enormous faith in your ability to weasel it out of any file or hiding place where the numbers are buried."

Donny's shoulders went back, preening. He corrected the move at once: no one was supposed to notice that he could be flattered.

7

Melanie Horvath bore her grief quietly, in the middle of a very quiet subdivision on the outer reaches of Chicago's exurbia. We don't dress for mourning anymore; she greeted me in skinny jeans covered by a man's white shirt.

She took me to a sunroom at the back of the house, which overlooked a flower garden. Beyond it a field stretched away into the hills.

"I didn't want to see his body, not when the police described it to me, but then it showed up on social media. A kind neighbor thought I should look at it. Will I ever get that image out of my head?"

It was a rhetorical question, but I assured her it would fade in time. "If the picture comes to you, try to think at that moment of a time when he was laughing or intent on a project. Some people find that helpful."

I apologized again for disturbing her but explained that there were ongoing questions about the murder—in particular, what time her husband went to the warehouse.

"The crew on the floor say he was often there in the middle of the night, that he liked to work on accounts undisturbed. It seems as though he could be pretty peaceful here."

She smiled, a small bleak smile. "I worried at first that he was using that as an excuse for an affair. I worried so much that I followed him several times, but, in fact, he'd go into the warehouse and leave after a few hours. I never saw anyone else there, except sometimes Harvey Roccamena."

A trio of horses appeared at the fence behind her garden. Horvath saw me looking at them.

"My hobby. My lifesaver now: you cannot leave animals unattended. They force me to get dressed and go outside."

I made a sympathetic noise, but I wondered about the income that supported three horses, a house that might include five thousand square feet, and the BMW I'd parked next to in the driveway.

We continued a desultory chat. She had last seen her husband when he left for work the morning he died. "He told me he had a dinner date and that he would probably be late. I finally went to bed at midnight. The police woke me at six with the news."

Her voice was steady with an effort; the tendons in her neck stood out and she twisted the ruby on her right hand until the prongs caught on a knuckle and made her bleed.

I asked if she could look up her husband's credit card on the chance he had paid for dinner. She did so, but he hadn't charged anything to his personal cards that day. She didn't have access to his corporate cards.

"I hope your coworkers or your neighbors are looking after you," I said as I left.

"My coworkers. Yes, it would be good if I had a job, something besides the horses to get me out of bed in the mornings. I'll think about that."

When I got back to my office I found a message under the door: *parking lot across from warehouse midnight.* It was in the rough handwriting of someone who seldom wrote; I took for granted it was from Donny Litvak.

8

At midnight, most of the massive warehouses and plants were down to skeleton crews. The parking lots were nearly empty. I left the Mustang near a twenty-four-hour diner so it wouldn't stand out and provide a target for the knots of teens who swarmed and evaporated through the area.

The Roccamena warehouse was about half a mile away, across a vast stretch of asphalt. The empty lot unnerved me. I walked along the perimeter, keeping away from the circles of light the streetlamps created, but close enough to the road I could sprint from danger if I had to.

When I got to the lot entrance, facing Roccamena, I squatted on the pavement. I was wearing a black cap, loose black clothes, running shoes with the white trim painted black.

A few semis were still huffing in the loading bays, a few cars still parked nearby. It was one before the last truck drove off, the last worker jumped down from the dock lip and into his car. One SUV remained, a late-model Lincoln. After another twenty minutes, Harvey Roccamena himself came through a side door, typed the code into the pad next to it, and took off in the Navigator.

After its taillights vanished, two figures walked down the road toward me. They were both bulky, broad shouldered, but I waited for them to get near before I got to my feet. When they reached the entrance to the lot, I could hear one say, "She'd damned well better be here, after you dragged me into Gregory's mess."

"Present and accounted for," I said softly, from my shadow.

"Fuck, Warshawski!" Donny swore. "You fucking gave me a heart attack."

"Wanted to make sure this wasn't a setup," I said. "Is this Reggie?"

The second man grunted. "Yeah. Donny can't handle technology. Has to come to little brother. Slobbering and groveling."

"You could have come up with the bail money," Donny said.

"I could not come up with two hundred thousand in cash. Stop playing on that string, Donny, or I'll head back to Elgin. In fact, I'd like to be there right now instead of running the risk of arrest with you. And what kind of lawyer did you grow up to be, Warshawski, breaking into warehouses in the dead of night? You could be disbarred if you're caught."

"Then we'd better not get caught," I said. "And the easiest way to avoid that is to stop arguing on a public street where no one else is loitering. I saw both Chicago and Bedford cruisers roaming through the lot while I was waiting."

I took gloves from my pocket. I offered some to the brothers, but they'd brought their own. I put on mine and followed the pair across the road to the warehouse. Despite their bulk, the Litvaks moved quickly. At the side door where Roccamena had exited, we flattened ourselves against the wall while Donny stuck up an arm to put a piece of chewing gum over the camera eye. Reggie held his camera lens over the keypad. Whatever app he'd installed communed with the keypad's brain; in another minute a light flashed green, and we were inside.

The warehouse had security lights in the ceiling tiles. Their glow was just bright enough that we could see the crates and ladders cluttering the aisles.

Donny knew what arcs the security cameras traced. Reggie and I followed his lead, getting down on the floor and sliding, snake-like, between the edges of the camera ranges. We were all out of breath, holding back adolescent giggles, when we reached the door that led to the warehouse offices.

Reggie once again held his phone to the keypad. On the other side of the door, we tiptoed up a metal stairwell to a small room that overlooked the warehouse floor. Here were the computer monitors, showing the cameras at work. I watched as they tracked the shelves, checking for pilfering, but not sweeping low enough to have seen us on the floor. A big monitor with a keyboard in front was connected to the company's main computer.

This room didn't have any windows to show a light to the outside; we turned on the desk lamps.

"Okay, nerd, work your magic," Donny said to Reggie.

"Right, punk. Go beat someone up and don't bother me."

Reggie settled himself at the monitor, removing his gloves to make it easier to type. Donny entertained himself by going through the drawers in the small desk. I stood behind Reggie, watching the screen.

It took him about twenty minutes to get into the system and to find his way around the files. I watched, impressed, as he found the reports from the night Horvath was killed.

Action began at 2:32 A.M. It showed a forklift emerging from the back of the warehouse, from the area around the loading bay. It was impossible to see the driver but easy to follow the action:

Godzilla going through New York City, picking up high shelving and toppling it.

At one point, the driver stuck his torso out at right angles to the machine and waved at the cameras. He was masked, wearing work gloves. You couldn't see who it was, but if the state was basing Gregory's arrest on his prints on the machine, this frame showed he didn't leave them that night.

A few minutes after that, the machine started down aisle ninety-seven. We saw the driver pick up a shelf, try to resettle it, and back away as it crashed in front of him. He maneuvered through the wreckage and disappeared into the service bays.

"Poor bastard—must have seen Horvath's body," Donny said.

I swerved to look at him. "How do you know that, Donny?"

He met my gaze with a limpid smile. "Police report; dude was found in aisle ninety-seven. Must have been a hell of a shock to see a body on the floor."

"Right." My voice was as dry as glass dust. "As you pointed out, Gregory's alibi could embarrass someone."

I waited another minute, but he wasn't going to say anything else; I turned back to the monitor.

The program only played camera activity if something triggered their motion detectors. A clock at the top of the screen reported how many minutes they idled between reports. Twelve minutes had passed before the warehouse was filled with cops.

Roccamena appeared, talking to whoever was leading the patrol unit.

"Back that up," I told Reggie. "Where did he come from?"

He backed up the video, but Roccamena seemed to appear from nowhere.

"You can't get inside the offices from the outside staircase, so he had to still be in the building," I said. "If he'd come in through the side entrance or the bays, he'd be on camera four or seventeen. Go back to the start of the night. When did the last person leave the building?"

Reggie found someone bolting the last of the loading bays at 11:00 P.M. He left through the side door, shutting off the lights on his way out. After that, nothing triggered the sensors until 11:30, when a man came in through the side door. The cameras went black.

Reggie went through all his file-revival tricks, but the cameras hadn't found anything until 2:32, when the forklift appeared from the loading bays.

"Was that Horvath? Can we look at him again?"

Reggie went back to 11:30 and froze the frame. None of us knew Horvath by sight, but his picture had been all over the news immediately after the murder.

"Send all these files to me, will you?" I said to Reggie. "We need these pictures if we end up going to court. Of course, the real driver of the forklift may step forward."

"I wouldn't count on it," Donny said. "He'd be afraid of being framed for the murder."

"Maybe he'll grow a conscience," Reggie growled.

"Maybe his overgrown conscience led him to the warehouse that night," Donny growled back.

"We'll turn the alibi holder over to Sonia in the morning," I said. "Right now, I want to make sure we have our own copy of the camera footage. And then get out before someone finds us in here."

"Sonia," Donny said in a strangled voice.

"Your sister is my client. She needs to know about Gregory's alibi." I grinned in a friendly way.

Reggie muttered curses at Roccamena's IT administrator—he couldn't find file compression software. "They've got 7-Zip now and they'd better thank me for it."

He closed the files he'd opened, used an alcohol pad to wipe off the keyboard, and followed Donny out the door. I was behind them when I realized Donny had left one of the drawers he'd been fiddling with open.

When I couldn't get it to shut all the way, I squatted and saw a sheaf of crumpled paper had slid between the back of the drawer and the desk wall behind it. I eased the pages out. It was a printout of financial data, as far as I could tell—most of the paper was so crusted in dried blood I couldn't read it.

9

I was between the stairs to the office and the side door when I saw the flashlight dancing across the floor.

"I know you're in there. I have a gun and I'm prepared to use it," a deep voice cried.

"And I have the blood-covered report on your pension fund. Which I am prepared to use," I called back.

I'd stood in the office too long, trying to read through the dried blood. I'd finally seen that this was a printout of the Roccamena pension fund activity for the past six years. Names that I couldn't decipher were highlighted.

I'd heard the side door shut behind Donny and Reggie; Donny

texted me to hurry it up, they wouldn't wait forever. I stuck the report into an envelope and left the office—about five minutes too late.

Harvey Roccamena charged around the corner of aisle 114, gun out. I hit the floor, rolled up against the shelf. He lifted his hand to fire and I swept all the bottles from the bottom shelf into his path. He sidestepped and his shot went wide, shattering the whiskey behind me.

I scrambled to my feet and flung a bottle at him. It went high, flying over his head to shatter against the shelf behind him. I threw again as he fired. My fourth bottle hit his shoulder and he dropped the gun. He scrabbled for it as I tried to kick it. My toe slammed into his hand, but he held on to the gun and pointed it at my head.

I twisted around, swung my left foot into his gut. Dropped to the floor as he fired, grabbed his leg, upended him into the broken glass.

The gunshots were so deafening that I didn't hear the forklift engine until it was almost on us. Donny was screaming at me. I jumped onto the forks and clung to the mast as the lift made a tight circle and trundled to the loading bays.

One of the doors was open, waiting. We jumped from the machine and ran. Roccamena stood in the doorway shooting at us.

10

They should never have fired Gregory," Donny said.

"So you decided to destroy Roccamena's inventory in revenge?" I said.

"Of course not." That was Sonia. "Donny was with me that night. I needed help filling out my tax return."

"And Donny, tax whiz that he is, was just the man for the job," I agreed politely. "Reggie would have been a better choice, but he was with Donny at the warehouse, using his snazzy app to undo the keypads at Roccamena's."

"I most certainly was not," Reggie huffed. "I was right here at home with Cassie, wasn't I, darling? Our home security photos prove it."

He showed me the date-and-time-stamped pictures on his monitor, Cassie working on a quilt in the family room, him at his desk, doing something on his computer. Their two sons were playing a video game.

"You do remember that I grew up with you, I hope. I remember when you and Stanley worked a racket with the numbers runners outside U.S. Steel. That guy, what was his name? Lime Pit or something—he ratted you to the cops, and each of you claimed it was the other until Sonia stepped in and said you'd both been with her."

"So?" Reggie said. He sounded blasé, but his shoulders were tense.

"So I learned the only way to tell you apart was Stanley's birthmark on his left temple." It was tiny, barely the size of a sunflower seed, but visible in the security photo.

"Stanley drove straight through from Sedona, stayed here with Cassie, and drove home."

"You can't prove that," Sonia cried.

"I can't prove the driving part," I agreed, "but the birthmark is there. Anyway, the SA had to release Gregory. The documents

I pulled from Roccamena's desk were Harvey's printout showing how Horvath had been defrauding the pension fund.

"Horvath created phantom employees. He was sending their benefits to a bank in Saint Kitts. Roccamena finally figured that out—he had a forensic accountant audit the books. He confronted Horvath, killed him, and left him on the warehouse floor. When Donny came in an hour later and started knocking over the inventory, it was gravy. No way to prove how Horvath died or who killed him, but Roccamena and Harvey must have fought—blood from both was on the report. It was good enough for the cops. They figured Roccamena did the damage to the warehouse himself to cover the crime."

"So Sonia and Donny saved me again." That was Gregory. He looked better in jeans and a T-shirt than he had in the jail, but he was still slouched in his chair, looking at the floor. "I'm such a fuckup."

Sonia went over to him and put an arm around his neck. "You're not a fuckup, Gregory. You just need a little extra support. That's what we're here for."

"What I'd really like to know, Sonia, is why the hell you put me through that song and dance of hiring me, when you Litvaks already had the whole story covered."

No one spoke for a long moment until Donny said, "She didn't know. It was all I could do to talk the clean virtuous twins into helping out. Reggie made me promise not to tell Sonia—he didn't want word getting back to his investors."

"I have a life," Reggie snapped. "You can't grow up, Donny. I gave up all that crap when I left South Chicago. It was only when you told me you were going ahead regardless that I got Stanley involved, and he hated it as much as I did. But we needed him here for the time stamp, and so he came, but he sure as hell won't do it again, and neither will I."

"Oh, Reggie," Sonia said reproachfully. "Your own brother? If he was in danger again I can't believe you'd let him suffer."

"Then keep him out of danger." Reggie scowled.

After another pause, Donny said, "I hear the whole company has shut down. I thought Roccamena's kids could keep it going."

"They could if they had the capital," I said. "Ajax canceled the bridge loan they'd provided while they waited for their adjusters to figure out the bottom line on the claim. Roccamena's is gone, which is sad. They had a wonderful whisky supply."

Donny grinned. "Someone told me you were a whisky drinker. I just happened to have a case of Oban delivered to me. I kept a bottle for you. Along with whatever Sonia's paying you, of course."

II

I set the bottle of Oban on my dining room table, in between two of the red wineglasses my mother had brought with her from Italy all those years ago. Next to them I set my framed photo of my parents, not the formal one—Tony in his dress blues, Gabriella in her burnt velvet concert gown—but a snapshot I'd taken with the Brownie camera they'd given me for my tenth birthday. They were sitting in plastic garden chairs in our minute garden on South Houston, fingers loosely linked. Tony was watching her, his beloved wife, while Gabriella smiled at some private thought.

I wondered what my dad would have done with Donny, if he'd

have let him off the hook or made the arrest. Would he have seen him as someone protecting his vulnerable brother, or just the punk who never even committed grand enough crimes to qualify for a federal prosecutor?

"It was the dress, Mama," I explained to Gabriella. "Why couldn't Mr. Litvak let Sonia have that one beautiful thing? Maybe her life would have moved onto a different track if she'd seen herself as someone special, someone who got to wear that dress."

Note

Although I grew up in rural Kansas and V.I. Warshawski on the South Side of Chicago, I always feel most at home, my freest in writing about her, when I mine her memories of her old neighborhood. Three of the stories in this collection are based in South Chicago ("Death on the Edge" and "Wildcat" are the other two). This story grew out of my own revenge fantasy over a close friend who suffered a wrongful firing. I thought if I was half as good a friend as I wanted to be, I would have wreaked havoc on the offending business. Instead, it all came out on the page, and in the Litvak family, who turn dysfunction into an art form.

MISS BIANCA

Abigail made her tour of the cages, adding water to all the drinking bowls. The food was more complicated, because not all the mice got the same meal. She was ten years old and this was her first job; she took her responsibilities seriously. She read the labels on the cages and carefully measured out feed from the different bags. All the animals had numbers written in black ink on their backs; she checked these against the list Bob Pharris had given her with the feeding instructions.

"That's like being a slave," Abigail said, when Bob showed her how to match the numbers on the mice to the food directives. "It's not fair to call them by numbers instead of by name, and it's mean to write on their beautiful fur."

Bob just laughed. "It's the only way we can tell them apart, Abby."

Abigail hated the name Abby. "That's because you're not looking at their faces. They're all different. I'm going to start calling you Number Three because you're Dr. Kiel's third student. How would you like that?"

"Number Nineteen," Bob corrected her. "I'm his nineteenth student, but the other sixteen have all gotten their PhDs and moved on to glory. Don't give the mice names, Abby: you'll get too attached to them and they don't live very long."

In fact, the next week, when Abigail began feeding the animals on her own, some of the mice had disappeared. Others had been moved into the contamination room, where she wasn't supposed to go. The mice in there had bad diseases that might kill her if she touched them. Only the graduate students or the professors went in there, wearing gloves and masks.

Abigail began naming some of the mice under her breath. Her favorite, number 139, she called "Miss Bianca," after the white mouse in the book *The Rescuers*. Miss Bianca always sat next to the cage door when Abigail appeared, grooming her exquisite whiskers with her little pink paws. She would cock her head and stare at Abigail with bright black eyes.

In the book, Miss Bianca ran a prisoners' rescue group, so Abigail felt it was only fair that she should rescue Miss Bianca in turn, or at least let her have some time outside the cage. This afternoon, she looked around to make sure no one was watching, then scooped Miss Bianca out of her cage and into the pocket of her dress.

"You can listen to me practice, Miss Bianca," Abigail told her. She moved into the alcove behind the cages where the big sinks were.

Dr. Kiel thought Abigail's violin added class to the lab, at least that's what he said to Abigail's mother, but Abigail's mother said it was hard enough to be a single mom without getting fired in the bargain, so Abigail should practice where she wouldn't disturb the classes in the lecture rooms or annoy the other professors.

Abigail had to come to the lab straight from school. She did her homework on a side table near her mother's desk, and then she fed the animals and practiced her violin in the alcove.

"Today Miss Abigail Sherwood will play Bach for you," she announced grandly to Miss Bianca.

She tuned the violin as best she could and began a simplified version of the first sonata for violin. Miss Bianca stuck her head out of the pocket and looked inquiringly at the violin. Abigail wondered what the mouse would do if she put her inside the violin. Miss Bianca could probably squeeze in through the f-hole, but getting her out would be difficult. The thought of Mother's rage, not to mention Dr. Kiel's or even Bob Pharris's, made her decide against it.

She picked up her bow again but heard voices out by the cages. When she peered out, she saw Bob talking to a stranger, a small woman with dark hair.

Bob smiled at her. "This is Abby; her mother is Dr. Kiel's secretary. Abby helps us by feeding the animals."

"It's Abigail," Abigail said primly.

"And one of the mouses, Abigail, she's living in your—your—" The woman pointed at Miss Bianca.

"Abby, put the mouse back in the cage," Bob said. "If you play with them, we can't let you feed them."

Abigail scowled at the woman and at Bob, but she put Miss Bianca back in her cage. "I'm sorry, Miss Bianca. Mamelouk is watching me."

"Mamelouk?" the woman said. "I am thinking your name 'Bob'?"

Mamelouk the Iron-Tummed was the evil cat who worked for the jailer in *The Rescuers,* but Abigail didn't say that, just stared stonily at the woman, who was too stupid to know that the plural of *mouse* was *mice,* not "mouses."

"This is Elena," Bob told Abigail. "She's Dr. Kiel's new dishwasher. You can give her a hand, when you're not practicing your violin or learning geometry."

"Is allowed for children working in the lab?" Elena asked. "In my country, government is not allowing children work."

Abigail's scowl deepened: Bob had been looking at her homework while she was down here with the mice. "We have slavery in America," she announced. "The mice are slaves, too."

"Abigail, I thought you liked feeding the animals." Dr. Kiel had come into the animal room without the three of them noticing.

He wore crepe-soled shoes, which let him move soundlessly through the lab. A short stocky man with brown eyes, he could look at you with a warmth that made you want to tell him your secrets, but just when you thought you could trust him, he would become furious over nothing that Abigail could figure out. She had heard him yelling at Bob Pharris in a way that frightened her. Besides, Dr. Kiel was her mother's boss, which meant she must never *ever* be saucy to him.

"I'm sorry, Dr. Kiel," she said, her face red. "I only was telling Bob I don't like the mice being branded, they're all different, you can tell them apart by looking."

"*You* can tell them apart because you like them and know them," Dr. Kiel said. "The rest of us aren't as perceptive as you are."

"Dolan," he added to a man passing in the hall. "Come and meet my new dishwasher—Elena Mirova."

Dr. Dolan and Dr. Kiel didn't like each other. Dr. Kiel was always loud and hearty when he talked to Dr. Dolan, trying too hard not to show his dislike. Dr. Dolan snooped around the lab, looking for mistakes that Dr. Kiel's students made. He'd report them with a phony jokiness, as if he thought leaving pipettes unwashed in the sink was funny when really it made him angry.

Dr. Dolan had a face like a giant baby's, the nose little and squashed upward, his cheeks round and rosy; when Bob Pharris had taken two beakers out of Dr. Dolan's lab, he'd come into Dr. Kiel's lab, saying, "Sorry to hear you broke both your arms, Pharris, and couldn't wash your own equipment."

He came into the animal room now and smiled in a way that made his eyes close into slits. Just like a cat's. He said hello to Elena, but added to Dr. Kiel, "I thought your new girl was starting last week, Nate."

"She arrived a week ago, but she was under the weather; you would never have let me forget it if she'd contaminated your ham sandwiches—I mean your petri dishes."

Dr. Dolan scowled, but said to Elena, "The rumors have been flying around the building all day. Is it true you're from Eastern Europe?"

Dolan's voice was soft, forcing everyone to lean toward him if they wanted to hear him. Abigail had trouble understanding him, and she saw Elena did, too, but Abigail knew it would be a mistake to try to ask Dr. Dolan to speak more slowly or more loudly.

Elena's face was sad. "Is true. I am refugee, from Czechoslovakia."

"How'd you get here?" Dolan asked.

"Just like your ancestors did, Pat," Dr. Kiel said. "Yours came steerage in a ship. Elena flew steerage in a plane. We lift the lamp beside the golden door for Czechs just as we did for the Irish."

"And for the Russians?" Dolan said. "Isn't that where your people are from, Nate?"

"The Russians would like to think so," Kiel said. "It was Poland when my father left."

"But you speak the lingo, don't you?" Dolan persisted.

There was a brief silence. Abigail could see the vein in Dr. Kiel's right temple pulsing. Dolan saw it also and gave a satisfied smirk.

He turned back to Elena. "How did you end up in Kansas? It's a long way from Prague to here."

"I am meeting Dr. Kiel in Bratislava," Elena said.

"I was there in '66, you know," Dr. Kiel said. "Elena's husband edited the Czech *Journal of Virology and Bacteriology* and the Soviets didn't like their editorial policies—the journal decided they would only take articles written in English, French, or Czech, not in Russian."

Bob laughed. "Audacious. That took some guts."

Abigail was memorizing words under her breath to ask her mother over dinner: *perceptive, editorial policies, audacious.*

"Not so good idea. When Russian tanks coming last year, they putting husband in prison," Elena said.

"Well, welcome aboard," Dr. Dolan said, holding out his soft white hand to Elena.

She'd been holding her hands close to her side, but when she shook hands Abigail saw a huge bruise on the inside of her arm, green, purple, yellow, spreading in a large oval up and down from the elbow.

"They beat you before you left?" Dr. Dolan asked.

Elena's eyes opened wide; Abigail thought she was scared. "Is me, only," she said, "me being—not know in English."

"What's on today's program?" Dr. Kiel asked Abigail abruptly, pointing at her violin.

"Bach."

"You need to drop that old stuffed shirt. Beethoven. I keep telling you, start playing those Beethoven sonatas, they'll bring you to life." He ruffled her hair. "I think I saw your mother putting the cover over her typewriter when I came down."

That meant Abigail was supposed to leave. She looked at Miss Bianca, who was hiding in the shavings at the back of her cage. *It's good you're afraid,* Abigail told her silently. *Don't let them catch you, they'll hurt you or make you sick with a bad disease.*

RHONDA SHERWOOD'S HUSBAND had been an account manager for a greeting card company in town. His territory was the West Coast. When he fell in love with a woman who owned a small chain of gift shops in Sacramento, he left Rhonda and Abigail to start a new life in California.

It was embarrassing to have your father and mother divorced; some kids in Abigail's fifth grade class made fun of her. Her best friend's mother wouldn't let her come over to play anymore, as if divorce were like one of Dr. Kiel's and Dr. Dolan's diseases, infectious, communicable.

When her husband left, Rhonda brushed up on her shorthand and typing. In May, just about the time that school ended, she was lucky enough to get a job working for Dr. Kiel up at the university. Rhonda typed all his letters and his scientific papers. Over dinner, she would get Abigail to test her on the hard words she was learning: *Coxiella burnetti, cytoblasts, vacuoles.* Rhonda mastered the odd concepts: gram staining, centrifuging. Dr. Kiel was not a kind man in general, Rhonda knew that, but he was kind to her, a single mom. Dr. Kiel let Rhonda bring Abigail to the lab after school.

There were eight scientists in Dr. Kiel's department. They all had graduate students, they all taught undergraduate classes at the university, but Abigail and Rhonda both knew that none of the other scientists worked as hard as Dr. Kiel. He was always traveling, too, to different scientific conventions, or overseas. Rhonda hadn't been working for him when he went to Czechoslovakia three years ago, but she was making travel arrangements for him now. He was going to Washington, to San Francisco, and then to Israel.

Even though Dr. Kiel had an explosive temper, he had a sense of camaraderie that his colleagues lacked. He also had an intensity about his work that spilled over into the lives of his students and staff. His students and lab techs were expected to work long hours, do night shifts, attend evening seminars. Perhaps in exchange, he took a personal interest in their families, their hobbies, took his male students fishing, bought his female students records or books for their birthdays. When he went to New York in August, he brought Rhonda back a scarf from the gift store in the Metropolitan Museum of Art.

Dr. Kiel had a wife and five lumpy, sullen children: Abigail met them when Dr. Kiel had everyone in the department out to his house for a picnic right after school started. He never seemed to think about his children the way he did about his staff and students.

It was Dr. Kiel who suggested that feeding the animals might make Abigail feel that she was part of the team. He seemed to sense her loneliness; he would quiz her on her classes, her music. He also knew better than to tease a ten-year-old about boys, the way Dr. Dolan did.

When Rhonda worried about the diseases the animals were infected with, Dr. Kiel assured her that Abigail would not be allowed in the contamination room. "And if some Q Fever germ is brave enough to come through the door and infect her, we keep tetracycline on hand." He showed Rhonda the bottle of orange pills in one of his glass-doored cabinets. "I've had Q, and so has Bob Pharris. Watch out for a high fever and a dry cough, with aching joints; let me know if either of you start having symptoms."

"High fever, dry cough," Abigail repeated to herself. Every day when she went in to feed the animals, she checked Miss Bianca for a fever or a cough. "Do your joints ache?" she would ask the mouse, feeling her head the way Mother felt her own head when she was sick.

ELENA MIROVA'S ARRIVAL unsettled the lab. She was quiet, efficient; she did whatever was asked of her and more besides. She worked with Bob and Dr. Kiel's other two graduate students, often giving them suggestions on different ways to set up experimental apparatus or helping them interpret slides they were studying.

"Czech dishwashers know more science than ours in America," Bob said one day when Elena flipped through the back pages of the *Journal of Cell Biology* to show him an article that explained apoptosis in *Rickettsia prowazekii*.

Elena turned rigid, her face white, then hurriedly left the room, saying she heard the autoclave bell ringing.

"It's the Communists," Rhonda explained to her daughter when Abigail reported the episode to her.

"It was so weird," Abigail said. "It was like she thought Bob was mad at her. Besides, she was lying, the autoclave bell didn't ring."

"The Russians put her husband in prison," Rhonda said. "She's afraid that they'll try to find her here."

That frightened Abigail. Everyone knew how evil the Communists were; they wanted to take over America, they wanted to take over the whole world. America stood for freedom and the Communists wanted to destroy freedom.

"What if they come to the lab to get Elena and kill you instead?" she asked her mother. "Are the mice safe? Will they want the mice?"

Dr. Dolan came into Dr. Kiel's office at that moment. "Of course they want the mice; the mice are our most important secret."

Abigail rushed down to the animal room to make sure Miss Bianca was still safe. The mouse was nibbling on a piece of food, but she came to the front of the cage as soon as Abigail arrived. Abigail was about to take her out when she saw that Bob was in the contamination room.

Instead, she stroked the mouse's head through the cage door. "I wish I could take you home, Miss Bianca," she whispered.

When Bob came out and went into the back room to scrub himself down in the big sink, Abigail followed him.

"Do you think Elena is a Communist spy?" she demanded.

"Where do you come up with these ideas, short stuff?" Bob asked.

"Dr. Dolan said the Communists want our mice, because they're our most important secret."

"Dr. Dolan talks a lot of guff," Bob said. "There's nothing secret about the mice, and Elena is not a Communist. She ran away from the Communists."

"But she lied about the autoclave. She didn't like you saying how smart she was."

Bob stopped drying his arms to stare at her. "You're as small as the mice, so we don't notice you underfoot. Look: there's nothing secret about our mice. We get a grant—you know what that is? Money. We get money from the army, so we do some work for the army. The disease Dr. Kiel works with can make people very sick.

If our soldiers got sick in Vietnam, they wouldn't be able to fight, so Dr. Kiel and I and his other students are trying to find a way to keep them from getting sick."

"But he has that drug, he showed my mom," Abigail said.

"That's great if you're already sick, but if you're in the middle of a battle, it would be better not to get sick to start with. It would be hard for the army to get enough of the drug to our soldiers out in the jungles and rice paddies while the Vietcong were firing rockets at them."

"Oh," Abigail said. "You're trying to make a shot, like for polio."

"And the mice are helping us. We give them some of Dr. Kiel's disease, and then we study whether we've learned any way to prevent them from getting sick."

After Bob went back to the lab, Abigail took Miss Bianca from the cage and let her sit in her pocket, where she had a lump of sugar. "Even if the mice can help win a war with the Communists, I think it would be better if you didn't get sick."

She practiced her violin for half an hour. The scratchy sounds she got from the strings sounded more like the squeaks the mice made than Bach, but neither she nor the animals minded. When she finished, she took Miss Bianca out of her pocket to ride on her shoulder. When she heard voices outside the animal room door she crouched down, holding Miss Bianca in her hand.

"Mamelouk is here," she whispered. "Don't squeak."

It wasn't Mamelouk, it was Dr. Kiel with Elena. Elena's face was very white, the way it had been when she first came into the lab. She fumbled in her handbag and produced a vial with something red in it that Abigail was sure was blood.

"I hope is sterile. Hard job doing self. *My*self," Elena said.

Abigail bent her head over her knees, so Miss Bianca wouldn't have to see such a dreadful sight. After Dr. Kiel and Elena left the animal room, she stayed bent over for a long time, but finally went up to the floor where the labs and offices were.

Her mother wasn't in the outer office, but the typewriter was still uncovered, which meant she was either taking dictation from Dr. Kiel or in the ladies' room. The door to Dr. Kiel's inner office wasn't shut all the way; Abigail walked over to peer through the crack.

Dr. Dolan was there. He had a nasty look on his face. The vein in Dr. Kiel's forehead was throbbing, always a bad sign.

"I got the library to order back copies of the Czech *Journal of Virology,* and no one named Mirov is on the editorial pages," Dr. Dolan said.

"I didn't know you could read Czech, Patrick," Dr. Kiel said. "I thought you moved your lips when you read English."

Abigail wanted to laugh, it was such a funny insult. Maybe she could use it the next time Susie Campbell taunted her about her parents' divorce.

"Don't try to change the subject, Kiel," Dr. Dolan said. "Are you or aren't you harboring a Communist here? What kind of background check did you do on your protégée before you let her into a lab doing sensitive work for the government?"

"I met her husband in Bratislava three years ago," Dr. Kiel said coldly. "We were correspondents until the tanks rolled in last year and the Soviets put him in prison as an enemy of the state. Elena came here in danger of her life."

"Correspondents? Or lovers?" Dr. Dolan sneered.

Abigail put a hand over her mouth. Lovers, like her father and the new Mrs. Sherwood out in California. Was Elena turning Mrs. Kiel into a single mom for the five lumpy Kiel children?

"Maybe you grew up in a pigsty," Dr. Kiel said. "But in my family—"

"Your Communist family."

"What are you, Dolan? A stooge for HUAC?"

"The FBI has a right to know what you were really doing in Bratislava three years ago. You work with a weapons-grade organism, you speak Russian, you travel—"

"The operative word here being *work*," Dr. Kiel said. "If you worked on *listeria* as energetically as you do on spying on my lab, you'd have won the Nobel Prize by now."

Mother came into the outer office just then and dragged Abigail to the hall. "Since when do you eavesdrop, young lady?" she demanded.

"But, Mom, it's about Elena. She's lying all the time, her husband didn't work for that magazine in Czechoslovakia, Dr. Dolan said. He says she's stealing Dr. Kiel away from Mrs. Kiel, like that lady who stole Daddy from us. And Elena just gave Dr. Kiel something funny in the animal room. It looked like blood, but maybe it's a magic potion to make him forget Mrs. Kiel."

Rhonda stared down at her daughter in exasperation, but also in sadness. "Abigail, I'm not sure it's such a good idea for you to come here after school. You hear things that are outside your experience and then you get upset by them. Elena is not going to break up Dr. Kiel's marriage, I promise you. Let's see if I can find someone to stay with you after school, okay?"

"No, Mom, no, I have to come here, I have to look after Miss Bianca."

Elena came into the hall where they were standing. She'd been in the lab but they hadn't seen her. Rhonda and Abigail both flushed.

"Sorry," Elena murmured. "I making all lives hard, but I not understanding, why is Dr. Dolan not like me?"

Rhonda shook her head. "He's jealous of Dr. Kiel, I think, and so he tries to attack the people who work for Dr. Kiel. Try not to pay attention to him."

"But Dr. Dolan said your husband's name wasn't in—in the Czech something, the magazine," Abigail piped up, to Rhonda's annoyance.

Elena didn't speak for a moment; her face turned white, as it had in the animal room earlier in the afternoon. "No, he is scientist, he is reading articles, deciding is science good or not good? He telling editor, but only editor name in *Journal,* not husband."

Dr. Dolan stormed out of Dr. Kiel's office, his round cheeks swollen with anger. "You were quite a devoted wife, Elena, if you studied your husband's work so much that you understand rickettsial degradation by lysosomal enzymes," he said sarcastically.

"I married many years, I learning many things," Elena said. "Now I learning how live with husband in prison. I also learn acid rinse glassware, forgive me."

She brushed past Dolan and went down the hall to the autoclave room, where the pressure machine washed glassware at a temperature high enough to kill even the peskiest bacterium.

OVER THE WEEKEND, Bob and the other graduate students took care of the animals. On Monday, Abigail hurried anxiously back to the lab after school. Bob was in the animal room with a strange man who was wearing a navy suit and a white shirt. None of the scientists ever dressed like that: they were always spilling acids that ate holes in their clothes. Even Mother had to be careful when she went into the lab—once Bob accidentally dripped acid on her leg and her nylons dissolved.

"But she has access to the animals?"

Bob was shifting unhappily from one foot to the other. He didn't see Abigail, but she was sure the man in the suit was talking about her. She crept behind the cages into the alcove where the big sinks stood.

Bob was putting on a mask and gloves to go into the contamination room, but the man in the suit seemed to be afraid of the germs; he said he didn't need to go into the room.

"I just want to know if you keep it secure. There are a lot of bugs in there that could do a lot of damage in the wrong hands."

"You have to have a key to get in here," Bob assured the man, showing him that the door was locked.

When the two men left, Abigail went out to the cages. Miss Bianca's cage was empty. Her heart seemed to stop. She had the same queer feeling under her rib cage that she'd felt when Daddy said he was leaving to start a new life in California.

A lot of the cages were empty, Abigail realized, not just Miss Bianca's. Bob and Dr. Kiel had waited until the weekend so they could steal Miss Bianca and give her a shot full of germs while Abigail wasn't there to protect her.

Dr. Kiel had given Mother a set of keys when she started working for him. Abigail went back up the stairs to Dr. Kiel's lab. Mother was working on Dr. Kiel's expense report from his last trip to Washington. Abigail pretended to study Spanish explorers in the 1500s, sitting so quietly that people came and went, including Bob and the man in the suit, without paying attention to her.

Dr. Kiel was in his lab, talking to Elena as they stood over a microscope. The lab was across the hall; Abigail couldn't hear what anyone said, but suddenly Dr. Kiel bellowed "Rhonda!" and Mother hurried over with her shorthand notebook.

As soon as she was gone, Abigail went to the drawer where Mother kept her purse. She found the keys and ran back down to the animal room. She didn't bother about gloves and masks. At any second someone might come in, or Mother would notice her keys were missing.

There were so many keys on the key ring it took five tries before she found the right one. In the contamination room, it didn't take long to find Miss Bianca: slips of paper with the number of the mouse and the date of the injection were attached to each cage door. 139. Miss Bianca. The poor mouse was huddled in the back of her cage, shivering. Abigail put her in her pocket.

"I'll get you one of those special pills. You'll feel better in a jiffy," Abigail promised her.

When she got back upstairs, Mother and Dr. Kiel were inside his office. He was talking to her in a worried voice. Elena and Bob were in the lab. Abigail got the bottle of pills from the cabinet. The bottle said four a day for ten days for adults, but Miss Bianca was so tiny, maybe one tablet cut into four? Abigail took ten of them and put the bottle away just as Mother came out.

While Mother was preparing dinner, Abigail made a nest for Miss Bianca in a shoe box lined with one of her T-shirts. She took a knife from the drawer in the dining room to poke air holes into the box, then used it to cut the pills into four pieces. They were hard to handle and kept slipping away from the knife. When she finally had them cut up, she couldn't get Miss Bianca to take one. She just lay in the shoe box, not lifting her head.

"You have to take it or you'll die," Abigail told her, but Miss Bianca didn't seem to care.

Abigail finally pried open the mouse's little mouth and shoved the piece of pill in. Miss Bianca gave a sharp squeak, but she swallowed the pill.

"That's a good girl," Abigail said.

Over dinner, Abigail asked her mother who the man in the suit had been. "He was with Bob in the animal room," she said. "Is he spying on the animals?"

Rhonda shook her head. "He's an FBI agent named Mr. Burroughs. Someone sent an anonymous letter telling the FBI to look at Dr. Kiel's lab."

"Because Elena is a Communist spy?" Abigail said.

"Don't say things like that, Abigail. Especially not to Agent Burroughs. Elena is not a spy, and if Dr. Dolan would only—" She bit her lip, not wanting to gossip about Dolan with her daughter.

"But she did give Dr. Kiel a potion," Abigail persisted.

"Whatever you saw was none of your business!" Rhonda said. "Clear the table and put the dishes in the machine."

If Mother was angry, she was less likely to notice what Abigail was doing. While Mother watched *It Takes a Thief,* Abigail cleaned up the kitchen, then brought a saucer from her doll's tea set into the kitchen and put some peanut butter in it. Before she went to bed, she stuck some peanut butter onto another piece of the pill and got Miss Bianca to swallow it. When she brushed her teeth, she filled one of her doll's teacups with water. The mouse didn't want to drink, so Abigail brought in a wet washcloth and stuck it in Miss Bianca's mouth.

She quickly shoved the shoe box under her bed when she heard Mother coming down the hall to tuck her in for the night.

ABIGAIL DIDN'T SLEEP well. She worried what would happen when Dr. Kiel discovered that Miss Bianca was missing from the lab: she should have taken all the mice, she realized. Then the FBI might think it had been a Communist, stealing their secret mice. What would happen, too, when Mother realized one of Abigail's T-shirts was missing?

In the morning, she was awake before Mother. She gave Miss Bianca another piece of pill in peanut butter. The mouse was looking better: she took the pill in her little paws and licked the peanut butter from it, then nibbled the tablet. Abigail took her into the bathroom with her and Miss Bianca sipped water from the tap in the sink.

All this was good, but it didn't stop Abigail feeling sick to her stomach when she thought about how angry Dr. Kiel would be. Mother would lose her job, she would never forgive Abigail. She put the mouse on her shoulder and rubbed her face against its soft fur. "Can you help me, Miss Bianca? Can you summon the Prisoners Aid society now that I've saved your life?"

The doorbell rang just then, a loud shrill sound that frightened both girl and mouse. Miss Bianca skittered down inside Abigail's pajama top, trying to hide. By the time Abigail was able to extricate the mouse, she was covered in scratches. If Mother saw them—

The doorbell rang again. Mother was getting up. Abigail ran back to her bedroom and put Miss Bianca into the shoe box. She peeped out of her room. Mother was tying a dressing gown around her waist, opening the front door. Dr. Kiel was standing there, the vein in his forehead throbbing.

"Did you do this?" he demanded, shaking a newspaper in Mother's face.

Mother backed up. "Dr. Kiel! What are you—I just got up—Abigail! Put some clothes on."

Abigail had forgotten to button her pajama top. She slipped back into her room, her heart pounding. Dr. Kiel had come to fire Mother. Her teeth were chattering, even though it was a warm fall day.

She flattened herself against the wall and waited for Dr. Kiel to demand that Mother turn her daughter over to the police. Instead, Mother was looking at the newspaper in bewilderment.

"'Reds in the Lab'? What is this about, Dr. Kiel?"

"You didn't tell the paper that the FBI was in the lab yesterday?" he demanded.

"Of course not. Really, Dr. Kiel, you should know you can trust me."

He slapped the paper against his hand so hard that it sounded like the crack of a ball against a bat. "If Bob Pharris did it—"

"Dr. Kiel, I'm sure none of your students would have called the newspaper with a report like this. Perhaps—" She hesitated. "I don't like to say this, it's not really my place, but you know Dr. Dolan has been concerned about Elena Mirova."

Dr. Kiel had been looking calmer, but now his jaw clenched again. "Elena is a refugee from communism. She came here because I thought she could be safe here. I will not let her be hounded by a witch hunt."

"The trouble is, we don't know anything about her," Mother said. "She knows a great deal about your work, more than seems possible for a dishwasher, even one whose husband was a scientist."

Dr. Kiel snarled. "Patrick Dolan has been sharpening his sword, hoping to stick it into me, since the day he arrived here. He's not concerned about Communist spies, he's studying the best way to make me look bad."

He looked down the hall and seemed to see Abigail for the first time. "Get dressed, Abigail; I'll give you a ride to school."

Dr. Kiel drove a convertible. Susie Campbell would faint with envy when she saw Abigail in the car. When she started to dress, Abigail realized her arms were covered with welts from where Miss Bianca had scratched her. She found a long-sleeved blouse to wear with her red skirt. By the time she had combed her hair and double-checked that Miss Bianca had water, Mother was dressed. Dr. Kiel was calmly drinking a cup of coffee.

Abigail looked at the newspaper.

The FBI paid a surprise visit to the University of Kansas campus yesterday, in response to a report that the Bacteriology Department is harboring Communists among its lab support staff. Several members of the department work on microorganisms that could be used in germ warfare. The research is supposed to be closely monitored, but recently, there's been a concern that a Communist agent has infiltrated the department.

The newspaper and the FBI both thought Elena was a spy. Maybe she was, maybe she really had given Dr. Kiel a magic potion that blinded his eyes to who she really was.

"Rhonda, we're going to have every reporter in America calling about this business. Better get your makeup on and prepare to do battle," Dr. Kiel said, getting up from the table. "Come on, Abigail. Get to school. You have to learn as much as you can so that morons like this bozo Burroughs from the FBI can't pull the wool over your eyes."

Abigail spent a very nervous day, frightened about what would happen when she got to the lab and Bob Pharris accused her of stealing Miss Bianca. She kept hoping she'd get sick. At recess, she fell down on the playground, but she only skinned her knees; the school nurse wouldn't let her go home for such a trivial accident.

She walked from school to the Bacteriology Department as slowly as possible. Even so, she arrived too soon. She lingered at the elevator, wondering if she should just go to Dr. Kiel and confess. Bob Pharris stuck his head out of the lab.

"Oh, it's just you, short stuff. We've been under siege all day— your mom is answering two phones at once—someone even called from the BBC in London. A guy tried to get into the animal room this morning—I threw him out with my own bare hands, and for once Dr. Kiel thinks I'm worth something." He grinned. "Number Nineteen cannot get a PhD, but he has a future as a bouncer."

Abigail tried to smile, but she was afraid his next comment would be that he'd seen that Number 139 was missing and would Abigail hand her over at once.

"Don't worry, Abby, this will blow over," Bob said, going back into the lab.

Dr. Kiel was shouting; his voice was coming up the hall from Dr. Dolan's lab. She crept down the hall and peeked inside. Agent Burroughs, the bozo from the FBI, was there with Dr. Kiel and Dr. Dolan.

"What did you do with her?" Dr. Dolan said. "Give her a ticket back to Russia along with your mouse?"

Abigail's heart thudded painfully.

"The Bureau just wants to talk to her," Agent Burroughs. "Where did she go?"

"Ask Dolan," Dr. Kiel said. "He's the one who sees Reds under the bed. He probably stabbed her with a pipette and threw her into the Kansas River."

Agent Burroughs said, "If you're hiding a Communist, Dr. Kiel, you could be in serious trouble."

"What is this, Joe McCarthy all over again?" Dr. Kiel said. "Guilt by association? Elena Mirova fled Czechoslovakia because her husband was imprisoned. As long as she was in Bratislava, they could torture him with the threat that they could hurt his wife. She was hiding here to protect her husband. Your jackbooted feet have now put both her and his lives in danger."

"There was no Elena Mirova in Czechoslovakia," Burroughs said. "There are no Czech scientists named Mirov or Mirova."

"What? You know the names and locations of everyone in Czechoslovakia, Burroughs?" Dr. Kiel snapped. "How did you get that from the comfort of your armchair in Washington?"

"The head of our Eastern Europe bureau looked into it," Burroughs said. "The Bratislava institute is missing one of their scientists, a biological warfare expert named Magdalena Spirova; she disappeared six weeks ago. Do you know anything about her?"

"I'm not like you, Burroughs, keeping track of everyone behind the Iron Curtain," Dr. Kiel said. "I'm just a simple Kansas researcher, trying to find a cure for Q Fever. If you'd go back to the rat hole you crawled out of, I could get back to work."

"Your dishwasher is gone, whatever her name is, and one of your infected mice is gone," Burroughs said. "I'm betting Mirova-Spirova is taking your germ back to Uncle Ivan, and the next thing we know, every soldier we have below the DMZ will be infected with Q Fever."

Abigail's book bag slipped out of her hand and landed on the floor with a horrible noise, an earth-ending noise. The men looked over at her.

Dr. Kiel said, "What's up, Abigail? You think you can be David to all us angry Sauls? Play a little Bach and calm us down?"

Abigail didn't know what he was talking about, just saw that he wasn't angry with her for standing there. "I'm sorry, Dr. Kiel, I was worried about the mouse."

"Abigail is the youngest member of my team," Dr. Kiel told Burroughs. "She looks after our healthy animals."

The FBI man rounded on Abigail, firing questions at her: Had she noticed Elena hanging around the contamination room? How hard was it to get into the room? How often did Abigail feed the mice? When did she notice one of the mice was missing?

"Leave her alone," Dr. Kiel said. "Abigail, take your violin down and play for the mice. We have a lab full of Fascists today who could infect you with something worse than Q Fever, namely innuendo and smear tactics."

"You signed a loyalty oath, Dr. Kiel," Agent Burroughs said.

"Calling me names makes me wonder whether you really are a loyal American."

Dr. Kiel looked so murderous that Abigail fled down to the animal room with her violin and her book bag. She felt guilty about taking Miss Bianca, she felt guilty about not rescuing the other mice, she was worried about Miss Bianca alone at home not getting all the pills she needed. She was so miserable that she lay on the floor of the animal room and cried.

Crying wore her out. Her head was aching, and she didn't think she had the energy to get to her feet. The floor was cool against her hot head and the smells of the animals and the disinfectants were so familiar that they calmed her down.

A noise at the contamination room door woke her. A strange man, wearing a brown suit that didn't fit him very well, was trying to undo the lock. He must be a reporter trying to sneak into the lab. Abigail sat up. Her head was still aching, but she needed to find Bob.

The man heard her when she got to her feet. He spun around, looking scared, then, when he saw that it was a child, he smiled in a way that frightened Abigail.

"So, Dr. Kiel has little girls working with his animals. Does he give you a key to this room?"

Abigail edged toward the door. "I only feed the healthy mice. You have to see Bob Pharris for the sick mice."

As soon as she'd spoken, Abigail wished she hadn't; what if this man wrote it up in his newspaper and Bob got in trouble?

"There aren't any foreigners working with the animals? Foreign women?"

Even though Abigail was scared that Elena was a Communist spy, she didn't feel right about saying so, especially after hearing Dr. Kiel talking about witch hunts.

"We only have foreign witches in the lab," she said. "They concoct magic potions to make Dr. Kiel fall in love with them."

The man frowned in an angry way, but he decided to laugh instead, showing a gold tooth in the front of his mouth. "You're a little girl with a big imagination, aren't you? Who is this foreign witch?"

Abigail hated being called a little girl. "I don't know. She flew in on her broomstick and didn't tell us her name."

"You're too old for such childish games," the man said, bending over her. "What is her name, and what does she do with the animals?"

"Mamelouk. Her name is Mamelouk."

The man grabbed her arm. "You know that isn't her name."

Bob came into the animal room just then. "Abby—Dr. Kiel said he'd sent you—what the hell are you doing here? I thought I told you this morning that you can't come into the lab without Dr. Kiel's say-so and I know damned well he didn't say so. Get out before I call the cops."

Bob looked almost as fierce as Dr. Kiel. The man in the brown suit let go of Abigail's arm.

He stopped in the doorway and said, "I'm only looking for the foreign woman who's been working here. Magdalena, isn't it?"

Abigail started to say, "No, it's—" But Bob frowned at her, and she was quiet.

"I *thought* you knew, little girl. What is it?"

"Mamelouk," Abigail said. "I told you that before."

"So now you know, Buster. Off you go."

Bob walked to the elevator with Abigail and called the car. He stood with a foot in the door until the man got on the elevator. They watched the numbers go down to "1" to make sure he'd ridden all the way to the ground.

"Maybe I should go down and throw him out of the building," Bob said. "He was here when I opened for the day. Elena took one look at him and disappeared, so I don't know if he's someone who's been harassing her at home or if she's allergic to reporters."

He looked down at Abigail. "You feeling okay, short stuff? You're looking kind of white—all the drama getting to you, huh? Maybe Dr. Kiel will let your mom take you home. She didn't even break for lunch today."

When they got to the office, Bob went in to tell Dr. Kiel about the man in the animal room, but Rhonda took one look at Abigail and hung up the phone midsentence.

"Darling, you're burning up," she announced, feeling Abigail's forehead. "I hope you haven't caught Q Fever."

She went into Dr. Kiel's office. He came out to look at Abigail, felt her forehead as Rhonda had, and agreed. "Better get a doctor to see her, but I can give you some tetracycline to take home with you."

Rhonda shook her head. "Thank you, Dr. Kiel, but I'd better let the pediatrician prescribe for her."

Mother collected her book bag and violin where Abigail had dropped them on the floor of the animal room. "I never should have let you work with the animals. I worried all along that it wasn't safe."

In the night, Abigail's fever rose. She was shivering, her joints ached. She knew she had Q Fever, but if she told Mother, Mother wouldn't let her stay with Miss Bianca.

Mother put cold washcloths on her head. While she was out of the room, Abigail crawled under the bed and got the mouse. Miss Bianca needed more of her pills, but Abigail was too sick to feed her. She put Miss Bianca in her pajama pocket and hoped she wouldn't make the mouse sick again.

Mother came and went, Abigail's fever rose, the doorbell rang.

"What are you doing here? I thought it would be the doctor! Abigail is very sick."

"I sorry, Rhonda," Abigail heard Elena say. "Men is watching flat, I not know how I do."

She was a terrible spy; she couldn't speak English well enough to fool anyone.

"You can't stay here!" Rhonda said. "Dr. Kiel—the FBI—"

"Also KGB," Elena said. "They wanting me. They find me now with news story."

"The KGB?"

"Russian secret police. I see man in morning, know he is KGB, wanting me, finding me from news."

"But why do the KGB want you?"

Elena smiled sadly. "I am—oh, what is word? Person against own country."

"Traitor," Rhonda said. "You are a traitor? But—Dr. Kiel said you had to hide from the Communists."

"Yes, is true, I hiding. They take my husband, they put him in prison, they torture him for what? For what he write in books. He write for freedom, for liberty, for those words he is enemy of state. Me, I am scientist, name Magdalena Spirova. I make same disease that Dr. Kiel make. Almost same, different in small ways.

Russians want my *Rickettsia prowazekii* for germ wars, I make, no problem. Until they put my husband in prison."

Rhonda took Elena out of the doorway into the front room. For a few minutes, Abigail forgot how sick she felt, how much every bone in her body ached with fever. She slid out of bed and went into the hall, where she could hear Elena's story.

When Elena learned that her husband was being tortured, she pretended not to care. She waited until she could take a trip to Yugoslavia. She injected herself with the *Rickettsia* she was working on right before she left for the airport.

In Sarajevo, Elena ran away from the secret police who were watching her and hitchhiked to Vienna. From Vienna, she flew to Canada. In Toronto, she called Dr. Kiel, whom she had met when he came to Bratislava in 1966. He drove up to Toronto and hid her in the back seat of his car to smuggle her to Kansas. He gave her tetracycline tablets, but she didn't take them until she had extracted her infected blood to give to Dr. Kiel. That was the magic potion Abigail had seen in the animal room; that was why her arm was all bruised—it's not easy to take a blood sample from your own veins.

"Now, Dr. Kiel have *Rickettsia prowazekii,* he maybe find vaccine, so biological war not useful."

The words faded in and out. Miss Bianca had a bad Russian germ, now Abigail had it, maybe she would die for thinking Elena-Magdalena was a Communist spy.

The front door opened again. Abigail saw the brown suit. "Look out," she tried to say, but her teeth were chattering too hard. No words would come out.

The brown legs came down the hall. "Yes, little girl. You are exactly who I want."

He put an arm around her and dragged her to her feet. Mother had heard the door; she ran into the hall and screamed when she saw the brown suit with Abigail. She rushed toward him, but he waved an arm at her and she stopped: he was holding a gun.

He shouted some words in a language that Abigail didn't understand, but Elena-Magdalena came into the hall.

"I am telling Dr. Spirova that I will shoot you and shoot the little girl unless she comes with me now," the man said to Rhonda. His voice was calm, as if he was reading a book out loud.

"Yes, you putting little girl down." Elena's voice sounded as though her mouth were full of chalk. "I go with you. I see, this is end of story."

Elena walked slowly toward him. The man grinned and tightened his grip on Abigail. It took Rhonda and Elena a moment to realize he was going to keep Abigail, perhaps use her as a hostage to get safe passage out of Kansas. Rhonda darted forward, but Elena shoved her to the ground and seized the man's arm.

He fired the gun and Elena fell, bleeding, but he had to ease his chokehold on Abigail.

"Miss Bianca, save us!" Abigail screamed.

She dropped the mouse down the man's shirtfront. Miss Bianca skittered inside in terror. The man began flailing his arms, slapping at his chest, then his armpits, as the mouse frantically tried to escape. He howled in pain: Miss Bianca had bitten him. He managed to reach inside his shirt for the mouse, but by then, Rhonda had snatched the gun from him. She ran to the front door and started shouting for help.

Abigail, her face burning with fever, fought to get the mouse out of his hand. Finally, in despair, Abigail bit his hand. The man punched her head, but she was able to catch Miss Bianca as the mouse fell from his open fist.

The police came. They took away the KGB man. An ambulance came and took Elena to the hospital. The pediatrician came; Abigail had a high fever, she shouldn't be out of bed, she shouldn't be keeping mice in dirty boxes under her bed, he told Rhonda sternly, but Abigail became hysterical when he tried to take Miss Bianca away, so he merely lectured Rhonda on her poor parenting decisions. He gave Abigail a shot and said she needed to stay in bed, drink lots of juice, and stay away from dirty animals.

The next morning, Dr. Kiel arrived with a large bouquet of flowers for Abigail. Rhonda made Abigail confess everything to Dr. Kiel, how she had stolen Miss Bianca, how she had stolen tetracycline out of his office. Abigail was afraid he would be furious, but the vein in his forehead didn't move. Instead, he smiled, his brown eyes soft and even rather loving.

"You cured the mouse with quarters of tetracycline tablets dipped in peanut butter, hmm?" He asked to see the pieces Abigail had cut up. "I think we're going to have to promote you from feeding animals to being a full-fledged member of the research team."

A FEW MONTHS later, Dr. Dolan left Kansas to teach in Oklahoma. A few years later, Bob Pharris got his PhD. He was a good and kind teacher, even if he never had much success as a researcher. Magdalena Spirova recovered from her bullet wound and was given a job at the National Institutes of Health in Washington, where she worked until the fall of the Iron Curtain meant her husband could be released from prison.

Miss Bianca stayed with Abigail, living to the ripe old age of three. Although Rhonda continued to work for Dr. Kiel, she wouldn't let Abigail back in the animal lab. Even so, Abigail grew up to be a doctor working for Physicians for Social Responsibility, trying to put an end to torture. As for the five lumpy Kiel children, one of them grew up to write about a Chicago private eye named V.I. Warshawski.

Note

When Jeffery Deaver and Raymond Benson asked me to contribute a story for *Ice Cold: Tales of Intrigue from the Cold War* (Grand Central Press, 2014), I knew at once that I wanted to tell this story—not the story of Abigail and the white mouse, Miss Bianca, but the story of my father's efforts to bring a sample of a microorganism the Soviets were trying to use in germ warfare to his Kansas lab. He actually did what Elena does in the story: when he was invited to an international conference on *Rickettsiae* in Czechoslovakia in 1966, he somehow got hold of a sample of the Soviet organism and persuaded a Czech lab tech to inject it into him. He got off the plane in Kansas City with a raging fever but refused to start antibiotics until his lab tech took a blood sample from him. This story grew into *Fallout*, my 2017 V.I. Warshawski novel. I couldn't work in Abigail, and Dr. Kiel morphed into a much less attractive man, for which I'm sad.

IS IT JUSTICE?

I

I hit the street, arms over my head, when I heard the report. Thunder may sound like a gunshot, but a rifle never sounds like anything else: you know a weapon has been fired.

People were screaming. It was impossible to tell where the shot had come from, or if anyone had been hit, but the thicket of cameras that had sprouted outside the courthouse, waiting for the verdict in *Illinois v. Cordell Breen,* was trained on the stairs in front of the entrance. A crowd gathered behind them.

Twenty-Sixth and California is lousy with cops and sheriff's deputies; they were already swarming, outfitted with riot helmets and assault weapons.

A car honked furiously, rubber squealing as it missed me by an inch. That was when I realized I had dropped for cover in the middle of the street. The driver stuck his head out the window to swear at me.

"You'd better get out of here before the road is blocked off," I said, getting to my feet, but my advice came too late: squad cars, their goose horns honking, were covering all the intersections near the courthouse and jails. They also were blocking the exit to the parking garage across from the courts. I was going to be here for a while, so I went back to the west side of the street, where the cameras and cops and everyone else was jammed.

The police were clearing a path for an ambulance crew; I followed the stretcher bearers to the TV cameras. Murray Ryerson had persuaded Global Entertainment to let him cover the trial. He's six-four, with red hair, easy to spot. I used the bruising elbows I'd perfected as a child with my hockey-playing cousin to force people out of my way.

"What happened?" I asked.

Murray glanced at me but kept speaking into his microphone. "Just moments after the jury declared him 'not guilty' on all but one of twenty-seven counts of a criminal indictment, Cordell Breen has crumpled on the stairs in front of the Cook County Criminal Courts, apparent victim of a gunshot. An ambulance crew is on the scene, and we'll keep you updated as events unfold.

"Meanwhile, here with me is Chicago investigator V.I. Warshawski, who played a major role in getting the state to bring charges against Breen. She was also a key witness for the state. Vic, what were your thoughts when the jury brought in their 'not-guilty' verdicts?"

My thoughts had included fury at the outcome, followed by how much I disliked watching Richard Yarborough in victory. I had wanted to flee the courtroom, but I was wedged into the middle of one of the benches and couldn't get out. I fumed while my ex-husband turned a dazzling smile on Cordell Breen. He clasped Breen's forearm with one hand and put the other around his client's shoulder. While he man-braced Breen, Dick scanned the courtroom, nodding at journalists, but really looking for me, wanting to gloat in person.

He released Breen and walked through the swinging gates to the benches. He had to lean across several people, hitting them with his jacket, but he ignored their protests: What were the spectators ever going to do for him?

"Vic, you know how much respect I have for you. You did a heck of a job." His smile managed to combine pity with arrogance.

Dick hadn't been the lead on the defense—he doesn't do criminal law—but as a senior partner at Crawford, Mead, he showed up most days. After all, Breen was one of the firm's most important—i.e., richest—clients, and he was on trial for counts ranging from criminal fraud to accessory to murder.

My final thought on hearing the verdict: if I'd stayed married to Richard Yarborough I'd be in the Logan Correctional Center for Women right now, serving natural life for murder. I didn't say any of this with a live mike under my nose.

"I thought the state's attorney brought the case in well," I said to Murray. "It's always disappointing when you have rock-solid evidence and the jury votes against you, but of course the jury system is the bedrock of our democracy."

"Someone didn't agree," Murray said. "Cordell Breen was shot as he stood on the top step, straightening his necktie."

"You don't know that he was the target," I objected. "There are a lot of guns around here. You have angry husbands, betrayed wives, and a whole freight car full of drug dealers. Breen could have been hit by accident."

Murray narrowed his eyes at me but didn't say anything: he was listening to a voice inside his earpiece. "The Chicago Fire Department is taking Cordell Breen to Stroger Hospital, where the city's top trauma surgeons will be waiting. This is Murray Ryerson, live at the Cook County Criminal Courthouse." He switched off his mike and glared at me. "Are you running for office, Warshawski? 'The jury system is the bedrock of our democracy'?"

"I hope you don't disagree, Murray—you'd have to go back to Miss Motley's remedial civics class."

"And that clap-doodle about the state's attorney bringing the case in well—by the end of the third day, I was prepared to think someone had paid her to look as ineffectual as possible," Murray said.

The same thought had crossed my mind, as Sonia de Winter fumbled her cross-examination of one of the defense's key witnesses from Breen's R&D department. She'd been equally uncertain when she interrogated Breen's estranged wife, Constance, who was testifying on our side.

I certainly wasn't going to say as much to Murray Ryerson, though, even with the mike turned off. Time was when I could trust him with my private thoughts on the criminal justice system, but those days had disappeared along with his job at the *Herald-Star*. Now, as he scrambled for face time on cable news, he was willing to say almost anything. In fact, the wilder the statement the better—that helped him go viral on YouTube.

"I don't suppose you shot Breen yourself, did you?" Murray asked hopefully.

"Don't you need to get over to the hospital?" I asked. "You wouldn't want Fox or ABC to scoop you with word about Breen's condition."

His crew had the same concern; I could hear someone's voice coming scratchily from his earpiece. His camerawoman was tapping his arm impatiently.

"Cops are letting news crews out, but they're inspecting everyone's equipment, so we need to get going," the camerawoman said.

I tagged along behind them. It would be hours before I'd be able to get my own car out of the parking garage. The whole area was under tight security by now. The cops waved us into the Global Entertainment van, giving our bags a cursory check for weapons.

As we nosed around the police cordon, we heard a loudspeaker announcement from the CTA: the California Avenue bus was being rerouted to Western, half a mile to the east. People who'd spent a long day in court to support a loved one were trudging along the side street, faces bleak. Some were towing small children, who whimpered at the long walk. One woman, with a corona of unkempt white hair, was slowly pushing a walker with the bowed face of someone long inured to hardship. I suggested to Murray that we give her a lift—it would be a good human-interest story—but he wanted to get to the hospital along with the rest of the rat pack.

2

What do you know about this?" Richard Yarborough was in my office, whining and petulant. I can't say I liked his whiny petulant persona, but it was a lot easier to take than his gloating.

He'd called as I was packing up my office for the day. He tried to order me to visit him at Crawford, Mead's offices near the river, but I refused, on the simple grounds that I didn't want to talk to him; if he was desperate to see me, he could slum it in my Humboldt Park warehouse.

"As for what I know, Cordell Breen was killed by a single bullet that went through the middle of his face at four-seventeen yesterday afternoon. I learned it from reading the paper this morning. You probably know more, being the guy's counsel and privy to all his secrets."

Breen had been dead when the ambulance picked him up. They'd taken him to the hospital for tactical, not medical reasons. The police hadn't found the murder weapon, but the bullet had come from a hunting rifle, not an assault weapon.

Dick's nostrils twitched. "I wouldn't put it past you to have done it yourself, just because you hate to lose."

I let silence build for a moment. "Dick, that had better be a joke."

He flushed, but muttered, "You always bring out the worst in me."

"You slandered me because I made you do it? That's the most feeble apology I've ever heard. If you came here to accuse me of murder, you'd better go right now, or believe me, you will leave here on a stretcher yourself."

"It's true, though," he insisted. "You can't stand losing."

"Whereas you embrace it? Come on, Dick. You know we couldn't stay in the same room together when we were studying for the same test back in law school. Why did you really want to see me so urgently?"

"Breen dying like that, just at the moment we cleared his name—who besides you could have such a grudge against him, or against us for that matter?"

"Breen's wife. Your team made her look like a bitter drunken has-been. Martin Binder—your client murdered his grandmother—"

"Breen was found not guilty," Dick interrupted me hotly.

"Oh, please, Dick. Your client's henchman and a bent sheriff's deputy murdered Kitty Binder on Cordell's orders. Ditto Julius Dzornen. Ditto Derrick Schlafly, not that he's any loss to society. Ditto for Bowser—"

"Bowser?" Dick said.

"Schlafly's dog," I said. "And then, you have all of Breen's shareholders, furious with Cordell for ruining their investment. When he was indicted, the stock tanked. It did not show any bounce when the verdict came in: the market thinks your guy was guilty and the shareholders are a peevish and embittered bunch."

"So you think Martin Binder killed Cordell?"

I got up. "Leave, Dick. You are an insane person this afternoon and I don't have the patience for it."

"I'm not leaving until you answer my questions."

"You don't have questions. You have offensive accusations. First me, then Martin? Why do you need to pin the murder on anyone?"

He pursed his lips, pushed his cuff back to look at his watch. He was trying to figure out what excuse I would buy.

"My partners are concerned," he said. "They know you have special contacts with the police and the media."

"You want me to call Murray Ryerson and tell him Crawford, Mead's partners are concerned, so please release your private video foot—oh." I interrupted myself. "You're billing Breen's company, not Breen as a private individual. And the board is balking at the bill. Must run to about six million, doesn't it?"

"We could be tied up in litigation for years," Dick said plaintively.

"My heartstrings are truly tugged, but I will not confess to a murder I didn't commit just to clear your profit center for the year. Go home to Terri, let her tell you what a handsome hero you are and what a bitch I am."

He glared again. "I'm sorry I misspoke. My partners are hoping you know something."

"I'm not working for you, Dick. You know that would be a total disaster."

"We'd pay a good five figures for any information you have," he said.

"You're way too used to having your own way. Even a good six or seven figures wouldn't tempt me. I really do not care who killed Cordell Breen. The police will jump through hoops for you; that has to be enough, even for your vanity."

3

It was true: I didn't care who killed Breen. His father had been with the U.S. Army of Occupation in Europe after World War II where Breen, senior, had stolen a patent from a Holocaust victim. He'd used it to build an electronics empire in the 1950s and 1960s.

The victim, a physics virtuoso named Martina, had managed to slip her design into a collection of papers that survived the war. Martina's great-grandson Martin Binder inherited her gifts. When he stumbled on Martina's papers and found her design—created in hellish conditions during the Second World War—Martin tried to talk to Cordell Breen about his great-grandmother's work. Cordell Breen knew his father had stolen the design from Martina; he thought it was a good joke, because he believed his family was entitled to whatever came their way.

Cordell pulled out all the stops, including murdering Martin's family, to protect the Breen fortune, but Martin had managed to flee. I had spent much of the previous fall looking for him—and ducking a lot of Cordell's bullets in the process.

It had been one of the hardest jobs of my professional life to persuade the state's attorney to bring charges against Cordell. If his wife hadn't decided to testify against him, we might never have gotten as far as the courtroom. I don't believe in vigilante justice, really, I don't, but I wasn't going to lose sleep over Cordell Breen's death.

His murder was certainly a nine-day wonder, not just in Chicago but internationally, given that Breen had headed one of the world's largest electronics companies, but my own work was keeping me busy. When the murder receded from the front pages, I stopped thinking about it.

That changed the afternoon Alison Breen came into my office. She was Breen's daughter, distressed at finding out what her father had done, distressed at seeing her parents' marriage unravel under the relentless light of the cable news cameras. When I first met her, she'd had the assurance and good looks that wealth and a quality education provide. Today, though, her chestnut hair had lost its glossy sheen, her nails were bitten down to the quicks, and her eyes were red rimmed and puffy from lack of sleep.

"Vic, please, you have to help me."

I ushered her into the armchair in the alcove I've created for client meetings. "What's the problem?" Besides her father getting murdered, her mother testifying against him in court, what else could be wrong?

"I think—the police have been acting really weird—they're talking like—" She kept interrupting herself, and then stopped altogether.

"Like what?"

"Mother came over this morning. Really, like three in the morning. She was—she'd been drinking, she wasn't herself—but this one detective, the way he's talking, she's afraid they think *she* killed Daddy."

I shut my eyes, trying to remember the courtroom at the moment the verdict came in. "She was there, wasn't she? And her friend, that woman—what's her name?"

"Leila. Leila Mitchum. I really can't stand her. She's always talking like some dreary political slogan, how Mother is an archetype of the oppressed woman, how Daddy tried to buy her and then broke her spirit, all this stuff that is just stupid and horrible to listen to. And then she likes to go drinking with Mother, which I hate even worse. But, yeah, Leila and Mother were there when the verdict came in."

"Does your mother know how to shoot?"

"We all do," Alison said. "Mother grew up with guns, and she and Daddy used to go target shooting, back—well, before—before everything turned crazy. Daddy felt, since we were kidnapping risks, we should know some basics of self-protection, so Mother and I took kung fu together when I was in high school."

"Aside from the fact that your father's lawyers made your mother look bad on the witness stand, does she have any reason to have shot your dad?"

"Vic! I came to you for help, not for you to build a case against her."

"I can't do anything to help until I understand why the police suspect her. Didn't your father try to strip her assets?"

"He tried to take away her voting shares in the company," Alison whispered. "We were having a big argument about that while the trial was going on. He was so angry that she was testifying against him. It was horrible in court. Daddy sort of apologized to me, but he was in a red rage, you know, and he kept telling me it was my fault for trying to fight him when he only wanted what was best for me and for the company."

Her puffy eyes filled with tears. Alison had been subpoenaed by the state, which treated her gently. My ex-husband's team had been less forgiving. If they'd painted her mother as an embittered drunk, they tried to make Alison look like a greedy young woman grasping for control of a fifty-billion-dollar business.

"Anyway, Daddy's lawyers were trying to tie up her shares, but I don't think they've been able to. Mother gave up the Lake Bluff house as part of their divorce, not that it had become final before—" Her mouth worked. "Last week, you know, when Daddy— but, anyway, Mother gave up the house."

"Who inherits it?"

Alison shook her head. "I don't know. Mother, if she hadn't signed anything. Or me, I guess."

I could see why the cops were interested in Constance Breen. She hadn't seemed like the kind of person who wanted to be involved in a bitter fight over assets, but perhaps her husband's attitude drove her into a more vindictive position. Or perhaps her friend Leila pushed her there.

"I'm sorry to talk to you about it clinically, Alison, but the shot that killed your father—that took a really skilled marksman. Is your mother that good a shot?"

"I don't know. I don't know!" she cried. "I thought I knew my father, but it turned out he was like some kind of monster, killing people who got in his way. So how can I say what I know about my mother?"

"Is that what you want me to do? Find out what your mother is really like?"

"If she turns out to be just as monstrous"—Alison tore at her cuticles, her voice a hoarse whisper—"how can I know what I might be like? Maybe I'm just as able to switch from nice girl to killer."

"Alison, you're true blue and disaster isn't going to change that," I said, "but I'll find out what I can."

4

Bobby Mallory is a police captain, with a secretary and a couple of sergeants at his beck and call, but in his rookie year, he was partnered with my dad. The two remained close until my father's death: my Jewish mother was godmother to Bobby's eldest Catholic daughter; Bobby was one of Gabriella's and then Tony's pallbearers.

When I started as an investigator, it felt like a slap to him— Bobby didn't like to see women in nontraditional roles. He's changed with the times, though, seen women become good police officers, seen me land on my feet in tricky situations, and the affection he felt for me because of my parents has lost its angry edge. Still, my arrival in his office at police headquarters didn't make his face light up with joy.

"You must be in worse trouble than usual if you're coming to see me," he growled.

I bent down and pecked his cheek. "I'm not in trouble at all. I'm here as a very virtuous citizen giving you a heads-up. Alison Breen has hired me to find out what role, if any, her mother played in Cordell Breen's death."

"I knew the investigation could only get worse," Bobby said. "I don't suppose I could ask, plead, beg, or order you to tell Ms. Breen that we have the situation well in hand and no one will railroad her mother?"

I couldn't help laughing, but I treated the question as rhetorical. "Is Constance Breen a person of interest? Can she shoot well enough to get one shot into a man from five hundred yards away?"

"How do you know the distance?" Bobby demanded.

"I figured the shooter had to be in the parking garage; there's no place to take cover on the street, and there must be a hundred surveillance cameras on that stretch of California. Did you find the shell casing?"

"Every punk in America watches too many *NCIS* and *CSI* episodes; they all know they're supposed to pick up their shell casings after they've murdered someone. But I don't suppose it will derail the investigation if you know that the bullet came from an older hunting rifle, not from a fancy assault weapon. The shooter was either lucky or very good. It was a hell of a shot. Heck of a shot." He corrected himself hastily: he's accepted the fact that I'm a competent investigator, but not that I can listen to vulgarity and swearing without collapsing.

"And is Constance Breen that kind of shooter?" I asked.

"Hard to believe, but she won medals at the gun club she and Breen belong to. Belonged to. Of course, killing a man is different from hitting skeet, but shooting at a distance, you don't see the blood or hear the lungs groaning for air, you could imagine it was one more clay target."

"Does she have the weapon?"

"Her father did," Bobby said. "It was a Mannlicher. Forensics says an antique, probably dating to the 1920s. Kind of thing Hemingway liked to carry around Africa."

My eyes widened: Bobby had never struck me as a reader. He saw my expression and made a face. "That's what the forensics chief said, not me. You could kill a lion with it, and Constance Breen's father bagged his share."

"So Constance Breen came from money as well as marrying it?"

"Her family was old money that they lost. It's like something out of some crappy novel or movie: Cordell Breen the brash million-aire, Constance Hargreave the artistic last descendant of someone who came on the *Mayflower* or the *Pinta* or something. Breen's dough let Constance's father spend his life drinking whiskey and killing endangered animals. He died, oh, maybe ten years ago, and she got the gun collection because that was all Hargreave had to leave her."

"You got enough to make an arrest?"

Bobby scowled at a fat file on his desk. "She's a better candidate than anyone else we're looking at. Breen was playing hardball over the divorce, and he was a smart and quick and dirty fighter. Your ex, of course, was a big help in that department. You never collected any alimony, did you?"

I made a face. "We didn't have assets to parade for Global Enter-tainment's benefit. But I didn't want his alimony." I'd like to think I could have beaten Dick in court, but probably not over a divorce set-tlement. Anyway, I hadn't been able to beat him over Cordell Breen.

Bobby gave a half-smile: I guess he was entitled to a little smirking at my expense. "So Breen, or your ex, was able to shut down a lot of Constance's accounts. Of course, she still has a few million, enough to buy a stable of her own legal advisers. And the kid, if she likes her mom, can bail Constance out to any tune you want to name."

Meaning, justice may be blind, but she has an acute sense of touch: she knows when she's about to bump into the kind of influence that makes a cop's life hard.

When I got up to go, Bobby said, "You know something that will make us look in a different direction?"

"No. I know nothing. Where does Constance say she was when her husband was killed?"

"She was waiting for someone to pick her up. Potty-mouthed woman who won't leave her side. Constance can't prove it, but we can't disprove it. No witnesses except the potty-mouth, who we figure would say anything."

"You're sure Cordell was the intended target?" I asked.

Bobby's blue eyes narrowed to slits in his round face. "You *do* know something. What?"

"I really know nothing, Bobby. Just—the street's lousy with drug dealers coming to see if their homeys are ratting them out. Someone could have missed, that's all."

"Be your age, Vicki,"* Bobby said. "Someone who could nail Breen over the heads of eleven camera crews and God knows how

---

* NB: Bobby Mallory is the only person who is ever allowed to call V.I. Warshawski "Vicki." To everyone else, she's Vic, V.I., Victoria or, when they're annoyed, "Warshawski."

many flashing strobes was not missing a shot directed at a Latin King. If Breen had had a bull's-eye painted between his eyes, she couldn't have done better."

5

I called Murray from my car. "I want to see all the video footage you have of the street."

"Any particular street, oh She Who Must Be Obeyed?"

"California Avenue, the day of Breen's murder."

"The cops have already subpoenaed copies and come up dry. What do you know that they don't?"

"I've been told someone from the Cubs pitching rotation had a good enough aim to hit Breen. I don't believe it, but I want to see if any of their starters were outside the courthouse."

He was silent, thinking it over, wondering what I was hiding, but he finally agreed to show me the footage. "But I get to watch it with you. And you feed and water me."

Murray drank Holstens, five bottles. I primly sipped Black Label. Murray objected that the bag of pretzels I set on my office worktable didn't constitute food, but I told him I didn't want grease or sauce on my big computer screen.

We looked at footage for two hours, slowly, stopping sometimes for a frame-by-frame view. Murray's camerawoman had shot a lot of street footage while the crews waited for word to filter down from the jury room. Bobby was right—there was no sign of Constance Breen on the street.

The courtroom had been filled with senior staff from Breen's company as well as families of people whose death Cordell Breen had helped engineer. I watched the head of one of the software divisions come down the stairs. Neighbors of Martin's grandmother, who raised him, came to the trial. Members of the Dzornen family turned out in force—Herta, whose father had been a Nobel Prize–winning physicist, and who thought young Martin was trying to blackmail her: her father's prize had been based on Martin's great-grandmother's work, which he'd never acknowledged. Herta's children and grandchildren had flown up from Arizona, eager to protect the family name.

I saw Herta in court with her family every day of the trial: her younger brother Julius had grown up with Cordell Breen. He'd been one of the people killed in Cordell's ferocious campaign to protect his billions. The day of the verdict, she seemed to have been alone. At least, on the video footage we were watching, she came out of the courthouse alone, walking slowly with the aid of her cane, her white hair sticking out around her head like dandelion pollen. Perhaps the daughter had gone to get the car to spare her mother a longer walk.

The woman I'd seen slowly pushing a walker up California Avenue the afternoon of the shooting had also had a corona of white hair.

"What are you staring at?" Murray demanded. "Herta Dzornen? You think someone with fingers like that could aim a rifle and pull a trigger?"

"I think you missed a chance to get a human-interest story out of her when you were fleeing the scene right after the murder."

"You fled with me," Murray said.

"Yep, so I did."

We watched the cops push the camera crews back from the foot of the steps as the doors opened for Cordell Breen and his entourage. He stood at the top of the stairs in his ten-thousand-dollar custom tailoring, looking energetic, youthful, a man ready to go back to the boardroom and make new history in electronics, not like a ruthless killer in his seventies.

He exchanged some kind of joke with my ex-husband. The lawyers all laughed in a polite fakey way, and then Breen pushed them away and stood alone on the stairs for a moment, straightening the knot in his tie, looking straight at the cameras. When his face exploded, it happened almost in silence: the cameras were trying to pick up his conversation with his lawyers, and so the mikes didn't catch the bullet and the recoil. Bobby was right: no one else could possibly have been the target.

"So what did you learn?" Murray demanded.

"It's horrible to see a man die in front of your eyes. That image will stay in my head a long time."

"But who killed him?"

"The cops think it was Constance Breen, but she must have left by a side door. The deputies will do that to keep someone out of the camera range, you know."

"I know they're looking at Constance's bank accounts, and they're inspecting the little arsenal she inherited from her old man. Tiger Hargreaves, that was what they used to call him."

"'They' being all the hearty boys at his club who liked the spectacle of beaters shoving a tiger in front of a man with an arsenal."

Murray glared at me. "Why do you have to be such a frigging killjoy all the time?"

"I didn't like Cordell Breen, but that shot, the kill shot. That's hard to watch. I guess the TV crews were kind of beaters, too, weren't they, setting him up for someone with a rifle."

"That is the fucking last straw, Warshawski. I did not lose a night's sleep from covering his death, and I'm not going to have you guilt me into it now."

"I wasn't trying to," I said. "I was thinking of something else and that came out."

It wasn't much of an apology and I didn't blame Murray for stalking away in a major huff. When he'd left, I stared for a long time at the whisky in my glass. The cops were taking Constance Breen seriously as a candidate for murder. The evidence might be unsatisfactory, but people have been tried on less evidence than owning the right caliber rifle. They've been convicted on even less than that.

I swallowed the rest of the Black Label and drove over to the Gold Coast, to Herta Dzornen's building. The doorman knew me by sight and didn't like me, but when he called to announce me, Herta told him I could come up.

"The walker," I said when we were sitting in her living room. "It had that little box thing that you can sit on. That's where you put the rifle after you'd shot Breen, but where did you park the walker during the trial?"

She kneaded her hands, the gesture she and her half sister Kitty had in common. "How did you know?"

"I saw you pushing it up California, after they blocked off the street, but you came out of the courthouse just using your cane."

"They inspect everything when you go in," she said. "I knew I'd never get it past the metal detectors. I left it in the parking garage, chained to a railing with a bicycle chain up on the fifth floor. I thought it would be an omen: if someone stole it while I was in the courthouse, then Breen was intended to live. If it was still there, then, well, the opposite."

"Where did you learn to shoot?"

Herta looked at me for a long pause, then said, "My mother's father had been an officer in the German Army during the First World War. He taught my mother to shoot using his military rifle, and she taught me. It's a Mannlicher; we brought it with us when we had to flee Vienna. Even after a century, it still handles beautifully. It's Greek made, actually, not German, but the machining is perfect."

"Why?" I asked. "I didn't think you cared that much about your brother."

Her mouth worked. "I cared about him deeply. How he was before Cordell Breen destroyed him, I mean. You don't know what he was like—a sensitive joyous boy. He was passionate about science and music, and then he became a shell of himself.

"When you told me what the Breens had done, how they'd forced Julius to be part of their lies and murders, I thought my heart would break. And I thought, this one time, Cordell won't succeed, I was sure he would be found guilty, but as the trial progressed, I could see that the jury didn't like the state's attorney, or didn't trust her.

"I thought I would have one chance, that it would be too hard to find him in the open any other time than when he left the courthouse. I told my daughter I needed to hear the verdict alone, that I would be too upset to be with anyone if he were found not guilty.

"I left as soon as the foreman started saying 'not guilty.' When you're old and disabled, no one looks at you. I made it into the garage and—it was amazing to me. I hadn't been hunting since we moved to Chicago—we used to shoot when my father was at Los Alamos, my mother and sister and I used to go up into the mountains and shoot at small game, and I became very good. It was so strange, picking up the Mannlicher again, feeling it come to life. I cleaned it, found some shells, but I only needed one. And then I took it apart again, put it in the little sitting box of the walker, and became an invisible old woman again. The police were searching handbags and briefcases, but they wouldn't bother an old lady with a walker."

She blinked away tears. "Poor Julius. My poor brother."

We sat in silence for a time. She finally wiped her eyes with a lace handkerchief.

"What will you do now?" she asked.

"I am an officer of the court. I cannot commit or condone perjury, but I am also not required to repeat everything I know. However, Constance Breen is under danger of arrest for her husband's death. If you saw her, or think you saw her, get into a car and drive off before he was shot, I want you to tell this to the police. You're an old invisible woman, you say, but you also have considerable stature in this city because of your father's fame. They will listen to you."

Herta blinked at me. "And then what will you do?"

"And then—I will spend a long time wondering if I've made a terrible mistake."

I drove from Herta's apartment to the lake and watched the black water break up and refract the moonlight. It is always best to follow the law in its confining constructs. If you start thinking you're the equivalent of God, entitled to mete out justice as it suits your own interpretation, you leave a swath of destruction behind you.

I finally drove home, but I didn't sleep much that night, nor for many nights to come. Alison Breen tried to pay me when the cops told her that her mother was no longer a person of interest. I couldn't take the money. A few weeks later, there was a small paragraph in the paper, announcing Herta Dzornen's death. The story recounted her family's history in fleeing Europe, her father's prize. I can't say that brought me much comfort, either.

Note

Critical Mass (2013) was my homage to my husband and his friends' and mentors' work in their quest to find the heart of the atom. All the characters in this story were involved in the novel, but a lot of readers wrote to say they were unhappy that Cordell Breen walked away unscathed. I wrote this story as a present to these readers. "Is It Justice?" was first published in *Suspense Magazine,* December 2013.

FLASH POINT

I

He was waiting outside my office when I arrived that morning, a tall lean man with a hint of sandalwood aftershave about him. It was the smile that got to me, though, that lazy, lurking smile that says, "We both know this is a game, but it's fun to play it."

"Knock it off, Warshawski," Murray Ryerson said. "I want to know how you got involved with the Teichels."

"He had legs that wouldn't stop," I said, "and those soft bronze curls—"

"That tell us your client was a giraffe," Sal Barthele interjected. "Are you writing a zipper ripper or giving Murray deep background on the case?"

I was at her bar, the Golden Glow, with Murray, recovering from an exhausting day. I didn't feel like talking about the Teichels, but I had promised Murray an exclusive.

"It started with sex, or with me misinterpreting a question about sex," I said. "And knowing Murray, or his corporate masters, I figured men whose glinting good looks make bishops kick holes in stained-glass windows—"

"Philip Marlowe said that about a blonde. A woman," Murray objected.

"I've known a number of blond men," I said. "My ex-husband for starters. Igor Palanyuk for another. Both made me want to kick things, but the passion they inspired was about as far from lust as you can get."

"Begin at the beginning," Murray said. "And I'd like another beer."

"You're buying, remember?" I said. But I began at the beginning, a Tuesday afternoon in Minna Simms High School.

2

Have you ever, like, slept with a suspect to get information?"

A titter ran through the room and the kid turned crimson. The guidance counselor on the stage with me stiffened and glared at the youth, but I answered gravely.

"It's important to stay alert, even on dull assignments. Booze, drugs, sex, anything that might make you sleep, especially with a suspect, should always be avoided."

A snicker and some catcalls arose from the back of the room on the right. "Maybe that's how losers get a sex life, Cory," one guy yelled. "That makes this a good career for you."

"Suspect has to be trying to get in his pants, dude, what self-respecting girl wants to be there?" another clever guy chimed in.

I'd misjudged the question and the questioner. Cory turned red; he blundered along the row of kids, heading for the exit.

"Cory, I'm sorry," I said into the mike. "I assumed you were with the feral group in the back. Please don't leave."

It was too little, too late. He stumbled up the aisle and out the auditorium door.

I was taking part in a career fair at Minna Simms High School on Chicago's northwest side, describing life as a private investigator. I'd explained to the room full of slouching adolescents that solo ops were a rare breed; most investigators work for giant firms like Tintrey, which require a background in law enforcement or an advanced degree in law or criminal justice. I'd finished covering old-fashioned tailing—how to blend in with your surroundings—when Cory had stood to ask his question.

"That's a good example of the wrong way to conduct an investigation," I said to the now-silent room. "Jumping to conclusions about where a conversation is going. The more you can exhibit empathy with a witness, the more easily they'll talk to you. When you make fun of someone instead of listening to them, you lose the chance to gain information."

At the end of my hour, when students had asked about guns and data mining, and how to protect your own privacy if you were the target of an investigation yourself, I asked the guidance counselor how to find Cory.

Cory Teichel should have been in third-semester calculus, but he'd left the high school campus without saying anything to anyone. The guidance counselor who'd been chaperoning me said it was against school policy to give out an address or phone number. I left a note for Cory with her and went back to my office.

Impulse control. I should have told the kids impulse control was a good quality in an investigator. Follow hunches, take quick decisive action, but don't let the chip on your shoulder fly into your eye and blind you. In other words, I was annoyed with myself, but I had a heavy workload, and by the end of the afternoon I'd put Cory Teichel and my gaffe out of my mind.

I was forced to think about him again the next afternoon. As I was shutting down for the day, someone rang the bell to the outer door. I looked at my security camera feed and saw a young woman in leggings and a layer of tank tops and shirts, carrying a backpack almost as big as she was. Her hair was thick and fell over her eyes and cheeks, so that it wasn't possible to make out her expression.

I buzzed her in and went down the hall to meet her.

"You're the detective?" Her voice was unexpectedly deep.

I nodded.

"You're the one who made fun of Cory yesterday?"

I nodded again. "Were you at the career fair?"

"I went to the session on architecture. But I heard about you from someone at your session. It was very unfair of you to say what you did."

"You're right, at least up to a point," I agreed, "the point being that the question was pretty snarky. Did you come here to chew me out?"

She bit her lip. "Cory disappeared. No one knows where he went."

I didn't say anything.

"You need to find him."

I cocked an eyebrow at her. "Who are you, and what's your relationship to him?"

She flushed. "I'm a friend."

"Well, friend, here's the scoop. I don't know who you are, I don't know if Cory Teichel is missing, and if he is, I don't know if you have a legitimate interest in having him found."

Her flush deepened. "I see exactly how you behaved to Cory.

That's why he ran away. If this is how you treat everyone who wants help, I'm surprised you stay in business."

"Do you always leap to conclusions like a young chamois in the Caucasus?" I was exasperated. "You come in demanding that I find Cory Teichel, but for all I know, this is a scam you and he have put together to embarrass *me* for having embarrassed him. I go looking for him and he's sitting in your basement playing video games."

"Oh." She deflated. "I hadn't thought of that. If I tell you my name, will you keep it secret?"

"Keep it confidential, you mean. Yes, unless you've committed a felony."

She came into my office, scuffing her toes like a six-year-old going to the doctor. When I showed her to the alcove where I see clients, she dumped her backpack on the floor, kicked off her boots, and sat cross-legged on the couch. Under the cascade of dark hair, she still had the soft round face of childhood, but the expression in her eyes was fierce and intelligent.

After another demand that I not tell anyone she'd come to see me, she gave me her name: Erica Leahardt. She and Cory had known each other since middle school because they lived only five blocks apart. They usually rode the Peterson Avenue bus together in the mornings, but Cory hadn't been on the bus and he hadn't been in any of the classes they had together.

"And you know he's not home sick?" I asked.

"He's not answering his phone and then I went to his place, but no one was home."

I suggested different possibilities—a family emergency had

taken him out of town, for instance, or he was brooding with his earbuds in and didn't hear the bell.

"It's just Cory and his father. His mother took off when he was little, he doesn't even remember her, and he doesn't have any other family."

"Why don't you ask Mr. Teichel where Cory is?"

She made a horrified face. "I couldn't, it would be too weird."

"You don't think it would be extremely weird if I asked him? I don't work for the school, I don't have a legitimate reason to call him out of the blue to ask him about his son."

"You couldn't, like, hack into Cory's cell phone to find out where he is?"

"That's illegal, Ms. Leahardt, even if I knew how, which I don't. It wouldn't be weird for you to call your friend's father to say you need to talk to Cory about—anything. Your calculus assignment, your upcoming camping trip, whatever it is the two of you do together. You don't have to say you think he's missing, just ask the question. He'll tell you where Cory is."

"You don't know why that would be really hard for me."

I invited her to tell me, but she clammed up mulishly and finally left, with a sullen comment about my incompetence.

I took a moment to look up the two families. Mike Teichel—original name Dmitri Teichel—had come to this country from Ukraine as a teenager before the fall of the Soviet Union. If he'd married Cory's mother, there wasn't a record of it. If his own parents were still alive, I couldn't find them. He was a freelance designer of computer games who rented office space near Northwestern University's Evanston campus—he apparently taught a seminar in their computer engineering department every winter.

Erica's parents were divorced. She lived with her mother, a systems analyst at Metargon, the big electronics firm in Northbrook. Her father was in Seattle running an art gallery.

Single dad a game designer, single mom at a big electronics firm. I thought back to Cory's question about sleeping with a suspect. Had Cory Teichel been worried that Erica's mother slept with his father to wangle gaming secrets from him? Maybe he suspected Erica was sleeping with his father. Or, à la Dustin Hoffman, was Cory sleeping with Erica's mother?

The possibilities reminded me of Professor Wright's efforts to teach me the mathematics of permutations and combinations. The possibilities were all there, but the probabilities were impossible to calculate.

In the morning, I called Candace Mehr at Simms High School. She was the guidance counselor who'd shepherded me through the career fair two days ago.

"Candace, V.I. Warshawski. I've been feeling bad about the kid I embarrassed on Tuesday. Any chance I could meet with him in person, apologize, find out what was on his mind when he asked his question?"

She said she'd check with him, get back to me, but when she called an hour later, it was to say that Cory hadn't been in school for two days. "In fact, his father was just in the principal's office, trying to find out where Cory is. He hasn't been home, either. I gave him your name."

Mike Teichel called almost as soon as I'd hung up: he needed to see me at once to discuss his son.

"At once" when you have to cover four miles during Chicago's morning rush means three quarters of an hour. I had time to finish a report and reorganize my morning meetings before Teichel showed up.

He was belligerent. Like Erica Leahardt yesterday afternoon, he blamed me for Cory's disappearance. He'd heard from Candace Mehr how I'd embarrassed his son in front of the school; it was my job to find him.

"Have you talked to the police?"

"Absolutely not. If I wanted to go to the police, I wouldn't be coming to you!"

I sat back in my chair. "Mr. Teichel, your son asked an absurd, and on the surface, insulting question in front of the school. There's a myth about the world of private eyes, that they're hard-bitten lonely men who have sex with glamorous and dangerous women. When Cory asked if I ever slept with a suspect, I thought he was trying to draw a laugh from his classmates by playing into that myth. He obviously had something else on his mind. You're his father—you tell me what that was."

Teichel breathed hard through his nose, a kind of bull-in-the-ring sound. "Cory's seventeen. That's not an age where someone confides in his father," he said at last.

"Who would he confide in? His mother?"

The bull-ring snort grew more pronounced.

"Friends?" I finally asked, when it was clear the mother wasn't going to be talked about.

"He's a loner. I don't think he has friends."

"Erica Leahardt?"

"That lying little bitch?" he shouted. "Are you a friend of hers, or that mother of hers?"

"Let's see where we are so far, Mr. Teichel: you say your son is missing. You claim I'm responsible. You won't go to the police. You won't discuss his mother. You don't know who his friends are. Is Cory really missing?"

Teichel's lips were pressed in a thin angry line. "He is really missing. Now tell me how you know the Leahardt females."

I shook my head. "People tell me you're a software designer—gaming software, right?"

"So she *is* trying—"

"I can't believe you can write code if you work on untested assumptions. I won't talk about the Leahardt *women* because you're not asking a rational question about them. And unless you want to hire me to find your son and to answer some questions yourself, there's no reason for us to continue speaking."

I pulled out my phone and started returning emails, or at least pretended to. Teichel walked to the door, hesitated, walked back again.

"Very well. I wish to hire you to find Cory. But only if you are not playing some game with those Leahardt fe— With the Leahardts."

He was still making tiresome assumptions, but I let it pass. "I met Erica Leahardt briefly, once, and don't know her mother. When Ms. Leahardt told me she was worried about your son, I told her to talk to you, but she said she couldn't."

His nostrils flared again, cornered bull. "Damned right. Not since the day I found her snooping in my home computer."

I raised my brows.

"Her mother works for Metargon. They are notorious thieves of other people's work. Erica claimed she was looking for a document that Cory had created—she had come over on the pretext of a study date with my son. That was the last time she was allowed in our home."

"How did Cory feel about you banning her from the house?"

"He didn't say anything about it. He probably realized she was using him, but it didn't seem to bother him."

"Maybe it did him terrible damage for you to exclude his friend," I suggested. "She seems to like him—she came all the way down here on the bus to ask me to find him."

That didn't set well with Teichel, but he wasn't stupid, only angry and confused. After railing at me for a moment, he stopped and thought.

"I suppose. After all, it's her mother who wants my files. Berenice Leahardt could have been exploiting her daughter's interest in Cory."

I asked what proof he had that Berenice Leahardt was trying to steal his designs.

"The work I do is on the edge, where AI meets traditional gaming. Defense industries are among my clients, and anything you do for defense rouses interest around the globe. Metargon is a player, anyone who works for Metargon—"

"In other words, more assumptions, but no proof," I snapped. "Do you think your son's disappearance is connected to your work?"

He suddenly became very still, as if his entire mind had retreated to a remote place. When he spoke again, it was quietly, without bluster.

"I hope not. But—if it is—the faster you find him the better. And without police, FBI, none of them. They will care more for the software than for Cory."

I talked him through the basics—when had Teichel realized his son was missing?

He hadn't become seriously concerned until this morning—he'd been in San Francisco Tuesday, meeting with a corporate client, got home late yesterday. "I thought maybe he'd gone to bed early—I didn't land until eleven last night; his room was dark, I didn't try to wake him up. Then this morning, I saw the message from the school, that he hadn't been to his classes yesterday. He wasn't in his room, he wasn't at school. I drove there at once, of course, and they told me about you. Your humiliating him."

"Yes, we've covered that," I said. "You're sure he wouldn't be with his mother?"

He went quiet again. "Cory's mother disappeared from our lives before Cory's third birthday. She has never written, she has never been in touch, but someone told me she returned to Ukraine, to Simferopol, where we both grew up. Except that city is now in Russia, not Ukraine."

The only detail Teichel had, or at least was willing to share, was his ex-wife's name: Nina Lavrentovna. "I don't know what last name she is using now—mine, Teichel? Her birth name, Serova? Maybe she even married again. Since I never have heard from her, I don't know."

He didn't know if she'd remarried, and whether she worked, but the two had met in the States as engineering students, gravitating to each other since they were both from Crimea. "Russian and Ukrainian women work, as a rule. If she has a job, it is in electrical engineering."

I went back to the question of Cory's friends. Teichel finally dredged up the names of two kids who Cory sometimes went with to nature preserves. "He likes that kind of thing, wetlands, birds, the ecosystem. He volunteers in a prairie restoration project."

I asked if Teichel monitored his son's whereabouts. After another round of defensive hostility, he admitted that he'd put stealth software into Cory's Android, but that he hadn't been able to track him past yesterday afternoon.

"He went to the Sulzer Regional Library yesterday morning and he spent the day there. And he left his phone there. I picked it up this morning on my way to the school."

"Do you have it? Did you see who he was calling or texting?"

"No one since Tuesday afternoon." He stopped, then added reluctantly, "He texted Erica: 'The PI totally bricked me. Hope the architect was better.' I still think she was trying to use Cory to steal my secrets. Took a computer gaming class to make sense of what she saw in my office."

Bricked, as in dropped a ton of bricks on him, I supposed.

I sidestepped another argument about the Leahardt women. "What's been on Cory's mind lately? He came to my session for a reason. He wanted to know if it was okay to have sex with someone in order to get information from them. Who would he have been wanting information from?"

Teichel said he couldn't possibly know, but he only spoke after a pause and his tone was uneasy.

"You know something. You need to tell me."

"I know—that I don't know my son. Always a hard thing for a parent to admit," he said harshly. "Give me whatever paperwork you need. I need to know what's happened to Cory."

"You would be much better off with the police," I said.

"Absolutely no police," Teichel hissed.

"Or a big firm. Tintrey, Balladine, they can put a lot of resources into a search. I can't. Especially not with so little to go on."

Teichel didn't want a big firm—who knew who owned whom when you were with a multinational? He wanted someone loyal to him and his son. We finally signed a contract, me reluctantly, and demanding a $2,500 deposit, more than I usually required, but I didn't like the setup. Teichel also texted me a couple of somewhat recent photos of his son. And, very reluctantly, let me borrow Cory's Android.

When he left, I checked my police and hospital sources. No un-identified white male teens had been found in the last several days. It didn't mean Cory was still alive, but I could use it as a working assumption.

I started at the Sulzer Regional Library, since that was Cory's last known location. The reference librarian was helpful; she re-membered Cory, mostly because he was using the pay phone, unlike every other teen glued to their handhelds. She'd been on the late shift on Tuesday; she hadn't noticed him leaving, because a second wave of heavy users started pouring in around seven, after supper. She'd been swamped until almost closing, but he was definitely gone by then. She sent me to the security staff, who didn't remember him but said there hadn't been any rough busi-ness in the library that day.

"Every now and then we have kids who think the library is an extension of the schoolyard or their gang turf and start mixing it up, but nothing like that happened Tuesday," the head of the detail said after consulting his logs.

As for where the Android had been discovered, Mike Teichel had found it with his locator app: Cory had stuffed it behind the pay phone he'd been using.

I sent Teichel a text, saying that the cops could get a warrant to find out what numbers Cory had called from the pay phone, but I couldn't. *NO POLICE* came back in all caps, followed by a dozen exclamation points.

I looked at Cory's Android, at the texts he'd exchanged with Erica. His last outgoing text, about being bricked, had been in response to a query from Erica. She had sent him several dozen messages from Tuesday evening through last night. None this morning.

As I looked at the log, I saw she initiated 90 percent of their contacts. Maybe more. She was chasing him, poor puppy, and he was indifferent. Unless Mike Teichel was right and she was using Cory as a way to get into his dad's study and steal code. Maybe Cory was gay. Maybe he didn't like her.

Cory's initiating texts were messages to the guys he went hiking with, or to members of a school photography club he belonged to. His Facebook page showed seventeen friends. Despite the photography club, he had almost no pictures on the phone—a few dozen of the prairie and the wetlands, a few selfies taken there, a few with his buddies. None of Erica, nor of any other girls. Whether gay or straight, he had the kind of thin, interesting face that attracts a lot of people, male or female. However, the lack of pictures was odd, very un-teenlike.

When I called Mike Teichel, he couldn't tell me his son's sexual orientation. "I've never seen signs he was interested in anyone, boy or girl, not even Erica. If he's seeing anyone, it's very secretly."

I mentioned the puzzling lack of photos on the Android. Most teens like pictures of themselves and their friends, especially pictures of themselves and their lovers.

Teichel snorted. "I hope I raised Cory to be better than that; my family made it out of Ukraine with the clothes on our backs, not with Androids and selfies and all that self-indulgent crap."

"I'm sure it's a help to his confidence to know that," I said dryly. "He belongs to the school photography club. I'd at least expect photos he'd taken for the club."

Cory was a serious photographer, his father told me; he had two cameras, a pocket digital and a 1975 Nikon that he'd found at a flea market. As to whether he had a photo cache online, Mike couldn't say. If he did, he'd probably hidden it deeply, to avoid charges of immaturity and self-indulgence, but I kept that wry thought to myself, saying instead that I was on my way over to Teichel's to look myself.

Mike Teichel tried to argue me out of it: looking for a teen's art shots was a waste of time when I should be out beating the bushes for him.

"The way to find a needle in a haystack, or in the bushes, is to use a magnet," I said. "I need to find someone Cory felt able to confide in."

"It won't be in a roomful of negatives," Teichel snapped. After a pause, he grudgingly allowed that Cory might have talked to the adviser to the school photography club. Teichel didn't know his first name; Cory only referred to him as "Mr. Spiro."

3

Of course, if the needle is made out of plastic, a magnet won't work and you're doomed, I realized. I was waiting in the principal's office for Mr. Spiro, who also taught chemistry; when I showed the staff the contract that Mike Teichel had signed for me to find his son, they were eager to help in any way they could.

While I waited for Spiro, I texted the nine people in Cory's message list, telling them Cory was missing and asking them to tell me the last time they'd seen or heard from him. I wanted to talk to Erica face-to-face; the assistant principal said she'd organize that for me once I was through seeing Spiro.

Mr. Spiro—Antony Spiro, he told me as he briskly shook hands—was a wiry man in his late thirties who smelled of carbolic. He had the friendly inquisitive face of a terrier, even the same high wide cheekbones; I could see that adolescents might confide in him.

He was distressed to hear that Cory was missing. "That explains why he hasn't been in class or the club. I thought he might have gone home sick."

I told Spiro the same thing I'd said to Mike Teichel, about Cory's question in my presentation. "I think now it was a cry for help: he'd had sex with someone to get information, or maybe his father was having sex with someone inappropriate, and what should he do about it."

Spiro slowly shook his head. "He didn't confide in me, at least not directly, but there's a photo in a recent batch he took—he seemed to be trying to draw my attention to it, but I thought it was about the setting, not the people in it."

He looked at the wall clock. "I have another class in ten minutes, but I think I can find it pretty quickly."

He set off down the hallway at a fast clip, greeting students by name. I trotted behind him along the long corridors favored by early-twentieth-century school designers. Partway down the third hallway, Spiro pulled out his keys and unlocked the door to a small room. The musty smell of developing chemicals hit us. When Spiro flipped on the lights, the walls were so full of pictures that I shrank back; they seemed to make the space too small to breathe in.

Spiro didn't pay attention to me or to the pictures but unlocked a cupboard in the far corner and pulled out an artist's portfolio with Cory's name on it. Spiro riffled through a set of black-and-white shots until he found the print he was looking for. I leaned over his shoulder as he laid it on a light table. Two men were embracing in a parking lot at night. Their stance was ambiguous. Were they lovers? Combatants? The faces were hard to make out in the poor light, but I thought the man on the right was Mike Teichel.

I bent over it, trying to get one clue to where the picture had been taken. A tan brick wall with cracks was in the left of the photo, a Dumpster in the background with some slats sticking out of the top, but nothing that would help me identify the building.

"I thought he wanted advice on the focus and the lighting, but from what you're saying, I'm wondering if it was the two men."

I nodded, pointed at Cory's father. "Can you make me a JPEG of this so I can email it?"

Spiro looked at his watch and the clock on the wall, called the principal to say he'd be a few minutes late for his 1:50 class. He found the negative in Cory's folder and made a fresh print, getting as sharp a contrast as he could, then scanned and emailed it to me.

He hustled me out of the room, pointing me toward the principal's office, before trotting in the opposite direction to his waiting chemistry class.

As I walked, I texted the photo to Mike Teichel—this made me blend in with the students, who were almost all focused on their devices yet seemed able to hurry down the hall toward lockers or classrooms without bumping into anyone.

Cory took this shot. Does this explain his running away? Who were you with?

Teichel called me before I reached the principal's office. He was furious; he told me to stop my search and to mind my own damned business.

"If I'd known you would take that contract as a license to invade my privacy I'd never have come to you. Send me back my retainer and stop at once."

"It's not that simple, Mr. Teichel," I said. "Seeing you with this man apparently upset Cory. If you want to find him—"

"I'll find him on my own. You stop *now!*" He broke the connection.

4

Cory is really missing?" Erica asked.

We were alone in the assistant principal's office. The assistant had been reluctant to leave us alone, but I wasn't a cop, nothing Erica said to me could be taken down and used in evidence, and Erica had insisted she wanted to speak to me privately.

"Really missing," I said. "His father won't call the cops, which makes me wonder what Mr. Teichel is afraid of. He says you were snooping in his home office. What was that about?"

Erica was mortified, she didn't want to talk about it, but I reminded her Cory's life could be on the line; I needed to know everything, and she was the only person who might know something vital.

It came in small whispered pieces. Yes, she had a crush on him, he didn't know she was alive, well, of course, they rode the bus together, they did homework together, but—*you know*.

I gave a wry smile: I knew. The adored object did not return the love.

"I thought if I got his dad all wound up, maybe Cory would say something or do something, notice me as more than a homework buddy. It was pretty pathetic. All it did was make Mr. Teichel say I couldn't come to the house—he was sure I was trying to steal something my mom could use at Metargon."

"Does he work on something she would be interested in?"

Erica flung her hands wide. "I don't think so, but I don't know. My mom doesn't work on anything secret. She's not an engineer, she does flow charts for smart home appliances. Mr. Teichel, he's like a game theory person. The software I saw was for some company in California with a weird name. Knee Ice, Ice Knee, something like that. I asked if he was making portable ice for sports injuries, because I wrecked my knee pretty good last summer and I can't play soccer now, and he acted like he was going to murder me. Like he couldn't take a joke," she added resentfully.

Knee Ice, Ice Knee. "*I-C-E-N-I?*" I spelled.

"Yeah, that's it."

"Iceni is one of the country's biggest defense contractors. No wonder he got so bent out of shape when he saw you looking at the file. You didn't actually take any of the code?"

"It didn't mean anything to me!" she cried. "And afterward, Cory, he—he wouldn't talk to me about it, and then he started acting all weird, not coming home after school, going off with his camera."

"Where did he go?"

She turned scarlet; how would she know.

"If you followed him, it would be great for me to know, and believe me, I won't rat you out."

At first, Cory had taken off for the forest preserves on his bike. She'd followed him on her own bike, and seen that he was taking nature photos, sometimes with one of his buddies from the photography club.

"But then, like, five days ago, he went on the L. It was so creepy—he got off at Pulaski and went to this horrid motel down near the expressway. I was totally freaked, but I hid behind a Dumpster." She giggled nervously. "I was watching him watch a parking lot, but then I started getting, like, a thousand texts from my mom, ordering me to come home. She could see where I was because like an idiot I hadn't turned off my phone.

"She knew I wasn't with Melanie and Caitlin, which is what I'd told her. She was in flamethrower mode. I started to leave, but then Mr. Teichel drove up. Cory didn't do anything, I mean, he didn't, like, run over and talk to his dad, he just started photographing him, which seemed totally weird. Mom threatened to call the cops. I had to leave, sneaking all the way around the back of the building so neither of them could see me. And it was—gross. Hookers, I guess. Drunks. I—it was awful."

I showed her the picture I'd gotten from Spiro.

"That's, like, the place, at least, I think it is. It was this old building with that funny kind of hinge for the bottom of the fire escape. That's Mr. Teichel, but I didn't see the other man, I left before he showed up."

Her soft round face looked gaunt and haunted. "Is that Mr. Teichel's lover? Is that why Cory ran away?"

I shook my head: I didn't know.

Erica didn't remember the name of the hotel where she'd tracked Cory, but she could tell me the location: Pulaski Street, just north of the Lake Street L stop.

I squeezed her hand with a reassurance I didn't feel, told her to leave it all to me, but not to talk to anyone else about Cory. "And don't follow me. I may be moving fast around the city and I don't want to leave you in a place where you wouldn't be safe."

5

The Ditchley Plaza on Pulaski was all that Erica had reported and then some. I left my car on the street but approached through the parking lot, stopping to look at the hinged fire escape that had caught Erica's eye. It was so badly rusted I hoped the residents never had to depend on it for their lives.

I kicked a few needles aside when I crossed the lot to get to the front entrance. The hotel had a pseudo-Byzantine facade underneath its layers of dirt, and the lobby was a large high-ceilinged space, where half-dead palm trees sat in dusty tubs next to armchairs in front of an unused fireplace.

A high grille separated the hotel staff from junkies and other customers. I pressed an old metal bell. Five minutes went by while I watched a spider move lethargically along a frond on one of the palm trees. I dinged the bell again and a woman appeared, slowly, from the back. She was thin, with deep disapproval lines gouged along her nose.

"I heard you. You need to learn some patience. You want a room?"

"I'm a detective. I'm looking for—"

"Detective? You have a warrant?"

"I'm private. No one issues warrants for me."

"Then you need to go someplace else to look."

She twitched and scratched her arms while she spoke. Liver damage, probably, especially when I saw how yellow her eyes were. I'd made copies of my key photos, Cory's and Mike Teichel's faces and the shot Cory had taken of his father embracing another man. I slipped these under the grille with a twenty. The clerk pocketed the twenty but didn't look at the pictures. I sighed and put another twenty on the counter.

"Never saw him before." She stabbed a finger on Mike Teichel. "This one, he came last week." She stabbed the man with Teichel. "The kid showed up Tuesday night"—that was Cory—"waited in the lobby until the other guy showed, followed him into the elevator. Haven't seen the kid since Tuesday night, but the other one comes down periodically to get a bottle or a pizza."

She jerked her head across the street, where a couple of fast-food joints and a liquor store were flashing their lights. A clutch of men were lounging near the liquor store doorway. Panhandling, maybe, or dealing, or both.

"Kid hasn't shown?" I asked.

"I just said, I haven't seen him. 'Course I'm only here two till midnight. Could be Major's seen him. You come back at midnight, you can ask him."

"Room number?" I asked.

"People come here to be private," she said. "I don't tell their business, I leave them alone."

I had one twenty left. It wasn't enough to buy me the room number, but the clerk slipped it into her flat chest anyway. And then told me I couldn't wait in the lobby: people who stayed at the Ditchley valued their privacy.

I went outside and moved my car down the street, where I could still see the front of the Ditchley but not be watching in an obvious way. I wasn't there ten minutes when the clerk emerged, heading for the liquor store. I got out of the car for a better view. She was showing one of the loungers two of my twenties. He took them and hustled her out of sight, around to the back of the building.

I pulled my picks out of the glove compartment and ran back to the Ditchley. A prim notice, BACK IN 5 MINUTES, sat in front of the bell I'd rung for service. I went past the counter, around the side, and found the door to the office and front desk. The lock was modern but not difficult.

The office was just big enough for a desk with two computers and a phone. One of the computers was hooked to security cameras that covered the lobby, a back door, and the front exit. The other held data. It was password protected, but someone had written down the password on a Post-it and stuck it to the keyboard tray.

I logged in and searched the guest list. More people were staying there than I had thought, especially since I hadn't seen anyone coming or going. I didn't know the name of the man in the picture, but only two people had been there longer than two nights, Gene Nielsen in 227 and John Smith in 631. I voted for John, but just in case, I made keys for both rooms—the instructions were helpfully taped to the keyboard tray next to the log-in code and the combination for the wall safe.

I just had time to get out of the office, skirt the lobby's security camera, and slide into a chair behind one of the dying palms when the clerk returned. My money had bought her a certain degree of calm: she moved languorously across the lobby without looking around.

The chair gave me a good view of the elevator in the far wall and a sort of view of the parking lot, but not of the front desk. I guessed from the noises that the clerk had reinstalled herself in the office, and I didn't hear any shrieks that showed I'd left some trace behind.

I put my phone on silent and leaned back in the armchair to minimize my visibility. The chair was upholstered in a frayed and faded fabric steeped in so many decades of dust that I kept having to choke back sneezes.

A trucker pulled his rig into the parking lot and came in to get a room for the night. The clerk was floating in some happy place and only appeared when the trucker had shouted her name several times. Florence. He was a regular, a long-haul driver on his way to Phoenix from Bangor. When he'd gone upstairs, a young woman booked a room. The phone rang twice. And then the elevator doors wheezed open and the man in Cory's photo emerged.

He walked toward me and I braced myself, but he was merely going to a window behind me to squint at the street. He looked to be in his forties, with thick bronze curls and arms that held enough muscle to pack a serious blow if he tried to hit anyone.

He lowered the blind and went out. I went to the window myself, lifted an edge of the blinds, and saw him cross the street, heading for a pizza place on the far side of the liquor store.

I glanced at the registration counter, but didn't see Florence. The elevator stood open. I hurried over and slipped inside just as the doors started wheezing shut. Florence appeared, shouting at me in a high querulous voice: "You, PI, get out of there!"

I swore under my breath: I'd forgotten the security cameras.

I didn't know what Florence's next move would be but mine involved the agony of a ride in an elevator that had read the tortoise and the hare way too many times. When I finally reached the sixth floor, I saw a pile of discarded pizza boxes in the hall and stuffed those between the doors to keep the elevator from moving. As I knocked hard on the door to room 631, the elevator alarm began jangling.

"Housekeeping," I called, although I wasn't sure there was such a thing at the Ditchley. "We have your clean towels."

I didn't hear any movement inside the room. Knocked again, then used the card-key. The lock clicked open. I moved quickly, shoulder against door, pushing my way into the room.

Cory Teichel sat on the bed, wearing his Jockeys and a T-shirt. He pulled the sheet over his legs when he saw me, his thin young face registering fear, not relief.

"I'm V.I. Warshawski," I said. "The detective who was stupid when you asked about sex at my presentation on Tuesday. Do you want to be here, or do you want to leave?"

He blinked, didn't move—my appearance, my sharp questions, he was having trouble following me.

"Can you get dressed?" I asked.

"He took my clothes," Cory muttered.

"Okay, we'll take his."

The man hadn't brought a suitcase, but a gym bag on a card table in the corner held a pair of sweatpants and some T-shirts. I tossed the sweats to Cory. They'd be big on him, but they'd get him out of the hotel.

The guy's passport was in the bag, too: Russian. Igor Palanyuk, written in Cyrillic and Roman. Inside was folded the photograph of a woman of about thirty-five or forty.

"He said if I leave, he'll call the FBI and they'll arrest my dad and then kill my mom. That's my mom, that picture."

"He's not going to call the FBI," I said. "Whoever Igor Palanyuk is, he kidnapped you."

Cory looked up from fumbling with the sweatpants' waist-string—his skinny adolescent body would have fit into one leg. "I came here. He didn't kidnap me. I wanted to find how to get my mom out of Russia."

"You want to stay with him?"

"No, but—"

"There's no but. He's keeping you against your will. We'll figure out your mother when we're safe and have room to act."

We both heard the tread outside the door. Cory froze. I put the chain bolt into place and ran to the room's only window, above the bed. I wrestled with the lock, but it had been painted into place. Igor began banging the door methodically to and fro against the chain. I picked up a chair and shattered the window. I half-carried Cory to the broken window, wrapped a sheet around him, thrust him outside onto the fire escape.

"Get down that ladder. When you get to the bottom, stay out of sight, do not show yourself for anyone except me."

He stood on the platform, eyes big with fear.

"Move!" I screamed.

He skittered down the escape just as Palanyuk forced the bolt screws out of the doorframe. The door flew open. Palanyuk's ferocious forward momentum made him stumble. When I flung the chair at him, he tripped and fell heavily.

I scrambled through the broken glass on the bed and went down the fire escape. I found Cory on the bottom platform, two stories above the ground, huddled against the wall. I grabbed his hand, led him to the edge of the platform, climbed onto the first rung of the ladder. Shut my eyes, prayed. A bullet whined past us. I jumped up and down on the top rung. Igor had emptied a whole magazine when I felt the mechanism slowly release.

I shoved Cory in front of me, forced his terrified body down the ladder. We crossed the parking lot at a shuffle, Cory trying to keep the giant sweats in place.

Blue-and-whites started swarming, but we were out of searchlight range. A few drunks stared at us apathetically from the curbs. They'd seen every possible permutation and combination of men and women along Pulaski to be startled by a half-naked teenager with an older woman.

I led him to my car and drove him to his father's house.

6

And that was it?" Murray said.

"'That' was far from 'it,' but once we got to Teichel's place, the story unspooled pretty easily. Palanyuk was with the Ukrainian mob; he—"

"You said his passport was Russian."

"Pay attention to geopolitics, Murray. He's from Simferopol, Crimea, now part of Russia, but he's ethnic Ukrainian. Mike Teichel's wife, Nina, was Crimean."

Once he had Cory safely home, Mike Teichel had felt able to call a contact at the National Security Agency. In a surprisingly short time, he'd tracked down Nina Lavrentovna, now surnamed Batitsky.

Her current husband was an oligarch wannabe. None of their get-rich quick, or even slow, schemes had worked out, but Nina had kept track of what her ex-husband was up to. When she learned about the game theory he was applying to defense systems, and how well his new generation of software worked, she and Batitsky concocted a strange plan to get hold of it.

Batitsky told Teichel that he was a coworker of Nina, that she had been imprisoned for anti-Russian activities in Crimea. He said Nina realized she had made a terrible mistake in abandoning Cory and Mike. If Mike would get them a flash drive with the Iceni software on it, Batitsky could barter it for Nina's safety.

In addition to the sob story, Batitsky sent his friend Palanyuk over to Chicago to try to force Teichel into parting with the system.

"Mike was behaving so oddly that Cory started following him, and saw him embracing Palanyuk outside the Ditchley Plaza. That was the first night Palanyuk arrived, when Teichel believed the sob story about Nina. At first, he embraced Palanyuk out of joy— until he found out what the price of her safety was."

"Meanwhile, Cory thought his father was there to have sex with men. He took the photograph he showed his teacher, but went back to the Ditchley two nights later to see if his father showed up there again. That's why he followed Palanyuk into the elevator and why he ended up a prisoner in the hotel room.

"Batitsky then offered to trade Teichel Cory's safety for the flash drive—that was when Teichel fired me. He was scared Cory would be killed if I got too close."

"Why did Cory ask if you ever slept with a suspect?" Sal put in.

"When he first followed his dad to the Ditchley Plaza, he thought Mike and Palanyuk were lovers. He thought maybe he could seduce Palanyuk and find out what his hold was on his dad. That ploy didn't work well—Palanyuk wasn't interested, but he realized with Cory, he had a more potent pawn to play with Mike Teichel than a long-absent wife."

"So why did Teichel fire you?" Murray demanded.

"He'd been in San Francisco when Cory took off. He didn't connect his son's disappearance with his own troubles, not until I texted him the picture Cory had taken of him with Palanyuk outside the Ditchley."

"Which one of them would have made you kick a hole in a stained-glass window?" Sal poured my drink, cocking an eyebrow seductively.

"Cory, of course. I did kick a hole in a window for him."

"Too bad Erica wasn't with you," Murray said. "She could have administered some TLC."

I didn't tell him Erica had shown up at the Teichel house, ostensibly to fill Cory in on homework assignments he'd missed. Cory thanked her politely but told her he needed to be alone with his father. I escorted her home, and agreed with all her bright superficial chatter. There is nothing worse than someone telling you "This, too, will pass." You have to learn your own route out of agony.

"I'll take another Oban, Sal," I said.

"Why do you have to drink expensive malts on my tab?" Murray grumbled.

"Oh, Murray, you know—everything tastes twice as good when someone else is paying."

Note

I wrote this story originally as "A Family Affair" for Bob Randisi's collection, *Fifty Shades of Grey Fedora* (Riverdale Avenue, 2015). Our brief was to create a story with a sexual theme that fit in with the craze for *Fifty Shades of Grey*. I started with Murray and V.I. at the Golden Glow and V.I. using one of Chandler's notable sexual lines about Velma—a blonde who could get a bishop to kick a hole through a stained-glass window.

I've rewritten it for this anthology, adding about a thousand words and hopefully making the storyline easier to follow. The sex is actually nonexistent, but it's the fear that his father is having an affair that drives young Cory Teichel into action.

ACID TEST

I

She hadn't known her life could unravel so fast. Yesterday morning, her biggest worry had been the phone calls from Ruth Meecham, complaining about the noise:

("Are you running a hippie commune in there, Karin?"

"Yes, Ruth."

"I'm complaining to the alderman: you're renting rooms to people without meeting the building code for separate entrances."

"Fine, Ruth.")

Also Clarence Epstein's threats to sue her for harassment. In fact, when the cops arrived—all thirteen of them, at midnight, with enough cars to run Indy right there on the spot—she'd assumed it was because Clarence had made good on his threats.

Chicago's Hyde Park neighborhood was filled with people Karin had known since first grade. Ruth Meecham was one of them—they lived side by side in the same outsize houses where they'd grown up. Clarence was another. In high school, he'd just been another grade-grubbing faculty brat, but when Karin got back from her time in India, he'd turned into a power-grubbing economist.

He and Ruth and Karin had all lost their parents relatively young, and they'd all inherited their childhood homes. Clarence Epstein had donated his family's brick home to the Spadona Institute. Of course, Spadona's main offices were in Washington, but so many of their fellows were on the University of Chicago faculty—most in economics or business, some in law—that Spadona needed a home near the university.

Ruth Meecham had inherited a portfolio along with her house. She lived alone in eighteen rooms, and kept them up with a meticulous round of repairs, gutter cleanings, and tuck-pointings. Gardening was her acknowledged hobby, but meddling ran a close second.

Ever since her own parents' death brought Karin back from India twenty-six years ago, Ruth had been monitoring her. She'd noticed Karin's pregnancy before Karin admitted it to herself, admitted that the nausea she'd suffered since coming home wasn't due to changing back to Western food, or even grief at the loss of her elderly, remote parents, but a souvenir of the ashram in Shravasti.

Karin so missed life in the ashram that she turned her parents' mansion into a kind of co-op. Unlike Ruth, she hadn't inherited money to keep up the house. The co-op helped pay the bills, besides giving her a chance to practice the nonviolent activism of Shravasti. Karin typically had three or four tenants, usually young activists who stayed a year or two before moving on.

Right now the most intense tenant was a young environmentalist with a toddler. Jessica Martin had shown up at Karin's door when the baby was only a month old. Remembering her own trials as a young single mother, Karin took her in, adopted baby Titus as an honorary grandchild, and tried to keep peace between Jessica's volatile moods and the rest of the co-op.

Jessica had made Clarence's Spadona Institute her particular project, tweeting about it, posting photos on Instagram, and running a podcast. She also staged sit-ins, helped a group of nuns with prayer vigils, and invited a lot of police surveillance of Karin's home.

After Clarence Epstein's death two days ago, the surveillance had grown to round-the-clock squad cars in front and in the alley. Every now and then a detective came in to talk to one or another resident, always beginning by cross-examining Karin on what she knew about the person and why she'd rented them a room.

And then—she herself had been arrested for conspiracy to commit murder. Karin sat cross-legged on the jail cell's steel bed, palms up, thumbs and forefingers forming an O, trying to chant, but despite decades of practice, she couldn't keep her focus on her breath.

She'd been arrested before, but for demonstrations against wars, or the kind of trespass that Clarence had been so exercised about. She'd never been alone in jail, though—it had always been with friends, and never for a charge like murder. She couldn't comprehend it, even though she was choking on cigarette smoke and gagging on the other smells—stale urine, vomit, the iron stench of drying blood.

Empty the mind. Swami Rajananpur used to say, "Karin, caught between hope and fear, the spirit is liked a trapped bird frantically beating its wings, and going nowhere. Empty the mind, join yourself to the great Now."

"*Eka leya*," she chanted softly, *harmony*. A woman rattled the bars of the cage and screamed for a guard. A trapped bird, let it out, let it fly away. "*Eka leya, eka leya*," she kept repeating, trying to set free all the birds whirring in her head, but last night's interview with the young state's attorney kept flying back in.

"We know you had a major fight with Dr. Epstein two nights

before his death." The state's attorney had been a young man, wearing navy pinstripes even at two in the morning, and trying to intimidate her by leaning over her and talking in too loud a voice.

"We didn't fight," Karin had answered, trying to explain that even if Clarence was angry, she, Karin, was too committed to non-violence to fight with him. Nor would she add that everyone in the house had been angry, because it was also against her principles to shield herself at someone else's expense.

Had it only been five days ago? Clarence had come over in person—usually he sent a student or an intern with his complaints—and he'd seemed angrier with young Jessica Martin than with Karin herself. That wasn't so surprising, given Jessica's protests at the Spadona Institute. Conversation had been heated but civil until Jessica's little boy, Titus, toddled in, moving uncertainly on his chubby legs.

Clarence tried picking him up, and Jessica snatched Titus away, shouting, "Don't touch my child. I won't have him covered with the blood that's on your hands."

Clarence had turned white with fury. "At least everyone knows what I stand for. I hate to see a child raised by a hypocrite."

Titus was usually a sweet and happy baby, but the angry voices made him start to howl.

"You two know how to calm down," Karin said, taking Titus from Jessica. "Don't you see, if two smart grown-ups can't talk calmly, there's no hope for the world?"

"Karin, don't tell *me* what to do, you overgrown hippie," Clarence growled. "You never had a sense of values and you haven't got them now, letting anyone and everyone camp out here, and using your father's house as a base for violating my privacy!"

Jessica started to shout something, but Karin shook her head. "Insofar as I can, I run this house on principles of nonviolence. That means nonviolent verbal reactions, too, Jessica. If someone comes in here who's out of control, it's his problem, not ours. I will not allow you to shout at him in here or call him names. You can take it outside if you have to do it, but think how much happier you'll be if you can stay calm."

"Be as sanctimonious as you want, Karin," Clarence snarled, "but keep this in mind while you practice your heavy breathing: if you let this flip-flopping radical stage a protest out of your father's house one more time, I will be suing you for intent to injure me and my institute. I came over to tell you I've been getting legal advice on this matter and my attorney is prepared to act."

Karin laughed. "It's my house, Clarence. Are you trying to say my dad would have supported your institute if he were still alive? Maybe so, but I bet your mom would hate to know what you do in there."

And then she'd felt ashamed, because in one second all her training, all her values, had gone out the window at the chance to score on him. Jessica had given a harsh laugh and yelled, "Right on, Karin," which made Karin leave the room abruptly, still holding the baby. At least she'd defused the encounter—Clarence had stayed another half hour, and Karin hadn't heard any shouting coming from the big common room where he and Jessica were talking. That was the last time she'd seen him, and she'd been shocked, even if not grief-stricken, when she learned of his death two days later.

The state's attorney hadn't believed Karin. He thought the threat of Clarence's lawsuit was enough to make her drop all her principles, figure out how to make a bomb and how to set it off just when Clarence and his crony, the Spadona constitutional scholar Roger Brooke, were having an early morning meeting on Tuesday.

"I don't know anything about explosives," she'd protested.

"But your daughter does, doesn't she?"

"Temple?" Karin had been astonished. "She's an engineer. She knows how to calibrate things, and wire a house, and make heating and cooling systems go. She doesn't know bombs!"

"Anyone could have built this one."

Karin shook her head. "Not me. And I'm sure not Temple, either."

Although, really, where her daughter was concerned, Karin was sure of nothing. How could you love someone and know so little about her? She had raised Temple in the relaxed, accepting atmosphere she herself had longed for in her own rigidly controlled childhood, and Temple had grown up tidy, precise, so compulsive she changed her voice mail message every day—as Karin realized when she'd made a frantic call to her daughter as the police were arresting her. Listening to Temple give the date, her whereabouts, when she'd return calls, Karin had moaned, "Darling, please, just answer, just answer," and when the beep finally came, had time only to cry out, "Temple, come as soon as you get this message— it's urgent!" before the cops snatched the phone from her.

2

Temple had been in the water lab at the Cheviot Engineering Institute when the Spadona building blew up. She was conducting tests on a grooved end-fitting that had come loose in a water main break to see whether the fitting was defective or had simply been improperly installed. She was covered in waterproof gear, happily reading gauges and jotting down notes to take back to the computer, and didn't hear the news until later.

"Isn't that the place where your mom leads protests?" Alvin Guthrie asked when Temple got back to her desk. "I thought I saw her on TV when Abu Graib hit the news, because she said that some of the Spadona fellows were training torturers, or justifying them or something."

"Your mom is totally amazing," Lettice announced. "Still living the hippie life after all these years. My mother is, like, obsessed with her body, you know, getting into a size two instead of a size six. I like how your mom just enjoys life and eats what she wants."

"It would be better for her health if she worked out and didn't eat so much dal and curry," Temple said—although her suggestions along those lines to Karin had made her mother tilt back her head, with its rope of graying blond hair, and laugh. (She'd stroked Temple's cheeks an instant later, because she hated cruelty in herself as much as in others, and said, "Darling, I can't be the kind of woman you see at your health club. I do yoga every day, you know, and even if I'm twenty pounds overweight, that doesn't stop me from making a tree *vrksasana*." And she raised her right foot to press into her left thigh, while little Titus clapped his hands and tried to imitate her.)

"Anyway, I don't have enough memory in my phone to keep track of all the places Karin goes on protests," Temple added to Alvin, when he repeated his question. "I think I was born at a rally or protest of some kind."

She could picture her mother, giving birth in the street, wrapping Temple in a banner, and continuing to march. Temple's earliest memories were of painting signs for protest marches, or the marches themselves. Whether the cause was peace, farmworkers, or reproductive rights, Temple's childhood was spent waking to a house full of strangers, tiptoeing around throwing out beer cans and scraping leftover curry into the garbage while the activists slept until noon.

She told her coworkers this, and Lettice once again exclaimed in envy about how open Temple's mother was. The idea of a house full of empties didn't make them gag, the way it did Temple herself. She'd gone to engineering school as the culmination of an obsession both with order and with making things work properly, but Alvin and Lettice were both good engineers with a high tolerance for mess—as Temple knew, since they'd all roomed together as students.

"If you'd grown up in my family, you'd welcome your mother's open-house outlook," Alvin said. "My parents only entertain once a year, when they have my father's family to Thanksgiving, and that is an evening in hell, let me tell you."

While Alvin and Lettice argued which one of them had the more neurotic family, Temple slipped into the hall to call Karin. "You weren't at the Spadona Institute today, were you?"

Karin laughed. "You don't think I blew it up, do you? We had a gazillion fire trucks on the street; Titus was in heaven—you know how little boys are with loud machines. But we had a teen reading circle at the house this morning, so I couldn't go to the protest. Jessica was there with the sisters, and I hope you don't think a group of pacifist nuns could blow up a building. Thank goodness none of them was injured—they were kneeling out front when the place went up."

"Temple!" Her boss, Sanford Rieff, had suddenly appeared behind her. "I hope that conversation is about the threads on Rapelec's pipe valve, because we need a report for them by the end of the day."

Temple felt her cheeks grow hot and fled back to the office. While she wrote up her results, her office mates kept up a running commentary on the Spadona bombing, which the news sites were covering with an orgiastic glee.

Terrorism Strikes Chicago and *Al-Qaeda in the Heartland,* they trumpeted. A few hours later came the reports that police had discovered the bodies of Clarence Epstein and Roger Brooke in the building rubble. This seemed to pin the blame securely on al-Qaeda: the two men had been heavily involved in the interim government in Iraq, Epstein as an economist, Brooke giving advice on how to draft a new constitution. The FBI figured that Epstein and Brooke were targets of the blast, since they often met early in the morning before any of the administrative staff arrived.

The news reports expressed astonishment at the Institute's location, but the *Herald-Star* did a sidebar explaining that the University of Chicago had taken over a lot of mansions on Woodlawn and Kimbark Avenues to house some of their auxiliary activities; the Spadona Institute, from its beginnings among the economists of the Nixon era, had always had close ties to both the university and the national government.

When Sanford Rieff came in at three to see whether Temple had finished her analysis, she was glad she had Rockwell hardness charts up on her screen—it was to Lettice and Alvin that Rieff said dryly, "Have you been assigned to the Spadona bombing? I didn't realize anyone had retained Cheviot Engineering on that case yet.

Temple, are you finished? And Alvin, don't we have anything productive for you to do? You can go assist them in the crash lab."

Temple surreptitiously watched the news on her phone. Whatever clues the FBI's forensics team had picked up in the building they were keeping as secret as possible, although they did concede it wasn't a typical bomb—something more homemade, which made people think about Oklahoma City. On Thursday, Temple, egged on by Alvin and Lettice, went down to see what Karin knew, and to inspect as much of the damage as the police barricades allowed.

The trio stopped at the Spadona Institute first. Like Karin's house and other homes along Woodlawn Avenue, it had been an outsize brick mansion, with some twenty rooms, standing on a double city lot. Set well back from the street, with a couple of old maples and an ash in the front lawn, it had done nothing to attract attention to its activities, at least until it blew up.

When the three engineers got close to the house, they could see that a number of windows had shattered; behind the glass they could make out charring from the fire. The main destruction was on the roof and third floor of the building, but they could see black scarring underneath the second-floor windows, as if the house had been tied up in a giant black ribbon.

"Odd kind of destruction pattern," Alvin said.

The two women nodded, and moved cautiously around the building to the back, which looked much like the front. Although all three were engineers, none of them had training in explosives; Lettice, a chemical engineer, came the closest, but she had never examined a bomb site. Temple was a mechanical engineer, which meant she knew a lot about furnaces and heating/cooling systems; at the Cheviot lab, she'd mostly been working with pipes and valves.

"Have they said where the bomb was planted?" Lettice asked. "Because it looks as though it was under the roof, which would be really weird if you were trying to kill someone. Maybe whoever set it off just wanted to disrupt the Institute—maybe one of your mom's nuns didn't know enough to realize she'd got hold of something powerful."

Temple shook her head. "It can't have been set under the roof, not with that burn pattern around the second story. Fire goes up."

"Doh," Alvin said. "I missed class the day they talked about fire."

Temple swatted him with her briefcase. "It wouldn't burn downward, at least, not along that very precise route—you'd see fingers of charring. This looks like it followed the pipes."

"So maybe it started on the second floor and traveled upward," Alvin said.

"Along what route?" Lettice asked. "Temple's right—the burn pattern doesn't make sense."

A police car pulled over; the man at the wheel didn't bother to get out, just broadcast over his loudspeaker that the area was off-limits. He waited at the curb until the three engineers went around the block to Karin's house.

The front door stood open: so many different people used the common rooms of the house for meetings that Karin never locked up during the day. When Temple and her friends walked in they heard a woman shouting.

"You and your stupid protests. You *look* stupid with all this adolescent behavior, your marches, your prayer vigils, wearing your hair as if you were still twenty-something instead of fifty-something. You hated Clarence so much you'd let anyone into this house who was ready to hurt him. You never thought to ask any questions, but believe me, he did, and I did."

The first speaker shouted, "You made his last days on earth miserable! Don't tell me to calm down."

"That's Ruth Meecham," Temple said. "She lives next door; she and Karin and Clarence Epstein all grew up together. Karin hates people shouting, but when she says 'calm down,' it sometimes makes you want to hit her."

Temple led the way into a large common room, where her mother stood, a toddler in her arms, facing her neighbor. Temple suddenly saw her mother through strange eyes: she did dress like an old 1960s hippie, in her Indian pajama trousers. Her graying hair hung unbraided to her waist. She was barefoot this afternoon, too.

Almost as if she were deliberately accentuating their differences, Ruth Meecham had dyed her hair black and wore it severely bobbed around her ears. She was wearing makeup, and the open-toed espadrilles showed she had polish on her toes.

"Hi, Karin. Hi, Ms. Meecham. Hi, Titus," Temple added as the little boy squirmed out of Karin's arms and toddled over to her. "Where's everyone else?"

She bent to pick up Titus, but he wriggled away and made a beeline for a chest in the corner where Karin kept toys—not just for him, but for all the children whose parents brought them to the many meetings held in the house.

"Jessica Martin left as soon as I came." Ruth Meecham bit off the words as if they were cigar ends. "She knew I'd let her have what-for, the way she treated Professor Epstein."

"Clarence had so many resources," Karin said. "The president, the Congress, all those billionaire Spadona donors. Was Jessica really more than he could handle?"

"Not even letting him touch the baby!"

"And how do you know that?" Karin asked.

Ruth Meecham hesitated, then muttered that it was all over the neighborhood. Karin didn't reply to that; after an awkward silence, Ruth started to leave. She paused in the doorway long enough to say, "Do you ever investigate the people you give house-room to?"

Karin laughed. "I hope you're not suggesting Jessica is a fugitive from justice. She's a little aggressive, it's true, but she's still very young."

"Oh, grow up, Karin!" Ruth Meecham stomped down the hall to the door.

"Did Jessica and Mr. Epstein have a fight?" Temple asked. "Oh—Karin—you remember Alvin and Lettice, don't you?"

"Of course." Karin gave them a warm smile. "Jessica is too hot-tempered; she wouldn't let Clarence hold the baby. But Ruth was lying, wasn't she, on how she knew."

"I bet she was listening under the window," Temple said. "She does, you know. At least, when I was a kid, I sometimes saw her with binoculars, studying the inside of our house."

"That's a little different from listening under the window, Temple!"

"She might have a remote mike," Alvin suggested. "Something with two point four gigahertz could pick you up from next door without her leaving the comfort of her home."

"If she wants to listen in on our pregnant teens book group, she's welcome," Karin said. "Maybe it'll make her decide to volunteer. I suppose, though, Clarence told her. She always had a crush on him and he knew she'd see his side of things, no matter how crooked that side might seem to me."

Lettice and Alvin started asking her questions about the explosion. Temple wandered over to a battered coffee table whose surface was covered with flyers and books, old mail and unread newspapers; she started sorting them.

"Leave those alone, Temple," Karin called out. "Whenever you tidy up, it takes me forever to find my notes."

Temple bit back a reply. She wasn't going to argue with Karin in front of her friends, but really, how could anyone stand to live in this kind of chaos? She controlled the urge to pick up the papers that had drifted to the floor and looked at Titus, who was trying to fit a rubber ball into a plastic jug. The jug's lips and handles were misshapen— from being put on the stove, Temple imagined. In her mother's haphazard home, the kitchen always was the site of small catastrophes.

"That's quite an engineering problem you've set yourself, little guy." She squatted next to him to watch, then said sharply, "Where did you get that?"

When she pried the jug from his grasp, Titus began to howl—at which moment his mother appeared in the doorway.

"What are you doing to my child?" Jessica demanded.

She was a tall woman; Temple, who was barely five-two, always felt invisible next to Jessica. She craned her head back and said firmly, "I was taking this from him. It's had something nasty in it, and I think it's pretty irresponsible to let a baby play with it."

Karin interrupted her own description of Clarence Epstein as a high school student to say guiltily, "Oh, dear: I found that in the trash and meant to put it out with the recyclables. Titus must have picked it up from the kitchen table before I got around to it."

"Oh, everyone around here is so fucking pure! Couldn't you just leave it in the garbage for once? I picked it up in the backyard and threw it out!" Jessica grabbed Titus, who howled even more loudly.

"Sorry, sweetie." Karin smiled at Jessica. "Sometimes we're myopic, putting recycling ahead of baby's curiosity. And the recycling—oh, dear—I promised I'd look after that along with the seedlings, and I completely forgot to take them out last week. Sandra and Mark will be so upset when they get back."

"I'll take it out to the recycle bins." Temple picked up the container, giving her mother a level glance that stated her unspoken opinion of the sloth that let the container stay in the house.

Karin pursed her lips and turned away. Temple knew what she was doing—a mini-meditation, a mini-letting-go of anger with her own daughter, not with Jessica, who couldn't look after her baby and then got pissed off with someone who was paying attention to his welfare.

Temple walked through the house to the kitchen, which as usual had pots and papers and bags of organic granola on every surface. A blender was on the floor, where Titus could conveniently slice off his fingers; Temple put it next to a precarious mountain of bowls in the sink.

Karin had never appreciated her tidiness, even when she was eight, and making the chaotic house livable. Maybe Jessica was the daughter Karin had always wanted—an activist, the daughter who could tolerate mess—unlike Temple, in whose stark white apartment every pen and paper clip was in a tidy accessible drawer.

She blinked back self-pitying tears and went out to the recycle bins, where she removed newspapers from the bin for glass. Who knew what the papers had been used for—they were streaked with white powder. Surely no one was using cocaine in Karin's house. Temple rubbed a little of the powder in her fingers, which began to burn. She quickly wiped them on the grass.

A few minutes later, Alvin and Lettice joined her. Alvin wanted to see the greenhouse where Karin grew herbs, in case she had any medicinal marijuana. The greenhouse sat in the back of the garden, next to a compost heap where wasps were hovering.

"Knock it off, Alvin. If my mom was breaking the law she wouldn't be doing it where people like you could barge in on her. Anyway, the greenhouse is the responsibility of one of the other house members who's big on organic gardening—she starts all her seedlings out here."

Temple was annoyed with all of them, with Jessica for being such a dimwit, with her mother for running such an idiotic household, and with her friends for treating Karin like a sideshow in the circus. Her annoyance made Alvin clown around more, pretending that the oregano he plucked in the greenhouse was reefer. He staggered up the sidewalk past Ruth Meacham's house, and Temple's anger increased to see that the neighbor was watching them all with a kind of voluptuous malevolence.

It was six hours later that the police came for Karin.

3

What's she doing in handcuffs?" Temple demanded.

She had found Karin in a side room, where prisoners were held after their bond hearings until court ended, when they would be put on buses to Cook County Jail.

The sheriff's deputy bristled. "It's the law, and if you want to talk to her, you won't carry on in here."

Temple sized up the deputy, the gun, the attitude, and squatted next to her mother, who gave her a wobbly smile. Temple was overcome with shame: she had heard her mother's message when she got home at one, and decided if there was a crisis, it had something to do with Temple's visit earlier in the evening. She didn't feel like hearing a lecture on why she needed to treat Jessica with more consideration, so she'd erased the message and gone to bed.

It was only when she was dressing for work the next morning that she'd heard the news: her mother had been arrested for murder. Traces of the explosive used at the Spadona Institute, a common household cleaner mixed with fertilizer, had been found in the greenhouse at the back of the garden.

"I don't believe it, any of it," Temple announced to her kitchen. "This is insane."

She had called the house to try to find out where her mother was. The phone rang a dozen times before Jessica answered it. She was surly, as if annoyed that Temple wanted to talk about Karin. The police raid had totally freaked out Titus, she said: he'd cried until three in the morning.

"I don't know where Karin is and she's not my responsibility. If she blew up the Spadona Institute, then I am out of here—I am not getting involved in her crimes."

"Sheesh, Jessica, after all my mother's done for you, all the babysitting, letting you run off when you need your own space, or whatever sob story you lay on her. What happened? What grounds did they have for arresting her?"

Jessica bristled at Temple's criticism, but she did confirm the news reports, that the cops had found what they were looking for in the greenhouse.

Temple frowned. "I was in that greenhouse yesterday afternoon, and didn't see any buckets or bottles of cleaner. And you know Karin doesn't use that kind of product, or let anyone in the house use it—didn't you tell the police that?"

"It was the middle of the night, the baby was howling, what was I supposed to do, give them a lecture on nonviolence and green gardening?"

Temple pressed the off button hard enough to bruise her finger. In her head she could see a spreadsheet with a to-do list, the items filling in as if written with invisible ink. Number one, evict Jessica, had to be moved to number four, she decided: number one had to be to find a criminal lawyer for Karin. Number two was to find out what evidence the state had, and number three was to see if Karin was guilty.

Since Cheviot Engineering was a forensic lab, her boss, who'd testified in a gazillion or so criminal cases, surely knew a good criminal lawyer. She caught him on his way to a meeting. He thought for a minute, said that Freeman Carter was the best, if he was available, and that Carter could also find out exactly where Karin was. Carter wasn't in when Temple called, but his paralegal traced Karin and told Temple that Carter or one of his associates would meet her in Bond Court as soon as possible.

Temple was still squatting in front of her mother, rubbing her cuffed hands, and sniffing out an apology for not responding to Karin's SOS last night, when Freeman Carter arrived. He was such a model of the corporate attorney, from the bleached hair cut close to his head to the navy suit tailored to his tall body, that Temple was sure her mother would reject him. She was astounded when Karin got to her feet, awkwardly because of the cuffs around her ankles, and held out her chained hands to Carter.

"Freeman, of course! If I hadn't been so rattled last night, I'd have thought of you myself. Bless you—that is, I assume you've come for me?"

"Of course, I should have known it was you." Carter turned to Temple. "Our parents had adjoining cottages in Lakeside when we were growing up. I knew your mother before she went to India and changed her name to Shravasti. Let's get you out of here."

"They set bail at a million dollars," Karin said. "Even if I take out a higher line of credit on the house, I can't come up with that much money."

"That's why you've hired me. Or why your daughter has. Million-dollar bonds for felons are just part of our complete service."

4

I won't pretend that I'm going to wear black and sob at their funerals, but I didn't kill Epstein and Brooke," Karin said.

"I don't want any hairsplitting here," Freeman Carter said sternly. "If you placed an explosive device in the house, intending to blow it up before the guys got there, you're still liable for their deaths."

"Freeman! I don't know word one about explosives, and I am utterly and completely committed to nonviolence."

"That's really true," Temple said. "And besides, she's totally green, you know. They're saying she mixed ammonia with fertilizer from the compost heap, but Karin wouldn't buy a cleaning product with ammonia in it."

"But they found her gardening gloves in the greenhouse and they're saying they had traces of the ammonia and some fertilizer on them," Jessica put in.

They were sitting in Karin's private parlor. When she turned her house into a co-op, she'd kept a suite of four rooms for herself at the back of the second floor. Normally at a meeting like this, all the housemates would have taken part, but Jessica—and Titus, happily banging away on a drum improvised out of old milk cartons—were the only ones at home. Three were trekking in Uzbekistan and the fourth, an elderly civil rights lawyer, was visiting his daughter in northern Michigan.

"But I don't garden," Karin said. "Maybe I have some old work gloves, I guess I do, but Sandra—one of our housemates—looks after the greenhouse, and she's one of the ones away trekking right now. In fact, it's been on my conscience that I haven't looked at her seedlings to see if they've been watered."

"It's impossible to prove, Karin." Freeman held up a hand as Karin and Temple both began to protest. "I'm not saying I doubt you, but I can't prove it in court, which is where it matters. If you're innocent, someone planted your work gloves in there, coated with ammonium nitrate. Who could have done that?"

"Anyone," Temple said. "Karin keeps an open house. Doors are locked at night, but I bet you never lock the gate leading to the alley, do you?"

"Of course not, darling, why would I? It just makes twice as much work. It's bad enough that people are always losing house keys, without worrying about the garden, too."

"Are you sure it was an ammonium bomb?" Temple said. "I'm surprised it behaved like this one did."

"What do you mean? How does an ammonium bomb *behave*?" Jessica gave the word a sarcastic inflection.

Temple saw Karin mouthing "let it go" and took a deep breath before she answered. "Ammonium nitrate bombs leave a big hole. The house would have fallen in on itself if the bomb had been set inside, and if it was outside, the front or the back would be missing. The Spadona building just has roof damage and a pattern of burn marks around the second floor."

"Are you an expert?" Freeman asked.

"No, but that's the kind of thing everyone knows," Temple said.

"Everyone?" Jessica sneered.

"Everyone who thinks logically about fire and burn patterns," Temple said. "What about the samples from the house? Where was the bomb set? What was it made of?"

Freeman jotted a note. "I'll see what the Feds are willing to say. Going back to who could have planted this on you, do you have any ex-tenants, or old enemies in the neighborhood, who might have it in for you?"

"Just Ruth Meecham," Jessica said. "She's always calling the alderman's office about the number of people living here."

"Oh, Ruth—" Karin said dismissively, but Temple interrupted her.

"There's something I need to check on. I'll talk to you later, but get some rest, go to the Buddhist temple, do something for yourself, okay? Today isn't your day for being Titus's babysitter."

She darted from the room without waiting for anyone's reaction—just as well, Karin thought, given Jessica's furious expression. A moment later, they heard the clatter of metal lids. Jessica and Karin went to the window, followed by Freeman. They looked down to see Temple rummaging through the recycling bins. A flash of light made Karin look across the yard. Ruth Meecham also had her binoculars trained on Temple.

5

Alvin and Lettice had spent the whole morning discussing Karin's arrest, and how she'd managed to plant the bomb. When Temple finally arrived at the lab, a little after noon, they pounded her with questions.

"My mother did not put a bomb in that building," Temple snapped at them.

She pulled a couple of specimen bags from her canvas briefcase and laid them on Lettice's desk. One held the distended plastic jug, the other a newspaper. "Can you analyze these?"

Alvin came over to look down at the bag. "Hmmm. Small print, lots of words, a screed about liberals in the media, must be the *Wall Street Journal*."

"Please don't joke about it, Alvin—these might help with Karin's defense."

"What are they?" Lettice asked.

"The *Wall Street Journal* and an empty water jug," said Alvin, unrepentant.

Lettice picked up the specimen bags. "What am I looking for?"

"Yes, what is she looking for, and why are you giving her the assignment?" It was their boss, Sanford Rieff, who had materialized in the doorway.

"Oh, sir, it's—you know, the Spadona building, my mother was arrested, they planted false evidence in her greenhouse, I'm sure of it, and I want—"

"Slow down, Temple. I can't follow you. Give me a step-by-step picture of what this is about."

Temple shut her eyes. Where Karin chanted for harmony, Temple saw her to-do list, laid out in her head like a spreadsheet. It was so clear to her that she had trouble putting it into words, so she went to her computer and typed it all out.

Sanford Rieff looked at it and nodded. "And who is the client? Who is going to pay for time on the mass spectrometer, and for Lettice's time?"

Temple swallowed. "I guess that would be me, sir."

Sanford looked at her for a long minute, then walked over to her computer and typed a few lines. "Okay. I've added you to the client data base. You can finish Lettice's tests on the water in the Lyle township pool—you know enough chemistry for that, right? And do you know what you expect Lettice to find?"

Temple took a deep breath. "I don't know if these are connected to the explosion, but—I'd look for ammonium nitrate, to see if the stuff they found in the greenhouse is on these, and check for acetone in the jug. I knew it smelled funky when I took it away from the baby yesterday, but it was only just now I realized it was nail polish remover, I mean, I never use it, and I'd forgotten, I had a college roommate who was always doing her nails, but what I ought to do is go back to the Spadona building and get samples."

"You're not making sense again, Temple," her boss said, "but what you ought emphatically *not* to do is go back to a closed-down explosion site to get samples. You could be arrested, or even worse, injured. Someone has taken samples and we'll see if we can find their reports."

Sanford Rieff pushed her gently toward the door. "You have the makings of a forensic engineer, Temple, but we need the swimming pool analysis this afternoon. Alvin, what are you doing, besides trying to best Temple's time at Candy Crush? Get me all the reports that are available on the Spadona bombing, then go back to the electronics lab to give Dumfries a hand with the timing problem he's working on."

It was six before Lettice was able to get time on the spectrometer. Temple, who'd finished her work on the swimming pool an hour earlier, stood next to her while Lettice read the bar graphs into her computer.

Temple pointed at a peak on the graph. "Would C_3H_6O spike there?"

"Temple, I swear, you are hovering like a bumblebee, and if you don't stop, I am going to swat you. I'm not going over these with you—I'm taking them to Sanford first, and he's left for the day, so get out of my hair!"

"I'm the client," Temple objected.

"And you're like every other annoying client, trying to run the investigation for us. Can't you do something useful? A yoga headstand or something?"

Temple stepped away, fiddling with her watchband, and looked at the samples she'd brought in. Lettice had returned the *Wall Street Journal* to its protective bag, but the jug was standing open on the counter. Come to think of it, who at her mother's house read the *Journal*? They got their news from *The Nation* and *In These*

Times. And if she was right, if that was acetone in the jug, well, that came from nail polish remover, and she was sure no one in Karin's house used polish or remover—Karin didn't approve of environmental toxins, whatever use they were put to.

But Ruth Meecham—that was another story. Temple had seen the polish on her toenails earlier this week, and Ruth, supporter of Clarence Epstein and the Spadona Institute, she surely read the *Journal.*

She walked over to her desk and called her mother. Jessica answered the phone and told her Karin was resting. "Do you want me to give her a message?"

Temple hesitated, trying to balance her jealousy of Jessica with her need for information. "Where did you get that jug, the one that I took away from Titus yesterday?"

"I told you—I found it in the backyard! Did you call up to give me another lecture on child safety? Because I don't need it."

"Don't yell at me, Jessica. I'm trying to figure out how to clear my mom's name, and I think that whoever planted the ammonium nitrate in her greenhouse made a bomb out of something different, probably out of acetone. I don't know how it worked, but if a fire had gone up through the air-conditioning vents, it would have left the kind of burn pattern you can see on the outside of the house, following the track of the vents around the perimeter, and acetone would be a really good fast-igniting agent. We're waiting on the test results, but I'm wondering if Ruth Meecham might have tossed the jug into our—into Karin's yard."

Jessica paused before answering, then said, "If she did, what motive could she possibly have for blowing up the Spadona Institute? She adored Clarence Epstein, she talks about him as if he were a saint. I think they were lovers or something back in college and she kept mooning over him even when he obviously had moved on to bigger and better things. He was a star, but she was only a moon." She laughed at her own pun.

"I don't know motives," Temple said impatiently. "Ms. Meecham hates the way Karin uses the house as a commune, she hates the causes Karin supports—maybe she's deranged and figured if she could plant a big crime on Karin and send her to prison, the house would shut down. But I need to go through her garbage and see if I can find any traces of the ammonium nitrate before she gets rid of it, or even worse, dumps all of it in Karin's trash. I think I'll come down tonight and have a look, before it's too late. Don't tell Karin—she doesn't like people thinking vengeful thoughts."

Before leaving, she checked back at the spectrometer lab, but Lettice had disappeared. She wandered back to Lettice's desk and looked at her computer. Lettice probably used her cat's name as a password. Temple's fingers hovered over the keyboard, then withdrew. She knew it was acetone in the jug; she bet it was some kind of dried acetone compound on the newspaper that had burned her fingers yesterday afternoon. It was more important that she get down to Ruth Meecham's house and go through her garbage before Meecham decided to move it. And despite what Sanford Rieff had said, she'd go through the basement at the Spadona Institute and get some samples there. She had a hard hat in her trunk, she had a briefcase full of specimen bags, and she had a camera in her glove compartment.

The late-summer dusk was turning from gray to purple when she reached Hyde Park. She left her car on a side street and came up behind her mother's house through the alley—other neighbors were probably just as nosy as Ruth Meecham, and she was less visible in the alley. Ruth Meecham's back gate was locked, but Karin's—naturally—stood open to anyone who wanted to come in that way.

Temple came through the gate as quietly as she could. The fence that separated her mother's and the Meecham property ended at her mother's greenhouse; there was just enough space behind the greenhouse for her to squeeze past. When she reached Ruth Meecham's side of the yard, someone tapped her on the shoulder and she almost screamed out loud.

"Temple? Sorry to scare you." Jessica's face loomed over her in the dark. "Something worrying has happened."

Temple could still feel her pulse thudding against her throat.

"Right after we talked, Ruth Meecham called Karin, and Karin went over to Ruth's house and—I don't know. If Ruth was really crazy enough to blow up the Spadona Institute just to get back at your mom, I'm worried what she might be up to now."

"We should call the police," Temple said.

"To tell them what? That Karin has gone to visit a neighbor and we don't like it?"

"I guess I could go in and see what's going on," Temple said uneasily.

"I'll wait here. If you're not back in ten minutes, I'll call the police and tell them I saw someone breaking in," Jessica said.

"Where's your little boy?" Temple suddenly remembered Titus.

"He's asleep. He's okay by himself for a few minutes. Don't worry about him—you're as bad as your mother, fussing over me!"

Temple shut her eyes briefly: let it go. Jessica was a major pain in the ass, but she was helping, so don't waste valuable energy fighting her. She didn't say anything else but walked around Ruth's house to the front door and rang the bell. Jessica stayed behind her at the bottom of the steps, squatting so she couldn't be seen from the front door.

After she'd rung twice, Temple cautiously tried the knob. The front door was unlocked. She turned to wave at Jessica and moved inside. Her heart was still beating too hard, so she stood inside the doorway for a minute, picturing a decision tree: where she would look for Ruth and Karin, what she would do, each decision with its "yes" and "no" forks visible in her mind.

She'd only been in the house a few times and didn't know the layout, but she moved quickly through the ground floor without seeing anyone. Stairs to the basement led from both the kitchen and the front hall. Since she was right by the kitchen stairs, she went down those, but the house was so quiet she was beginning to worry that Ruth might have persuaded her mother to drive off with her somewhere.

She turned on her phone flashlight. She was in a small laundry area, with doors leading out of it to other parts of the basement. She swept them with her light. An instant later, she heard her mother call for help.

"It's me, Mom, it's Temple, I'll be right there."

The voice had come from her left. In her haste, she tripped over a basket of towels, but when she got back to her feet she managed to find a light switch. At first she saw only the furnace and other mechanicals, but when her mother called to her again, she found her in the back of the room, by the water heater, bound hand and foot. Next to her was Ruth Meecham, also tied, but unconscious.

Temple knelt next to her mother and started to undo her hands;

her own were shaking so badly she could barely use them. "Karin! What happened? I thought Ruth—"

"Temple, look out!" Karin shouted.

She turned and saw Jessica standing over her, a piece of firewood held like a club. She tried to roll out of the way, but shock slowed her reflexes, and the wood hit the side of her head as she rolled.

6

She blacked out for only a minute, but when she came back to a nauseated consciousness, she found herself lying bound on the floor next to Karin. Jessica was placing a wrinkled copy of the *Wall Street Journal* on the floor next to the water heater, her motions as precise as a temple goddess laying out a sacrifice.

"Jessica, what are you doing?" Temple knew she was slurring the words: everything was blurry, the lights, her voice, the giant standing over her clutching the *Wall Street Journal*.

"I'm solving the Spadona bombing," Jessica said. "Poor Ruth— her hatred for your mother had grown to such outsize proportions she brought the two of you here for a funeral pyre."

"But, Jessica, why? Why do you need to kill all of us? We don't wish you any harm, or at least, if it was you who blew up the Spadona building, why do you want to harm us on top of killing Mr. Epstein and Mr. Brooke?"

"Because you were meddling!" Jessica spat. "You had to go taking my supplies to your stupid lab. This way, it won't matter what they find, because all the evidence will point here! To the jealousy between Ruth and Karin."

"My God, you're foul!" Ruth had regained consciousness and now tried to sit up. She fell over again but said vehemently, "You thought no one would pay attention to your harassment of Clarence, but I saw it for what it was. I tried to warn Karin, but she's too holy for warnings and doubts."

"Let it go, Ruth, let it go, it doesn't matter."

"Let it go?" her neighbor said. "For five cents I *would* leave you to blow up here if I could, you and your unending chanting. Jessica worked for Clarence in Washington. Titus was his baby. She came here to Chicago to taunt him with it, and you let her use you as a dupe! If you ever asked the questions I'm prepared to ask, you'd never have given her house room!"

Temple felt a bubble of hysterical laughter rising in her, like a bubble floating on a fountain in a child's water experiment. She still felt dizzy, dizzy and ditsy. She thought, what a way to go, and she laughed helplessly.

"So you think it's funny?" Jessica snapped. "You're little Miss Perfect, aren't you, living your life according to so many rules you're like a walking computer, so I don't suppose you've ever even thought of having sex with a married man. Professor Conservative, the economic saint of the neocons, tried to force me to have an abortion. He didn't want a child on his résumé—at least, not one belonging to one of his interns, not when he has a perfectly respectable wife in their Potomac mansion. When he was here last week, he threatened me, threatened to take Titus away from me. He said he could prove I was an unfit mother and get me put in prison."

"But, Jessica, I would have helped you," Karin said. "You didn't need to kill him. You can stay calm, I know you have it in you, we can work this out together."

"Oh, *fuck* you and your calm!" Jessica screamed. "Read the newspaper—it'll forecast the end of the world for you."

She ran from the basement. Karin began chanting softly, *"Eka leya, eka leya." Harmony.*

Ruth told her to shut up, she didn't want her last minutes on earth to be filled with Karin's hippie crap. Overhead, Temple heard water running in the pipes.

"Is someone in the house? Who's running water?" she demanded, opening her mouth to scream.

"No one, I'm not like your idiot mother, running a commune in my parents' beautiful—"

The newspaper. That was it, Jessica had made explosive paper, soaked it in acetone, left it to dry, made a perfect torch. She was running hot water somewhere upstairs, and when the water heater pilot flicked on—it would at any second—the paper would go up like a napalm bomb. Temple rolled over painfully and flung herself at the heater. The drain tap, she needed to open it, she couldn't get her hands in front of her, damn it, seconds not minutes. She clenched her teeth around the tap and jerked hard, again, a tooth cracked, jerked again, and a stream of hot water flooded her, the paper, and Ruth Meecham, lying in its path.

7

Y ou're going to be okay, darling." Karin stroked Temple's bandaged head. "You got burned on the side of your face, but not too badly, and the surgeon says there will only be a faint scar, once they operate. You were so brave, my darling, so clever. How did you know what to do?"

"I'm an engineer," Temple said. "They teach us that stuff."

"But what was on the paper?" Karin asked.

"Acetone, with mineral oil and something called PETN, that's kind of a detonator," Alvin said.

Lettice and Alvin had come to the hospital to see Temple. They had brought a video game that they assured her was impossible to solve so she'd have something to do while she waited for her surgery. "Now the Feds are agreeing it's what Jessica used in the Spadona building—anyone can get the details from the *Anarchist Handbook*—you don't have to be an explosives engineer. It was smart of you to guess how the fire went up the mechanicals— Sanford says you did well for a beginner, even if you stuck your head in where you shouldn't have."

"I didn't know," Temple said. "She made me think Ruth was behind it all."

"Oh, Ruth, she's just a confused and angry person," Karin said. "She got us out of there—once she saw you use your teeth to open that valve or tap or whatever it was, she used her teeth to pull the knots apart on my wrists. Even though she was still woozy from the blow to her head, she got upstairs to phone for help."

"Jessica must have been totally insane," Lettice said. "How could she imagine she'd get away with it all?"

"Poor Jessica: she's going to have a hard time in prison. I didn't do well my one night in jail, despite all my years of training, but unless she starts wanting to find a place of balance, she's going to have an angry hard time of it."

"Poor Jessica!" Temple said. "Can't it ever be 'Poor Temple,' or even 'Poor Karin'? Don't you care as much about me as you do about her? She was a murdering bully, and I saved your life!"

Karin knelt next to the bed and put her arms around her daughter. "Darling, I love you. You're the moon and the sun goddess in my life, but you're never 'Poor Temple.' You'd never be so weak and so scared you'd have to kill someone to make yourself feel better. How could I insult you by feeling sorry for you?"

"See?" Lettice said. "My mom would never say something like that to me. It'd be, 'Lettice, get out of your hospital bed and bring me a glass of water.' Your mom is the coolest, Temple, get used to it!"

Note

When Christine Matthews asked me to write a story for *Deadly Housewives* (Avon, 2006) I'd been thinking about my generation of Second-Wave feminists and wondering what kind of children we might raise. I was never given the gift of children of my own, but I began thinking of someone who went to India, spent time—years, in Karin's case—at an ashram, and the effect this would have had on her child. Temple doesn't reject her mother's outlook on the world, but she does grow up revolted by the chaos in her mother's house.

In the V.I. novels, whenever the detective needs forensic advice she turns to the Cheviot Engineering company, which does forensic engineering. Temple works there. V.I. Warshawski's account manager, Sanford Rieff, is Temple's boss.

The homemade bomb is something I got out of *The Anarchist Handbook*. I have been told that this is a completely unreliable guide to homemade explosives. I myself have never been interested in chemistry experiments, so I can't tell you whether this works or not. If you know that it doesn't—please don't tell me. I like the story too much to want to have to change it.

SAFETY FIRST

She guessed cameras, or at least microphones, were hidden in the cell. Possibly in the showers, the cafeteria, even the attorneys' meeting rooms. From the moment of her arrest until the day of the trial, she said nothing inside the prison, except immediately after her arrest, and that was only to repeat a demand for a phone call. Finally, when she'd been kept sleepless and could no longer be sure of time, a guard handed her a cell phone and told her she had thirty seconds, and if she didn't know the number, they weren't a phone directory, so tough luck.

Once she'd made the call, she became mute. She didn't speak to the assistant attorneys for the Northern District of Illinois sent to interrogate her, nor to the guards who summoned her for roll call four times a day, or tried to chat with her during the exercise period. Because she was a high-risk prisoner, she was kept segregated from the general population. A guard was always with her, and always tried to get her to speak.

The other women yelled at her across the wire fence that separated her from them during recreation, not rude, just curious: "Why are you here, Grandma? You kill your old man? You hold up a bank?"

One day the guards brought a woman into her cell, a prisoner with an advanced pregnancy. "You're a baby doctor, right? This woman is bleeding, she says she's in pain, says she needs to go to the hospital. You can examine her, see if she's telling the truth or casting shade."

A pregnant woman, bleeding, that wasn't so rare, could mean anything, but brought to her cell, not to the infirmary? That could mean an invitation to a charge of abuse, malpractice. She stared at the pregnant woman, saw fear in her face and something less appetizing, greed, or maybe unwholesome anticipation. She sat crosslegged on her bunk, closed her eyes, hands clasped in her lap.

The guard smacked her face, hard enough to knock her backward. "You think you're better than her, you're too good to touch her? Didn't you swear an oath to take care of sick people when they gave you your telescope?"

In the beginning, she had corrected such ludicrous mistakes in her head. Now she carefully withdrew herself from even a mental engagement: arguing a point in your head meant you were tempted to argue it out loud.

She sat back up, eyes still shut, took a deep breath in, a slow breath out. Chose a poem from her interior library. German rhymes from her early childhood: *Über allen Gipfeln ist Ruh*. English poems from her years in London schools: *Does the road wind uphill all the way?*

WHEN HER LAWYER finally arrived, three weeks after her arrest, she still didn't speak inside the small room set aside for attorney-client meetings. The lawyer explained that it had taken them that long to discover where the doctor was being held. "They're fighting very dirty," the lawyer said.

The doctor nodded. *Come back with an erasable board,* she

wrote on an edge of the lawyer's legal pad. When the lawyer had read the message, the doctor tore off the handwritten scrap and swallowed it.

She was being held without bond because she was considered a flight risk, the lawyer explained. "We tried to fight for bail, but these new Homeland Security Courts have more power than ordinary federal courts. We are challenging the Constitutionality of both your arrest and your postarrest treatment. We have our own investigators tracking down information and witnesses in your support. Keep heart: there are hundreds of thousands of people in America and across the world who are aware of your arrest and are protesting it."

After the lawyer left, the guards took the doctor to a new cell, one with three other inmates. Those women were noisy. One had a small radio she played at top volume at all hours. Another heard voices telling her to pray or scream or, on their third day together, to attack the doctor. The radio player was shocked into calling for a guard. When no one came, the radio player grabbed the woman hearing voices; the fourth cellmate joined her. Together they subdued the voice-hearer.

"You gotta file a complaint," the radio player said. "You can't let people try to kill you. That's what they want, you know: they told us they're hoping you'll die, or that we'd annoy you so much, you'd attack one of us. They didn't say you was an old lady who wouldn't hurt a flea. So you gotta file a complaint."

The doctor almost touched the radio player's shoulder, remembered in time that a touch could be turned into a sexual caress by clever camera editing and clasped her hands in front of her. The following day, she was back in her old cell, one bed, just her, alone.

After that, she was sent to exercise with the general population. The woman who'd attacked her tried to do so again, joined by several others who liked to prey on the old or friendless—including the woman who'd been brought to her with a problem pregnancy. "She's a doctor but she only treat people with money!"

The radio player intervened. She had plenty of friends or at least followers within the prison, and she summoned enough help that the attackers withdrew.

"You a doctor?" the radio player demanded. "Why you in here?"

The doctor shook her head. Because they were outside, presumably far from microphones—although these days you probably were never far from a camera or a mike—she risked a few words.

"I don't know." Her voice was hoarse from disuse.

"How come you don't know? You know if you killed a patient, right? You know if you stole money from Medicare. So what you do?"

The doctor couldn't help laughing. "True, I'd know if I did either of those things. I didn't do them. I don't know why the United States government arrested me."

"You got some big fish pissed off." The radio player nodded sagely.

After that, people approached the doctor during exercise in the yard. The radio player served as an informal triage nurse. Swollen nodes in necks or armpits, varicose veins, heavy periods, no periods, bruises, knife wounds.

The doctor had limited ability to treat, no way to conduct a proper exam, but she would recommend the infirmary or a demand for hospital care or in most cases, wait it out—which is what the inmates would have to do in any event, even the women whose swollen abdomens didn't indicate pregnancy but ovarian tumors.

Finally, seven months and twenty-three days after her arrest and arraignment, the trial began.

THE CLERK OF the court: "Docket number 137035, *People v. Charlotte R. Herschel, MD,* Homeland Security Court, Justice Montgomery Sessions presiding.

"Dr. Charlotte Herschel is accused of violating United States Act 312698, an Act to Guarantee the Security of the Borders of the United States, known as "The Keep America Safe Act," ¶¶ 7.183 through 7.97 inclusive, relating to the medical treatment of undocumented aliens and to the willful concealment of undocumented aliens from the federal government. She is charged further with violating ¶¶ 16.313 through 16.654, relating to the sanctity of the life of all United States–born citizens, from the moment of conception."

Justice Sessions: "Today's hearing is held in camera. Because the Security of the Borders Act addresses Homeland Security, neither journalists nor civilian observers can be present. I must ask the bailiff to clear the courtroom of everyone but the lawyers and their assistants."

Some forty people from the Ex-Left were in the courtroom. Predictably, they raised outraged howls at being ordered to leave. In fact, many of them lay limp on the floor. The bailiff and federal marshals didn't suppress their grins as they banged the protestors into the benches or against the doorjamb on their way out of court.

About the only legislation the 115th Congress had passed was the Keep America Safe Act, and its follow-on, the law funding the Homeland Security courts. Dr. Herschel's case was one of the first to be heard in a Homeland court.

The law was sketchy on what defendants could do to support

themselves. They could not have a trial by jury—a tribunal of five federal judges was empaneled for each trial. Defendants could call witnesses, but it wasn't clear on the presence of citizens in the courtroom. Justice Sessions had decided that matter, at least for Dr. Herschel's trial.

From the moment of her arrest, Dr. Herschel's case had been drawing attention from the Extreme Left and their fake news machines. The *New York Times* huffed and puffed so often that a Real News cartoon, showing the paper as the Big Bad Wolf unable to blow over the government's case, went viral. Of course, in response, the Ex-Left tried to paint the government as a trough full of pigs, but everyone agreed that the *Times* response was a lame knockoff of the Real News original.

However, the *Times* coverage meant that the Ex-Left fat cats put up so much money for the doctor's defense that Ruth Lebeau had agreed to take the case. Lebeau was a formidable Constitutional lawyer with a team of experienced research lawyers at her side. Except for the court reporter and Dr. Herschel, she was the only woman in Justice Sessions's courtroom, and the sole African-American. She seemed to pay no attention to that distinction, nor to the insults lobbed by Real News, comparing her to a talking chimpanzee.

OPENING STATEMENT OF Melvin Coulter, federal attorney for the Northern District of Illinois:

"Dr. Herschel is well known to federal agents throughout the Northern District. She runs what she calls a medical clinic, but is in reality a squalid den where the most vile crimes are committed. She not only harbors known enemies of the United States, but is a self-proclaimed murderer of the most innocent lives in our midst. So heinous are the crimes, and so intent is this so-called *doctor* on keeping them from public view, that she spent a small fortune in turning her abattoir into an armed fortress."

Coulter droned on for over an hour. Ruth Lebeau, dressed in navy suiting with an Elizabethan collar framing her face, made a few notes, but spent most of Coulter's speech either smiling reassuringly at her client or mouthing comments to her chief associate, a young man whose impeccable tailoring matched her own. He seemed to find Lebeau extremely witty. The court reporter noticed that he often covered his mouth to keep from laughing out loud—a gesture that made Justice Sessions scowl with fury. The court reporter was surprised that Sessions, who was known for his short fuse, hadn't expelled the lawyer from his courtroom.

Dr. Herschel was a small woman, with graying hair cut close to her head. She wore no makeup and no jewelry. The court reporter thought she looked like the kind of doctor you could trust, not the formidable monster described in the government's brief.

It troubled the reporter that the doctor didn't look at Coulter or Sessions during the opening statement. The reporter believed innocent people could stare down their accusers. She didn't know that sociopaths could also stare down their accusers and that innocent people might look at their clasped hands so that judge and prosecutor couldn't see the furious contempt in their eyes.

When the prosecutor sat down, Ruth Lebeau made her own opening statement. She sketched Dr. Herschel's history: an orphan, a refugee, who had dedicated her life to the health and welfare of women in the United States. The many awards she had received for her humanitarian work, for her innovations in perinatal medicine and in surgery. Lebeau spoke about the Constitution, as well, and how the law under which Dr. Herschel was charged set up two classes of people.

"We're skating perilously close to Nuremberg laws here. Americans reject the idea that one class of person has higher value than other classes, whether the division is between black and white, Christian and Jew, foreign born or native born. We will show that Dr. Herschel's whole life and career have been devoted to caring for women and children who most need help, and that she has used her own resources to bring free medical care to Americans who can least afford it, but need it most."

The court adjourned for lunch. Melvin Coulter was seen eating with Justice Sessions and the other judges on the tribunal. A photograph of them together in the Potawatomi Club circulated on Fake News websites, but Real News assured Americans that there was nothing wrong with two old friends meeting for lunch. The Ex-Left also put up videos of the federal marshals dragging protestors from the courtroom; Real News showed patriots cheering the marshals.

IN THE AFTERNOON, the evidence part of the trial began. The government had been surveilling Dr. Herschel and her clinic for many months. Even before the Keep America Safe Act, ICE agents had paid particular attention to her Damen Avenue clinic because she treated so many low-income women, not just immigrants from Muslim countries and Mexico, but poor Americans as well.

Coulter began with photographs of the Radbuka-Herschel Family Clinic projected onto the three screens in the courtroom. These days the clinic was padlocked, the windows covered with obscene graffiti, as well as swastikas and "death camp" in jagged capital letters, but the pictures had been taken during the surveillance and data gathering phase of the case.

The clinic stood near the corner of Damen and Irving Park Road in Chicago. The sidewalks were dirty, the nearby storefronts run-down or boarded over. The court watched two women in headscarves approach the building, one with toddlers in a double stroller, the other carrying an infant while an older child held her skirt. The women glanced around furtively, then rang the clinic bell.

"You can see the armor-plated glass"—Coulter tapped the windows in the photograph—"and the video cameras. Once the women gained entrance through the first door, they were sealed in the equivalent of an airlock while clerks videoed them. Only then did they gain admittance to the death chambers inside."

The testimony of all the Immigration and Customs Enforcement Agents, along with the FBI, took close to two weeks to hear. The most dramatic testimony actually came from one of Dr. Herschel's own nurses: Leah Shazar had worn a tiny body camera to record many of Dr. Herschel's patients and procedures, even patients she herself was examining.

When Ruth Lebeau rose to cross-examine her, Shazar broke down into sobs. "They threatened to deport my own mother, my sisters, back to the men who raped them. What else could I do?"

"Find someone to help you fight them," Lebeau said. "What did you think you were doing to the patients entrusted to your care?"

After Shazar's weeping went into its second inarticulate minute, Justice Sessions ruled that Lebeau was badgering the witness and to stop such an emotional line of questioning. When Shazar stepped out of the witness box, she tried to approach the doctor, but Dr. Herschel turned her head away and refused to look at her.

The court reporter didn't know how to react. If she'd been a patient in the clinic, she sure wouldn't have wanted her own private business shown in a courtroom. Had it been fair for the FBI to coerce Shazar into recording people? At the same time, the nurse was truly sorry—shouldn't Dr. Herschel at least accept Shazar's apology?

During Shazar's testimony, Coulter showed videos that she had taken. "Yes, Dr. Herschel routinely performed abortions in her abattoir. And she helped illegal immigrants avoid federal agents."

The five male judges, the bailiff, the clerk, and the two armed marshals gasped in delighted indignation as a camera focused on a woman's vulva, where the doctor was inserting a speculum. A nurse, back to the camera, was bathing the woman's forehead with a towel. After a moment, blood flowed. The camera zoomed in on a blood clot, which Coulter identified as a dead baby.

After letting Justice Sessions and the rest of the all-male court lick their lips for a long moment, Coulter showed a video of the alley behind the clinic. A dark van was backed up to the clinic's rear door.

"We can't see who is coming out at this particular moment, but we do know that Dr. Herschel used this and other vehicles to whisk away illegals before ICE agents could demand their papers. Of course, once we spotted the ruse, we stopped the vans and arrested the occupants."

Here, the video showed Immigration & Customs Enforcement agents stopping several different vehicles. They pulled out women and children, cuffed them, and thrust them into government cars.

Dr. Herschel's lawyer directed a contemptuous smile at the prosecution table and made a point of writing an exceptionally long note. She whispered something to her own chief associate. The young man once again bit back a guffaw, earning yet another frown from Justice Sessions.

The final charge against the doctor claimed she'd helped spirit away the notorious immigration activist Sofia Pacheco. Since appearing on the FBI's ten most wanted list, Pacheco had been hidden in churches and attics by sympathizers across the nation. Every time the government seemed poised to make an arrest, it turned out they had the wrong information, or, worse, someone at the FBI or ICE had leaked the raid and given Pacheco time to make her getaway.

Finally, thirteen months ago, they were sure they had cornered Pacheco in a Chicago garden shop. The shop made a delivery of gladioli and daylilies to Dr. Herschel inside a long carton; Pacheco, apparently, lay underneath the flowers.

At the clinic, someone, perhaps the doctor, perhaps one of her staff, styled Pacheco's hair to resemble the doctor's own, streaked it with gray dye, put her in a lab coat, and brazenly sent her outside.

"The agent detailed to follow the doctor had stepped away from his post for three minutes—even our dedicated ICE agents sometimes have a call from nature." (Laughter from Sessions and the other four judges.)

"The clinic staff seemed to be watching our agent, because they used that window of time to send Pacheco out; she drove off in Dr. Herschel's own Audi."

The Audi had been found in the meatpacking district; the doctor was in surgery all day and claimed to know nothing about Pacheco. "Of course she knew about Pacheco: why else did she leave her Audi at the clinic instead of driving herself to the hospital?"

Ruth Lebeau cross-examined the agent to no avail: Wasn't it true that Dr. Herschel often used a car service between the clinic and the hospital? Wasn't it true that she was often in the operating room for ten or even fifteen hours, so that she was too fatigued to drive herself at the end of surgery?

"You're arguing generalities," Justice Session rebuked Lebeau. "We're looking at a specific day and a particular crime."

At the end of the eighth day, the prosecution rested. "The government has irrefutable evidence that warrants that Dr. Herschel be stripped of her U.S. citizenship. However, we believe her crimes rise to the level of deliberate treason against the United States by refusing to acknowledge the power of the Government to pass the Keep America Safe Act and to enforce its provisions."

Coulter wiped his mouth with the red handkerchief he kept in his breast pocket for such moments and resumed his seat. Justice Sessions adjourned the court and said they would hear the defense in the morning. He and Melvin Coulter rode down the elevator together and were later seen yet again at the Potawatomi Club, laughing over their drinks—martini for the prosecutor, iced tea for the abstemious justice.

ALL DURING THE final day of the prosecution's case, Coulter had been smirking with his juniors at the prosecution table, watching as Ruth Lebeau sent her own young team members out in flocks.

In the morning, it became clear that the defense was in trouble, and why: their key witnesses had disappeared. The detective V.I. Warshawski, who had gathered much of the defense's evidence, was in prison herself: she'd been arrested two days earlier, charged under the same sections of the Keep America Safe Act as Dr. Herschel.

The court reporter thought Dr. Herschel was going to faint. Her dark, vivid face turned pale and waxy and she swayed in her seat. Ruth Lebeau, her attorney, asked if she needed a break.

"I require water," the doctor said.

Ruth Lebeau's chief associate produced a large thermos of hot water from his case and poured a cup for the doctor. Since the rest of her witnesses had been disappeared, Lebeau called the doctor to the stand.

As the doctor spoke, her vocal cords gradually regained their flexibility. The court reporter had strained to understand her at first, but after half an hour, the grating harshness left the doctor's voice. She spoke clearly, almost musically: the reporter realized it was a pleasure to listen to her after all the men she'd been recording during the prosecution phase. Too much bullying and swagger, none of this evenness, this effort to be clear that the doctor exhibited.

"I treat everyone who comes to my clinic," Dr. Herschel said. "I don't need to see a driver's license or a passport to diagnose measles or an ectopic pregnancy."

On cross-examination, Coulter demanded to know why she'd refused to treat the pregnant woman who'd been brought to her jail cell.

"I am curious about your knowledge of this woman," the doctor said. "Did you direct the guards to bring her to my cell?"

The members of the tribunal seemed to gasp, but Justice Sessions said, "You are on the stand, Doctor. You don't get to ask questions."

The doctor bowed her head.

"You must answer the attorney," Sessions said.

"The woman was not pregnant," Dr. Herschel said.

"You refused to examine her, so how can you possibly know this?" Coulter asked.

"How many pregnant women have you examined in your legal career, Mr. Coulter?" the doctor said. "Oh, yes, I must not ask you questions. But we will assume it is one woman, your wife, who produced two children with you. I have seen thousands. I know the difference between an abdomen with a fetus inside it, and a body with a pillow buckled to it. Perhaps you would have been fooled, but I was not."

"You can't know that!" Coulter snapped.

The doctor shrugged but remained silent.

"Have you nothing to say?" Sessions demanded.

Before Lebeau could jump to her feet to remind the court that Coulter had made a statement, not asked a question, the doctor said, "I have lived a long life. I have seen governments taken over by ravening weasels, I have watched them incite bored or ignorant or fearful mobs to violence. That you would bribe or coerce a woman to pretend a pregnancy does not surprise me, but it does sicken me."

Coulter sat down again. There was a moment of silence and then Ruth Lebeau asked the prosecution to put up one of their videos of a couple of women being pulled from an SUV in handcuffs. She zoomed in on their faces and asked the doctor if she recognized them.

"Yes, they were patients, first in my clinic, and then, because the daughter had complications, I saw her in surgery at Beth Israel."

"And can you identify them, by name, I mean?" Lebeau asked.

"I can, but I will not. It is enough that these strange men can look at them and know they sought medical help, but I will not violate their privacy further by naming them."

"Did you know that the older woman was Justice Sessions's housekeeper?" Lebeau asked.

The doctor's eyes widened: the court reporter, barely keeping back a gasp herself, thought the doctor hadn't known. "I did not know that, but I do not discriminate among those I treat."

"And did you know the daughter, whose abortion you performed, had been raped by the justice?"

At that, Sessions slammed his gavel and demanded an end to the proceedings. "The defense will rest. They cannot call independent witnesses to this calumny—"

"Yes, we cannot call your housekeeper, who looked after you for twenty-three years, because she was deported last week, was she not?" Lebeau said.

"That was a decision by Immigration and Customs, not by me. The court is adjourned for today. The tribunal will meet tomorrow to discuss a verdict."

THE COURT REPORTER couldn't sleep that night. She was shocked by today's testimony. Abortion was evil, and the doctor was wicked to perform them. But Justice Sessions—when the black lady lawyer said he'd raped his housekeeper's daughter, he'd ended the trial. If he'd been innocent, surely he would have denied the accusation.

The court reporter had a high security clearance, which required her to sign papers promising never to speak to anyone of the proceedings she attended. She thought of her oath; she thought of the doctor, the presiding justice, the men licking their lips at the video of the naked woman's vagina.

At five in the morning, she got up and went down the street to her local drugstore. The clerk was yawning, barely awake, counting the seconds until her overnight shift would end. The reporter, her hands shaking, paid cash for a cheap phone. She made a call to the cousin who had helped get her the job with the federal courts.

IN THE MORNING, the tribunal met for less than an hour before summoning the prisoner. The court reporter could see that the doctor had probably not slept any more than she had herself. The doctor's walnut-colored skin was pale, her eyes a pair of black holes sunk deep in her face.

Justice Sessions said, "The court has voted four to one to find you guilty on all counts under the Keep America Safe Act. We debated stripping you of your citizenship and deporting you, but we are well aware that your native country, Austria, is prepared to make you an international heroine and martyr, and so we are sentencing you to natural life in a federal prison in the United States. The Federal Bureau of Prisons will inform your attorney when they have decided where to house you. For now, you will remain in Chicago in the care of the Metropolitan Correctional Center. Court is adjourned."

A marshal seized Dr. Herschel and marched her through the side door that led to the fenced-in yard at the back of the building where prisoners were transferred into the buses that returned them to the various jails around town.

Her lawyer and the lawyer's chief associate walked with the

doctor as far as the exit: they weren't permitted beyond the doorway. As she tried to thank the lawyer, the doctor seemed to stumble. Lebeau's young associate caught her as she fainted.

He pulled his thermos from his briefcase and unscrewed the top. No one could agree on what happened next, but one of the marshals thought the young lawyer poured a glass bottle labeled SUGAR into the thermos. Smoke billowed out. It covered the doctor, the lawyer, the marshal, and spread through the fenced-in courtyard. The marshals pulled their weapons and began firing into the thick fog, but someone screamed: they'd hit the driver of the prison van, who'd been standing behind it, waiting to lock the doctor inside. By the time the fog cleared, the prison van was gone.

Later that day, the van was discovered at Belmont Harbor on the Chicago shore of Lake Michigan. The Coast Guard began a search of all boats on the lake, but they didn't find the doctor, Lebeau's chief associate, or the federal marshal who'd handcuffed the doctor as she was taken from the courtroom. No one noticed that the court reporter had also disappeared.

Months went by; the Department of Justice kept close surveillance on anyone who might be in touch with the doctor, including the imprisoned V.I. Warshawski, who'd been the doctor's close friend for decades. They monitored the doctor's family members in Canada, her medical colleagues, even some of her high-profile patients. No one spoke of her. No one heard from her.

Time passed. Crops were rotting in the fields because the immigrants who used to harvest them were denied entry or had been deported from a safe America. Construction sites languished. The 117th Congress overturned the most stringent sections of the

Keep America Safe Act, although the criminal penalties for performing abortions on U.S.-born women remained in place.

Somewhere along the way, V.I. Warshawski was released from prison. She, too, disappeared without a trace, despite the FBI's continued monitoring of her actions.

Every now and then, the FBI or ICE would follow up on a report of a small, black-eyed doctor performing miracle cures among indigenous Americans, or in Congo or Central America. She had a few assistants, who helped trace rapists or murderers or thieves in whatever village or jungle they found themselves, but by the time U.S. agents were dispatched across the deserts and mountains, these legendary figures had moved on.

Note

This story was written for the anthology *It Occurs to Me That I Am America*, Jonathan Santlofer, ed., Touchstone Books, 2018. The fifty-two writers and artists who contributed work did so without pay so that all income from the book could support the American Civil Liberties Union. This is a dystopic story; the Homeland Security courts and Keep America Safe Act are imaginary. However, women all over the country are in real life, real time, being denied access to reproductive health care under laws which are ever more punitive.

TRIAL BY FIRE

I

"Yes, we'll gather at the river, the beautiful, the beautiful river . . ."

When she'd shut the window twenty minutes ago, they'd been singing "Throw out the lifeline" with the same ragged tunelessness. Sophia couldn't stand the hymns or the loud, lackluster singing. Most of all, she couldn't stand the tent revival on her land. She wanted to stay inside with the curtains drawn, but the heat was too heavy to leave the windows shut.

A bonfire on the far side of the tent gave her a shadow play of the figures inside, the preacher waving his arms in an orgy of rhetoric, the sinners going forward to kneel in an ecstasy of self-abasement.

This was the fourth night of a six-night revival. Attendance had been small the first night, but the preacher had passed out leaflets in all the surrounding towns, and each night more people pulled up in Model-Ts or horse wagons. Sophia had tried to get Lawyer Greeley to force the tent to move onto the Schapen property—after all, it was Rufus Schapen who'd given them permission to set up.

Lawyer Greeley had patted her hand. "Miz Tremont, they're not doing you any harm and they're bringing comfort to a lot of people. Why don't you just let that sleeping dog lie? They'll be gone in a week."

"You try sleeping with a hundred hysterical people on your land, lighting a bonfire in the middle of a drought," she'd snapped. "And it's high time Rufus Schapen learned that this is not his land to do with as he wishes. I'm not sure I want him to inherit it when the time comes. After all, Amos has nephews who would care for the land."

"Maybe this isn't the best time to make a decision like that," Greeley said. "Tempers are already high enough in the county. Let's wait for cooler weather and cooler minds."

The conversation still rankled. Women had the vote now, but men like Lawyer Greeley talked to her as if she were a child, not the person who had made this farm go almost on her own for most of its existence. She was rehearsing the grievance in her mind, wondering what she could do to force Rufus to move out of the house, when she caught sight of a slim silhouette rising and kneeling in the tent.

Georgie. If she was in the tent meeting, she had only gone to torment Rufus. Ever since she'd arrived on the farm six weeks ago, she'd been looking for ways to amuse herself; taunting Rufus was one of her favorites. Not that drinking and bareback riding on Sophia's cart horses didn't also entertain her. Rufus rose time and again to her bait, but her arrest had definitely been the last straw. If Sophia hadn't heard the shouting and come running, Rufus might well have beaten Georgie past recovery.

Sophia walked out of the house, wondering if she should go into the tent to remove the girl, but she stopped halfway across the yard. The silhouette with the bobbed hair had disappeared. She must have realized the crowd would think she was a true penitent, carried away by the Holy Spirit. They might try to put a white robe on her and carry her away to be baptized.

Perhaps it wasn't Georgie, anyway: her cousin wasn't the only young woman in Douglas County to bob her hair and paint her lips.

Sophia's own hair hung to her waist when she unpinned it. Even though it had gone gray, it was still thick and heavy, hair that Amos used to wrap around his hands to pull her toward him. He'd been dead so many years now she'd almost forgotten those nights.

"Yes, we'll gather at the river, that flows by the throne of God."

Sophia turned back to the house, away from the singing. The Kaw river was so low that you could walk across it on the sandbars, but no one wanted to; the mud stank of rotting fish.

She husbanded her well and rainwater carefully, bathing sparingly, washing clothes every second week instead of every week. The deep wells were for watering the stock and keeping some of the wheat and corn crops from dying. She used water from dishwashing and laundry on her truck garden, and the Grellier farm was doing better than many, but it was a hard summer for all of them; Sophia couldn't blame her neighbors for calling on Jesus for help. She just didn't want them calling from her property.

2

I don't know how you've borne it all these years." Her cousin Fanny had shuddered melodramatically when she came down for breakfast on her first morning at the farm. "Still using kerosene lamps and a coal stove, milking a cow with your own hands, and look at your skin—it's tanned like leather."

"The heat is unbearable," Georgina moaned, appearing at the table in a silk chemise.

Rufus's face turned mahogany under his sunburn. "Get some clothes on. You may think you've come to an Indian reservation, but this is a civilized farm. You don't sit at my dinner table in your undergarments."

"He's right," Fanny decreed. "You have a family reputation to uphold out here; don't get off on the wrong foot."

Georgina shrugged and poured herself a cup of coffee. "Pottery mugs. How quaint. Tell me you're not eating dinner at eleven in the morning, cousin Sophia, not when it's barely breakfast time. I'd like an egg and some toast. And if you have an orange or grape-fruit?"

Sophia gave a tight smile. "We ate breakfast while you were still in bed, Georgina. Dinner is our midday meal on the farm, but you can make yourself an egg—they're in the larder—that door to your right off the kitchen."

"Dinner before noon? I *am* in the wilds of America. Coffee is fine, thank you, Cousin Sophia. But I prefer to be called Georgie, not Georgina."

"Slang and nicknames are unbecoming a young lady, Georgina," Fanny said.

Georgie smiled brightly. "If I'm to be 'Georgina,' then you must be called 'Frances.'"

"Since to you, I am your grandmother, my first name doesn't come into the equation. Sophia, would you pour me more coffee?"

After a long pause, while Georgie stirred cream around in her mug, Rupert slammed down his knife and fork and headed back to the fields.

Sophia watched him leave without a word. She certainly was annoyed with Georgie, but it was really her son-in-law, claiming it was *his* dinner table, that set her teeth on edge. The farmhouse and the land were Sophia's, and she had the documents to prove it, locked prudently in a box at the bank, key hidden on a hook behind the old coal stove, but Rufus kept thinking the farm as good as belonged to him. He took for granted that her acres would pass to him when Sophia died. Give him his due, he worked the land as carefully as if it were, indeed, his, but what her beloved Anna had ever seen in that soulless lump, Sophia had never fathomed.

Fanny and her granddaughter were the first members of the Entwistle family to come west since Sophia's mama, Anna Entwistle Grellier, and her husband, Frederic, had emigrated in 1858 to undo the chains of the bondsmen and bring Kansas free into the union. Sophia had been ten then, an only child: all her younger siblings had died before the age of five.

"The Lord has called him home," her grandmother Entwistle said at baby Frederic's funeral the year before they left for Kansas Territory.

"It is not by the will of any god that my son died," her father had replied in his accented English, his eyes bright with tears over baby Frederic's coffin. He was a freethinker and was outraged that Mama's family organized a Christian funeral over his objections.

He and Mama differed on Jesus, but they agreed on the need to free the bondsmen. They answered the call from the antislavery society in Lawrence for a teacher in their school for children of all races. Even Indian children were welcome there.

All the Entwistle clan were antislavery, but none of them was willing to join Mama and Frederic in the perilous journey west. Mama's brothers worked for Grandfather in the bank; they couldn't possibly abandon their heavy responsibilities.

Sophia herself had been furious at leaving Boston. Grandmother invited Mama and Papa to leave Sophia with them, in the white ruffled bed where Mama herself had slept as a girl, but her parents would not give her up.

It took Fanny and Georgina little more than a day to travel by train from Boston to Lawrence. In 1858, the journey took over six long hard weeks. Sophia and her parents rode by train to Cleveland and then wagon to Saint Louis, where they transferred all their belongings, including Mama's piano, to a steamboat on the Missouri River for the week's journey to Kansas City

They waited in Kansas City for another two weeks, the time it took for an armed escort to assemble and accompany them past the slavers who controlled access into Kansas Territory. While they waited, Mama gave birth to her third baby boy.

The baby died on the two-day wagon ride from Kansas City to Lawrence. Little Joseph, going into the wilderness, his grave was one of the first dug in the new town. With Mama weak and grieving, and Papa unable to deal with anything practical, it fell to Sophia to find the ferryman, give him a precious dollar to load and unload their goods and carry them to Lawrence.

Six miles from Lawrence, they'd crossed the Wakarusa River on another ferry, but once on the other side the wagon had splashed through water almost all the way to the town. The wagon driver told her and Papa to walk alongside the wagon, as he did, to spare the oxen: they were in wetlands, with water too shallow for a ferry, but muddy and a strain for the animals. At one point the water rose to Sophia's waist; Papa picked her up and carried her for a time so as not to add her slight weight to the suffering beasts.

Too much water, not enough, that was the story of Kansas—

drought, floods, drought, locusts, blizzards—everything that nature could send to destroy the human spirit had descended on them. Neither of her parents knew anything about farming and Papa wasn't interested: he cared only about his school. The homestead they'd laid a claim to Sophia and Mama learned to care for, with the help of neighbors.

Sophia always assumed she would return to Boston as soon as she was old enough to live without parental decree. But then Papa was murdered by border ruffians during the Civil War, and she and Mama took over the school and still tried to run the farm, and then the Tremonts arrived from New York state with enough money to set up a ten-thousand-acre bonanza farm.

Young Amos Tremont helped Sophia, the Grellier farm began to succeed, they married, had one child who lived to adulthood and married Rufus Schapen. And now—Amos was dead, their daughter and her baby long dead in childbirth, and it was just Sophia and Rufus. She wished it were just Sophia.

Sophia had recently joined the Congregational church as a place to find companionship away from her son-in-law, and she was happy to drive the horses into town every Sunday. Rufus didn't like the Congregationalists; he found them cold and unfeeling, lacking in the genuine Spirit that he found in tent revivals. This was the church her mother and grandparents had belonged to; she always made a silent apology to Papa during the sermon, wondering if his freethinking ideas were wrong and he was actually with Jesus in heaven. Not sure of her own ideas on the subject.

It was in the midst of Sophia's loneliness that Fanny wrote: her granddaughter needed a change from Boston; could she spend the summer in the country with Sophia?

Rufus objected: a city girl on the farm, no doubt spoiled, the last thing they needed, but Sophia had written back at once to welcome Georgina. A young girl around the place was just what she needed to revive her spirits. She did caution her cousin that the amenities Georgina was doubtless used to in Boston would be sadly lacking.

"And if we are to feed her for three months, then a dollar a week in board would be welcome."

She and Fanny used to spend every Sunday together at Grandfather Entwistle's tall narrow house on Beacon Hill. They'd fought, played, shared the white ruffled bed on Sunday nights, and then, when they were ten, they were suddenly torn apart. They had written letters at first, the stilted letters of children:

Every thing here is covered with dirt and we must wash our own close in tubs there are no servants. The work is hard, but we are setting free the bondsman. We see Indyans every day and rackoons and sometimes wolfs.

She did not add that they barely had food to eat, especially since Papa was a vegetarian who would not allow murdered birds to be cooked in his house. Indeed, without the barrel of supplies Grandmother Entwistle sent them, they might well have starved to death. "Write nothing to excite pity," Mama said, editing her letter before she mailed it. "We are here for a high moral purpose and we should be envied, not pitied, for a few material lacks."

As time passed, the cousins' correspondence dwindled. They sent each other news of their marriages, of their parents' deaths, of the birth of their children and then grandchildren. Sophia had been vaguely aware of Georgie's birth to Fanny's younger son, but time passed and she hadn't realized the girl was now twenty years old.

She also didn't know that the Boston family was sending Georgie west not for her health but for the family's. She was cutting a wide swath in Boston nightlife that was raising questions at the bank where Entwistles had been a presence for almost a century. The final scandal, which resulted in a forced stay in a high-priced sanitarium in the Berkshires, caused the whole family to gather on Beacon Hill to discuss what to do with Georgie.

It was Fanny who suggested sending her to Kansas for the summer. She hadn't seen her dearest Sophia in sixty-five years; she'd bring her recalcitrant granddaughter west, catch up with Sophia, and then return in time to join the family at their summer compound in Newport.

Much as she scorned Sophia's primitive cooking and plumbing out loud, after a few days on the farm, Fanny wrote to her daughter-in-law in Boston that "it couldn't be better. Sophia doesn't own a car: she has a gasoline tractor for the farm, but still uses horses and a buggy to go into town. And the only man on the place besides the handyman is a hulking Caliban of a son-in-law of about fifty-five. Georgina will not have much opportunity to sow her wild oats here."

3

Georgie did not enjoy country life, at least, not life in the Kansas countryside. She described all the primitive plumbing, cooking, and work chores that she was expected to share in in extravagant letters to her chums back in Boston.

Give this country back to the Indians. No sane person wants to live without a telephone or an automobile. They have motion pictures in town but neither Sophia nor Rufus ever goes. Every dime is counted four times before it's spent, so we do nothing as frivolous as motion pictures. Once one of the neighbors had a barn dance and I was so desperate I actually went! My bobbed hair and painted lips caused quite a furore. Very entertaining.

Rufus made no pretense of welcoming Georgie. As he told Sophia, almost every morning, Georgie was exactly the self-centered, frivolous brat he'd expected. One morning he came back from the fields to find her sunbathing on the grass in front of the house. She was wearing the same kind of bathing costume that everyone in her set in Boston wore.

"How dare you?" he thundered. "This is a Christian household. We don't lie around naked like heathens and Indians."

"Do you have a tape measure on you, Rufus? Are you hoping to join the Modesty Police?" Georgie grinned up at him. "They patrol the beaches and measure how much leg we're showing. My friend Susan Whitney had to pay a ten-dollar fine, but as you know, I don't have any money with me. You'll have to send the bill to my papa, who will be appropriately enraged."

Rufus's head seemed to swell. Sophia feared he might suffer a stroke and moved to silence Georgie, but too late: Rufus carried her inside. She went limp in his arms and made the job as hard as possible, but he dumped her on the parlor sofa and stomped back out to the yard.

After that, Georgie went out of her way to taunt him, dressing as skimpily as possible, jutting her hip out as she walked past him, leaning over him to offer to pour him fresh hot coffee, her cleavage practically in his nose, and laughing as he started to roar at her. She would skip out of his reach when he tried to hit her.

"She needs to go back to Boston," Rufus said to Sophia after four days of this behavior. "I'm going into town to buy her a ticket."

"Rufus, this is my house and she's my cousin. She's welcome here this summer. Neither of us is used to having a young person around, but if it's that hard on you, why don't you go across the field and stay with your parents until Georgie goes back home in September?"

He looked at her in shock for a long minute, trying to absorb what his mother-in-law had just said. "You know I can't do that," he finally muttered before going out to the barn.

Rufus's parents farmed five hundred acres on land just to the north of Sophia's farm. His two unmarried sisters lived in the farmhouse with them, along with his younger brother, whose wife and three children were also crowded in. If Rufus moved to his parents' home, he'd sleep on the living room sofa and not have any privacy.

Sophia had let him stay on with her after Anna and the baby died, first out of pity for his grief, and later out of pity for the misery of the Schapen house. She saw now she'd made a colossal mistake in doing so: it would have been better to hire a farm manager to do the work that Rufus did than to have him thinking the house belonged to him.

She turned wearily to Georgie, who'd been in the parlor during her exchange with Rufus. "I thought your coming out here would be a welcome break for me, but you want it to be a failure, don't you? You're trying to punish Fanny or your parents, but you're only turning me against you and not gaining anything for yourself."

Georgie was silent for a moment before saying, "Did Grandmother or any of the others tell you what my rest cure was supposed to heal me of?"

Sophia sat. "Nothing specific, no. Fanny—your grandmother—said they thought you were running wild. Were you?"

"Maybe. Probably. Dancing, speakeasies. Bad company." She spoke flippantly, but the tendons in her neck stood out.

"You fell in love with someone unsuitable?" Sophia suggested after another long silence.

"Not quite." Georgie smiled brightly. "Let's say some of the boys thought they knew what love was all about. My father thought a trip to the farm for the summer would be best for him if not for me. Or for you."

"It will be what you make it to be, Georgie. But it's a farm, not a country resort." Sophia hesitated, trying to find the right words. "Rufus—is not an easy man. Baiting him is easy, but you don't gain from it. Pitch in with the chores. It will make the time pass more pleasantly."

"Slops and chickens." Georgie's bright smile became even tighter. "Of course, Cousin Sophia."

After that, she did pitch in to a certain degree. She'd been emptying her slop bucket from the start, because there was no one to do it for her. She'd refused point-blank to learn to milk cows, but she did halfheartedly hunt for eggs; she dutifully spelled Sophia at the mangle on laundry days and even tried, very inexpertly, to iron.

She still taunted Rufus, but in subtler ways that he found hard to pin down—no more sunbathing, no more appearing at breakfast in her chemise. If Rufus commented on the weather or the state of the crops, Georgie would clasp her hands and look at him soulfully and say, "So wise." At the end of the day, if he complained of fatigue, she would coo, "Big strong man, he needs his dinner and his sleep."

Rufus would react angrily, but there was nothing in her words to object to—it was the mockery in her eyes, which she revealed only to him. If he snapped at her, she would gaze at him even more soulfully and say a man needed a vent for his strong feelings.

One Sunday afternoon after church, Georgie walked two miles along the gravel roads to an Indian college southeast of town. She'd seen a notice in the *Douglas County Herald* that the students were holding a kind of powwow and wanted to see it.

She'd been hoping for naked dancing around a bonfire, war cries, body paint, and was disappointed by the tameness of the display. It's true the students wore buckskins, but men and women were all completely clothed. The men's hair was cut short in the same style that European men used, the women's long hair was pinned up in braids.

The students sang standard hymns of the kind Georgie had been hearing all her life in her family's Boston church. The dancing was sedate, nothing like the war dances she'd seen in motion pictures, let alone the Charleston, which Georgie had been dancing recently at home. After the dancing, the students served lemonade and cake that the young women had prepared in the school kitchen as part of their domestic skills training.

The white audience was small: the Europeans in the county had little interest in Indian life and culture. They had a vague sense that the Indian school was doing a good thing, civilizing the savages, and except for making sure that Indians, like the local colored population, didn't eat in their restaurants or sit next to them at the motion picture theaters, the Europeans didn't pay them much attention.

The *Douglas County Herald* had sent a reporter to cover the powwow, a bored young man who spied Georgie sitting on the grass, her legs drawn up under her so that her skirt covered her knees. With her bobbed hair and painted lips, Georgie would have stood out at any gathering, but here she was especially visible. Two of the young Indian men were talking to her, and she was laughing.

"I'm Arthur Jarvis from the *Herald*," the reporter said. "Looks like you're having a good time at the show."

"The boys and I were just talking," she said. "Will Garrison here from the Dakota people lent me the blanket his mother wove for his pony, but I'd better give it back. The pony races will start soon and you need it, don't you?"

She looked up at one of the Indians, smiling in a way that implied intimacy. He put down a hand and helped her to her feet, flashing a return smile.

"Come with us, miss: we'll see you get the best view."

Jarvis trailed after the trio. He waited until the two Indians disappeared toward the school stables, leaving Georgie in the shade of a giant cottonwood, near the open field where the races were due to be run.

"I haven't seen you around here before," he said. "Where you from?"

"You want to do an interview with me?" she said.

"Sure, why not? Tell me your name and what brought you to the powwow today."

"Georgie Entwistle, and I came here on my own two feet." She looked down at them and added mournfully, "Don't think I'll ever get the dust and the scratches from the gravel off them, and they cost me eight dollars."

"You walked here in all this heat? You must really love the Indians, Miss Georgie. But you want to be careful not to love them too much."

"What's that supposed to mean?" she demanded. "They were just a couple of nice boys."

"They look like nice boys, but you know, they're this close to still being savages." Jarvis held his thumb and index finger up so that they almost touched.

"I've seen white boys who were even closer than that to being savages," Georgie said. "Don't you worry about it."

"Just the same, Miss Georgie, your reputation—"

"Is this an interview for a paper or for the Modesty Police?" she interrupted. "My reputation is none of your business, Mr. Reporter."

Other visitors began strolling up to the fence next to the field. The school superintendent, with his wife, daughters, and a few select dignitaries, were escorted to benches that had been set up for them farther along the railing.

At the west end of the field, near the stables, Georgie saw the ponies line up. She couldn't make out her new acquaintances at this distance, but when the starting gun went off, she clapped and screamed as the ponies streaked past the crowd. One of the white women, who had met her at church with Sophia, tapped her reprovingly on the shoulder. Georgie moved away. Arthur Jarvis followed.

Ponies and riders grew small in the distance, then rounded a curve in the makeshift track and galloped back. The youths on horseback didn't make a sound, which disappointed Georgie: she had expected at least in the races she would experience an authentic Indian war cry.

The riders pulled up in front of the superintendent. Georgie went over to watch the superintendent's wife give a blue ribbon to the winner; the red second-place ribbon went to her new friend, Will Garrison. When he saw her applauding, Garrison trotted over and handed her the ribbon. Sweat ran down his face into the bandanna he'd tied around his neck, but he grinned down at her happily.

"They'll all be drinking joy juice at the School House tonight," Jarvis said sourly as Garrison rode back to his classmates. "You know Indians love their joy juice."

"What is joy juice, Mr. Jarvis?" Georgie asked in the soulful voice she used on Rufus.

"I thought a girl like you knew all about things like that." Jarvis was still sour.

"Like what? Is that a special Indian beverage that they make here at the school? I'm from out east where we don't have any Indians, so I don't know anything about their customs."

"Indians don't have any head for liquor, but they love to drink it."

"Oh." Georgie made her lips round with shock. "But with Prohibition—"

"Don't tell me that out east there aren't people who know how to bypass Prohibition." Jarvis looked at her suspiciously.

"Maybe they do." Georgie shrugged, as if she had never shared a flask with a group of Harvard men and their girls. "My family are descended from the *Mayflower* Puritans. We have an obligation to uphold moral standards." If she had heard her father and grandmother say that once, she'd heard it fifty thousand times, especially during the last year.

"I take it the School Yard is a place where Indians can get specially created liquor?" she added.

"School House," Jarvis corrected. "The sheriff raids it every now and then, but people keep coming back."

"The School House?" The superintendent's wife came over. "That place is an abomination in this county. I keep telling Mr. Macalaster that he needs to get it shut down. Our boys are too well mannered to frequent it, but their parents and cousins, who lack their good fortune in education, become sadly inebriated."

"And you, young lady." She turned to Georgie. "Don't get too friendly with Will Garrison or his friends. It's not appropriate for our Indian boys to be seen with white girls."

4

The School House was seven miles from Sophia's farm. By the time she'd left the powwow she'd managed to learn the exact location. Georgie waited until Rufus and Sophia were asleep and then tiptoed out of the house to the barn.

The horses that Sophia used to drive into town or for minor hauling around the farm weren't trained for riding, but they were placid animals. Georgie brought a blanket with her, filched earlier from Sophia's linen closet. She put a bridle on the horse, which he didn't like, but dried apples from Sophia's storeroom calmed him down while she adjusted the straps and climbed onto his back.

He snorted uneasily but finally walked out of the barn and down to the road.

She didn't try to make him do anything fancy, just guided him toward the road she wanted, let him set the pace, let him nibble at the dusty weeds in the ditches. She saw the School House easily from a distance, a grim cube of a building with lights flickering at the windows, and tied Sophia's horse a prudent four hundred yards away. As she walked up to the door she saw the yard was full of cars, Model Ts, some of the new Model As, and even a Stutz Bearcat.

Georgie didn't have money for drinks, but she knew that was never a barrier. She also knew that some men would see a single woman in a speakeasy as someone who wanted physical attention, but she was used to that as well.

In back of the building was a metal cube with cables running from it to the School House. It smelled of oil and hot metal, like the electric streetcars at home. Georgie stepped away from the smell, but saw that the cables must be providing light to the speakeasy. Why couldn't Sophia install one of those? Then she could power the fans in her rooms all the time, instead of just when the stupid windmill put out enough energy.

Georgie walked around to the entrance, which was locked. She was used to that, as well: there would be a special knock, a code word, but again, a young woman on her own would be let in without much bother.

While she waited for someone to answer her pounding on the door, she saw the words carved into the lintel: KAW VALLEY DISTRICT FOUR SCHOOL HOUSE. A bar built into a school; that thought made Georgie laugh out loud. The door had a spyhole on the inside;

whoever was looking through it saw Georgie laughing, head tilted back, and let her in, with a grin of his own.

"Share the joke, sister, and first drink's on the house." He pinched her bottom as she sidled past him. She knew the rules of the game, knew she was supposed to pout, pretend outrage, give him a playful slap. For some reason, she couldn't bring herself to do it tonight, but pushed past him into the packed room.

Not much had been done to the schoolhouse when it was turned into a bar, but the cables from the generator out back powered the flickering electric lights. There was also a ceiling fan. One of the blades was bent, brushing against the ceiling slats as it turned.

From Arthur Jarvis's snide comment at the races this afternoon, Georgie had thought the Indians she'd met would be there, drinking joy juice. She'd pinned Will Garrison's red ribbon to the brim of her hat and began poking and prodding her way through the mob, looking for them. The only person she recognized was Jarvis himself. He'd drunk a fair amount already. When he saw her he got unsteadily to his feet.

"It's Little Miss Mayflower, come to play Carrie Nation with the drunks. You going to give me your lecture on Pilgrim purity?"

Several drinkers stopped midswallow to guffaw.

"Buy me a drink, Mr. Reporter, and I'll lecture you personally."

Jarvis nodded at the bartender, a thickset man in an open-necked shirt. The bar itself was just a couple of slabs of wood laid over sawhorses. The bartender poured something into a heavy mug. Georgie took a swallow and made a face—it was a quick-brewed beer, thin and bitter.

She slapped the mug on the sawhorses. "We Pilgrims only drink gin."

"That'll cost you a kiss, Mayflower."

Jarvis put an arm around her and tried to kiss her, but she reached behind him for the mug she'd put down and poured it over his hair. The crowd loved it.

"Why'd you go and do that?" Jarvis pulled out a handkerchief and wiped his face.

"Why'd you go and do that, yourself?" Georgie said.

"If it had been your Indian friend, bet you'd have been cuddling right into his red arms," he said resentfully.

"Probably so," Georgie said. "We Mayflowers and the Indians go back three hundred years together."

"Then I guess you don't know those Indian boys have a curfew and everything and Superintendent Macalaster makes sure they spend their nights locked up in their school dormitory. But there are some redskins around here if you have Jesus power to raise the dead."

Jarvis pointed at a corner of the room where two men were slumped on the floor, the wall behind them keeping them from falling over completely. Their clothes were dirty, and someone had taken the bandanna one of them wore at his throat and tied it around his head, sticking in a piece of rubber tubing in lieu of a feather.

One of the men at the bar took over a mug of beer and shook them awake. "Hey, chief, wake up. Got a lady who says she knows your great-grandmother. Have a beer and talk to her." He poured the beer over the two men, to an uproar from the crowd.

Georgie pretended to laugh, but turned her back. She had seen drunks before, more than once, but these two men looked so naked she found it unbearable.

She put her drink down and tried to push her way through the door. Over the noise of the drinkers and the clacking of the fan as its bent blade brushed the ceiling, Georgie heard a siren. She froze, looking for a back door, but there wasn't one. A moment later, a sheriff's deputy came in, accompanied by two revenue officers.

5

Georgie had had other bad days, but none had ever included a night in police custody. The county didn't have a women's prison, so the deputy locked Georgie in the sheriff's office overnight, with a matron to look after her. She told the matron that her cousin Sophia's horse was tied to a tree near the School House.

"He needs to be taken back to his stable. Can someone look after him? Please? It's too hot for an animal to be out this long. I don't even know if there's water within his reach."

"You should have thought of that before you took him bar crawling with you," the matron said.

However, the sheriff, when he came in at seven in the morning, sent a deputy out to the Grellier farm. The sheriff knew Sophia, he knew two of her dead husband's nephews. He didn't want her to lose a horse just because she had a drunk cousin visiting for the summer. He moved Georgie into the courtroom with the other arrestees and told her to wait until her cousin arrived to pay her fine.

"What if she doesn't come?" Georgie asked.

"Then you'll be assigned to a county crew to work off the fine," the sheriff said.

About twenty detainees waited in the courtroom with Georgie. Not everyone who'd been in the School House had been brought in. Arthur Jarvis, the *Douglas County Herald* reporter, was missing, Georgie noticed. The judge gave everyone a choice of a fine, thirty days in the county jail, or a week on a county work detail. At the end of the morning, only Georgie and the two Indian men remained.

At lunchtime, Will Garrison, the Dakota who had come in second in the pony races, arrived. He was covered with dust: he'd walked the two miles from the school to the police station to pay the fine for the two Indians.

When Georgie saw Garrison, she turned crimson with shame and huddled deep in her chair. She didn't look up, so she didn't know if he looked at her or not.

Around mid-afternoon, Sophia drove the buggy into town. Her lips were tight and white with rage, but she kept her temper to herself until they were on the road out of town. She was driving with only one horse.

"You stole my horse, you left him tied up near a busy road. What is the matter with you? You come from a good home, you never wanted for anything! Why are you acting in this fashion, doing everything you can to turn me, and Rufus, too, against you? I can't keep this from Fanny: that ten-dollar fine is a lot of money for me. Your father is going to have to pay me back. And then what will you do? Where else can you go?"

Georgie didn't try to say anything in her own defense: she didn't feel guilty about going to the speakeasy, but she wished she had never taken Sophia's horse.

"Is he—is the horse hurt?" she asked timidly.

"One of the neighbors saw him when he was out mulching at five this morning. He brought him home, undamaged but tired, which is why we're driving one horse this afternoon."

Georgie's contrition over the horse wasn't as deep as her shame that Will Garrison had seen her in the courtroom. She kept that thought tucked away below her diaphragm—she certainly wasn't going to share it with Cousin Sophia.

When they reached the farm, Sophia said, "You go muck out the stable. You will make the care of these two horses your mission for the remainder of your time on the farm. I want the stalls spic-and-span, I want the horses' coats glossy, I want them to have the water and food they need. You will *never* ride them again. Do you hear me?"

Georgie nodded. "Yes, Cousin Sophia."

Sophia gave her a pair of men's overalls. Not Rufus's, which would have swamped Georgie, but a pair of her own. She ordered them from the Sears catalog to wear when she was doing farmwork herself.

Georgie thought the worst was past, but when she washed herself off under the outdoor pump after working the rest of the afternoon in the barn, Rufus was waiting for her, shaking the evening paper under her nose.

"How dare you? How dare you take advantage of my hospitality?"

Georgie just had time to see the headline: MAYFLOWER DESCENDANT DESCENDS TO PUBLIC DRUNKENNESS, before Rufus slapped her head so hard she was knocked off her feet.

"Whore," he grunted. "Rutting, drunken whore."

He yanked her to her feet, but she wriggled away before he could strike her a second time. Standing just out of his arm's reach, Georgie pulled the top of her dress down under the overalls, flashing her breasts.

"You want these, don't you, Rufus? That's why you're so cranky all the time. You want them and you know I'll never give them to you."

Rufus started after her, but before he reached her Sophia appeared in the yard.

"I don't know what game you two are playing, but stop it at once."

Sophia's voice was even colder and angrier than when she'd lectured Georgie in the buggy. "The next time either of you behaves like this, you will both leave the farm, if I have to get the sheriff to remove you."

It was later that afternoon that the itinerant preacher appeared. He saw Rufus and got his permission to set the tent up on the Grellier property.

6

Georgie waited until Sophia and Rufus had gone to bed before reading the article in the *Herald*. As she read, her own temper rose up: Jarvis hadn't mentioned that he was drunk as ten skunks. Instead, he made it sound as though he had merely gone to the School House as a reporter so he could let Douglas County know what went on inside its pure borders. And he'd spent a number of paragraphs on Georgie, the *Mayflower* Descendant in love with the Indians.

> Miss Entwistle consorted with some of the young bucks at our local Indian school after yesterday's powwow. Superintendent Macalaster's wife tried to speak to her about the dangers intimacy between

> white girls and Indian boys holds for both races,
> but Miss Entwistle seems to think that her Puri-
> tan ancestors protect her from following normal be-
> havioral conventions—as she demonstrated at the
> School House that same night. She ordered gin from
> the bemused bartender, and made herself quite the
> spectacle for all the rowdies who usually frequent
> such a place.

Georgie tore the paper into spills and laid them in with the coals in the stove. When Sophia lit the fire in the morning to make Rufus his fried eggs, the story would go up in smoke. She lay in bed in her stuffy room but couldn't sleep. She wanted revenge on Arthur Jarvis, but couldn't think of anything drastic or punitive enough.

Around dawn her thoughts shifted to Will Garrison at the Indian school. They had been flirting in a harmless way, not consorting, but she wondered if he was in trouble with the school because of Jarvis's story. She thought of writing to the superintendent's wife or to the superintendent himself, but Mrs. Macalaster was a cold woman. She seemed to look down on the Indian students and she definitely looked down on Georgie.

At five, she heard Rufus go out the kitchen door. She watched from the window as he went into the barn to do the morning milking, and then heard Sophia go down the stairs to the kitchen. She smelled the smoke as the fire started. At least Jarvis's hateful words weren't in the house any longer.

There was a small table in the room where Georgie kept her toiletries and a pitcher and basin. She sat there to write a note to Will Garrison:

Dear Mr. Garrison, I apologize for any trouble I may have brought into your life. I enjoyed meeting you at the powwow on Sunday and thought you were a super rider. I am living on my cousin Sophia's farm, the Grellier farm, about two miles south of your school, near to Blue Mound. At the big crossroads between us and your school is a mailbox held into the ground with a couple of big rocks. If you would let me meet you to apologize in person, or if you would like me to return your red ribbon, leave a note for me under one of those rocks. Ever yours sincerely, Georgie Entwistle

As soon as Rufus had headed to the fields where he and the handyman were haying, Georgie came down the stairs. Sophia was washing the breakfast dishes. She nodded at Georgie but didn't speak.

Georgie drank her coffee, ate a piece of toast with tomato preserves, put on her overalls to go out to the barn. The overalls had pockets; she slipped the letter into one of them and walked past the barn, grabbing one of the big straw hats that hung just inside the door as she passed. She made a detour across a field where she couldn't be seen from the house or from the quarter section Rufus was working.

The July heat was fierce and she was sweating heavily under the straw hat, but when she took it off, the sun glare made her eyes ache. She went to the school's front door, forgetting that she wasn't in Boston where her name and privilege got her past most barriers, forgetting that she was dressed like a farmhand.

"Go out to the barn, boy, if you have a message from the farmer." It was Mrs. Macalaster herself who answered the door.

Georgie bit back a laugh. The overalls and hat were a perfect disguise, even hiding her sex. She walked around the main building to the barn, where some of the Indian boys were pitching down hay for the ponies and cows. Will Garrison wasn't among them, but one of them took the letter from her and promised to give it to him. He eyed her narrowly; she was sure that, unlike the superintendent's wife, his keen hunter's instinct knew not just that she was a woman but also that she was the woman who'd been at the powwow.

She scuttled away from the barn but stopped at a pump in the yard long enough to sluice her hot head and neck. Her overalls and the blouse she wore underneath them were dry by the time she got back to Sophia's barn.

She led the two horses out to a shady place in the enclosed field where Sophia usually left them for the day. The stalls were relatively clean from her previous day's work. She shoveled the manure into the compost area behind the barn, put out clean straw, and rinsed off her overalls under the pump in the yard.

She bypassed the kitchen when she came into the house: Rufus was at the table, eating corn bread and a fried pork chop. The hot food on the hot day made Georgie queasy. She took a cold bath, despite the interdiction from Sophia not to use water wantonly, and lay down to sleep.

Rufus went over to the revival tent after supper. He urged Sophia and Georgie to go with him.

"A good sermon that brought you to a sense of your sins would be the best thing you could do for your immortal soul," he said to Georgie.

"You have such a good sense of my sins, I expect Jesus will pay more attention to what you have to say about them than he will me," Georgie said.

Rufus glowered at her but left for the meeting without saying anything back. Georgie sat in the parlor with Sophia and watched her darn socks. Finally she went up to bed, waiting for Sophia to turn out the lamp in the parlor. When she heard her cousin climb the stairs, she slipped down the stairs in her stockinged feet and then out the back door.

The house was between her and the tent, but she could see bonfires shooting up flames, and could hear the singing and some of the excited cries from the sinners. She walked to the mailbox she had described in her letter and lifted the rocks. No answer had come from Will Garrison.

As she walked back to the house, automobiles began coming toward her: the damned and the saved leaving the revival. She stumbled into the ditch to keep from being seen and tore her good silk stockings on the nettles.

Georgie went to the mailbox faithfully for three nights, and on the Thursday was rewarded: Garrison himself rose from the shadows.

Georgie wanted to say something bold, the kind of comment she was used to making to the boys she knew at home, but she felt embarrassed and unlike herself.

"You came yourself?" she finally blurted.

"I was leaving a note for you, but then I saw you walking down the road."

"They told me you have a curfew."

"Yes, but the windows open. It's not so hard to jump out. Harder, maybe, to jump back in."

"Are you in trouble because of me?" Her voice had gone up half a register, making her sound like a child. She hated it but couldn't seem to control it.

"In a small way," he said. "The superintendent knows that Indian boys are weak in the face of temptation, and that a white woman is a powerful temptation. Almost as strong as drink. He and Mrs. Macalaster blame you for trying to lead me astray."

His voice was steady, and in the dark she couldn't tell if he was teasing or if he truly believed it. She felt her face grow hot.

"I didn't want to lead you astray," she said in her little-girl voice. "I wanted—my family in Boston sent me here because at home I— they didn't like how I acted. Too wild. And on my cousin Sophia's farm I have been so bored. I thought the powwow would be exciting."

"You hoped for wild Indians who would let you behave wildly. I can't be a wild person for you, Miss Entwistle."

"Georgie," she said.

"For Georgie, either." He turned to walk away.

"You looked happy galloping on your pony," she called after him. "Happy to be wild for a minute. And that's what I want, a minute to be happy."

He came back and put his hands on her shoulders. "Miss Georgie, for you this is a vacation or maybe it is a rest cure, but for me this is life. I am at this school, with all the rules that I find stupid, because I need to help my family. We are helpless against the white men. As Little Crow truly spoke, you keep coming with your guns and your own laws that you twist and turn for your own advantage.

"Do you know that the land where your cousin farms was under water and home to many thousand waterbirds only sixty years ago? My family were driven here from lands to the north and the east, but we learned to live with those birds. Now you have drained the land and made it white people's farms. To help my family I cannot be wild. I must be the tamest of all tame Indians. My mother and my grandmother sent me here with that mission."

He bent and kissed her and turned and left.

When Georgie got back to the farm, the revival seemed to be at a fever pitch. She went into the tent. The smell of all the sweaty bodies, the smell of sex, the people bowing and kneeling and moaning, swept across her and she began to shout and kneel and writhe with them. No cocaine and Charleston party had ever been this full of hot raw emotion.

"Sister, what's your name, sister?" the preacher shouted at her.

"I'm a wild bird," she said. "Birdie is my name."

"Birdie, come forward, confess your sins to Jesus."

People gathered around her, chanting, "Confess, confess, confess to the Lord and be saved."

"I confess," she said. "I confess to wildness."

7

Georgie slept late the next morning. When she came down, Rufus was crossing the yard to the kitchen; it was close to eleven, time for the fried chicken whose smell made Georgie sick, not hungry.

Sophia wished her good morning and reminded her that the horses needed to be cared for.

"Yes, cousin," Georgie said.

She swallowed her coffee and started to pull on the overalls that were hanging by the back door. She was stiff in every limb and almost fell over as she hoisted her legs into the heavy denim.

Rufus grabbed her forearm before she could go down the stairs to the yard. "You were in the tent last night, confessing the sin of wildness. Everyone wants to know, was that a mockery or was it a true confession?"

Georgie pulled her arm free. "That's between me and Jesus, Cousin Rufus. None of your business."

"If it was genuine, and you've really repented your wildness, why did you call yourself 'Birdie'? Why not give them your real name?"

"Thanks to that reporter, everyone in your county knows my name. When I'm confessing to the Lord, he knows who I am, but your friends and neighbors don't have to. Now if you'll excuse me, Cousin Rufus, your mother-in-law's horses need tending to."

"Just so you know, Georgina, if that was a true confession, if you've given your heart and soul to the Lord, we're having a group baptism here at the horse trough on Sunday afternoon."

"I'll keep that in mind."

Sophia had stood at the screen door listening, but she didn't comment. That had been Georgie in the tent last night. What was the girl up to? Ragging Rufus, going to Jesus, or something else? Sophia had seen those tent revivals, she knew the emotions that swept through them. They were like prairie fires—easy to start, impossible to control.

In fact, the fire was already spreading, a plume of smoke here, a lick of flames there, because there is always fire if there's smoke. One of the people driving away from the revival Thursday night had seen Will Garrison with his hands on Georgie's shoulders. Wild girl, wild Indian, she had come to Jesus but he was a savage interfering with a white girl.

By Saturday afternoon, the story was all over the county. Men confronted Rufus that night in the tent.

What are you going to do about it, Rufus Schapen? Your own cousin, your own home, you going to let that savage get away with it?

As the meeting revved up in intensity, Rufus glared down the men around him. "Anyone can talk, but who can act? If I act, am I on my own or are you with me?"

"With you," they shouted eagerly.

They piled into their Model-Ts and As, bringing Rufus into the lead car. They drove to the school, knocked down the door, found the dorm, found Will Garrison, and dragged him to the school yard. To a tree.

Georgie heard about it at the social hour after church the next morning. Indian boy hanged in the night. A lynching, but he'd been seen out on a county road with a white girl. Sidelong glances at Georgie, who said nothing. On the drive home, Sophia tried to talk to her about what had happened, but the girl had disappeared into a remote place, so deep inside herself that she seemed not to hear a word. She had turned a pasty white and gave off the smell of vomit. Sophia touched her forehead; it was cold, despite the hot day.

When they got to the house, Sophia told Rufus she did not want the baptism on her land, in her horse trough.

"No way to stop it, Mama Sophia," he grunted. "Don't even know who's fixing to come, couldn't get word to them if I wanted to. Got a white robe laid out on Georgie's bed for her. Wash yourself in the blood of the Lamb and your wild ways will come to an end."

Sophia helped Georgie up the stairs.

"You lie down, you stay in bed. I'm bringing you up a cup of tea, and then you sleep. Don't go out to that trough, don't make another public display of yourself. Please, Georgie."

Georgie might have heard her, hard to say. She took off her shoes and her silk stockings, though, and lay under the covers. Sophia put the white robe on a chair. The group baptism wasn't for another three hours; with luck Georgie would sleep through it.

Sophia was worn herself and went to her bedroom to rest. As she hung her dress in the wardrobe she watched Rufus cross the field to his parents' house. He knew she was angry about the Indian boy; he was hiding with his mother, as he usually did when Sophia was angry. He'd be back at five, though, swelling with importance at the trough—*her* trough.

Afterward, Sophia asked herself why she'd left the robe in Georgie's room. Why she hadn't stayed with Georgie. Afterward, when the preacher showed up with his eager penitents, and preacher and penitents all screamed hysterically to see the body in the trough, weighted down with the heavy rock Georgie had carried up the road from the mailbox.

Afterward, when Lawyer Greeley refused to redo her will so she could leave the Grellier farm to the Indian school—*I can't let you do that, Miz Tremont. No, it's not because of what people will say. It's because Rufus can make a good case in court, overturn the will, eat up the value of the farm in lawsuits.*

Afterward, she looked at the farmhouse, gray, worn, as she herself was gray and worn. Her whole life given in service to a piece of land. She'd never danced the Charleston or inhaled cocaine or even drunk as much as a thimble of wine.

She looked at the tintype of her father and mother in pride of place on her mother's piano, the picture taken by an itinerant photographer four months before her father's murder.

"Are you with Jesus, Papa? Is there a heaven, is there a Jesus, who cares that you were murdered and I grew up without a father? Does he care that somewhere there is a mother crying for a dead Indian boy? Did anything you or Mama or I did matter in the least bit?"

She took a splinter from the wood box and set it alight, touched it to the kitchen table and kitchen curtains, moved to the parlor curtains, traveled on to the barn, where the animals were in their stalls for the night. Led the puzzled cows and horses to the field, climbed to the loft and set the hay on fire around her. Rufus, stumbling out of the house in his nightshirt, feet and hands singed, saw her outlined in the opening to the loft, flames riding up her long hair to form a halo around her face.

Note

I wrote this story for Larry Block's 2019 anthology *From Sea to Stormy Sea* (Pegasus). I had originally imagined writing a trilogy about the families who make up my nonseries novel, *Bleeding Kansas* (Putnam, 2008). I wanted to trace them from their arrival in Kansas in the 1850s as antislavery emigrants to the current period; this story is part of the middle story. I still hope to write the beginning narrative.

Although this is a work of fiction and all the people named in here are imaginary, some things are based on fact. Haskell Institute, now the four-year Indian Nations college, was set up on the outskirts of Lawrence, Kansas, mostly to train young Indian men and women in the domestic arts. The town of Lawrence practiced unwritten segregation against members of Indian nations as well as against African-Americans.

As Will Garrison says, part of the land in the area was marshland, drained for farms as European settlers moved into the area in large numbers.

Modesty Police, sometimes called Modesty Censors, did patrol beaches around the country in the 1920s. They did fine women whom they judged were showing too much skin.

MURDER AT THE
CENTURY OF PROGRESS

I

23 May 1933

Miss Charlotte Palmer
c/o Stevens Hotel, Chicago
Letter to Mrs. Ben (Chlotilde) Milder
The Vicarage, St Clement-sur-Mare
England

Now that we are finally arrived in Chicago I have leisure to write you a proper letter. My nephew may have been foolish enough to lose a fortune to a plausible rogue, but he is gentleman enough to know how to look after a dithery elderly woman. From the moment he met my train at Paddington until I was ensconced today in the Stevens Hotel, every attention that could be paid to my comfort was paid. He even had champagne waiting for me shipboard! And when I gave him a gentle scold for his extravagance, he reminded me that our American cousins still practice their absurd Prohibition and that it would be some time before I could partake of alcohol again. Of course, I do not drink aside from the occasional sherry, but even my respected father saw nothing amiss in a glass of champagne for women on very special occasions. On the dear Queen's Golden Jubilee—well, that was long ago, and I was a foolish girl of eighteen, and those reminiscences are not the news you are hoping to read here.

We arrived only this morning, so I have had no time to look around me. At the station poor Eric could not make any of the porters understand him: the Oxford accent does not translate well in this city of immigrants. When I thought we might have to spend the entire day on the platform, a rude man from the second-class car shoved his way past us. I was about to utter a sharp rebuke when he obligingly carried all of our cases to a taxi! He disappeared before I could thank him. Although he was gruff in manner, I suppose one must label him a diamond in the rough.

How extraordinary that Eric should be your cousin on your mother's aunt's side, as well as my own sister's grandson. Life is filled with these most curious coincidences, but I am frankly glad that I have an intimate at home with whom to share my dismay at our relation's stupidity!

The city is in a great bustle with the World's Fair about to open, certainly an ideal setting for a confidence artist. Whether the man who "fleeced" Eric (I believe that is the police term for taking someone's money through a confidence trick) will be bold enough to show his face here, I cannot say. But Eric seems convinced such a man will want to "work" this exposition; he says a venue like this is irresistible to the confidence artist.

Miss Palmer did not add that she thought Eric had a letter that had persuaded him to come to the Century of Progress Exposition.

Every time she brought up the matter, he patted his jacket where his leather pocketbook resided. Whenever she taxed him with why he thought his swindler would be in Chicago, he would laugh.

"Oh, Aunt Charlotte! You're just as prim-seeming as Granny's other sisters on the outside, but you're very jolly underneath. Anyway, Chicago's just a notion I took into my head."

She had let it go, but she was convinced the man had either said something when Eric gambled away his father's rubber plantation or had written her nephew subsequently to lure him to Chicago: Eric had been absolutely set on coming.

An indiscreet young man, even if quite charming, Eric must have told their plans to all the world and its wife. Miss Palmer thought back. When had she received her own extraordinary letter? After they had booked their tickets, not before; she was sure of that. For a brief, idiotic moment she thought she could return to the scenes of her youth, perhaps even—

Miss Palmer clipped off the thought and continued writing.

Meanwhile, it is a beautiful day, and our hotel overlooks the great lake of Michigan, which sparkles in the sunlight. I can also see the north end of the fairgrounds; indeed, your cousin has rented an entire suite for me. If I can persuade someone to make me a proper cup of tea, I will feel quite ready to start exploring. The city has changed a great deal in the forty years since I was last here.

Miss Palmer crossed out that last sentence and laid down her pen. The fatigue of her long journey was making her garrulous. It was one thing to act the dithering maiden lady in public—one of

Sir Neville Burdock's "old pussies," as she'd overheard him call her—but quite another to start doing it in private.

She'd been twenty-three when she first saw the great White City on the Midway. She and Papa had traveled to Chicago on the cars from Arizona, where they'd left Mother to try the desert cure. A London specialist had recommended it for lung disorders, and Mother had come home two years later perfectly cured. During her own time in Chicago with Papa, he was tied up with some tedious business about railroad investments. As for her, for a few months she thought she had opened a new book on life, but it turned out to be a closed chapter.

Miss Palmer looked at the offending sentence. It was still quite legible behind the strong line she'd drawn over it. She would have to copy the whole letter again from the beginning. It would take a spill of ink to cover the line, and Mother would never have allowed her to send a letter with such an unsightly blot on it. Even in her seventh decade, Miss Palmer could not go against the teachings of that scrupulous educationist.

2

Race Williams, to himself

The Twentieth Century Limited blows me into Union Station at 2.08 on the dot. I pick up my hat and my overnighter from the rack and saunter off the train, only to find my way blocked by an old lady with enough luggage to sink the Titanic. She has a young whippersnapper with her who's trying to grab a porter. I oblige just so the rest of us poor saps can get moving. The old dame thanks me with so many words you might have thought she was writing a dictionary. They don't know me in Chicago yet, but anyone in New York could tell you Race Williams don't have a heart, or manners either.

Compared to Gotham, this burg is strictly a small potato, but you see the same guys lying on park benches and the same pathetic fools trying to cadge two bits for dope. They're about to open a World's Fair here that they're calling "A Century of Progress." We're like a bunch of apes walking backward into the sea, and they want the mugs to believe we're in a century of progress! There's thirty bucks trying to keep each other warm in my wallet, and they're all that's separating me from the boys on the corners with their cans full of pencils, so I walk across town until I find a place on Harrison Street where I can flop for a couple of bucks a night. It was those thirty slender dollars that persuaded me to leave the great city on the ocean for the small pretender by the lake.

If you're from west of the Hudson, you may not know the name Race Williams—may not know I'm the first and the best of the private investigators. Still, I hesitated when a gent calling himself Lionel Maitland waltzed into my office on Monday telling me he wanted to nail Jimmy "Red Dog" Glazer.

Now, Red Dog never did anyone a day's harm that didn't have money to lose. He's not the kind of guy who'd as soon plug you as look at you, and taking things altogether, I'd just as soon go after the uglier customers. Your true hoods are in oversupply, to use the economists' lingo, and there's no demand for them, whereas a skilled con artist is doing a hard day's work and getting paid for it. But I'd had to swallow my pride. My last thirty were limiting my options.

So this Maitland comes in, very British, down to the cane, the gloves, the thin mustache and of course the accent. But he sees he's dealing with a professional, and he don't try any tricks on me. He just tells me that Red Dog bilked him of five million in a phony bottling scheme, and if he don't get it back, well, he'll have to sell off the ancestral home. Which would make his ancestors rise from their graves and haunt him, I suppose. Anyway, he had enough left to buy me a ticket to Chicago, enough left to promise me a thousand when I spot the Dog, and twenty if I get the dough back. And he thinks Red Dog will turn up at the Fair—partly because it's filled with mugs and partly because Chicago's Red Dog's hometown.

It was my hometown, too, once upon a time, if you can call that orphanage down on Cottage Grove a home. I had hoped never to see this dim-bulb burg again after I hightailed it to the great city in 1907, but here I am—a fish out of water, so to speak.

3

4 June 1933

Miss Charlotte Palmer
c/o Stevens Hotel, Chicago
Letter to Mrs. Ben (Chlotilde) Milder
The Vicarage, St Clement-sur-Mare
England

We have been in a positive whirlwind of activity since the opening of the Fair last Saturday. Our second night, Eric struck up acquaintance with a compatriot, a Colonel Townsend, who is here with the British Industrial Council. We all had dinner together after the formal opening, but I am not entirely at ease with this new acquaintance. Colonel Townsend reminds me of Major Thorndike, who settled in St Clement-sur-Mare shortly before the Great War and persuaded poor Arnold Huxtable to open that garage with all his mother's savings. When Arnold discovered he had been defrauded, Thorndike broke Arnold's shoulder by flinging him from the roof of the garage. I always thought Thorndike meant to murder Arnold to keep him from talking, and I could only be happy that the police were on hand.

Now I can't help wondering why this Colonel Townsend has so much time to spend in bars with young men like Eric. The two of them have derived vast amounts of fun from watching the celebrated fan dancer Sally Rand appear from her boat as Lady Godiva every night.

By the way, I have had several conversations with this young woman, and despite the risqué nature of her entertainment, I believe Miss Rand is actually a highly moral creature—and one with more brains than most of the men around her.

Of course, because of Prohibition, the Stevens Hotel does not have a bar, so the gentlemen retire to other parts of town where they can imbibe in private. Eric and Colonel Townsend have been joined by several Americans, including the man who was so kind as to help us with our luggage when we arrived. They play a game called poker, at which I fear my nephew has his usual ill luck.

Since ladies do not frequent such places—called speakeasies— you may be wondering how I have acquired such knowledge.

It comes from the Negro woman who cleans my room. We fell into conversation the day after the Fair opened when I asked if she had attended the ceremonies.

"No, ma'am. That place is for white people, not Negroes."

"Excuse me, my dear, but surely in the North there are no laws forbidding members of your race to enter public places?"

She continued dusting the furniture without speaking for a moment or two, then said in a cold, clipped voice, "How many jobs do you think that Fair has brought the out-of-work Negro in this city? If I told you seventy-five out of the many thousands working there, would you think it was because no Negro applied for work?"

When I didn't answer she said, "I haven't been there, nor will I go." Noting the bitterness in her tone, I left her alone to clean the room.

After leaving my room, I rode the bus over to the fairgrounds. It had not struck me before that in this city of many million people, with many hundreds of thousands of African descent, how few were at the fairgrounds. Indeed, the only ones I saw were employed as janitors in the public lavatories.

My eyes have since been opened to many injustices here. No Negroes may stay as guests in this fine hotel or eat in any of its restaurants. Nor are they allowed to shop at Chicago's most magnificent store, Marshall Field's.

The list goes on, but to return to matters of more moment to you: when the maid saw I was sympathetic to the plight of her people, she came to warn me of the bad company my nephew has fallen into. Her uncle, it seems, plays poker at the same speakeasy Eric frequents and has talked to her of the gullible young

Englishman who seems a prey for any passing card shark, to use her uncle's term.

I tried to remonstrate with Eric, but he only laughed at me. He comes in very late now and sleeps until noon. When he gets up, he does not look refreshed. But when I suggest that we go home to England, he protests vehemently and says not until he has found the man who robbed him of his inheritance!

I can't help worrying that Eric may be compounding his problems by associating with Mr. Williams—for such is the name of our "diamond in the rough"—and another American named Mr. Redmond, who has lately joined them. Mr. Redmond represents a South American mining company and is in Chicago to find investors among the wealthy attending the Fair. Our diamond in the rough, however, reminds me of someone . . .

The memory was elusive. Miss Palmer stared sightlessly out the window at the light dancing on the lake as she tried to capture the fugitive resemblance. When it came, she gasped softly. She stared at the paper, then picked up her pen again and quickly continued:

. . . but not anyone who would be known to you in St Clement-sur-Mare.

Well, Mr. Redmond has offered to take me to church with him this morning, although I fear the sermon will not be as interesting as those I am accustomed to hearing from your dear husband.

Miss Palmer signed the letter and took it with her to the hotel's front desk. She had selected a number of gauzy scarves to drape around her neck and shoulders, which, with the wide brimmed hat, should keep the worst of the sun from scorching her. The cool weather of her first week in the city had suddenly changed to a stifling damp heat that she had never known at home. Dear Mother had suffered greatly from sunburn while she took the desert cure.

After their return to England those forty years ago, Miss Palmer had never been able to submit to her mother's parental authority again. When her father died, she and Mother had lived as uneasy strangers in the house in St Clement-sur-Mare, attending divine service together twice every Sunday and again on Wednesdays. Everyone said what a devoted daughter Miss Palmer remained, as twenty turned to thirty, then somehow to forty-four, and she spent middle age nursing wounded men sent back to the village from the trenches.

But a deeper, more complicated feeling tied Charlotte Palmer to her mother. Anger and resentment, yes—but it was a vindictive desire to prove she could be more upright, more thoroughly moral than Mrs. Palmer that had given them twenty-five exhausting years together and had taught Miss Palmer that even in a small village, the pond's surface hides more than it reveals.

Mr. Redmond thought she seemed a little fragile and was concerned about her walking more than a mile to divine worship, but the air, humid though it was, seemed to do her good. It happened to be Whitsunday, and Miss Palmer was struck by the Collect, with its prayer "to have a right judgment in all things and evermore rejoice in the Spirit's Holy Comfort." Only God, of course, had a right judgment in all things, but surely, if she avoided the sin of pride, she might find her reason properly guided.

On the way back to the hotel, she was willing to let Mr. Redmond hail a cab. "Too much mortification of the flesh is as bad as not enough," she commented.

"I'm glad you think like that, Miss Palmer. Young Master Eric would be mighty upset if you gave up your beautiful suite in the Stevens to stay in a lesser hotel. He's a relation, I take it?"

"My sister's grandson, Mr. Redmond, and my own godson, which makes me feel a special interest in his welfare."

Redmond eyed the fluttering scarves thoughtfully. "I only wondered, ma'am, because—well, not to put it too bluntly. I shouldn't like to think he was guiding your investments."

"Investments! Now you are asking me to speak of finance, Mr. Redmond, and my dear father held that women's brains could not encompass such a subject. I must say I am inclined to agree, although when one sees the sad squandering of family fortunes on the most injudicious investments, one cannot help asking whether the male brain is always suited for such deep subjects, either. Dear Eric . . . he is so impulsive. You will think this is most foolish, perhaps insulting to a young man of twenty-four, but he cannot sign any documents abroad without my co-signature. Still, it might keep him from pursuing some foolish-sounding venture to begin with, because of course it would be beyond me to unravel it."

In the earnestness of her discourse, Miss Palmer managed to spill the entire contents of her pocketbook on the floor of the cab. Despite her protests, Mr. Redmond got down on the floor in his clean linen suit and gathered up all the component parts. By the time he had presented them to her, the taxi had let them out in front of the Stevens Hotel. He walked away with a thoughtful frown.

The next day, Miss Palmer, carefully following the directions of the head porter, walked across downtown Chicago to the City-County Building. As she crossed the Loop—and why "Loop," she wondered, then decided it must be the elevated train circling the central business district—she fell prey to an unaccustomed melancholy. So much had changed since 1893—all these hotels and office buildings had been nonexistent then. And State Street, now jammed with cars and buses, had then been packed with horse-drawn wagons, carriages, and foot traffic. Even the City-County Building, which was old enough to show some signs of wear, had not been thought of on her previous visit. And she—she had changed as well, settling into the rut of one of Sir Neville's well-mannered, interfering pussies.

She fluttered earnestly from one official to another until she was finally able to consult the birth and death registers. She looked under every name she could think of but turned up nothing to the point. Of course, that was not conclusive proof—but something cold clutched around her heart. Why had she not done this years ago? Illness was never an excuse for feebleness of mind or purpose: dear Mother had taught her that by precept as well as example. And she might have spared herself much grief.

4

Race Williams, to himself

I can't figure the dame and the kid. I spotted him for a mark right from the get-go, and if you're looking for Red Dog Glazer, the best thing to do is hang out by a mark. Now the dame, she flutters around waving her veils and whatnot, so I do my best to calm her down, get her to take a sightseeing trip or go to church or whatever old English dames do when they're overseas, and she stares at me with those china-doll eyes and says, "Oh, too kind of you, Mr. Williams, but—now I know you wouldn't think it to look at me—I'm well able to take care of myself, so please don't worry about needing to entertain me." And on she hangs for dear life.

But getting the kid to a speakeasy did the trick. Miss China Doll Palmer may want to hold on to him twenty-four hours a day, but she's not about to follow him drinking on Rush Street, much less on to the "Streets of Paris" for Sally Rand's show. Although, peculiarly, I could swear I saw her leaving Miss Rand's dressing room—or should I say undressing room?—after the performance the other night, when all the sex-starved boys of Chicago were hanging around panting.

Sure enough, two days after I detach the boy from his aunt, we start to draw a crowd for poker. A breezy American with more luck at cards than is good for him, name of Doug Redmond. A large, middle-aged Negro named Sam Leyden who works as a stevedore during the day and has the devil's own skill at cards. And damn me if who doesn't turn up but my client Lionel Maitland, gloves, cane, accent, everything just like it was in New York except his name. He's calling himself Colonel Townsend. I take advantage of young Eric's excitement at winning a hand to haul Maitland outside.

"What the hell's your game, Maitland? You hired me to find Red Dog Glazer, and now you've blown into town to do the job yourself! You afraid to part with your money?"

"My dear chap! I can scarcely blame you for being distressed, but—can you kindly remove your hands from my weskit?"

"Not until I've had a look at your wallet, my friend." And I

pull it out of his vest pocket—or weskit, as he calls it. He wants to grab it back, but I never travel without my gun, and it's casually pointing at his watch pocket while I flip the contents of his wallet with my left hand. He's got cards in every name under creation— Colonel Townsend, Lionel Maitland, and three or four more besides. And enough cash to put me up in the Stevens for the rest of the summer. I pull out four fifties and tuck them into my inside jacket pocket before stuffing the wallet into his weskit again.

"I need some walking-around money, Colonel Townsend-Maitland. It'll help me draw Red Dog to my side. You can hold the rest until I've executed my mission. But what the hell are you doing here?"

He looks at my face, doesn't like what he sees, and transfers his affections to the gun. Father's helper is still pointing at his chest.

"It just seemed to me, old chap, that this feller Glazer being a master of disguise, it might be handy if I was on the spot, see if I recognize him, what?"

"He's much more likely to recognize you and spoil your game." I let go of his lapels and shove him backward, not gently, toward the alley. "Leave the detecting to me. If you can't trust me to do the job right, why did you hire the best investigator in New York?"

"No offense, old man, but what have you been doing besides tagging along with that milk-fed youth?"

"If you haven't seen me at work, that means I'm doing a good job," I snarl.

And I hadn't been idle. My first stop in town had been the Chicago American, *where I met a reporter named Reuben*

Levine, who was interested in the Dog. I got what pix there were of him and a basketful of tales of his doings. Around the time of the Great War, Red Dog had posed as a wealthy German looking for Americans to invest in land devalued by the war. He found plenty of suckers, all right, just as he had for running a shady betting scheme on some horses he controlled. His main gig lately, though, has been the one Maitland says he got caught on. Seems Glazer likes to pretend he's a bumbling idiot with a booze factory he can't handle, finds a mark who wants to make a fast buck on the shady side. He rents a warehouse, fills it for twenty-four hours with actors pretending to be bootleggers, gets a still, bottles, the works, and sells the lot, including the distribution routes. When the mug shows up the next day to take over, he finds an empty warehouse!

And I'd found the speakos Glazer liked to hang at when he was home—one of them being the very place I'd just pulled Colonel Townsend-Maitland from. But it's not my policy to let the client know what I'm up to. Keep an air of mystery and they think you're all-powerful. Let them in on your secrets and they always think you haven't done enough.

"I've done some digging," was all I told Maitland-Townsend. "And I've found out more than you realize."

He gives me a skeptical look, but he heads up the alley and away from me. I go back into the speako.

Young Eric, after his big victory ten minutes ago, is managing to lose a few bills, but he keeps joking around in his usual good-natured way. He may be a fool, but at least he's a well-behaved fool. Redmond is dealing, which kind of makes me wonder.

Redmond looks mighty uncomfortable when I come back in,

which has me even more curious about his system for marking cards. But he asks after Townsend-Maitland, and when I say the limey's taken a hike, he relaxes and orders a round for everyone at the table.

Meanwhile, I take advantage of the lull to exchange my own deck for the one Redmond was using. The big Negro gives me a long, hard look and demands a fresh deck from the houseman. We all take a turn inspecting the cards and play begins again. Pretty soon the luck has evened out, and Redmond is looking peevish. He breaks up the party a little after two and saunters into the night.

Now anyone who knows Race Williams will tell you he's not a sap, so don't think I'd turned into a soft touch when I took young Eric by the hand to lead him back to his auntie and his hotel. The old lady drives me crazy, but there's something about how she looks at me with those china-doll eyes that makes me think the way to minimize trouble is bring her little boy home and tuck him into bed, that's all.

On the way I try to pry into how Maitland-Townsend and Redmond act around each other—what kind of clues are they dropping about their past relationship. Of course the kid's never noticed anything. But just as I'm about to give up on him, Eric adds, in that accent I can hardly make out, "Now the funny thing is, Williams, I think I know Townsend myself from someplace. It's how he deals cards that makes me think it, but when I asked him if we'd ever met, he got quite huffy. He says he's spending his time working night and day for the Empire. Although I can't see how playing poker in speakeasies does the Empire much good."

Which just shows that even an innocent like young Eric isn't totally stupid. I deliver him into the care of the night man at the Stevens and hoof it back to my own flop. He calls after me to pick him up in time for Sally's entrance tomorrow night.

5

7 June 1933

Cable from Miss Charlotte Palmer, Stevens Hotel, Chicago
To Chlotilde Milder, The Vicarage, St Clement-sur-Mare

See no point in your crossing Atlantic. Will arrange for Eric's body to be sent home for funeral as soon as police complete investigation. Letter follows.

7 June 1933

Miss Charlotte Palmer
c/o Stevens Hotel, Chicago
Letter to Mrs. Ben (Chlotilde) Milder
The Vicarage, St Clement-sur-Mare
England

I cannot tell you how remiss I feel, for how laden with remorse I am over this tragedy. Had I the least notion of his being in danger, I would have overridden his protests about leaving

Chicago. And then for his body to be found by the janitors as they cleaned up the "Streets of Paris" venue early yesterday morning!

The police have arrested Samuel Leyden, a Negro who had played cards with Eric at the speakeasy they both frequented. In fact, Mr. Leyden is the uncle of my Negro maid, the one I wrote you about. I went to visit the unfortunate man in prison. I cannot believe him to be the perpetrator of this crime.

Mr. Williams, who brought me the news, seemed to think the murder had to do with a row over cards. Such a sad way to die, if indeed it is true, although how Eric happened to be in Miss Rand's pavilion without anyone the wiser, I do not know. When they took me to identify the body—

Miss Palmer broke off here. No need to distress poor Chlotilde with details. Or with the matter that had troubled Miss Palmer for the last twenty-four hours: the fact that Eric's billfold had been rifled. It was a large double-fold, almost too big for his breast pocket. He carried all of his documents in it, and that's what the killer had taken, no money or passport. These past weeks, Miss Palmer had seen Eric surreptitiously inspecting its contents. What had he hidden there all these weeks?

She could not believe the Negro, Mr. Leyden, would have murdered Eric over a dispute at cards and stolen his papers while leaving his money intact. The papers could be of no use to a third party unless there were something in them worth committing blackmail over. Miss Palmer felt suddenly chilly, despite the oppressive humidity of the June day.

Then, too, if the dispute had been over cards, why was Eric's body

found at the pavilion? He had been murdered elsewhere and taken
there. Even Captain Oglesby, the arresting officer, who had scarcely
been civil enough to take his cigar out of his mouth when speaking
to Miss Palmer, could acknowledge that. "Had there been blood-
stains at the speakeasy where Eric played cards?" she asked of him.

"The police know what they're doing, lady. If you'll take my advice, you'll mind your own business and leave me to mind mine."

"But the murder of my nephew must be my own business, Captain, and I cannot believe Mr. Leyden did this deed."

"Women's intuition?" Oglesby's mouth curled in an ugly sneer.
"We've had our eyes on this Leyden for some time. He's uppity, a
Commie, an agitator, and God knows what else besides. Leave the
police work to those who know how to do it."

She knew when it was futile to argue. But she was certain Eric
had not been killed over cards. It had to be about the confidence
artist he had come to Chicago to find. For a time, Miss Palmer
wondered whether Mr. Redmond was the man. He was certainly
American. He was a rogue, but not cruel. Now if it had been Colonel Townsend . . . but the colonel was so very definitely British, and
the man who had fleeced Eric in Malaysia was American.

Miss Sally Rand, a keen observer behind her ostrich-feather
fans, had taken a fancy to Miss Palmer. Looking into those blue
eyes, the dancer had seen a kindred spirit and a soul of steel, and
had taken to inviting Miss Palmer into her dressing room after her
shows, past the crowds of men who clamored for her attention. So
on Monday night, before the murder, Miss Palmer had looked for
Eric at his usual seat in the pavilion. When she couldn't spot him,
she had searched the crowd through her opera glasses, without
finding him or the men who were usually in his company.

Miss Palmer finished her letter with a brief description of Leyden's arrest and her own determination to stay in Chicago until all matters relating to Eric's death had been resolved. She pondered what steps to take. There was no point in telling Captain Oglesby that Sir Neville Burdock at New Scotland Yard would vouch for her. The police captain hated the English with all the usual passion of the Irish in America. Certainly he had no use for Scotland Yard. No, she would have to use her wits.

Eventually she put on a hat with a veil long enough to protect her face from the sun. Swathing her shoulders in voile, she gave the bellman a dime to find her a taxi.

6

Race Williams, to himself

I never should have left New York for this two-bit dump. The mark gets himself bumped off, and Leyden is arrested for the crime. A colored man killing a visiting Brit is bad for business, so he'll fry before the end of the year.

And what about my fee? Since the kid's body surfaced, there's been no sign of Doug Redmond, although my client, Maitland-Townsend, is hovering around, officious enough. Of course, I'd figured Redmond for Red Dog Glazer even before I saw Reuben Levine's pix. The name itself tipped me—not much of a disguise, almost as if he was flirting with discovery. But I didn't unmask him, and now the slicko's hoofed it. Why didn't I finger him and at least get my thousand, you want to know? Because

I wondered what game he was playing and how much of my client's story about the booze-factory scam to believe.

And since there's no fee waiting for me, I might as well get back on the Twentieth Century Limited. I've parlayed the Brit's four fifties into eight hundred cool ones at the poker table, so I can swank it with the rich folks in the sleepers going home.

I'm lying on my bed with only a flask to keep me company when a knock on my door is followed by the arrival of—of all people—Miss China Doll. Of course, I have my gun pointed at the door before the knocking stops. Does this make her jump? About as much as if it had been a silver platter for her to put her visiting card in.

"You come to chew me out for your nephew getting iced? Forget it. You want my condolences, you got them. Now take off. This flop is no place for a lah-ti-dah lady, so you'd better go where they can get you a cup of tea when you come all-over faint."

"Perhaps you could put the gun away, Mr. Williams. I assure you I am not going to shoot you."

And with that, seeing the dump doesn't run to chairs, she sits on the end of the bed. I lower the gun but keep hold of it while I swing my legs past her head and sit up on the side.

She keeps on nattering. "I know there are people, Mr. Williams—and doubtless you like to think you are one of them—who believe human life consists of kill or be killed. But I do have to confess that I doubt very much whether you truly believe that deep down. You remind me too much of a man I knew many years ago, a Mr. Guillaume, who, like you, was a diamond in the rough but a gentle man at heart.

"I would like to know how Eric came to be killed. Where he came to be killed, for that matter. I'm hoping you can tell me whether on Monday night he was at that drinking establishment you and he frequented."

I feel the blood rush to my head. "Ever since you blocked my path getting off the train two weeks ago, you've been slowing me down—you and your nephew between you. Now you want me to hang around this burg to clean up after him?"

She shakes her head. "Eric was an adult, even if not very wise, Mr. Williams. I truly regret his death, but I hold you no more responsible than I hold myself—less, if the truth be known, since his dear grandmother had entrusted him to my care. Of course, between ourselves, Eric had got into trouble in the Far East before returning to England in March. He had been sent there to look after his father's rubber plantation in Kuala Lumpur—or do I mean Rangoon? So much alike, these Asian places—but instead, he took up with a plausible rogue and lost the entire plantation at cards. I feared the worst when he began going to the speakeasy with you and—"

I interrupt her roughly. "You may be an old lady, but you're not the innocent you'd like everyone to believe. I've seen you hanging out in Sally Rand's dressing room, and no virtuous maiden aunt carries on like that. And I've seen a look in those china-doll eyes of yours that could stop a charging elephant."

"You are right, Mr. Williams, I am not a total fool. Only"—she makes a helpless, fluttering gesture that sends her scarves flying across the bed—"when the head of New Scotland Yard refers to one as an 'old pussy,' even though one has been most

helpful in solving several murders, it seems easier to play that role than to make people uncomfortable by acting differently from what they expect."

I pick her scarves out of my hair and hand them back to her. "So why are you here?"

"I find it impossible to think of Mr. Leyden as a murderer."

I cut in before she can go on. "You think he's a general in the Salvation Army, saving the down-and-outs? He's a Wobbly. Know what that is, lady? A labor agitator who ain't afraid to beat up someone who gets in his way."

"But does he cheat at cards, Mr. Williams? Has he murdered anyone in cold blood?"

"Cheating at cards—that'd be more Red Dog's game." Then I have to interrupt myself to explain to her about Doug Redmond really being Red Dog Glazer, and all about his phony bootleg warehouses, his fixed horse races, and fuzzing the cards. "A dyed-in-the-wool con man, and the top skinner of all time."

"Red Dog? What a fascinating and most unusual alias. I'm not doubting he is a highly skilled confidence artist, Mr. Williams. But is he a murderer? I fancy"—and here she coughs a little, as though what she is saying doesn't really count—"I fancy that if someone discovered what Mr. Glazer was doing, he would smile and find another . . . another mug. You see, I am *au fait* with the language of the criminal world! But I don't think Mr. Glazer would be concerned to murder his unmasker. Now if it had been Colonel Townsend—but Eric was convinced his scoundrel was American."

"One thing about Townsend: it's not the only name he

uses. *Maybe not the only nationality, either.*" I tell her what I know about my client, and what I don't know—which is a whole lot more.

"So either he is an American assuming a British accent, or an Englishman who can speak with a strong American accent," she says. "Now I incline to the latter. I would be able to tell if his British accent were spurious, but I doubt whether poor Eric could have detected a false American accent. Our job is to find out who he really is. And whether he murdered Eric."

"The cops have arrested Eric's murderer. It's an open-and-shut case, Oglesby says."

"But don't you think, Mr. Williams, that if a Negro of Mr. Leyden's size had come into the pavilion, the number of witnesses would have been very great? Most Negroes are boycotting the Fair because of its very unfair anti-African policies. The few that show up are instantly remarkable." She fiddles with the catch on her handbag for a minute, then says, "I'm assuming that they arrested Mr. Leyden because he was with Eric at the . . . the speakeasy where you and he played poker. I'm wondering whether Colonel Townsend was there Monday night as well."

"Can't tell you, lady. I had other fish to fry."

I don't see any need to tell her about my fish, but it came in the form of an anonymous letter suggesting that the dame who'd cold-bloodedly laid me in that orphanage thirty-nine years ago was in town wanting to see me. Well, I figured I have a score or two to settle with any dame who'd leave her kid to the kind of treatment I got, but when I showed up at that place down on

Cottage Grove, it was a bust. The orphanage was gone, see, and there was a gas station and a furniture store on the spot, but no dame waiting to meet me.

"But you know," I say to Miss China Doll as the idea comes to me, "now I have to wonder if someone was getting me out of the way deliberate. No one's going to mess with the kid with me around to see fair play done, so they had to ditch me. If it wasn't Leyden, then it had to be either Townsend or Red Dog."

She shakes her head. "I doubt very much that it was Mr. Redmond—or Mr. Glazer, as I suppose I should say. How hard it is to keep track of all these people and their different names! Mr. Glazer is so like—well, like a man in my village at home. If you stopped him from trying to defraud you, he wouldn't hurt you— just give you a cheerful bow and move on to someone else. But Colonel Townsend, now he is very like—well, another, much uglier man, who did try to murder a man once. No, if I had to choose from among the men with whom poor Eric associated here in Chicago, it would be Colonel Townsend."

"Why'd Townsend want to kill the kid?"

"If I knew that, Mr. Williams, I would be at the police station, not in your room. But no one is asking that question about Mr. Leyden. No, they arrested him without even really thinking."

She paused. "The first thing to do is to find out who Colonel Townsend really is. I can do that readily through friends at the British Consulate. Perhaps you could use your knowledge of weapons to find out about the gun that killed my nephew. Was it recovered? Did it have Mr. Leyden's fingerprints on it? And do they know where Eric was killed? Perhaps you can talk to men in the police department or the newspapers, maybe even go to

the speakeasy yourself. Why don't you come to my hotel tomor-
row for lunch so that we can compare notes?"

She gathers her scarves together and flutters out the door.
Now, I'm flopping in a part of town where they take dames like
that apart and put them together in their soup. So I follow her
down four flights of stairs and make sure she gets into a cab
without being molested. Don't go thinking that makes me a
softy. Just common sense. If she's right, and it's a mighty big if,
then she's going to help me nail a guy who sucker-punched me.
So it's in my interest to keep her in one piece, see.

After I get back to my room and commune with my flask,
I start to wonder if she's playing me for the biggest sucker of
all. So I call my friend Reuben Levine over at the Chicago
American *and ask him to cable London, get his pals there to*
say whether this Palmer dame really knows the head of Scotland
Yard, get someone there to cable back a description of her. I'm
tired of Brits waltzing into my life pretending they're person
X—Maitland-Townsend, say—and popping up in Chicago as
Y—Miss Palmer, say.

7

At the Century of Progress

Reuben Levine pulled his chair closer to Sally Rand's. "You what?"

"I stayed late after my show Monday night. I do sometimes, just to have some privacy. If I leave right away, I waltz into a crowd of mash-ers. Well, Monday I must have fallen asleep, because the pavilion was deserted and the Fair was closed when a loud noise woke me up. Now are you interested, or am I still just a crazy exhibitionist?"

Levine threw up a hand. "Sorry! Sorry I once wrote that about you, Miss Rand! I must've had some cheap bootleg and it went to my brain."

Sally Rand beamed at him and tapped his arm with an ostrich feather. "Listen, I know Sam Leyden didn't kill that kid because I saw the guy who dumped the body."

Levine sat bolt upright. "You . . . what? Who was it?"

Sally shrugged. "I couldn't make him out that clearly. After all, I was seeing him by moonlight. Which was definitely not romantic. But he was a white man—that much I'm sure of. And I bet I'd know him again."

"Why are you coming up with this story now?" Levine asked.

"Because I only just found out that they arrested Sam for the murder. I don't care what all those sharks do to each other, but Sam Leyden helped me load my horse onto the boat the first night I came here. He's always willing to help a working girl, and one good turn deserves another."

After the reporter left, the dancer called out, "How'd I do?"

"You were perfect, my dear." Miss Palmer emerged from behind the famous fans and helped Race Williams to his feet. "And now I think you'd better let Mr. Williams stay near you for protection until we flush our murderer."

"Who do you think it will be?" Miss Rand asked.

"I'm assuming either Colonel Townsend or Mr. Redmond—Mr. Glazer, I mean. But we could be surprised. It might be someone who is a stranger to both of us."

8

Race Williams, to himself

I straighten up from my position behind the dancer's costumes and try to brush the dust from my knees. "Miss Palmer likes people to think she's a lady, so she won't say we have a bet on the action. I think it's Red Dog Glazer; she's betting on the colonel."

Not that I'm going to reveal the stakes in front of Sally Rand, however much her curves appeal to my eyes. No, that all came up in Miss China Doll's and my luncheon conversation. I showed her my cable: "There is no detective in England equal to a spinster lady of uncertain age with plenty of time on her hands," the head of Scotland Yard said, "and Miss Palmer is the best of the bunch." She seemed tickled I'd suspected her of masterminding an international criminal gang, but in my line of work you see plenty of stranger things.

So we get down to brass tacks. I go to the speako last night and talk to some of the boys, but everyone is clamming up, and that gets me suspicious. I'm the outsider, see, the tough from New York, and they're going to protect their own from me. Townsend is an outsider too, but Red Dog is a hometown boy, and that makes me think they're protecting him. Where is he? I ask, and pretty soon the bouncer is trying to show me the outside of the door. So I leave and nose around the alley in back, and I see some signs of blood, all right.

In the morning I go back to Reuben Levine at the Chicago American *and get the lowdown on the police investigation. It seems pretty clear they nailed Sam Leyden without looking too hard for evidence. There was a big punch-up at the speako Monday night. From what the reporter says, no one knows who started it or why, but the smart money is on my client, Maitland-Townsend, trying to get ugly with Red Dog. The kid gets in the middle of it, trying to break it up, the Negro turns ugly, and the next thing they know, the boy is dead. I tell all this to the Palmer dame, and suggest the kid got plugged by mistake.*

"I fear not, Mr. Williams," she says, throwing her scarves all over the table for some poor waiter to come and sort out. "You see, I have received some definitive information from New Scotland Yard."

And damn me if the dame hasn't collected all our finger-prints from the first night we ate dinner with her and the kid at the hotel! She bribed the waiter not to clear the table, came back and collected our water glasses, packed them up as neat as you please, and shipped them back to home-sweet-home. And it turns out that Townsend-Maitland's real name is Thorndike. He's the son of a man Palmer hounded out of her home village fifteen years ago, and he and his old man have been bearing a grudge against her all these years.

So when they run into her nephew out in the jungle and see what a sap he is, well, they promptly set out to rob him of his life's savings. But they're not content with that: they lure him and the Palmer dame to Chicago.

"You see," Miss Palmer says, "I found an anonymous letter

in Eric's room when I searched it last night. I knew some kind
of missive had brought him here, because whenever I queried
him, 'Why Chicago?' he unconsciously patted his breast pocket.
As you know, all personal papers were missing from his pocketbook when his body was found, but I knew what a careless
young man he was and hoped he might have left something in
his luggage. And although the search took me some hours, I
was ultimately rewarded. He had put an earlier missive in his
trunk when he left England. I recognized the type—an e badly
out of alignment—from a similar document I had received myself, so I knew the same hand was drawing us here for no good
purpose."

And that's when my blood goes cold. Because that was the
same type on the letter that lured me down to Eighty-Ninth and
Cottage Grove on Monday night.

So the dame sees I know something, and I see she's got the
same correspondence, and the upshot is this: the person who's
wrong about who'll show up to croak Miss Rand has to show the
other their letter first.

Levine's scoop merits an early-afternoon extra, and long before Miss Rand is ready to load her horse onto the boat and head
for the pavilion, we've got every reporter in America wanting
to ask her questions. I sort them out, let her put her spiel on the
radio, and make the others go away: Miss Rand is an artiste
and needs her rest before she performs, see.

Of course Oglesby comes nosing around, but I tell him she's
asleep. "I need to talk to her," he says. "If you don't let me question her, I'll arrest her as a material witness in the murder."

"You and who else? You got Leyden under lock and key. You're too right to make a mistake, like confusing a white man and a colored, or an Englishman with an American, so what do you need Miss Rand for?"

He don't like it, and he threatens to come the heavy over me, but Miss China Doll flutters her scarves over him and he vamooses. But we can be sure he's going to have a front-row seat at the "Streets of Paris" tonight, my goodness, yes.

It all works out according to plan. We get Sally and her horse loaded on the boat, she makes her entrance at the pavilion right on schedule, begins her act, and the crowd goes wild. They don't care that reporters have flown in all the way from New York City and Los Angeles to see if someone kills her mid-dance.

At the height of her performance, a shot sounds out above the band, and so does a woman's scream. I muscle my way to the center of the melee. Miss Palmer is sitting next to the colonel, all right. She beaned him with her handbag as he was taking aim. She stunned him for a minute, but he's got his hands around her throat now. Ladies in the mob are screaming. I knock them out of my way and take a shot, cool as you please, that sends him to the deck. Then Oglesby shows up and tries to show some authority.

Townsend-Maitland-Thorndike isn't dead yet—I couldn't get a clean shot at him without winging Miss China Doll in the bargain. He's writhing on the floor, calling Miss Palmer every name in the book.

"You bitch! You got my father by a dirty trick, and now

you're trying to get me, too! Yes, I killed that precious nephew of yours, and I wish to God I'd killed you, too. Hounding my father out of town, costing him his commission, leaving us to a life of poverty while you lorded it over creation. Well, you smug old biddy, your mother talked about you plenty. Plenty, I mean, and I heard it all from my father. I bided my time, but . . . but. . . ."

And here his howls became incoherent and mixed with the great rattle of death itself.

Miss China Doll is looking mighty pale, but she is trying to ignore my client's outburst. Instead, she's breathlessly thanking people for retrieving her everlasting scarves. Miss Rand? Well, she just keeps dancing through it all.

Of course, the cops don't like having to let Leyden go. They never want to give up a body once they've got it locked up. And when it's the body of a Negro labor agitator, it just about takes an act of Congress. In the end, though, they release him to his niece, the hotel maid. I think I saw Red Dog in the crowd earlier, but he's melted. I never do learn whether Townsend-Maitland-Thorndike really had anything against him, whether he actually did get taken in by Red Dog's booze-factory scam. After Miss Palmer and I go off to share our mail, I have to guess my ex-client just wanted some excuse to bring me to Chicago.

Miss Palmer—well, she leaves for England and I go to Union Station for the train to New York. I hope to God I never see her again, or Chicago either. I belong in the great city. I plan to stay there.

9

Miss Charlotte Palmer
On the Twentieth Century Limited, Chicago to New York
Letter to Mrs. Ben (Chlotilde) Milder
The Vicarage, St Clement-sur-Mare
England

10 June 1933

I know I will never mail this letter, but writing to you has become the easiest way for me to organize my thoughts during this long trip to Chicago—by far the longest journey of my life, for it has taken me back in time, as well as exhausting my spirit in the present.

I had buried my past so deeply that I came to believe myself remote from the passions that actuate others. It is certainly true that strong passion impedes judgment; perhaps I judge more accurately than most because I have subdued such violent emotions within myself. Forty years ago it was a far different story.

My mother told me the baby had died shortly after birth. I was prepared to stay in America and raise him, far from the censorious eyes of her village intimates, giving her full permission to say I had drowned or disappeared in some other way, but I suppose my situation was far too shocking for her.

"A lady must never show either shock or surprise," she often told me. So the shock she felt was something she kept buried deep within herself. Or perhaps it was her rage at my having *stepped outside her tight bonds of confinement that led her to act as she did.*

She must have stolen my baby from his cot while I was still too weak to notice what she was doing, and taken him to the orphanage. She translated poor Robert's last name into English and told the nuns the boy's name was Williams, that the mother had died in childbirth—I suppose that had been her hope for me!—and the nuns gave him the first name Race as a representative of the human race.

Thorndike insinuated himself into the homes of numbers of old ladies during the Great War, and Mother's mind tended to wander in those days. She very likely shared her—and my—secret with him.

Robert had disappeared before he knew I was expecting a baby. He was an itinerant showman who took shooting galleries around the country to different fairs. At least his son inherited his marksmanship! And perhaps my instincts as an investigator. The loner detective on the edge of society—not the life one would choose for one's child. I had planned to look for Robert Guillaume once I got back on my feet, to show him his son and see if he wanted to make a life with us, but thinking my child dead, I saw no point in searching for his father.

Race and I had no touching reunion such as you find in novels or motion pictures. He is angry with me for abandoning him. "You're a better investigator than that," he said, "to take the word of your mother, an old lady who wants you and your kid dead. You looked at the death certificates last week and saw that no child named Palmer or Guillaume had died that winter. Well, if you'd really wanted to know, you would have looked years ago, before ever leaving Chicago in 1894. In the end, your conventional English morality made it convenient for you to believe your mother and return to your cozy little village."

Perhaps he is right.

"O cleanse thou me from secret faults," says the Psalmist in this morning's lesson. "Keep thy servant from presumptuous sins, lest they get dominion over me." I hope when I return to St Clement-sur-Mare I can remember the havoc my secret faults have wrought in others' lives, and try not to judge too presumptuously when I see the failings of my fellow men.

Note

"Murder at the Century of Progress" was first published in the *Mary Higgins Clark Mystery Magazine*, Summer 1999. The story had originally been commissioned—I can't remember by whom—for a collection of stories each involving two detectives. The commissioner turned down my contribution, because it didn't include V.I. Warshawski. However, I had set my heart on a story set in the 1933–34 World's Fair—the Century of Progress. The history of Sally Rand at the fair, and her support of African-Americans and of all out-of-work people, merits a bigger story than I gave her. I also wanted to bring Race Williams back onto the mystery scene. He was the first of the hardboiled detectives, created by Carroll John Daly in 1923.

Race Williams proclaimed: "Right and wrong are not written on the statutes for me, nor do I find my code of morals in the essays of long-winded professors. My ethics are my own. I'm not saying they're good and I'm not admitting they're bad, and what's more I'm not interested in the opinions of others on that subject."

I wanted to humanize Race, make him less two-dimensional. He needed a foil, and I decided the perfect foil to the ultimate hardboiled detective would be someone in Amelia Butterworth's or Miss Marple's mold. It would be impossible to rewrite the widely known and venerated

Jane Marple's story, but someone who seemed like her—an elderly spinster, dismissed by outsiders as a dithering old woman—deserved a passionate backstory of her own, and so I brought Charlotte Palmer (name courtesy of *Sense and Sensibility*) to Chicago for the World's Fair.

Note: I am indebted to Erin Mitchell for finding this story in the *Mary Higgins Clark Mystery Magazine* and making a Word document for me. It's a mystery to me, but my own copy of this story in all formats had disappeared.

THE CURIOUS AFFAIR OF THE ITALIAN ART DEALER

My wife having been called to the bedside of the governess who had been almost a mother to her, I was spending some weeks in my old lodgings on Baker Street. My wife's departure to Exeter, where her governess had for nine years run a select seminary for young ladies, coincided with my own desire to spend time with my old friend and flatmate, Mr. Sherlock Holmes. On the one recent occasion when we had persuaded him to dine with us, I had seen that Holmes had fallen into that state of nervous irritability he was subject to when no case or other intellectual pursuit occupied his mind.

As was typical of him in such states, he screeched away on his violin at all hours. I found the sound painful enough, but the occupants of the flat above threatened an action at law if he didn't desist between the hours of 2:00 and 6:00 A.M. "We know Mr. Holmes is a great genius who has often saved our monarch from acute embarrassment, but we must beg for a few hours' repose," their solicitor explained. Whereupon my old friend took up his pernicious cocaine habit once again.

I pled both as a friend and a medical attendant, to no avail: Holmes hunched himself deep in his chair and muttered that he had not inflicted his company upon mine, that I had chosen to come uninvited, when I could have been in uxorious attendance on Mary in Exeter. In states like this, my friend often displayed a petulant jealousy of my wife, or perhaps of my preference for her company: upon our marriage he was wounded by our refusal to take lodgings across the landing from his own.

In an effort to rouse him from his stupor, I tried to draw Holmes's attention to crimes reported in the sensationalist press. The stabbing of a cabman in Fleet Street "was banal beyond bearing," while the theft of the Duchess of Hoovering's emerald tiara "would prove to be the work of a criminal housemaid." When later reports confirmed he was wrong in both cases—the Hoovering cadet, bitter at the privations of a youngest son, had sold the tiara to fund a disastrous trip to Monte Carlo, while the cabman turned out to have been a Russian spy trying to overhear secrets of a Hapsburg diplomat—Holmes sank deeper into his drugged stupor.

I could not neglect my own practice, or perhaps I should say, my other patients, who were usually more willing to follow my advice than was my brilliant but capricious friend. It was at the start of the third week of my stay with him that I was summoned to the Gloucester Hotel to attend a man who had been violently assaulted in the night.

The hotel manager, a Mr. Gryce, was more anxious that my arrival should be kept a secret than he was for the welfare of his battered guest. "An Italian prince and a French countess are among our current guests," he said as he led me up to the second floor by way of the servants' staircase. "Any scandal or fear that assaults are part of everyday life at the Gloucester would be most detrimental to our business."

I turned around in the middle of the stairwell. "I hope your guests believe that your solicitude for their welfare would cause you to respect the medical man you brought in to examine them. If you can't take me up by the main stairs, then I will return to my surgery, where a number of patients no doubt await me already."

Mr. Gryce hurriedly begged my pardon, took me to the first floor and down the red-carpeted hall to the main staircase, which was filled at this hour with ladies on their way down to the street to shop or meet friends for coffee. On the second floor, the wounded guest lay in a suite near the hotel's northeast corner, a secluded part of the building that afforded but a poor view, since the flats on Cassowary Road obscured all but the tallest trees in Hyde Park. A secondary stair led from this wing to the hotel mews.

My patient was a man perhaps in his mid-twenties. Despite his Italian name—Frances Fontana, visiting from Buffalo, New York—he was a fair man, probably attractive when not swathed in bandages.

The sufferer had been badly struck around the face and had significant cuts in his fingertips. I could make no sense of the wounds, nor of the man's story. Fontana claimed he had been sound asleep when he was awakened around three by the lighting of the gas lamp in the main entrance to his suite.

"I got out of bed and instantly called out, demanding to know who was there. No one answered, but my attacker, his face covered by a mask, rushed through the sitting room and struck me about the head, demanding all the while where 'it' was. I hit out as hard as I could, but the man was clothed and I was in my nightshirt; he trod on my foot, demanding 'it.'

"Finally, it transpired he wanted a small painting I had brought with me from America. Family legend ascribed it to Titian and I had wanted an opinion from Carrera's on Bond Street. My assailant ransacked my luggage, looking for it, and found it in a secret compartment in my trunk. We fought for it, but he was stronger than I, and as I say, clothed and shod. As soon as he had left, I raced to the ground floor, where they thought I was perfectly demented, but when they saw my wounds, the night man bathed and dressed them. I lodged a complaint, of course, for how did the man get into my room, if not through their carelessness in giving him a key?"

Mr. Gryce looked reproachfully at Fontana. "We didn't, Mr. Fontana, you know we went into this very thoroughly with the night porter and the night manager both, and no one asked for a key to your suite last night. It's possible that you yourself failed to lock the door."

Fontana protested angrily, but I cut short his outburst by unwrapping the bandages and forcing him to sit while I examined his wounds. The one on his right cheekbone was the most severe: he seemed to have been struck with some heavy object, perhaps a truncheon. I bathed the wounds with peroxide, put on a salve that contained a small amount of an opiate to relieve the worst of the pain, and looked at his fingers.

"How did you come to injure your fingers? I have found a glass fragment in one of them and they all seem to have been cut with glass. At first I thought perhaps you had grasped a razor in your attacker's hands."

"What difference does it make? Are you as insensible as this man Gryce? Am I to be catechized when instead I need medical attention? I suppose the glass over the picture broke in our struggle. It's highly likely, after all."

I forbore to argue, simply checking each digit with my magnifying glass to make sure I had removed any minute glass fragments. I anointed his fingers with the same salve I used on his face and told him in a day he would be able to dress and eat without pain, but that for the next twenty-four hours he would do well to avoid using his hands.

He seemed to accept this with a good enough grace, said his man, who was lodged in the servants' wing, would take care of his most urgent needs, and would sleep in a truckle bed the hotel was bringing up so that he need not fear a second intrusion.

"And no word of this should get to my sister, mind you," he added as I restored my implements to the bag.

"Your sister?" I inquired. "Miss Fontana is also a guest in the hotel?"

"No. She is lodging with friends in Kensington. But she is likely to call, and I would have her believe I've gone to the country for a few days. It will alarm her greatly if word of this attack should reach her."

Mr. Gryce promised readily as did I, in case the sister should learn that a medical man had been called in to consult with her brother. "I foresee no complications," I said as I put on my hat and coat, "but should you need me, you may send word through Mr. Sherlock Holmes, whose guest I currently am." Holmes's name acted powerfully upon Fontana, as I confess I hoped it might. He said nothing, however, and I didn't press the matter further.

As Gryce and I left, I looked around the living room of the suite and saw the signs of struggle clearly enough: drawers removed from the bureau, cushions from the divan lying at cockeyed angles, and my patient's trunk, with the secret drawer smashed into splinters.

Gryce interpreted my gaze as criticism and hastily promised that a chambermaid would be sent up at once to put matters to rights.

When I returned to Baker Street that evening, greatly fatigued, for the day had included a most difficult lying-in, where I barely outwitted the Angel of Death, I had forgotten my American patient. I was startled, then, to see him fully dressed, outside our lodgings, in argument with a beggar woman.

"Ah, there you are, doctor. This wretched woman has followed me, I swear to heaven that she has been on my trail all the way from Hyde Park Corner. Begone, you harridan, or I'll send for a constable."

"Ah, you be a sly one, b'ain't you, mister? Thinking to do a poor beggar woman out of her widow's mite, but there be no need to call for a lawman. I ain't a going to do you no harm, no sir."

I stepped closer, to order her away from my patient, but the odor rising from her many shawls and skirts was as thick as her country accent. I took Fontana by the arm, instead, and bustled him into our entryway.

On the way up the stairs I asked how he came to be so imprudent as to rise from his couch. He said my mentioning Holmes's name had made him think his best course was to place his situation in the eminent detective's hands. "The police sent a Mr. Whicher, but I didn't care for his manner, no, not one iota. He seemed to blame me for being the victim of a crime."

The eminent detective, sprawled languidly in the armchair, still in his stained dressing gown, didn't look any more prepossessing than the beggar woman outside our door. Nor was the smell any more propitiating, although in Holmes's case it rose from the chemicals he'd been playing with all day. The dull eye he turned on me as we entered turned to anger when he realized I had brought a guest.

Fontana seemed to find nothing odd in the consulting detective's dress or manner—perhaps he had been warned that the great genius was eccentric to a degree. He plunged without invitation into a pouring out of his woes. As he spoke, my friend's eyes shut, but not, as I'd feared, in a stupor, for he pressed his fingertips together, as was his habit when he was concentrating intently on a narrative.

When Fontana finished, Holmes murmured, without opening his eyes, "And who knew that you were taking the painting from America to England with you?"

"No one," Fontana said.

"Not even your sister," Holmes said.

"Oh! Beatrice. Yes, of course she knew."

"Your father was a classical scholar," Holmes said.

"My father is a banker, sir, or at least was until a stroke deprived him of his faculties a year ago. It is my mother who has a great love of the Italian classics. But why is that relevant, and how did you know?"

"You are named for one of the great Renaissance poets, and your sister for the inamorata of another," Holmes said languidly, his eyes still shut. "But your accent surprises me: I hear it on the lips of graduates from Winchester College more than from Americans."

Fontana's lips tightened, but he said with a semblance of nonchalance that his mother, whose family hailed from Guilford, had caused him to be educated at Winchester.

"Yes, I thought as much," Holmes said. "I have composed a

monograph on the accents of the different public colleges of England and I am seldom mistaken. But to return to the business at hand, had you in fact called at Carrera's?"

"I had stopped at the gallery yesterday morning, but Signor Carrera was not in, and I had no wish to put such an important commission in the hands of an underling. I left my card and my direction and asked that he call on me, but, though I lay in bed all day per Dr. Watson's instructions, he never arrived." Fontana's tone was angry. "The English are famous for their manners, but few of the people I have encountered seem to have any consideration whatsoever, whether the police or the hotel manager, or even a gallery owner who might be interested in a large commission."

Holmes pointed out that Signor Carrera was not himself English, but added, "Perhaps he was your nighttime assailant. If he had wrested the painting from you, then he would know there was no need to call on you to examine it."

Fontana's eyes brightened at the idea: his shoulders relaxed and the choler in his eyes faded.

"And your sister, Miss Beatrice Fontana, she agreed with your mission to get a proper valuation of the painting?"

Fontana shifted uneasily. "She saw no point in calling public attention to it, should it prove valuable, nor of disappointing our parents, should it prove not to be the work of the great Titian."

"And she is staying with friends in Kensington, you say? Did she cross the Atlantic with you?"

"Yes; it was her voyage that decided me on my own. My mother felt that Mrs. Som—that is, an old friend of hers—could introduce my sister into society, since my mother herself is tied up wholly in care for my father." Fontana then reiterated his plea that his sister not be told; her worries for their father were sufficient. She did not need to know that her brother had been assaulted and the family's valuable painting stolen.

Holmes sat up slightly and looked at me.

"My dear fellow, you are all in—I see you have attended a difficult lying-in today—but perhaps, since he is here, you might examine your patient's wounds and change the dressing."

I wondered how he knew of my professional duties this afternoon, but knowing him as I do, assumed there was some aspect of my dress that was habitual with me on such cases. I unwrapped Fontana's bandages and was pleased to see that healing was already under way, judging by the deepening discoloration around the wounds, as well as the incipient scabbing. Holmes actually pushed himself from his armchair and looked on gravely as I bathed and anointed the injuries. While I rewrapped them in fresh bandages, my friend withdrew, and I heard the sound of water pouring into the bath—a welcome signal indeed!

I escorted Fontana to the street, but it took some time to hail a hackney cab. At length, I saw my patient safely bundled inside. I rather thought that the beggar who had accosted Fontana earlier was watching from a doorway at the corner, but as the nearness of Paddington Station makes Baker Street a popular spot for women of her ilk, I could not be certain in the dark streets.

By the time I returned upstairs, Holmes had finished bathing. For the first time in many days he was dressed, and in clean linen. Mrs. Hudson was just in the act of laying a plate of grilled kidneys in front of him, a sort of compromise meal of breakfast and supper, with potatoes and a dressed salad. For me she had grilled a steak.

My friend ate with all the relish of a man deprived of nourishment for some weeks.

"A very pretty problem, Watson, very pretty indeed."

"What did you make of his story?" I asked.

"It was the painting that interested me," Holmes said. "That, and the fact that his wounds were self-inflicted."

"Self-inflicted?" I repeated. "That blow on his cheek very nearly shattered the bone."

"He's left-handed, as I noted when he opened his card case," Holmes remarked. "You observed, of course, how much more severe the blow to his right cheek was than to the left, and yet the placement of the blows was symmetrical."

He picked up a sock stuffed with rags and handed it to me, instructing me to strike myself in the face. I reluctantly did so. The sock struck in both cases just beneath the eye socket. In my case, being right-handed, I felt the blow much more on the left than on the right side, and had to concede the point.

"And the glass in his fingertips? Did he do that to himself as well?"

"Ah, that's a most interesting point. I believe we have two calls to make, one on the Carrera Gallery in Bond Street, and the other to the home of Mrs. Chloë Someringforth in Cadogan Gardens, Kensington."

At my puzzled expression, Holmes held up his directory of London boroughs and street addresses. "There are seventeen households in Kensington with owners whose last names begin with 'Som,' but only one of sufficient size to admit of enough rooms to include a young lady making her society debut. And Mr. Neil Someringforth has a position in the Foreign Office, Undersecretary of

State for Oriental Affairs. He is at present in Cairo, leaving his lady with enough time to visit any number of balls and ridottos."

Now that Holmes had recovered his spirit, and had food inside him, he was ready to act on the instant, to go first to Bond Street and then to the Someringforth home in Cadogan Gardens.

I grumbled to Holmes that the gallery would be closed at this hour, that not everyone had the luxury of sleeping all day and imagining that the world was ready to conduct business at night.

"My dear chap, you've been badgering me for weeks to get up, to be active. Don't urge me to my bed now. And besides, it's Thursday, the night that new shows open in Bond Street's galleries. Carrera will be there, with wine and nuts and a desire to be accommodating, but if the fatigues of the day are such that you wish to retire, I can safely handle this business on my own."

Of course I made no further demur but changed my own soiled linen and prepared to set forth once again. At Bond Street, it was just as Holmes had foretold: a major new exhibit of paintings from France, works by the Impressionists who are all the rage there. I wasn't much taken with the blurry mess one named Monet had made of Waterloo Station, nor of a lady painter named Morisot, but Holmes studied the painting closely, until the gallery owner came over to us.

Carrera was a tall, muscular man, who looked as though he would be more at home on a sporting field than in a gallery, but he spoke fluently about Mlle Morisot's use of light and color.

"I find these Impressionists' work disturbing," I said. "This painting of Waterloo—the trains look as though they are as insubstantial as the smoke rising from their engines."

"I confess," Holmes said, "that my client here, Professor Samm-lung, is more interested in Renaissance art. We had been told that you might have recently acquired a Titian portrait, and would be grateful for the chance to view it."

I tried to compose my features to conform to a German intellectual with a taste for Renaissance portraiture.

"Titian?" Carrera held up his hands with a laugh. "No, no, I seldom deal in old paintings. They're outside both my expertise and my finances."

"*Ach,*" I said, "*aber* Herr Fontana, he spoke to me of his Titian that he wished to sell to you. You did not visit him to inspect it, Herr Carrera?"

Carrera stared at me with narrowed eyes, and said abruptly that he knew no one named Fontana, and that he'd best return to other patrons who had more interest in modern painting.

A woman of middle age, dressed in a richly figured silk, although cut without pretense to contemporary fashion, joined us in front of the Morisot painting. "I like this," she said forthrightly, in an American accent as plain as her high-necked costume. "She gets the woman's life just right, don't you think? The sense of fatigue, although perhaps neither of you two gentlemen has ever had occasion to look at domestic work from the female point of view."

Holmes and I muttered something disjoint, and the woman nodded in good humor. "Yes, I know, meddlesome middle-aged women are the devil, aren't we? But I will confess I was surprised to hear you were a German art collector—I imagined from your waistcoat and that eminently serviceable pocket watch that you were a doctor."

"Come, madam, a doctor who collects art is no rarity. My dear Sammlung, there's a second gallery we should visit before we dine." He bowed slightly to the woman; I clicked my heels, and we made good our escape.

We both laughed ruefully over the encounter in the cab. "A woman of such strong observational powers," Holmes said thoughtfully. "It's rare, rare indeed. I shouldn't like her as an adversary. But the gallery owner knows rather more than he's saying. He left us abruptly when you mentioned Fontana's name, Herr Sammlung."

"He knows I'm not German," I said with some asperity. "If you will saddle me with preposterous identities, do so before I suddenly find myself switching from fluent English to halting German!"

Holmes merely said he would set one of his street Arabs to watch Carrera's movements. "When he left us so abruptly, it wasn't to meet with other clients as he claimed, but to go into the little office in the back of the gallery. I think we can depend upon his visiting Fontana. I had best find Charlie before we go on to Kensington."

We swung down to the river, to the docks where the boys Holmes often used could be found, scavenging among the detritus that the Thames casts along her banks. Holmes gave a peculiar whistle, and after some moments, there came an answering whistle, and one of his street urchins, his Baker Street Irregulars, appeared. While our jarvey waited, most reluctant to keep his cab standing in such a dubious spot, Holmes gave the lad a shilling and told him where to go and who to watch for.

To the driver's relief, Holmes directed him next to Cadogan Gardens, a much more genteel location, and one where a wealthy fare might better be found. We alighted at the corner of the gardens, where the street connects with Pavilion Road. To my astonishment, as Holmes paid the fare, the cab was hailed by none other than our client.

"Mr. Fontana," Holmes cried, "I thought you were surely in your room at the Gloucester. You have had too much exertion for one with your recent injuries."

Fontana stared at us angrily. "What I do is none of your business, after all, and it was essential that I call on my sister."

"I thought your object was to keep your sister in ignorance of your injuries," I said.

"It was," he said, "but the attack on me was in the evening paper. That damned ineffectual manager Gryce, I suppose, although you'd think he wouldn't want his hotel to be known as a place where guests' bedchambers can be invaded in the middle of the night."

He climbed into the cab and we heard him give the driver the Gloucester as his destination.

Holmes chuckled. "It was not Gryce but I who put that story about. I telegraphed a stop-press to the evening papers, and both the *Times* and the *Examiner* picked it up."

"But why?" I demanded.

"If the man injured himself, he is covering some shameful secret. Or he is protecting someone else's secret. I hoped to prod him to action."

As we approached the house at 26 Cadogan Gardens, we saw one of the housemaids in the area, talking to a shabbily dressed woman. I pointed her out to Holmes, for I thought she might be the beggar who had accosted Fontana outside the Baker Street flat earlier this evening.

Holmes looked at her with keen interest, but when we came up to the house, we both realized she was merely a charwoman looking for rough work. She bore neither the filthy rags nor the malodor of the beggar woman, and on coming up to her I saw she was altogether younger and smaller than the woman I'd seen earlier.

"They told me as how you was down a hand here," we heard her say as we climbed the shallow steps to the front entrance, "and I got good references, sure I have. Clean the area stairs, empty slop buckets, nothing ain't beneath me."

I thought of the American woman we'd encountered at Carrera's and her comment on the French woman's painting, that it captured the fatigue women experience from their domestic labors. I wondered if I had ever considered the fatigues my own dear Mary subjected herself to in order to ensure my own domestic comfort, and found my thoughts so disquieting that I was glad when a manservant answered our ring.

My friend handed him a card. "Pray tell Mrs. Someringforth that Mr. Sherlock Holmes would like a word with Miss Fontana."

The servant looked at us doubtfully. "Mrs. Someringforth is dressing and Miss Fontana is indisposed."

"Ah," Holmes said. "That is sad news indeed. We are employed by Mr. Fontana, however. Dr. Watson here is Mr. Fontana's medical adviser, and if Miss Fontana's indisposition is related to her brother's recent visit, why, Dr. Watson will be delighted to assist her, I'm sure."

I produced my own card, bowing assent, much relieved that I didn't have to impersonate a Russian serf or Sufi fire-walker to suit my friend's whimsy.

The man bowed slightly and left us on the doorstep while he went to consult his mistress. The ill breeding in not inviting two gentlemen into the house annoyed me but caused Holmes to knit his brow. "Something is upsetting this household. Perhaps the fact that they're 'down a hand,' as the charwoman said. Or perhaps Miss Fontana is having an hysterical fit."

We hadn't long to wait, however, before we were invited to step into a salon on the first floor. We followed the man up a flight of carpeted steps into a small room where the newly hired charwoman was hastily building a fire.

"So Fontana was ushered up to his sister's room," Holmes observed, "not treated as a common visitor."

The manservant superintended the charwoman's fire making, including clearing the hearth of any stray ashes or kindling, then bustled her out of the room. Shortly after, Mrs. Someringforth appeared, dressed for the theatre in a low-cut gown of gold silk. The diamond drops that hung from her ears were no more lustrous than her dark eyes; she held out both hands to Holmes and, with a delightful smile, begged his pardon for keeping him waiting.

"My dresser has contracted the influenza, and the housemaid filling in for her is so fearful of making a mistake that she spends twice the necessary labor on the simple job of making a middle-aged woman appear half her age."

"If she has succeeded marvelously, it can only be because she had such excellent raw materials to work with." My friend bowed over her hands. "We had come to call on your houseguest, however, and beg you won't let us keep you from your evening engagement."

"Ah, poor Beatrice!" Mrs. Someringforth cried. "I fear it's from her that my maid acquired her illness; she dressed Beatrice last night, when the poor girl was already ill. I should never have permitted her to go with me to Lady Darnley's ball, but I thought she was merely fatigued; it wasn't until our return that I realized how feverish she was."

"She saw her brother when he called?"

Mrs. Someringforth shook her head so vigorously that the diamond drops swung like pendulums. "I wouldn't permit it. He is such an excitable young man, and she is so very feverish that I feared a visit from him would only make her worse, especially since he presents such a horrible vision, swathed as he is in those bandages."

"If she is indeed seriously ill, as my friend, Dr. Watson, is already here, it would be prudent to allow him to—"

"Oh, please, Mr. Holmes, just because I am going to the theatre you must not think me heartless or lacking in appropriate care for my charge. My own doctor saw Beatrice this morning. He left various draughts for her, as well as for my maid, and will return this evening. Now you must not let me detain you."

She rang the bell; the manservant must have been hovering nearby, for he came at once to usher us down the stairs, handing us our hats and coats so quickly that we barely had time to assume them before he had the front door open once again.

"They're expecting another visitor," was my friend's comment. "Or concealing something they don't want us to see."

We retreated to Pavilion Road, where Holmes flagged down a passing cab, instructing the jarvey to wait. While we watched 26 Cadogan Gardens, the charwoman left the house by the rear door. She looked up at the cab, as if puzzled by why it stood there, and we shrank back in our seats so as not to be visible from the sidewalk. The woman hurried on up Pavilion Road toward Hyde Park.

After a few minutes more, Mrs. Someringforth's carriage pulled up in front of her house; a footman helped her inside and her carriage bowled past us, heading north. Holmes told the cabman to follow her, and she led us directly to the Siddons Theatre in the Strand. Holmes proposed following her into the theatre, but I pled my long day and asked the cab to return me to Baker Street.

Back at my old lodgings, I fell instantly into a deep sleep, from which I was roused a little past one in the morning by Charlie, the lad Holmes had set to watch Carrera. He had banged on the street door until the noise finally roused Mrs. Hudson, who was much incensed by his visit.

"He shoved his way past me, the little wretch." She was panting from her efforts to catch the boy before he could make it to Holmes's door.

"Never mind that, missus," Charlie said. "Is Mr. Holmes about? There's been a terrible accident, to the swell that he set me to watch, beat up, he was, on his way from his shop to wherever he was next a-heading."

I came fully awake. "How is he? Where is he?"

"I whistled up my squad and they run for help, brung a constable, *which* took some doing, I can tell you that: *None of you boys is going to be making game of I,* he says to Freddie, and Freddie has to practically swear his soul to the devil before the constable come. I stayed close by till I saw him brung into some lady's house, and then come back here to tell it all to Mr. Holmes."

Just as I was saying that Holmes had not yet returned, we heard his step on the landing. Mrs. Hudson broke into further excuses and laments about the wretched lad, but Holmes cut her short and demanded a full accounting from Charlie.

"How many assailants?"

"Just two, but they was powerful strong, they was carrying clubs or somepin' like 'em. They swung 'em at me when I tried to stop 'em but when I whistled up my lads, then they took to their heels fast enough. We sent Freddie for the constable and Oliver went for to bring a doctor, who wouldn't come at all, not for *street rabble,* and we would have been done for except this lady come along. She says to the constable, just help him into my carriage and I'll see that he gets proper care."

I looked at Holmes, startled. "Good God! Was it Mrs. Someringforth?"

"It couldn't have been," Holmes said. "I sat in the box adjacent to hers; she stayed through the entire performance and then continued to a party at Stoggett House."

"The town home of the Duke of Hoovering," I said, trying to remember where I had recently heard the name.

"Yes. Her grace's grand ball, one of the high points of the London season. I gained admittance through the servants' entrance by passing myself off as Lady Naseby's footman, and spent the evening watching our friend. At one point she disappeared up a rear staircase, but she reappeared within a few minutes. She can't have been the person who bore off Signor Carrera. Charlie, do you have any notion where they went?"

"'Course I do, governor, like you taught me, I got up behind the lady's carriage and rode with them down to the river, over Chelsea way. Ann Lane they went to."

"Excellent." Holmes gave the boy a shilling for himself and a handful of sixpenny pieces for his "squad."

When the boy had gone, shooed down the stairs at high speed

by the incensed Mrs. Hudson—"Giving him money like that will just encourage him, Mr. Holmes," she'd warned, to which my friend replied, "Precisely, my dear Mrs. Hudson"—Holmes paced up and down restlessly.

"Who could have taken him in? A good Samaritan or an accomplice? It's past two now, but she's close to the river; she could smuggle him and a valuable painting away at a moment's notice."

He rummaged through the papers for the table of tides. "Yes, the tide will turn at four-oh-nine this morning. I think, yes, I think I'd best be on my way to Chelsea."

"But she rescued him from armed assailants, Holmes," I protested, by no means willing to leave my bed after a scant four hours' sleep.

"She came along mighty promptly, whoever she is. What if the assailants are in her pay, or vice versa, and by looking like a good Samaritan, she is able to worm the Titian away from him? This must be a painting of uncommon value." He rubbed his thin hands in front of the grate. "No, I must go to Ann Lane."

I retired to my room to change once more into day clothes, half sorry my friend had been roused from his torpor: I had forgotten how exhausting it was to keep up with his fevered pace.

We reached Ann Lane easily, the streets being virtually empty at such an hour. The cab deposited us on Cheyne Walk and I was glad I had chosen to accompany Holmes, for at this hour the denizens of the embankment were rats and human scavengers, some hunting for easy prey among homebound revelers.

The house where Charlie had seen Signor Carrera deposited was in the middle of a row of elegant town houses and flats. On inspection of the entryway, Holmes saw that there were three flats in the building. We assumed our quarry was on the first floor, for it alone among the buildings on the street still had a light burning.

While Holmes and I stood on the doorstep, carrying on a soft conversation about the best vantage point for watching front and rear entrances, we were surprised by the opening of the outer door. Holmes had his hand in his pocket, but it was a woman at the top of the stairs, carrying a lamp.

"No need to shoot me, Mr. Holmes, and no need to fuss about keeping an eye on things, either, for I can let you come in and see the poor beat-up signor for yourself."

It was the American woman we had encountered at Carrera's gallery last evening. I was too astonished for words but cast a glance at Holmes. His face betrayed no surprise, but I could see a muscle quivering in his temple as we followed the lady into the house.

She led us up the stairs to the first floor and into a drawing room that overlooked Ann Lane. One of the blinds was half drawn at a lopsided angle and our hostess excused us while she went to straighten it. She untied a black thread from the cord, and we saw that it led through the window to the street.

"I worried about someone surprising me here, Mr. Holmes, so I tied a length of embroidery silk to the blind and across the railing outside. Anyone passing through it would break it at once, the thread's so fragile, and the blind would come down to alert me."

She placidly wound the thread around a spool and placed it in an outsize workbasket.

"Madam," Holmes said, "you have the advantage of us. I am certainly Sherlock Holmes and this is Dr. Watson, but—"

"My land, how rude of me, Mr. Holmes. The day has been so filled with excitement that I've forgotten my manners. I'm Amelia

Butterworth of Buffalo, New York, and how I came to be involved in your adventure is quite a long story. May I make you a pot of tea, or perhaps a whisky? I believe the friend whose flat this is has one or two decanters, although I myself don't indulge."

"Tea would be welcome," I confessed, although my friend, impatient for an explanation, looked at me in annoyance.

Miss Butterworth went to the doorway and called out. A young servant, very quiet and well behaved, appeared. She reported that Signor Carrera was sleeping comfortably, and that she felt able to leave him for five minutes to bring us some tea.

"Now, you'll be wanting to know who I am, and how I came by this."

She walked over to a pianoforte and opened a massive volume whose cover proclaimed "The Ring Cycle, scored for Pianoforte and voices." This turned out not to be a musical score, but a hollowed-out book, and recessed within it sat a painting of a woman, whose auburn hair, floating around a swanlike neck, seemed so burnished, so real, that one wished to touch it.

The servant returned with a tray, which Miss Butterworth laid on a low table. "Yes, that's the Titian, or so we're led to believe," she said as she poured out cups for me and herself.

"Now, Beatrice Fontana, she's the daughter of my good friend Alice Ellerby, who married Mr. Fontana. I don't know what the man calling himself Frances Fontana may have told you, but Mr. Fontana is a banker. He used to be in a good way of business in Buffalo, but times have been bad with the recent slump. This painting has been in the Fontana family for centuries; they say the lady was his great-grandmother's great-grandmother and a mistress of one of those doges in Venice.

"Be that as it may, Mr. Fontana wants to prove the picture's value, for if it is by this Titian, then it will pay for a dowry for Beatrice and keep Mrs. Fontana in comfort besides. So when we learned about this Signor Carrera being a leading authority on Renaissance painters, Mr. Fontana decided he should come over and show the painting to the signor, get an opinion and a valuation. But he couldn't leave Buffalo with his business in such a bad way, so young Beatrice said she'd undertake the commission, and, as she's my goddaughter, and I enjoy foreign travel, I fixed to come with her.

"Another old friend of ours was quite a beauty when we were all young together. She married an English gentleman, and her daughter is the lady you've been following tonight, Chloë Someringforth. Chloë is a bit older than Beatrice, maybe ten years, and quite the society lady. When she learned from Mrs. Fontana that Beatrice was coming over, she offered to provide her a room and an introduction to society. That sounded good to Alice, that is, Beatrice's ma. I have another old friend here in London who's away this winter; she offered the use of this pleasant flat."

Holmes stirred his tea with his finger, impatient with all the chatter about who was married, who was whose friend, and so on. "How came you to have the Titian."

"Well, Mr. Holmes, I'm coming to that, and not a pretty story it makes, either. I got my goddaughter settled at Chloë Someringforth's, but when I went to call on her a few days later, I found her in some distress. It seems that while Mr. Someringforth has been serving his country in Egypt, his lady has been entertaining a young gentleman from the Hoovering family. And it didn't take a doctor's eye to notice that Chloë will be presenting her husband with an interesting event on his return."

I was so startled that I dropped my teacup, but when I bent to try to mop up the spill, Miss Butterworth told me not to mind it, that she would get to it after we left. "I can clean the area stairs, empty slop buckets, nothing ain't beneath me," she said.

"Yes." She laughed, seeing our amazement. "I was the charwoman looking for to help out at Someringforth's last evening, and I'd best get back there soon to light the morning fires and try to get my poor Beatrice out of their clutches, for it really is no laughing matter. And your help will be most welcome, Mr. Holmes, most welcome indeed.

"So to make a long story short, Chloë Someringforth has been entertaining this young lord who stole his ma's jewels and lost all the money at gaming. And when he learned that my young Beatrice had in her hands a valuable painting, worth maybe twice or three times the price his ma's emeralds had fetched, first he tried to sweet-talk her, and then he tried to rob her. And Chloë apparently helped him, along with her fancy-talking personal maid, or at least that's how I interpret the stories I got from the other servants last night.

"Beatrice managed to grab the painting away from this young Hoovering scoundrel and run out into the street. She somehow made it to Bond Street and got the picture in the hands of Signor Carrera. She had left the gallery and was in Oxford Street, trying to find a cab so she could get to me, when Chloë came upon her. Beatrice cried out for help, but Chloë used all her charms to explain to the crowd that the young lady was unbalanced."

"How can you possibly know this, unless you were there yourself?" I demanded.

"Some of it I had from the signor, and the rest I put together from what the other maids were saying when I was scrubbing the pots tonight. Chloë's dresser, she put out the story that my Beatrice was delirious with fever and that Chloë picked her up in Bond Street screaming her head off. The servants were beside themselves with the extra work, for the first housemaid was waiting on Chloë, while the lady's maid stayed in the bedroom making sure that Beatrice didn't get out.

"They were so upset by all this turmoil, they told me the whole story, not holding anything back. They said they didn't think Chloë's maid was sick, they'd had to bring her up a tray themselves and she looked in the pink of health, and this made them all crosser. Then that hoity-toity man who acts as the butler came into the kitchen and warned them all against spreading tales if they wanted to get paid at the quarter, so I reckon he's in on the plot, too. But anyone could guess the rest, and my word, servants do talk among themselves, as you know from your own work in disguise, Mr. Holmes."

My friend sat rigid, furious at the condescension he perceived in Miss Butterworth's compliment.

"Meanwhile, this Lord Frances Hoovering, he'd cut himself badly on the glass that was covering the painting. He went back to his hotel room and I guess he beat himself up, using one of those billy clubs that he attacked Signor Carrera with tonight. He had to alter his appearance, he's so well known in London society. Any newspaperman who saw him would report his whereabouts on the instant, so he checked himself into this Gloucester Hotel and used the side entrance, beat himself about the face, and then blamed it all on some intruder."

"But why would he need to disguise himself?" I asked.

"Because he knew that Beatrice was taking the painting to Carrera's—she'd let that slip before she realized what a pair of villains he and Chloë are—and he couldn't afford for the signor or anyone else to recognize him. I went to the gallery first thing yesterday morning, but the signor was on his guard: Beatrice had warned him that someone might try to steal the painting, and he didn't know me from Adam or from Eve. The best I could do was to keep track of everyone. First I dressed up as that foul-smelling beggar, following the young lord around, and then back to the gallery I went to see who might show up for the opening. And then away to Chloë's to find out what I could about my poor young Beatrice.

"I saw there was no getting near her last night, not with the manservant standing guard outside the door, so I came back to see what the art dealer was up to. He was trying to take the painting to his own home, where he could put it in a safe, when the young lord and some hired bully jumped him. The signor had buttoned the painting inside his shirt, and before they could find it on his person, those young street Arabs of Mr. Holmes up and frightened off the attackers. I was lucky enough to follow the clamor and take him up and bring him back with me here. He finally was brought to believe that I meant him no harm.

"And now, Mr. Holmes, you get out of your sulks. Even Shakespeare didn't always write perfect plays, and even you can't be right but nine hundred ninety-nine times out of a thousand. You and Dr. Watson come along with me and we'll get Miss Beatrice out of her captivity fast enough."

We did as Miss Butterworth commanded. While she changed into her charwoman's costume, I visited the unfortunate gallery owner, who was asleep in a spare bedroom. He had been well treated, his wounds properly bathed, and he was in a deep, drug-induced sleep.

As soon as I had finished my inspection of the dressings, I joined Holmes and Miss Butterworth and we set out for Cadogan Gardens, dismissing our cab on Sloan Street, for what charwoman can afford a hansom cab?

When the under-housemaid opened the area door, Miss Butterworth, and Holmes, disguised as a coal man, followed. I came in as a doctor, claiming that I had been sent for to treat the young lady with the dangerous fever.

We freed Miss Beatrice quickly, and not a moment too soon, for the bonds with which she was restrained were taking a toll on her circulation, as was the lack of food and water on her general health. The lady's maid and the butler we locked in the bedroom to await the arrival of Scotland Yard.

Miss Butterworth and I escorted Miss Beatrice back to the American woman's borrowed flat, where I tended the young lady, until I had the satisfaction of seeing her color somewhat restored. Signor Carrera was much improved as well. In fact, he was almost exuberant, for he was able to confirm that the painting was, indeed, by Titian.

Holmes, in the meantime, undertook to bring the difficult news of his wife's treachery to the Undersecretary for Oriental Affairs, sending a telegram to the Cairo office of the Foreign Secretary. When I returned to Baker Street, he was moodily playing his violin and cut off my attempts to report on Signor Carrera's assessment of the portrait.

"I shall retire, Watson. I am clearly no longer fit for this work. If I had taken your first suggestion to heart and looked into the theft of the Duchess of Hoovering's tiara, none of the rest of these events need have occurred. I should not have been shown up by an untrained middle-aged American woman."

Before I could do more than mumble some incoherent phrases, Mrs. Hudson came up the stairs in great excitement to announce the Duke and Duchess of Hoovering. The noble couple wished somehow to convey the shame they felt on having a cadet who had so disgraced their lineage and their country.

"We are sending him to Kenya to work on our coffee plantation there," her grace said, "in the hopes that having to work for his livelihood will give him a greater respect for the wealth that he squanders at play. In the meantime, Mr. Holmes, we hope you will undertake a most delicate mission for us in Budapest. As you may know, my sister is one of the Empress Elizabeth's ladies-in-waiting. My sister believes that someone is attempting to poison Her Majesty, but it is impossible for her to mount an investigation herself."

Holmes bowed and said he was, of course, her grace's servant to command.

My wife having telegraphed her imminent return to London, I stayed at Baker Street only long enough to help my friend pack his bag. I escorted him to Waterloo for the night train to Paris. You may imagine how eager I was to put the sorry business of Lord Frances Hoovering and Chloë Someringforth out of my mind, although I was of course delighted that my friend's weakness for royalty had caused him to put down his violin and return to the chase.

My one cause of unease was the sight of a beggar woman wrapped in numerous shawls boarding the third-class carriage of the Paris train. But surely, I thought as I sped through the streets toward my own home, Miss Butterworth would not leave her young charge alone in London.

Note

Amelia Butterworth was the amateur detective created by American crime novelist Anna Katharine Green (1846–1935). Miss Butterworth assisted and, indeed, outshone Green's investigative detective Ebenezer Gryce, whose methods of observation and deduction were similar to those of Holmes. The first Gryce novel, *The Leavenworth Case,* was published almost a decade before Sherlock Holmes first appeared. At the height of her popularity, Green's novels sold in the millions of copies. At the start of his career, Conan Doyle corresponded with Green, wanting to meet her in person to discuss her methods of publicizing her work.

I have always felt some annoyance that Green's work has disappeared from public awareness. Many of Holmes's methods were pioneered by Green's detectives, and so when Laurie R. King and Leslie S. Klinger asked for a story for their collection, *In the Company of Sherlock Holmes* (Pegasus, 2014), I seized on the opportunity to have Amelia Butterworth show up the Great Detective.

WILDCAT

I

The heat in the attic was so heavy that not even the flies had enough energy to move. The two children lay on the floor. Sweat rose on their skin, gluing their clothes to the linoleum.

Normally on a hot August Friday, they'd be at the beach, but Marie Warshawski had decreed that her son must remain close to home today. Normally the cousins would have disregarded this edict, but today Victoria was nervous, wanting to hear as much of the grown-up gossip as possible.

She and Boom-Boom—Bernard to his mother—often spent afternoons together: that was when Victoria's mother gave music lessons in the minute front room of her own South Chicago bungalow. If Victoria stayed home, she either had to read quietly in her attic room or sit primly in the front room to watch and learn from her mother's few good singers.

Just as a student was starting to warm up, Victoria would announce glibly that she would visit Aunt Marie, choosing not to notice her mother's prohibition against running wild with her cousin.

In the winters, Victoria followed Boom-Boom to the makeshift ice rinks where he played a rough brand of pickup hockey. No girls allowed, period, which caused some fights between the cousins—away from the other boys, Boom-Boom wanted Victoria to help him perfect the slapshot of his idol, Boom-Boom Geoffrion.

"Tough," she'd say before skating to the other side of the rink. "Girls can't play hockey, remember?" He'd skate after her, they'd argue and even wrestle, until he went down on one knee and said, "Victoria, please help me. When I'm a star with the Blackhawks, I'll get you free tickets to every game."

In the summers, the cousins spent hours together. With the rest of the neighborhood, they played pickup baseball in Calumet Park. Or they pooled their coins to take bus and train up to Wrigley Field, where they climbed over the wall behind the bleachers and sneaked into the park. Or they dared each other to jump off the breakwater into Lake Calumet, or rode their bikes past the irate guards at the South Works, playing a complicated hide-and-seek among the mountains of slag.

This Friday, Victoria was too worried about her father to stray from Aunt Marie's home. Tony Warshawski was a police officer. Along with every other cop on the South Side, Officer Warshawski had been ordered to Marquette Park to help keep the peace.

Martin Luther King had come to Chicago in January 1966. He was living in an apartment, a slum, the newspapers called it. All summer long, there had been marches in different parts of the city, with Negroes and their white supporters demanding open housing, an end to real estate covenants, access to Lake Michigan beaches, access to city jobs.

"What are real estate covenants?" Victoria had asked her mother.

"White people who own apartment buildings or houses made a

law that Negro people can only rent apartments in one part of the city," Gabriella said. "They cannot be our neighbors here in South Chicago, for example."

"And they don't want to be!" Aunt Marie exclaimed. "They know their place, or they did, until that Commie King showed up here. And we're supposed to call him a doctor and a reverend? He's just a troublemaker who can't live without seeing his face on TV or his picture in the paper. We don't need him here in Chicago, stirring people up, causing trouble."

And trouble there'd been, by the truckload. Everywhere the marchers went—Negroes along with their white supporters, including nuns and priests, to Aunt Marie's fury—riots had followed. White people, who'd only ever seen Negroes on public transportation or cleaning the bathrooms in their office buildings, were furious at the thought that Negroes might become their next-door neighbors, swim at the same beaches, even become bus drivers. They threw bricks and bottles and cherry bombs while the police tried to keep order. Tony Warshawski had been away from home for three days at a time, working treble shifts along with every other cop in the city.

Today would be worse, Tony had told his wife and daughter Friday morning before he left for work: everyone's nerves were on edge. Nothing Mayor Daley said could stop the marchers, and nothing Dr. King said could get the real estate board to change their laws against open housing.

Anger in the Lithuanian and Irish and Polish neighborhoods grew when the city's new archbishop, John Cody, made every priest read a letter to the parish on open housing as part of a Christ-like life.

"They kicked Cody out of New Orleans," Marie fumed. "He made the Catholic schools take in colored children, but the people hated him for doing it and forced him to leave the city. I don't know why the pope thought we need him here! When he left New Orleans, the priests sang a thanksgiving hymn as soon as they saw him get on the plane. He's been here a year and he thinks he knows better than us what we should be doing? We're the ones who built the church here! Why doesn't he listen to his priests?"

Her own parish priest at St. Eloy's read Archbishop Cody's letter, since he was a good soldier in Christ's army, but Father Gribac also preached a thundering sermon, telling his congregation that Christians had a duty to fight Communists and look after their families.

Aunt Marie repeated the gist of Father Gribac's remarks when she dropped in on Gabriella earlier in the week. "Everybody knows this King person is a Communist."

"He is a pastor. He cannot be a Communist," Gabriella objected.

"They chose to make him a preacher as a cover, that's how the Communists operate," Marie rebutted. "Father Gribac says he's tired of the archbishop sitting in his mansion like God on a throne, not caring about white people in this city. *We're* the ones who built these churches, but Archbishop Cody wants to let those ni—"

"Not that word in my house, Marie," Gabriella had said sharply.

"Oh, you can be as high-and-mighty as you like, Gabriella, but what about us? What about the lives we worked so hard to make here?"

"Mama Warshawski, she tells me always how hard it is to be Polish in this city in 1923," Gabriella said. "The Germans have been coming here first, next the Irish. They want no Poles taking their jobs away. Mama tells me how they call Papa Warshawski names when he looks for work. And Antony, he has to do many hard jobs at the police, they are Irish, they aren't liking Polish people at first. It is always the way, Marie. It is sad, but it is always the way, the ones that come first want to keep out the ones who come second."

Marie made a noise like the engine on the truck her brother Tomasz drove for Metzger's Meats. She pursed her lips and leaned over to ask Gabriella how she would feel if her precious Victoria brought home one of *them* as a husband.

All Gabriella and Marie had in common was the fact that their husbands were brothers. On politics, on child-rearing, even on religion, they were forever twanging each other's last nerve. Maybe especially on religion. Marie had a painting or statue of the Virgin in every room in her house. The Sacred Heart of Jesus inside her front door was a sight that shocked and fascinated Victoria, the large red heart, with flames shooting out the top and barbed wire crushed around its throbbing middle. (*"Those are thorns," Aunt Marie snapped. "If your mother cared about your immortal soul, you'd go to catechism like Bernard and learn about Jesus and his Crown of Thorns."*)

Gabriella wouldn't allow such images in her home. She told Victoria it was pagan to worship the heart of your god: "almost a cannibal, to want display the heart—*barberica!*" Gabriella didn't think like this because her father was a Jew; after all, her mother, and her aunt Rosa—who like Gabriella had migrated to Chicago from Italy—were Catholics. It was more that Gabriella despised all religion.

When Father Gribac from St. Eloy's came to visit Gabriella, to

288 • LOVE & OTHER CRIMES

demand that she have Victoria baptized, to save her daughter from eternal torment, Gabriella told him, "Religion is responsible for too many torments people suffer here in this life. If there is a God, he won't demand a few drops of water on my daughter's head as proof of her character. She should be honest, she should always work her hardest, do her best work, and when she says, 'I will do this thing,' she must do that thing. If she cannot live in such a way, no water will change her."

The priest had been furious. He tried to talk to Tony Warshawski about Gabriella.

Peace-loving Tony put up his big hands and backed away. "I don't try to come between my wife and my daughter. If you were a married man, Father, you'd know that a mother tiger protecting her young looks tame next to a mother human. No, I'm not lecturing my wife for you."

After that, Father Gribac glowered at Victoria whenever he saw her on the street. He tried to tell Marie to keep her own son away from the den of unbelievers, but Bernie Warshawski—who was usually as placid as his brother Tony—told the priest not to meddle in his family.

The sisters-in-law lived only four blocks apart; they needed each other's help in keeping an eye on two of the most enterprising children in a wild neighborhood. Tony and Bernie suspected, too, that Gabriella and Marie also needed the drama of their arguments. True, Gabriella gave music lessons, Marie worked in the Guild of St. Mary, but both led lives of hard work; they needed excitement, and recounting each other's monstrous deeds or words gave their lives a running drama.

The summer of 1966, there'd been too much excitement for anyone's comfort. Although today's riots were almost ten miles away, on this sticky August Friday, all the mothers had canceled their children's lessons with Gabriella: better keep them locked inside than run the risk of a stray cherry bomb flying in. At five o'clock, Gabriella walked to Marie's house to collect Victoria.

Marie was chopping onions for stew: even on a hot day she made a cooked meal for her husband and son. "Bernie works on the docks, he needs to keep up his strength," Marie said when Gabriella recoiled from the steaming kitchen.

In the attic, Boom-Boom and Victoria moved to the top of the steep staircase to listen to their mothers.

"Antony needs to keep up his strength, too, but not with roasted pork when it's ninety degrees outside. They are big men, Bernard and Antony. Oh, if only he does not get hurt today!" The last sentence came out as an anguished plea.

"Our people will protect him," Marie said. "Father Gribac is going to the park with some of the members of the church, to show solidarity."

"They are the ones I worry about!" Gabriella cried. "I have seen those faces this summer, the hatred, the words on the signs! I thought I was back in Italy watching the Fascists attack my father, when I saw the photographs in the paper."

"Oh, the press, the press," Marie said. "They just want to make good Christians look bad. They try to make the police look bad, too, when they're trying to protect our property."

"But in Birmingham, the police, they are going against little black girls. Is that right, to send a large dog onto a small child?

Besides, here in Chicago, Antony, he tells me the police have the strictest orders to protect Dr. King and all the marchers."

"Yes, I heard Tony say that, and I can't believe it!" Little flecks of spit covered Marie's mouth. "The police! They're collaborating with these outside agitators, instead of looking after the community. They should know that the community isn't going to take that betrayal sitting down!"

"Marie!" Gabriella's voice was quiet with fury. "What happens if this community attacks my husband, who is, after all, your own husband's brother, what then? What will Bernard do if Antony is injured in such a way?"

The smell from the kitchen, roast pork and onions, came up the stairwell with their mothers' voices.

"That smell makes me sick to my stomach," Victoria said.

She got up from the floor and went to the window, her Brownie camera dangling from her wrist on its leather strap. She had turned ten a week earlier and the camera was a special present from her parents; she took it with her everywhere.

Boom-Boom started to argue with her about the smell, just to be arguing, but Victoria cut him short.

"Your uncle Tomasz just drove up. Have you seen his car? White convertible, red leather. He's got the top down." She opened the screen to stick her head all the way out the window. "What is it? A Thunderbird?"

"Buick Wildcat," Boom-Boom joined her. "He talked about it last Sunday at dinner."

Tomasz got out of the car, stroking the steering wheel as if it were a dog or some other living creature. The cousins watched him disappear around the side of the house.

"How could he afford it?" Victoria asked. "Metzger's fired him last week."

"That was a crock," Boom-Boom said. "It never would have happened if Commie King hadn't come to town."

"But Uncle Tomasz was stealing from Metzger's," Victoria argued. "It's what Papa said. How could that be Martin Luther King's fault?"

"He was not stealing!" Boom-Boom fired back. "Uncle Tomasz was framed by the janitor, and he's a nigger like King and all those other Commies. Now that King is in town, they think they own everything."

"Boom-Boom! Mama says that's the worst word to say, worse than *God damn it* or any other swearword."

For a moment, the cousins forgot the argument downstairs in their own fight, which degenerated quickly to punches. Although Boom-Boom was a year older and bigger, he was also the one who'd taught Victoria to defend herself, which she was ready to do at a moment's notice. It was only when he tore her shirt at the collar that they stopped, looking at each other in dismay: what would Gabriella say when she saw the torn shirt, or Marie when she saw the bruise on Boom-Boom's shoulder?

Over their sudden silence, they heard Uncle Tomasz say to Aunt Marie, "Better enjoy that pork roast, Sis. Won't be more where that came from for a while."

"See?" Victoria hissed. "What did I tell you?"

"Nothing. You told me nothing! Everyone at Metzger's got cheap meat for their families; it was a—a, I can't think of the word, but Dad told me it was like an extra job benefit. I'm going down to look at the car. Uncle Tomasz will let me drive it around the block, you just watch. But no girls allowed!"

"No girl wants to ride in a stinky stolen car," Victoria shouted as her cousin thundered down the stairs.

She stayed at the open window, watching her cousin jump over the door into the driver's seat. She wanted to ride in that car so bad, almost bad enough to make up with Boom-Boom. But Mama had explained why the words of hate were wrong and dangerous.

"*Carissima,* you will never know *Nonno* and *Nonna* Sestieri because the Fascists arrest them, send them to prison for no crime, only for being Jews. My mother, your *nonna,* she was born as a Christian, but after my papa was arrested, she started lighting lights on Friday night, as Jews do everywhere. We had no money, no candles, nothing, but she found axle grease and rubbed it on old cardboard circles and set them to light, to say to the neighbors and the Fascists, *I will not bend to your hate-filled laws.*

"She sent me into hiding the day before they came for her. Both of them, they were sent to Germany to die. And it all started with hateful words and spitting and throwing rocks and making people drink a bottle of oil in the night. It starts with name-calling and ends with death, always. That is why we do not use ugly words when we talk about the Negroes or Dr. King, because our own family was murdered and it started with ugly names."

"I will not bend to hate," Victoria shouted out the window, loudly enough for her cousin to hear her.

Boom-Boom didn't look up but honked the horn and turned the steering wheel, twiddling the radio dial, even though the engine wasn't on and he couldn't make it play. He pushed a button somewhere on the dashboard and the trunk popped open. Victoria wanted more than ever to go down and see how the magic trunk worked.

Uncle Bernie came up the walk just then and stopped to talk to

Boom-Boom. Victoria couldn't hear what they said, but she thought her uncle looked worried, maybe even a bit angry. He slammed the trunk shut and went around the back and in through the kitchen, which is how they all came and went in the neighborhood.

Victoria heard him greet her mother and her aunt, and then tell Tomasz that they needed to talk. He took his brother-in-law out into the tiny hall that connected kitchen to front room. Victoria went back to the stairwell and lay flat to listen to them.

"That car, Tomasz, that set you back more than a buck, didn't it. I ran into Lucco on the bus this morning: he said Tony is very unhappy with you."

I bet he is, Victoria thought. Her father hated people like Uncle Tomasz stealing and acting like they were kings of the mountain instead of working hard and being honest.

"What's Tony got to do with it?" Tomasz tried to sound brave, but Victoria could tell from his voice he was nervous.

"He thinks you got rid of more meat than just the roasts you brought home to Marie," Uncle Bernie said. "He thinks you owe him something. That car is going to be a red flag to him. If I were you, I'd return the car before Boom-Boom gets a scratch on it, and I'd make nice with Tony."

"Why should I be afraid of Tony?" Tomasz said. "Did he stand up for me when that nigger janitor ratted on me? I'm going over to Marquette Park, which is where he said he'd be, and I'll teach him a lesson about loyalty he won't forget in a hurry."

Tomasz's feet pounded through the downstairs and out the front door. Victoria heard the door slam and ran back to the window, in time to see Tomasz shove Boom-Boom over to the passenger seat and take off.

"*Vittoria! Vieni! Usciamo!*" Gabriella called up the stairs. *Come, we're leaving.*

If she stayed to argue with her mother, Gabriella would order her point-blank to stay home, in which case, even if Papa was in danger, Victoria would have to stay home. But you didn't grow up in South Chicago without knowing exactly what a grown man meant when he said he was going to teach another man a lesson. Victoria needed to get to Marquette Park and warn her father.

She slid her legs over the windowsill, lowered herself so that she was hanging over the tiny roof that covered the front doorway, and dropped. She shinnied down the pillar to the ground, ran to the side of the house where she'd left her bike, and took off.

2

Even half a mile from the park, Victoria could hear the screaming: ten thousand throats open in hate. The cops at the intersection, uniforms wet under the hot sun, were so tense that they shouted at everyone—old women asking what the trouble was, even a priest riding up on a bicycle—the cops shouted at them all, including Victoria Warshawski darting under the sawhorses that blocked Seventy-First street.

She had ridden her bike the three miles to Seventy-First and Stony, where she'd chained it to a streetlight. A number 71 bus was just coming along, and she climbed thankfully on board. Her torn shirt was soaked with sweat; her throat was hoarse and dry. She had eight-two cents in her pockets. If she used thirty cents on the round-trip fare, she'd have plenty to buy a Coke when she found a vending machine.

Seventy-first Street was blocked off half a mile from Marquette Park. Cops in riot gear were diverting all traffic, even CTA buses, in a wide loop around the park. Traffic was jammed on Western Avenue in both directions. The cops told the bus driver that no one was allowed off the bus until it got to the far side of the park, but while they were stuck in the intersection, Victoria forced open the back door and jumped out.

When the cops at Western Avenue yelled at her, she was afraid they might be friends of her dad's. If they recognized her, they would make her leave the area before she found him. Still, she couldn't help turning around, to see if they were calling her by name. When she turned, she saw something that shocked her into immobility.

Uncle Tomasz's white convertible pulled into the intersection. Uncle Tomasz was at the wheel; another man, a stranger to Victoria, sat next to him. She stood on tiptoe, trying to look into the backseat, but her cousin wasn't in the car.

The stranger was blond, like Tomasz. Riding in the open car had boiled both their faces bright red, as red as the wild shirt the stranger was wearing. At first the officer tried to stop the car, but the stranger pulled out his wallet. The cop looked around, as if checking to see who was watching. He took a bill out of the stranger's wallet, then moved two sawhorses so the Wildcat could drive through.

The uniformed man was taking a bribe. This was terrible! Tony Warshawski talked about this over and over again, the people who tried to give him money to get out of traffic tickets, and how wrong it was, it gave everyone on the force a bad name.

Victoria took a picture of the cop moving the sawhorses and then of Uncle Tomasz and the stranger. Tomasz must have gotten someone to help him find her father. The two men would gang up on Tony and kill him, and then some evil cop would take a bribe to pretend not to see that it had happened.

Victoria started running. She couldn't beat the convertible to the park, but she had to get there as fast as she could, to find her father before Tomasz and his partner did. Even before she entered the park, she realized this was going to be nearly impossible. The crowds were so thick that a child, even a girl like Victoria who was tall for her age, couldn't see around them. She had to fight her way through them.

People were holding up signs with horrible words on them. One said KING WOULD LOOK GOOD WITH A KNIFE IN HIS BACK, but the others! They said things that you were never supposed to say about anyone.

Victoria used her elbows the way Boom-Boom had taught her and pushed her way through a massive wedge of people. They were yelling and screaming and waving Confederate flags. Some of them had sewn swastikas to their clothes or painted them on their faces. This was also very bad: people with swastikas had killed *Nonno* and *Nonna* Sestieri.

Even as she looked for her father, Victoria realized she couldn't tell her mother the things she was seeing—swastikas, people calling Martin Luther King by a name worse than a swearword. She hoped Tony wouldn't say anything, either. It would upset Gabriella terribly; Victoria and Tony had a duty to protect Gabriella from any further unhappiness in this life.

As she moved farther west into the park, Victoria saw a group of teenagers turn a car over and set fire to it. The people near them cheered. Six policemen in riot helmets ran to the teenagers, who spat at them and started throwing rocks and bottles.

Victoria pushed through the cheering mob to where the policemen were using their billy clubs, trying to arrest the boys who'd set the fire.

She tugged on one officer's arm. "Please, I'm looking for Officer Warshawski, do you know him? Have you seen him?"

"Get back, get out of the way. This is no place for a kid like you, go home to your mommy and daddy." The man pushed her out of the way.

"Tony Warshawski," she cried. "He's my dad, he's working here, he's a cop, I need to find him."

This time the men ignored her completely. They couldn't pay attention to her—the crowd was protecting the boys, throwing rocks and cans of Coke at the officers. One can hit an officer in the head; the crowd roared with laughter when the soda spilled into his eyes, blinding him.

"The niggers are on Homan," someone shrieked. The whole mob swerved west, chanting, "Find the niggers, kill the niggers!"

Victoria followed them, her legs aching, a stitch in her side making her gasp for breath. She couldn't pay attention to her pain, it would only get in her way. She had to find Tony. She elbowed her way past the screaming adults. One of them put out a hand and grabbed her, so hard she couldn't wriggle free.

"And where are you going?"

It was Father Gribac. With him were half a dozen people she recognized from her own neighborhood, two of them women carrying bags of sugar.

"I'm looking for my dad. Have you seen him?"

"Have you seen him, *Father*. Doesn't your Jew mother teach you to respect your elders?"

"You're not my father!" Victoria kicked him hard on the shin; he let go of her shoulder, swearing at her in Polish.

Victoria slithered away. The crowd was so thick that the priest couldn't move quickly enough to catch up with her.

"Daddy, where are you, where are you?" She realized tears were running down her cheeks. "Babies cry; you aren't a baby," she scolded herself out loud.

She came on a drinking fountain and stopped to drink and to run her head under the stream of water. Other people came up and pushed her out of the way, but she was cooler now and could move again.

For over an hour she pushed her way through the mob. It was like swimming in giant waves in Lake Michigan: you worked hard, but you couldn't move very far. Every time she came to a cop, she tried to ask about Tony Warshawski. Sometimes the man would take time to shake his head, no, he didn't know Tony. Once, someone knew Tony but hadn't seen him. More often, the overheated officers brushed her aside.

A cherry bomb exploded near her, filling her eyes with smoke. A rumor swept through the mob: someone had knocked King down with a rock.

"One down, eleven million to go," a woman cackled.

"King Nigger's on his feet, they're treating him like he's royalty while we have to suffer in the heat," a man growled.

Victoria saw the golf course on her right. It looked green, refreshing, and almost empty of people. She wrestled her way through the mob and made it onto the course. She climbed the short hill around one of the holes and came on the road that threaded the greens. To her amazement, Uncle Tomasz's white convertible stood there. Neither Tomasz nor Boom-Boom was in it, only the stranger who'd been with Uncle Tomasz back at Western Avenue. He was driving slowly, looking at the bushes.

Victoria was too exhausted to run; she limped up to the car and started pounding on the door. "What happened to Uncle Tomasz? Where's Boom-Boom? Where's my dad?"

"Who are you?" the stranger demanded. "Tomasz doesn't have any kids!"

"*My* dad, Officer Warshawski," she screamed. "Uncle Tomasz said he was going to teach Tony a lesson. Where is he?"

The stranger looked at her and then burst into a manic laugh. "Believe me, little girl, Tomasz is never going to teach anyone a lesson."

The stranger opened the door. The look on his face was terrifying. For some reason, the girl held up her camera, almost as a protection against his huge angry face, and took his picture. He yanked at the camera strap, almost choking Victoria; the strap broke and he flung the camera onto the grass. As she bent to pick it up, he grabbed her. She bit him and kicked at him, but she couldn't make him let go.

3

The battle between the cops and the protestors went on for many hours after Dr. King and his fellow marchers left the park. As sunset approached, every cop felt too limp and too numb to care about the cars that were still burning, or those that were overturned or dumped into the lagoons ringing the park. Firefighters were working on burning cars, but they were moving slowly, too.

Patrolmen returning to their squad cars couldn't get far: women had poured sugar into the gas tanks. After going a few hundred feet, their fuel filters clogged and the cars died. When a firefighter came on the body shoved under a bush, he called over to a cop uselessly fiddling with the carburetor of his dead squad car.

The policeman walked over on heat-swollen legs and knelt, grunting in pain as he bent his hamstrings for the first time in nine hours. The man under the bush was around forty, blond, sunburnt. And dead. The cop grunted again and lifted him by the shoulders. The back of the man's head was a pulpy mess. Not dead from heatstroke, as the officer had first assumed, but from a well-placed blunt instrument.

A small crowd of firefighters and police gathered. The cop who'd first examined the body sat heavily on his butt. His eyelids were puffy from the sun.

"You guys know the drill. Keep back, don't mess the site up any more'n it already is." His voice, like all his brother officers', was raspy from heat and strain.

"Guy here says he knows something, Bobby," a man at the edge of the ragtag group said.

Bobby groaned, but got to his feet when the other cop brought over a civilian in a Hawaiian print shirt. "I'm Sergeant Mallory. You know the dead man, sir?"

The civilian shook his head. "Nope. Just saw one of the niggers hit him. Right after we got King, one of them said he'd do in the first whitey crossed his path, and I saw him take a Coke bottle and wham it into this guy."

The police looked at each other; Bobby returned to the civilian. "That would have been about when, sir?"

"Maybe three, maybe four hours ago."

"And you waited this long to come forward?"

"Now just a minute, officer. Number one, I didn't know the guy was dead, and number two, I tried getting some cop's attention and he told me to bug off and mind my own business. Only he didn't put it that polite, if you get my drift."

"How far away were you? Close enough to see the man with the Coke bottle clearly?"

The civilian squinted in thought. "Maybe ten feet. Hard to say. People were passing back and forth, everyone doing their own thing, like the kids are saying these days, no one paying much attention, me neither, but I could make a stab at describing the nigger who hit him."

Bobby sighed. "Okay. We're waiting for a squad car that works to come for us. We'll drive you to the Chicago Lawn station, you can make a statement there, give us a description of the Negro you say you saw, and the time and all that good stuff. . . . Boys, you're as beat as me, but let's see if we can find that Coke bottle anywhere near here."

Turning to the man next to him, he muttered, "I hope to Jesus this guy can't make an ID. The whole town will explode if we arrest some Negro for killing a white guy today."

As they picked through the litter of cups and bottles and car jacks that the rioters had dropped, looking for anything with hair or blood on it, a squad car drove up near them. The uniformed driver came over, followed by a civilian man.

"Mallory! We're looking for Tony Warshawski. Seen him?"

Bobby looked up. "We weren't on the same detail. I think he's over by Homan—oh—" He suddenly recognized the civilian: Tony's brother Bernie.

Bobby Mallory had been Tony Warshawski's protégé when he joined the force. Thirteen years later, he'd moved beyond Tony with promotions the older man no longer applied for, but the two remained faithful friends. Bobby had spent enough time with Tony and Gabriella that he knew Bernie and Marie as well; Bobby was an enthusiastic supporter of Boom-Boom's ambition to supplant the Golden Jet with the Blackhawks. He wished he could also support the freedom Tony and Gabriella gave their own only child, but he hated the way they let Vicki run around with Boom-Boom, like a little hooligan. Thank God Eileen was raising his own girls to be proper young ladies.

"We're falling down, we're that tired, Warshawski," Bobby said. "What's up?"

"Boom-Boom and Victoria," Bernie said. "Marie's brother, Tomasz, he stormed out of the house saying he was heading over here. The kids are missing, and one of the neighbors says Boom-Boom drove off in the car with Tomasz and then Victoria, she followed after them on her bike maybe five minutes later. I—I watched all this on TV, I know it's World War Three in here—but the kids, Jesus—"

Bobby interrupted him as an ambulance threaded its way through the garbage and the remaining rioters. "Gotta get a body outta here, back in a minute, Warshawski."

Bernie followed him. As the ambulance crew picked up the dead man, he gave a strangled cry.

"That's Tomasz. Marie's brother! What happened to him?"

He shoved past Bobby Mallory to kneel next to Tomasz. "Come on, man, get up. You've had your fun, now get on your feet!" He shook Tomasz's shoulder roughly. "Where the fuck is my son? What kind of asshole are—"

He dropped the shoulder in horror as he saw the battered side of his brother-in-law's head. "What happened to him, Mallory? Did he crack his head on a rock?"

"Someone cracked his head with a rock, more likely."

"Boom-Boom. Where's my boy?" Bernie's voice was breaking. He began clawing around the underbrush where Tomasz had been lying. He saw a sneaker with the number 9 painted in red on the back. Bobby Hull's number: Boom-Boom had painted it on his ice skates, his sneakers, and even his lace-up church shoes.

"This here is his shoe. Find my boy, God damn you, Mallory, find my boy!"

Bobby didn't say anything. Even though the sun was setting, the park was still seething. Knots of fifteen or twenty rioters kept passing the area where Tomasz had been killed, screaming abuse at Mallory and the rest of the force. A troop of cops, so weary they could barely put one leg in front of the other, arrived to help secure the crime scene.

"Traitors! Traitors to your race and your neighborhood!" a woman screamed. "Tell your precious archbishop we're *never* coming back to Mass. All that money he's spending, he can get it from the niggers!"

Bernie Warshawski stared at her in shock: it was a woman from his own parish, and near her was the St. Eloy priest, Father Gribac. The woman took a rock out of her pocket, but Bernie reached her and held her arm before she could throw it.

"Bertha! Bertha Djiak, what would your children say if they saw you doing this?"

"Out of my way, High-and-mighty Warshawski. Because your brother is a cop, you turn traitor, too?"

Still holding her arm, Bernie turned to the priest. "Father—it's my boy! He's disappeared. Someone murdered Marie's brother, right here in the park, and I can't find Boom-Boom."

4

It was completely black inside the trunk, and very hot. For a few minutes, Victoria screamed and kicked as the car bounced along. When they stopped, the man yelled, "No one will hear you." His voice was muffled, but he was bending over, close to the edge of the trunk.

He was right. The screams from the mob were so loud, Victoria could barely hear the police and fire sirens above them. She would suffocate in here. No one would ever find her; Mama would be heartbroken. Papa, too, but it was chiefly of her mother that Victoria was thinking.

Now she knew how Mama had felt when she was hiding from the Fascists in a cave in the mountains. Thinking of Gabriella made her stop crying. Mama had been seventeen in 1944. Her papa, *Nonno* Sestieri, had been arrested almost a year earlier and sent by the Germans to their death camp in Poland. At three in the morning, a neighbor came into the room where Gabriella and her mother were living. The neighbor's brother worked for the police in the town of Pitigliano and he had told the neighbor to warn Gabriella's mother that she would be arrested for Jewish activities.

Gabriella had a cardboard suitcase under her bed, ready for her to leave at a second's notice. Underwear, a heavy sweater, and eight red Venetian wineglasses, part of Papa's family for two hundred years: she had a duty to keep them safe. Gabriella went to the home of another neighbor, who had offered to hide her in the basement, only to learn that this neighbor had been arrested earlier that night. And so Gabriella fled on foot into the mountains.

"How did you live, Mama?" Victoria asked.

"By my wits," Gabriella said. "There are three laws to survive: keep calm, think, and be lucky. You can't control luck, but you can stay calm and think."

In the trunk of Uncle Tomasz's car, Victoria stopped crying. Stay calm. Think. Pray for luck.

One night at dinner Papa had talked about stopping a car for missing a taillight. "The driver was so nervous, I went to look more closely at the missing light. He had twenty M14 rifles in the trunk and one of them had broken out the light—the barrel was sticking out."

If she could find the inside of one of the taillights, Victoria could break it and stick her arm out. Maybe someone would see her. Anyway, she would have air, she wouldn't choke to death in this horrible hot trunk. She needed to scooch down so she could pull up the carpet that covered the bottom of the trunk.

The car was new and the carpet was glued down firmly. Victoria couldn't find anyplace to stick a finger and start ripping. A sob shuddered through her.

"Stop!" she ordered herself. "Keep calm and think."

The spare tire was punching into her back. And under the spare tire there would be tools. The jack, the wrench for taking off bolts.

Slowly, sweating so badly in the oven of the trunk that her body was sliding inside her skirt and torn blouse, she turned over. She found the hooks that held the carpet over the tire. Undid them. She was thirsty and sleepy.

Sleep would kill her. Stay alert, that is what Mama did. If she slept, the Fascist patrols might sneak up.

She stuck an arm under the carpet but couldn't move the tire to get at the jack beneath it. *Are you going to start crying again? A voice seemed to come from outside her head. Don't. I have no use for babies.*

She maneuvered her arm and then her shoulders and head under the carpet. Her trembling fingers bumped into a set of wires. She didn't know what they were for, but she pulled on them, pulled with all her might. They cut into her palms and she pulled harder.

Suddenly she saw light through the thick carpet, felt cooler air on her bare legs. She was near the end of her strength, had just enough left to move out from under the carpet. The wires she'd pulled were connected to the trunk release. She blinked, blinded by the light of the setting sun, and managed to crawl over the lip of the trunk and roll onto the grass.

5

Boom-Boom had been all over the park, trying to find Uncle Tony. At first, when Uncle Tomasz roared up Route 41 to Seventy-first Street, he'd been having a great time. He knew his cousin was watching from the attic. He could picture his mother rushing to the sidewalk, yelling after him, and then trying to get his father to chase after him. In their old Ford, like to see him try to catch the Wildcat.

They stopped at a barbershop at Seventy-first and Euclid, where Uncle Tomasz knew the owner. He made a phone call and fidgeted around, joking with the barbers, but tense underneath. He kept looking out the window. After about fifteen minutes, a man with thinning blond hair came in. He looked around, saw Uncle Tomasz, and jerked his head toward the door.

Boom-Boom was following his uncle to the street, but the man stared at him with the meanest eyes Boom-Boom had ever seen. "You stay in the shop and wait for your uncle there," he said in a voice so cold Boom-Boom turned around and went back in.

He asked Uncle Tomasz's friend who the man was, but the barber only shook his head and gave Boom-Boom a dime for the Coke machine. The machine was next to the front door. As Boom-Boom bought his soda, he saw the stranger get behind the steering wheel. Uncle Tomasz was letting this complete stranger drive his car, while he sat stiffly in the passenger seat.

When they took off, Boom-Boom ran after, the Coke bottle still in hand. He almost caught up with the Wildcat at the stoplight on

Stony Island, but as soon as the light turned green, the car was gone. A westbound bus lumbered into view and Boom-Boom boarded it by darting in through the back door as passengers were exiting.

When the traffic gummed up near Marquette Park, Boom-Boom jumped off. He jogged along the street and caught a break: he saw the Wildcat make its way around the sawhorses, although he wasn't close enough to see money change hands. If he'd been looking for her, he would have seen his cousin before she was swept up in the crowds entering the park, but in his imagination, she was still leaning out his attic window.

He hadn't known how hot and tired he could get, pushing and shoving his way through mobs in the park, looking for the Wildcat. It wasn't that there were so many cars—almost no one except cops, firefighters, and journalists had been allowed to bring a car in—but the waves of people, yelling, charging in different directions, "Hunting niggers," as many of them shouted.

In the back of his mind, away from his fatigue and his fear for what the man with the mean face would do to Uncle Tomasz, Boom-Boom thought his cousin and Aunt Gabriella were right: those ugly words were worse than swearing. They turned ordinary faces into something monstrous, made them nonhuman.

At one point he saw people from his own neighborhood. Bertha Djiak, who poked him during Mass if he talked to one of his buddies, there she was, her hair clumped with sweat, her face redder than ketchup from the sun, her lips flecked white. He ducked behind some thick shrubbery. And saw the mean stranger.

Uncle Tomasz lay on the ground, so still he might have been asleep. Boom-Boom looked from his uncle to the stranger, and the stranger lunged for him.

"Oh, yes, the nephew, the up-and-coming Golden Jet. I think you and I need to talk about your hockey future, boy."

Boom-Boom turned to flee, tripped over a root in the shrubbery, and fell flat. The stranger lunged for him and grabbed his left foot. Boom-Boom kicked, wriggled, and felt his sneaker pop off. He jumped to his feet and ran.

After ducking and weaving through the shifting crowds, Boom-Boom stopped to breathe. The sun was setting, but the air was still thick and hot. His throat was raw from running. He needed water and started to look for a drinking fountain. As he scrambled to the top of a knoll, hoping for a fountain and to check on his pursuer, he saw the Wildcat, its trunk standing open. It was pointing nose-down at one of the lagoons. In fact, it would have gone in except someone had rolled a squad car into the water—the Wildcat's front left tire had caught on the squad car.

He stumbled down the hill to the car. He began to wonder if he'd died, if he was in heaven seeing visions, because his cousin Victoria was lying in the grass next to the trunk.

6

It was dark by the time the cousins and their fathers found each other. When Victoria saw Tony, she burst into tears.

"*Pepaiola, cara mia, cuore mio,*" Tony crooned, the only Italian he'd picked up from Gabriella—my little pepper pot, he called his daughter. "What's to cry about now, huh?"

"Uncle Tomasz said he would kill you because he lost his job," she sobbed. "I wanted to warn you, but this man, this friend of

Uncle Tomasz's, he picked me up and put me in the trunk. I was scared, Papa, I'm sorry, but I was scared, I didn't want you to die and I couldn't tell you, and I didn't want me to die, either."

"No, sweetheart, and neither of us is dead, so it all worked out. Let's get you home so your mama can stop crying her eyes out and give you a bath."

"What man, Vicki?" Bobby asked—the only person who ever used a nickname that Gabriella hated.

"The man with Uncle Tomasz. I saw them when they—Papa, they gave money to the cop at the intersection and he let them into the park. I took his picture—oh! my camera, he broke the strap and threw my camera away, my special camera you gave me, Papa, I'm sorry, I didn't look after it like you made me promise."

Victoria started to cry harder, but Bobby told her to dry her eyes and pay attention. "We need you to help us, Vicki. We need to see if your camera is still here, if no one stole it. So you be a big girl and stop crying and show your Uncle Bobby where you were when this man picked you up."

"It's dark," Tony protested. "She's all in, Bobby."

Victoria frowned in the dark. "It was where you come into the golf course. One of the hills where the holes are on the Seventy-first Street side of the park. I know, there was a statue near me, I don't know whose."

With this much information, Bobby set up searchlights near the statue of the Lithuanian aviators Darius and Girenas, although none of the cops believed they'd find one small Brownie camera in the detritus left in the park.

When Boom-Boom whispered to his cousin the news that Tomasz was dead and the cops needed to find the man who'd been with him, Victoria found some reserve of energy from childhood's reservoir. She tried to remember in her body how slowly she'd moved, where she'd twisted and turned on the walking paths, and finally cut across the grass to one of the knolls. Boom-Boom stayed with her; within another five minutes, they'd found the Brownie.

Bobby took custody of it, promising on his honor as a policeman that he'd give the camera back the instant the pictures were developed. The cousins finally got into their fathers' cars.

At home, they received varying receptions from their mothers: both women frantic, both doting on their only children, each showing it with tears, and then a slap for being foolhardy and disobedient. Gabriella instantly repented of the slap and took her daughter into the bathroom to shampoo her rough mass of curls herself.

"When I was locked in the trunk, Mama, I thought I would die. And then I remembered you hiding in the cave in the mountains, and you made me brave. Stay calm and think, you said that, and be lucky. I stayed calm, and I was lucky."

Victoria showed her mother the welts in her palm from where she'd tugged on the cable that miraculously released the trunk lock.

Gabriella hugged her more tightly. "I'm happy, I'm happy that I can protect you even when I'm not with you, because I cannot always be with you. But, *Carissima,* when will you learn to think first, before you run headlong into danger? This Tomasz, this brother of Marie's, he was a . . . *mafioso—un ladro,* a thief—he stole from Metzger's Meats for the Mafia and sold the meat to supper clubs in Wisconsin. He blamed the janitor, who is a Negro man, for losing his job, because the janitor reported seeing him taking all that meat out of the truck.

"But your papa is telling me, Tomasz also cheated his *capo* in the Mafia, and this was a man also named Antony. It is not such a rare name, Victoria. If you asked me, I would tell you this thing, that your papa is in danger from the *calca*—the . . . the mob, that is the word—in the park, but not from this brother of Marie, and then you do not get the most biggest frightening of your life. And also, then you are not giving *me* the same gigantic frightening."

And, of course, as it turned out, when Bobby got the pictures developed, the man who abducted Victoria, who flung her into the trunk of the Wildcat, which he got several spirited youths to push into the lagoon, was the Tony who worked in Don Pasquale's organization.

Tomasz had been stealing meat from Metzger's and selling it in Wisconsin for the mob, but he'd taken more than his share of the profits. Don Pasquale sent Tony in his red Hawaiian shirt to Marquette Park to kill Tomasz under cover of the riots. The Don wasn't happy with his hit man for letting a little girl with a camera get the best of him: he refused to post his bail.

When Tony Warshawski reported the successful arrest of Tony-the-killer, he brought a red rose to his daughter, to thank her for her share in the rescue.

"No, Antony, no," Gabriella protested. "I do not want her to think she is a heroine, who can go saving people in danger. She will only be in danger herself, she will be injured, she will break my heart. Victoria, you must promise me: you are going to study at a university, no? You can be a doctor, or—I don't know, anything, you can do anything in your life that you wish, perhaps you can even become a judge or the first woman president, but do not be putting yourself in front of killers and mafiosi. Promise me this!"

Victoria looked up at the dark eyes, filled with tears and love. She clung to her mother's thin body. "Of course, Mama, of course I promise you."

Note

This story was originally published as "A Family Sunday in the Park" in *Sisters on the Case* (Sara Paretsky, ed.), Obsidian, 2007. It was based on my own experiences as a volunteer in the civil rights movement in Chicago during the summer of 1966. I had grown up in Kansas, where racism took a southern form of discrimination not only in public facilities but also in housing, but I'd never been around the kind of hate that I experienced that summer. My coworkers and I were assigned to spend the summer in a neighborhood near Marquette Park. It was what demographers call "white ethnic." Our job was to use soft propaganda to change hearts and minds of some eighty children we worked with in a summer day camp. But on that hot August day, when race riots broke out in Marquette Park, we saw our neighbors turn into bestial creatures. The insults, the signs, the insignia I describe in the story are all well-documented parts of those riots. I apologize for repeated use of a horrifically offensive word, but it is there to emphasize the hate that spilled out everywhere on the streets that summer.

While many Catholic sisters and priests were ardent supporters of civil rights, Chicago was also home to the notorious block clubs, which sought to keep African-Americans out of Catholic churches in white neighborhoods. In my neighborhood, rioting parishioners set fire to the rectory after the priests preached that open housing and equal jobs opportunities were Christ-like endeavors.

The story laid the groundwork for my 2009 novel, *Hardball,* whose backstory lies in the rubble of the 1966 riots.

I rewrote this story and made substantial changes when I published it as an e-book, *Wildcat* (Morrow, 2017).

DEATH ON THE EDGE

I

God of Mirth or God of Mercy

I grew up knowing gunshots before I even understood the words "Get down. Shield Baby!" But the bullet that killed Tyrone Elgar was louder, sharper than any I'd heard before.

I was six. I was by no means the youngest child on my street to lose a family member to a bullet: crossfire, gang war, police shooting. It doesn't matter whether a cop or a gangbanger is firing the weapon. The bullet doesn't care as it finds the artery, the brain, the liver.

Uncle Ty was driving me home from Pee Wee Soccer. I was a skinny little thing, and he used to tease me.

"You got legs like matchsticks, Keisha. How can those bitty legs kick a soccer ball?"

He had a big laugh, almost as big as he was himself, and when he teased us kids—me and my cousins and our friends—his laugh would rumble in our chests and we couldn't help laughing along with him.

The bullets hit as we were stopped at a stop sign on the corner of my grandma's street. I heard the sound, I knew to crouch down in my seat, and then I heard the screaming and above it all the keening of my grandmother. Someone opened my door and unbuckled my seat belt. I shut my eyes tighter and clutched the seat belt, scared someone was going to kidnap me.

"It's okay, sweetheart. I'm a fireman."

I opened my eyes and saw the black rubber sleeve with a giant white stripe. The zebras, we used to call firefighters.

Uncle Ty's head was plopped over on his right shoulder, as if he'd suddenly gone to sleep at the wheel.

I shook his shoulder and my hand came away covered in blood. I started to scream but my fireman lifted me from the seat and carried me across the street, away from the shattered glass and my uncle's blood. Over his shoulder I saw my grandma kneeling by the car, pulling Uncle Ty's head toward her own breast.

I never played soccer or any other sport after that day. My matchstick legs grew wide and heavy until all that was left of that six-year-old child was a nickname whose origin no one understands, "Sticky."

2

"Tell me again why you wanted me down here today?" I demanded.

Marcena Love's brows were raised in hauteur. "It is exactly what I said to you yesterday: this is your patch; I hoped you could get me past the suspicion one encounters as an outsider."

When she'd said this to me the day before, I'd replied it hadn't been my turf for at least thirty years. "I don't know anyone down here now," I'd added.

"You went to school with Hana Milcek," Marcena said.

"Hana Milcek? She's still down there?"

"Teaching high school English at—" Marcena consulted her notes. "Yes, Mirabal."

Hana and I had taken AP English and history together. A dreamy girl with a love of poetry, she'd impressed the rest of us with the dozens of poems she knew by heart. She could recite whole passages from Shakespeare.

Even though we'd been among a handful of college-bound kids at our school, Hana and I had never been close. I'd lost track of her when we graduated. She took off for Illinois Normal to do a teaching degree the same fall I left for the University of Chicago. I hadn't even known Hana had returned to South Chicago to teach until Marcena came to see me yesterday.

Knowing Marcena Love was back in Chicago had not made my heart flutter with joy. The last time I'd seen her had been about five years ago, when she'd been shrouded in gauze to shield her face while skin grafts healed. She'd looked fragile and very nearly contrite—she'd lost skin on a third of her face and arms in an assault she'd endured after she crossed the line between reporting on crime and participating in it.

Contrition had vanished along with the gauze. Her auburn hair had grown in again; she'd swept the curls from her face with a clip. She was dressed in her usual skintight black, with a velveteen fuchsia bomber jacket and puffy faux combat boots that announced she belonged in the front of the fashion line along with any other line she might stand in.

"I'm working for *The Edge*," Marcena announced when I buzzed her inside.

"You mean you're working on an edge and you're hoping I'll keep you from falling off."

"Oh, please, Vic: *The Edge*. Brand-new. It's a Salanter venture— he's put up the seed money. We're the future of journalism: we're out on the edge. Streaming, online, audio, everything but print."

The Edge was based in London, but after the Parkland massacre, when the *Guardian* newspaper had turned their editorial room over to the Parkland students who were organizing the March for Our Lives, *The Edge* thought they needed to go one better. Or one different.

Marcena explained that *The Edge* had put together an essay competition, asking teens to write about gun violence. "My idea, but Chaim loved it and put up the money for the prizes and transport and so on."

Meaning Chaim Salanter, octogenarian billionaire and Holocaust survivor, who hoped before he died to save everyone in the world, from journalists to children whose lives were damaged by violence.

Marcena and her team had culled a dozen winners from among seven thousand entries. They planned to fly the kids to DC, where they would be filmed reading their essays in the rotunda of the Library of Congress.

"Most of the entries were filled with predictable bromides and calls to action," Marcena added. "Others were harrowing accounts by survivors of school or mall shootings, but too many of those didn't read well. And then we got one from a girl named Keisha Dunne here in Chicago that was flat-out amazing. It was about growing up with routine gun violence and how it affected the girl and her family—she was with her uncle when he was collateral damage in gang crossfire. Her story was also a reminder that we media types care more about affluent white kids than we do about people of color in the cities. She's my number one choice, but I have to vet the story, of course, make sure she didn't make it up and that the girl wrote it herself, make sure she's mediagenic—"

"If it's the best story and she wrote it herself, why does it matter how good she looks on TV?" I demanded.

Marcena smiled puckishly. "Vic, darling, you are so charmingly Victorian. Of course it matters. We're doing this for the kids, of course, but we're also doing it to put *The Edge* on the map. We asked our hundred potential finalists for video clips, but now we need to meet and vet the writers and the stories.

"Anyway, I'd like you to come down to South Chicago with me and help me figure out if there are any issues with the story. The family—mother, I should say; father isn't in the picture—were eager, but then I got a call from this Hana Milcek, with some questions which she wouldn't discuss over the phone."

"She's Keisha Dunne's English teacher?" I was trying to follow the story.

"No. Keisha goes to a private school, South Side Preparatory Academy. But the head of the English and Journalism departments at Mirabal High was one of our local judges. I'm guessing he must have shown Keisha's essay to your friend Hana. She called me this morning and said she had questions before I met with the Dunne girl. She was pretty stiff on the phone, but I remembered that you'd grown up down there. When I asked Milcek if she knew you, she thawed and admitted she follows your cases. She'll talk more frankly if you're with me."

"The last time I let you romp around that high school with me, you dug a pretty big ditch through a lot of people's lives."

"It won't be like that this time." Marcena looked at me so earnestly that I almost believed her.

3

I tried calling Hana as soon as Marcena left, but she wasn't answering her phone. I left a message on her voice mail before digging into the Elgar and Dunne family histories. In case Hana's questions for Marcena had to do with the facts in Keisha Dunne's essay, I looked up her uncle's murder. Marcena had given me his name: Tyrone Elgar, but his murder had merited a scant line in a paragraph summarizing all the violent deaths that same week.

He'd been killed ten years ago, apparently caught in gang crossfire at a stop sign on Escanaba and Ninety-sixth. I'd wondered if he might be a banger himself instead of an innocent bystander, but it wasn't possible to tell from the single sentence.

I didn't see anything about Elgar's niece, Keisha Dunne. A Fannie Lou Elgar had been one of the winners of the mayor's summer reading challenge three years in a row and had also been on the Mirabal chess team when they beat Whitney Young for the city championship—an upset on the David-Goliath metric. Mirabal is a poor, underperforming neighborhood school; Whitney Young, a magnet school, is one of the top five high schools in Illinois.

Michelle Obama is among Whitney Young's graduates. I went to Mirabal High.

The Mirabal website celebrated their chess team hoisting the trophy, a stylized queen about a foot high. Seven guys and Fannie Lou, the lone female on the team, a heavyset girl who stared at the camera with a kind of defiant seriousness.

I dug a little and found Tyrone Elgar's paid death announcement in the *Sun-Times:* survived by beloved mother Verena, cherished daughter Fannie Lou, sister Jasmine, niece Keisha.

I wondered why the niece, not the daughter, had written about Elgar's death, but maybe she could be more detached. Although if it was the niece who'd been with him when he died—maybe it wasn't detachment but a decade of pent-up fears that made Keisha write. I imagined an uneasy rivalry of grief and fear between the two girls.

They were both only children; Jasmine Elgar Dunne, older than Tyrone by two years, had divorced Albert Dunne when Keisha was three and never remarried. Her PR firm, Jasmine Speaks Success, with offices on Seventy-first Street, had a small but important client list. She lived in one of the historic condominiums on Sixty-seventh Street that overlook Lake Michigan to the east and one of Olmsted's parks to the north.

Fannie Lou Elgar lived with her grandmother at Ninety-second and Brandon, only a few streets from where I'd grown up. Looking at the addresses, I thought Elgar must have been taking his niece to the grandmother's house when he was killed.

I called Lieutenant Conrad Rawlings, the watch commander at the Fourth District. Conrad and I have a Byzantine relationship, meaning I never fully understand the rules that dictate whether we are at odds or BFFs. Today we seemed on a cordial footing: after a few minutes on why I cared, he looked up the file on Tyrone Elgar. The cops made an arrest about eight months after his murder, when the same gun was used in another gang shooting. Dirtbag was doing twenty-five-to-life in Pontiac.

"Is there any suggestion that Elgar was involved with the shooters? Rival gang, anything?"

"I know you wouldn't assume a black man who got shot had it coming," Conrad said stiffly.

"Thank you; I don't. Merely I don't want to get blindsided tomorrow when I meet with the niece and her mother down at Mirabal. There's some issue around the essay that's making the English teacher uneasy."

I heard Conrad typing and then he assured me that Elgar had led a blameless existence—bachelor's in environmental studies at Illinois-Chicago, a stint with the navy in the Persian Gulf, and then home to a job with the South Chicago Re-Development Foundation.

Conrad's friendly manner disappeared in flames the next afternoon when he saw me backstage at the Mirabal school auditorium: I was standing near Hana Milcek's dead body, giving a statement to the sergeant who'd answered my 911 call.

4

When Marcena and I pulled into the visitors' section of the parking lot an hour earlier, I'd been depressed by how shabby Mirabal High looked. It had been old when I went there, but at least the asphalt had been in good shape. Now it had buckled and cracked;

several windows were boarded up, and—true for all Chicago schools, at least in neighborhoods where people of color live—all the entrances were padlocked except for one side door.

The teachers' lounge still occupied space adjacent to the auditorium. The space had been a greenroom when the school was new—decades before my time—and kids put on elaborate musicals. The lounge's main entrance was via the auditorium's backstage—there was a second door through a janitor's closet that no one ever used. I sidestepped instruments, cables, and music stands to get to the lounge.

Marcena had arranged to meet Hana there at the end of the school day, along with Keisha Dunne and her mother. I'd suggested we bring in the cousin and the grandmother, in case there were questions about what happened the day Tyrone Elgar died, but Marcena vetoed the idea.

"The more people involved, the longer it will all take; you know that, Vic. Of course, I'll check with the grandmother once I know Hana's concerns, but let's get those cleared up first."

I eyed her thoughtfully. "You have a second tape running in your head. I'd love to listen to that along with the foreground sound."

"Tape?" Marcena said derisively. "It's all digital now, Vic."

She moved away from me to greet a newcomer entering through the auditorium door, calling her "Ms. Dunne," exclaiming how delighted she was to meet in person.

"This walkway is a lawsuit waiting to happen," Jasmine Dunne announced. "I tripped on a music stand, and those cables are lethal."

She was dressed in a dramatic turquoise suit whose jacket had a half cape over the left shoulder. Keisha arrived a minute or two later. With her high cheekbones and her own stylish outfit—a horizontal-striped cropped top over high-waisted leggings—I could see why Marcena wanted to film her.

"Miss Milcek said there were questions about Keisha's essay." Jasmine Dunne impatiently waved aside introductions. "If someone is accusing my daughter of something, I need to be here. I own a public relations firm, and I know what happens when journalists start making accusations—"

"No one's making accusations, Ms. Dunne." Marcena cut her off smoothly. "I'm going to every school in North America that our winning writers attend. I'm asking the same questions of each student and their teachers. It's excellent that you arrived today; it saves me time in trying to make an appointment with you for permissions and all those things we do with underage performers."

The posh British accent worked its usual magic on the Americans. Keisha, who'd been staring at the floor, looked up and smiled at the word *performer,* while her mother nodded warily but calmed down—an English journalist might not bring an American's racial bias to the meeting.

A half hour passed with no sign of Hana; Marcena tried her cell phone, the school secretary paged her. I don't know what made me go back to the auditorium, except some obscure thought that she might have tripped on the backstage cables on her way to join us.

Lights were kept on during the school day, but I still almost missed her: she was sprawled across a book cart that had been wheeled behind the school orchestra's drum set. As nearly as I could tell, she'd been shot twice at close range.

My first, illogical thought was that Marcena had shot her to protect her precious *Edge* competition. My next thought was that Hana Milcek looked young and innocent in death.

5

"What the fuck are you doing here?" Conrad stormed over to me. "That call to me yesterday, that was a fucking setup, wasn't it?"

The watch commander's arrival at a crime scene makes the rank and file nervous: they know it's a high-profile case and they can't afford a mistake. The commander's arrival spitting nails makes everyone from first responder to senior detective fade as far into the scenery as possible.

"You remember Marcena Love, don't you, Lieutenant?" I said formally. "Her company is holding an essay competition on kids affected by gun violence; Keisha Dunne wrote about the murder of her uncle, Tyrone Elgar. Ms. Love asked me to be part of a conversation about the essay with her mother and with Ms. Milcek, since something in it troubled Ms. Milcek. I called you yesterday as a routine fact check; I wanted to make sure the CPD thought Mr. Elgar had been murdered."

"My brother was most certainly murdered," Jasmine Dunne snapped. "Are you trying to say he wasn't?"

"We're fact-checking all the essays," Marcena said soothingly. "A whiff of 'fake news' will destroy the credibility of this important program."

Jasmine was saying she wanted to go with Marcena when she checked facts at white suburban schools, but she was cut short by a man with a deep voice loudly demanding to know if "it was true."

"Someone told me Hana is dead. What happened to her? We had lunch together a few hours ago. I thought she seemed perfectly healthy."

If Marcena wanted mediagenic, she didn't need to look further than the new arrival, a tall, square-jawed white man with a shock of dark hair. Like most contemporary teachers he wore jeans, but he also had on a blazer over an open-necked shirt. If the principal hadn't already been in the room—an African-American woman in her fifties—I would have pegged this man for the job. He had that authoritative energy that men in power, or aspiring to power, project like a force field.

"It is true, Dex," the principal said, "and the police are here, wanting us not to contaminate their crime scene, so please don't come farther into the room."

Dex ignored her. "Marcena. If I'd known you were in the building I'd have come at once. What's going on?"

I stared as he hurried to Marcena's side.

"This is Dexter Vamor," she said quickly. "He was one of my—our—The Edge's local judges. We only met in person yesterday."

Vamor held a hand out to me. "Chair of the English and Journalism departments here at Mirabal, for my sins. Are you with The Edge as well?"

"I'm a detective," I said.

"Private," Conrad snapped. "She's not with the police, she's not going to ask any questions, she's not going to touch evidence and prove that she's sharper than we are."

I prudently didn't say anything.

The next hour was a jumble of questions about who had seen what and who was doing what in the lounge. All of us, from Keisha and Jasmine to me, and not excluding the principal or Marcena, were tested for gunshot residue and searched for weapons.

Conrad talked to the principal and Vamor about students or

colleagues who might have been angry with Hana, but both were adamant that she didn't have that kind of history.

Vamor added, "Of course, there's always a student who thinks their work is undervalued, but frankly, our kids aren't looking for that extra decimal on their GPA to get them into Harvard. As for her colleagues, sure, some people liked her more than others, but she's been here twenty years without making enemies among the teachers. This must have been a random shooting. Maybe she interrupted someone selling or using."

"Dex," the principal said, "we're not in the business of pointing the cops at our students or our faculty and staff. I'd appreciate it if you didn't start speculating without any facts to back up your statements."

Vamor gave her a mock salute. From the expression on the principal's face, she wished it was *his* body on the book cart, but she only turned to Conrad to say that Hana worked hard with students who wanted to excel but didn't neglect anyone in her classes.

"If she had discipline problems, she usually sorted them out herself."

When Conrad finally decided to dismiss us, I said diffidently, "If the lieutenant would permit me one question first?"

Rawlings looked at me sourly. "Meekness isn't your best act, Warshawski. Ask away."

"Mr. Vamor, I'm here because Ms. Milcek apparently had questions about Keisha Dunne's essay. Since you were one of the judges, you probably have a sense of what she wanted to know."

"What questions?" Jasmine Dunne demanded, hands on hips. "I am tired of you insinuating—"

"Please, Ms. Dunne," Marcena said. "Keisha's work is brilliant. But I still needed to speak to Ms. Milcek. Did she know your daughter?"

"Of course not. Keisha doesn't go to Mirabal. Hana Milcek might have been my niece's teacher." Jasmine looked a question at her daughter, who nodded and muttered that "Fannie Lou adored Ms. Milcek."

"Fannie Lou surely wouldn't bad-mouth you to her English teacher," Jasmine said to Keisha.

"No, Mama," Keisha muttered, staring at her feet.

Vamor was annoyed that Marcena had talked to Hana without telling him.

"Milcek—Ms. Milcek—found what hotel I was in and called me there," Marcena said. "She didn't want to talk on the phone. Vic's question is a good one: Did she share her concerns with you?"

Vamor shook his head. "As I said, I saw her at lunch today. We talked about the competition—like a lot of our teachers, she had kids whose lives were hit by gun violence and she'd encouraged them to enter—and she knew I was a judge, so she wondered when she could find out about her students. I told her that was up to the people in London, and of course I couldn't release names until Marcena told us they were ready to go public."

"But you'd already spoken to Keisha and her mother," I said to Marcena.

"Of course," she said. "Under oath of secrecy, since no winners can be announced until we're dead sure of our finalists."

"How did you come to pick Vamor as a judge?" Conrad asked. "A rust belt school isn't exactly on international radar."

"But Dex is," Marcena said. "He writes a regular column for one of the best journalism school blogs and he's on the faculty for a summer journalism program that works with teens. We knew about him even before we were sure we were going forward with the contest."

The principal raised her brows. "Dex, that's news to me. I'm surprised it's not in your CV."

He looked a little embarrassed. "Doing it on my own time, Albertine."

"Usually we know when you're up to something high-profile. But if there are questions about an essay submitted by one of my students—"

"She doesn't go to school here, Albertine," Vamor interrupted. "She's at South Side Prep in Chatham."

"The essay dealt with the murder of one of your students' fathers," I said. "Fannie Lou Elgar."

"But Fannie didn't write the essay," Vamor said sharply.

"Fannie *Lou,* Dexter," the principal said. "Her father named her for Fannie Lou Hamer. If her cousin's work deals with Tyrone Elgar's death, I'd like to read it; it might give me insight into Fannie Lou. She's one of our most gifted students, but painfully shy inside her shell."

"The essays are not being made public yet," Marcena said. "And they're the property of *The Edge.*"

"It's mine," Keisha said. "I wrote it."

Marcena smiled at her. "The contest rules state that *The Edge* owns all the submissions, I'm afraid. Even the ones that don't win awards we may want to use in some other way."

"But you could print it out for us to take a look at," I said.

"So you can start questioning it and tearing it apart?" Jasmine said. "I don't think so."

"In that case, I'll get the state's attorney to give me a warrant," Conrad said. "Gun deaths on the South Side are usually about gangs, and if the lady had been shot on her way out of the building I might believe it was an initiation murder. As it is, I'm open to all ideas. Which means all of you can wait here until the state's attorney gives me a warrant for the essay."

6

Marcena was magnanimous in defeat. The principal took her to the school office, where Marcena printed out a half dozen copies of Keisha's essay, including one for me.

Conrad pulled me aside for a short talk before he left: he trusted if I knew anything that would shed light on the murder that I would not be a glory hog but would turn it over to him.

"Talk to Love over there," I said, pointing at where Marcena was conferring with Dexter Vamor. "She's the one who pulled me down here and I'm still not sure I know why."

Conrad looked at her, but suddenly smiled at me. "I don't know her, Ms. W., but I know you. You may have come down here for the reasons you state, but you're obsessed now with Milcek's death."

"Of course I am. Violent death is always a shock, and then, you know, we went to school together. I'm not a glory hog—since you know me, you must surely realize that—but I want to know why Hana died and who killed her." I shivered: Hana had gotten out of bed thinking about her class schedule, or what she wanted to ask Marcena, or whether she could make her insurance payments on time—the quotidian, not the thought that she would die before suppertime.

"Are the school's surveillance cameras working?" I asked.

Conrad nodded. "Tech teams will look at them to see if any strangers came into the school in the last twenty-four hours. Guards sure didn't sign anyone in, but a school hall can be chaotic; someone could have blended in during a class change. Keep me on speed dial, Warshawski."

When he'd left, I went back to the principal's office to talk to Albertine Diaz about Hana Milcek's next of kin. Hana had never married; she'd lived with her mother until the older woman's death three years ago. If she'd been close to anyone with whom she might have confided her concerns about Keisha's essay, Diaz didn't know who that might be.

As for enemies among students or staff, Diaz shook her head. "Despite what Dex Vamor was saying in the group, he and Hana didn't get along. She was a serious type and he's flamboyant. No one ever put together better lesson plans than Hana, but the students gravitate to Dex. Being a teacher is half dedication, half knowledge, and all showman. Sad to say. I often thought Hana would fit in better at a university; I tried to get her to go for the doctorate, but she loved being in the classroom. And every now and then, she'd find a student who responded.

"The Elgar girl, Fannie Lou, she was one of the ones who responded to Hana Milcek's style. She's a studious type, too. Shy, serious, super-bright. I don't know what Hana's death will do to her. Her mother died in childbirth, along with the baby, when Fannie Lou was two, then her father was shot and killed. I hope the cousin told Fannie Lou she was writing about her father's murder. It would be a nasty shock to find out about it from your English friend's online performance."

"Yes," I agreed, thinking about it. "I wonder if that's what Hana wanted to talk about with Marcena. If Fannie Lou was one of her own protégées, she'd have wanted to protect her. . . . You said Hana solved her own disciplinary problems. Did she have many? Did students gang up on her because of her scholarly style?"

Diaz smiled wryly. "The teenage mind remains a mystery to me, even though I've been teaching and administrating in their world for close to thirty years. Kids treated her almost like a pet, I think because she was one of the world's true innocents. She behaved the same to everyone, to me and her peers and the janitors and the students. She thought everyone shared her interest in poetry and literature, and she'd listen to anyone's opinion. She added writers like Audre Lorde to her curriculum, she'd let kids write on hip-hop. She didn't try to be hip, not the way Dex Vamor does, but she listened."

"What's Vamor doing here, anyway?" I asked. "Seems like a guy who wants a bigger stage."

Diaz's lips tightened. "Yes, indeed. He's been here three years, came when we added a media department. He's only thirty-two, but he had the credentials to be a department head. I'm sure he's already planning his next move."

Marcena came into the office at that moment, looking for me, hoping it wouldn't be an inconvenience, but she needed to get back to her hotel so she could communicate with her London colleagues on Hana's death and how that might affect *The Edge*'s competition. I'd noticed her taking pictures of Hana's body—those would probably be on *The Edge*'s website within the hour. What a scoop, journalist right there when her subject's dead body was found. I wondered again if Marcena had known anything about Hana's death before I found her.

At home, I curled up with a glass of Amarone and read Keisha's essay. She wrote with a high degree of sophistication, both in language and in structure. She covered seven funerals she'd attended for people dead from bullets.

Every story is different, but every story is the same: the same grief, the same incomprehension, the same anger, whether over the baby Nikwa Jonas, hit by a bullet that went through her father's kitchen window, or for Alan Wicherly, star forward on my school's basketball team, shot by a cop when he was putting a hand inside his pocket for his driver's license.

These deaths create a mountain of grief that presses down on me. There are days when it scarcely seems possible to rise from my bed, because the grief mountain grew another hundred feet higher in the night.

Family and neighbors call on Jesus for help or faith, but I always remember my grandmother, kneeling next to my Uncle Ty. She called him "my baby." It had never occurred to me that my big laughing uncle had ever been my grandma's baby, but when he died, he was in her eyes no bigger than Baby Nikwa.

"Why, Jesus?" she cried. "Why did you bring him
safe home from Iraq only to let him die in front
of me? Are you the God of mercy or God of mirth,
laughing at the contortions of the human heart?"

I sat for a long time when I'd finished reading, staring at nothing. The pain of lives like Keisha Dunne's seemed almost beyond bearing. And now her cousin's high mountain of grief had just doubled with the loss of a beloved teacher.

I finally stirred enough to pour myself another glass of wine. Keisha had been six when her uncle was shot. I wondered if her grandmother had really uttered those words—God of mercy or God of mirth. The fireman was carrying Keisha across the street, away from the murder scene. The words could have sounded like blasphemy to a bystander; they would have been repeated in a shocked or titillated voice. They would have become part of what Keisha was sure she remembered from that day.

How would Fannie Lou, the shy studious cousin, feel if her father's murder catapulted Keisha into international recognition? Betrayed and violated, or would she be glad that the story reached a wide audience? Those could easily have been the questions on Hana Milcek's mind when she spoke to Marcena about the competition.

I went to my laptop and looked up Alan Wicherly. He'd died two years earlier, but she had the details right: shot by a cop, community fury, no action by the city or the department. He'd been a senior forward on the Mirabal High basketball team, with a full ride to the University of Kansas's fabled basketball program, when he was killed outside a gas station at Eighty-third and Exchange.

Mirabal High. Keisha didn't go to school there, but Fannie Lou did. I shook my head. Fannie Lou's murdered father, her high school's murdered basketball star. To an outsider, it looked as though Keisha needed to take her cousin's experiences and make them her own. Of course, Keisha lived on the South Side. If Wicherly was a local star, she could easily have known him and been affected by his death.

Even so. Even so, I found the card for the Mirabal principal, Albertine Diaz, and called her cell.

"Ms. Warshawski! Have you learned something about Hana's murder?"

"I'm wondering if I've learned what questions she wanted to ask about Keisha Dunne's essay," I said. "Have you read it?"

Diaz apologized. "I just got home ten minutes ago. I wanted to break the news of Hana's death to Fannie Lou Elgar myself, and she was every bit as distraught as I anticipated. I got her home and sat with her and her grandmother for an hour. I just hope this doesn't derail her academics: we have high hopes for her, but losing Hana to a bullet, after a childhood that started with watching her father die—"

"She was there when Tyrone Elgar died?" I interrupted. "Keisha's essay doesn't mention that."

Diaz said, "It's my understanding she was in the car with him when he got shot."

"She was? Both girls were there? That sure doesn't come across in Keisha's writing." I asked Diaz about Alan Wicherly.

"It was a big story in South Chicago. All the kids were affected. Basketball star gets shot, no one is safe: that was how every parent and every child felt. I don't think it means anything particular that

Keisha Dunne wasn't in the same school as Alan." Diaz's tone was sharp. "I'm sure you're right," I said. "I was trying to understand what in the essay troubled Hana. If Fannie Lou felt close to her, she might have discussed relations with her cousin. A lot of the events Keisha describe seem to come from Fannie Lou's direct experience, and I can't help wondering about rivalry and jealousy between the two girls."

"I'll read the essay and get back to you," Diaz said grudgingly.

I wasn't expecting to hear from her, especially after more than an hour had gone by. I was on my way down the stairs to give my dogs their final outing of the day when Diaz phoned.

"We have a situation here. Is there any chance you could drive down to Fannie Lou's grandmother's place tonight?"

She started to give me directions, but I cut her off. "It's my briar patch, too, Ms. Diaz: I grew up three blocks away."

7

Once I passed the Loop I had the roads almost to myself—few people go to Chicago's South Side late at night. I was passing the park that covered the old U.S. Steel South Works twenty minutes after I left home.

Lights were on in all the rooms of Verena Elgar's bungalow on Brandon. The situation, as Diaz had called it, was so loud that I could hear the shouts as I got out of my car. The noise and lights had drawn neighbors to the street outside. They watched me curiously as I jogged up the walk, but no one spoke to me until I rang the doorbell.

"They can't hear you inside but the door's open," a woman called helpfully.

She was right; I pulled on the handle and walked inside to fury. I recognized Fannie Lou Elgar from her chess club photo, a heavy young woman with a wild halo of natural hair, her face swollen from crying. Next to her was an older version of Jasmine Dunne. The grandmother, I presumed. The pair were facing off against Jasmine and Keisha, the girls yelling so loudly I could only make out a handful of individual words, but those were charged: *Thief! Liar! Loser! Murderer!*

Albertine Diaz was on the perimeter of the battle zone, watching the combatants, her shoulders hunched with tension. When she saw me, she relaxed noticeably and took me into the narrow hallway.

"I've unleashed a firestorm here. When I read the essay I felt—"

"I want no more secrets or secret conversations about my granddaughters." Verena Elgar had left her daughter and was facing us in the doorway, arms akimbo. "Whatever you have to say or think you know, I want it right here in my living room. And you can start by telling me who you are."

I obediently introduced myself.

"I see—you're the woman Albertine says made her start asking questions about Keisha's essay."

"It's my essay," Fannie Lou muttered. "She stole my essay."

"You can't prove that!" Keisha said. "You think you've got the only brain in the family. I'm tired of 'Fannie Lou won the reading competition,' 'Fannie Lou is doing summer math camp, Fannie Lou this, Fannie Lou that.'"

"I'm tired of 'Keisha is such a gifted singer and dancer. Must be hard to have a cousin like her when you're so fat yourself,'" Fannie Lou blurted, on the verge of tears.

"You didn't even know about the competition until I told you."

"Liar!" Fannie Lou said. "Ms. Milcek told me about it. I wrote about my daddy and she said it was brilliant and I should make it into a whole essay for the competition."

"And then you'd send in your video clip and Ms. Love would swoon over your fat ass and put you on national television. I don't think so," Keisha sneered.

"Fannie Lou, are you sure Ms. Milcek submitted your essay?" Diaz asked. "Even the most dedicated teacher can drop the ball now and again."

"Not Ms. Milcek," Fannie Lou said. "When she said she'd do a thing, she'd do that thing."

"Fannie Lou—Ms. Elgar—" I said. "Did you watch Ms. Milcek submit your essay?"

She nodded, choking back a sob. "I sat with her as she filled out the form, because some of the information was about me. My birth date and other things that Ms. Milcek wouldn't know off the top of her head. Two other kids in my class wrote essays and she sent them all in on the same day. So it wasn't that she was treating me special," she added fiercely to her cousin. "Everyone mattered to her if we did the work."

"And you, Ms. Dunne," I said quickly before Keisha could fire back. "How did you submit your essay?"

"Mom helped me, but we took it to my high school counselor."

I asked the girls for the dates they'd made their submissions, but they couldn't remember—it had been back in the spring, before the end of the school year, and it was late September now.

I felt a bit like King Solomon with the baby—who was really the mother of the essay? I called Marcena.

"Your winning student has a rival for the same essay. Can you check your files at *The Edge* for a submission by Fannie Lou Elgar?"

"I'm in the middle of something right now, Vic. Can't it wait?"

"I'm not sure how you'd handle a public outcry if your winner was found to be guilty either of theft or plagiarism. That's where this is heading, though."

"What are you talking about?" Marcena demanded.

"Your winning essay, your mediagenic kid. It's possible she stole her cousin's work. I'm trying to figure that out."

Marcena wanted to know where I was, how I knew this, damn it, I should have called her as soon as I heard about the problem—did I think I was God Almighty on a throne dispensing justice to the rest of the human race?

"We can sort out later who I think I am and who I think you are, but in the meantime, can you get that information from your paper's database?" I said.

I heard a man's voice in the background, a smothered noise of annoyance, and then Marcena said she'd call me back in ten. It was actually a bit under that when she phoned to say she'd gotten *The Edge*'s nightshift tech department to do a search. Nothing from Fannie Lou, nothing from Mirabal High, sorry, Vic.

"But that can't be," Fannie Lou protested. "I watched her, and so did Jordan and Artiya."

"You just can't admit you or your precious teacher made a mistake," Keisha said. "Did you even do your video? Maybe your teacher didn't know how to upload that."

"Just because I don't go to a fancy school doesn't mean we all crawl around in the dirt down here," Fanny Lou said.

"Girls!" Verena's voice was a whip. "I will not have you turn yourselves into a public spectacle. That's enough of this for tonight. You, Ms. Detective, do you have any advice on how to find out what happened to Fannie Lou's essay?"

"Did Ms. Milcek do this at a school computer or on your laptop?" I asked Fannie Lou.

"At the school, in the computer lab, but I have my essay on my machine, and it has the date stamp on it. That will prove I wrote mine before Keisha wrote hers!"

"Only if Keisha's date stamp is later than yours, Missy," Jasmine said. "Why can't you let Keisha have a little glory for once in your life, Fannie Lou? You get your name in the paper every five minutes for some competition or other."

Fannie Lou said, "She's in the choir, she got a solo at the Youth Orchestra, she was an extra in Chi. Why can't she let me be best at this one thing?"

"Go get your computer, Fannie Lou," her grandmother said. "At least we can find out what date *you* put your essay in your machine."

Fannie Lou turned to go to the hall and up the narrow stairs to the second floor. Keisha was watching her, hands on hips, biting her lips.

"Sticky!" I called.

Fannie Lou stopped with her foot on the first step. She turned to look at me, but Keisha didn't move.

"I'm pretty sure that answers the authorship question," I said dryly. "We can get the computers and find Hana's and check all the dates, but I think we'll find that Fannie Lou wrote the original essay."

Principal Diaz and the grandmother both looked bewildered. "Why? What does 'Sticky' have to do with it?" the principal said.

"The start of the essay," I said. "The writer says the only remaining piece of the girl with 'matchstick legs' who was with Tyrone Elgar when he died is the nickname. Keisha went through the essay and found every reference to Mr. Elgar as 'Daddy,' or 'my father,' and changed them to 'Uncle Ty,' or 'my uncle.' But she forgot the rest of the context. Why, though?"

When Keisha didn't say anything, Verena Elgar demanded that she answer the question.

"Fannie Lou was, like, preening herself. 'My essay's so good, I'm going to win the big prize.' I couldn't take her boasting on herself."

"What big prize?" I asked.

"The scholarship money," Keisha whispered. "The winners all get scholarships to the college of their choice. I want to go to a real music conservatory, in New York or Boston, and it seemed like—I read Fannie Lou's essay and I thought, she'll win this competition just like she wins everything. But even without this, she'll get a scholarship to Stanford or Harvard or someplace, why can't I have this one chance?"

"But why, baby?" Verena went to Keisha and took her in her arms. "You know I would help you, you know I've saved my pennies and dimes so that you and Fannie Lou could both go to college."

"We don't know that, Mama." Jasmine's voice was like a whip. "The whole time I was growing up, everything was 'Ty, Ty, Ty.' He was so special, it was like I didn't even exist. And then after he died, you were the same with Fannie Lou. Keisha's accomplishments never mattered to you the way Fannie Lou's do. I work hard, but the money isn't there for the New England Conservatory or Cincinnati."

Albertine Diaz's jaw dropped in horror. "But, Ms. Dunne—surely you didn't encourage your daughter to steal her cousin's work!"

"No. But when she told me what she'd done, I thought, okay, why not? After all, Ty was my brother, but my grief never counted for anything. And he was like a second father to Keisha—her daddy left us when she was a baby. But it was always Fannie Lou's grief, Mama's grief, never what happened to us."

"You must have known this would come out if Keisha won," I said. "Didn't you have a plan?"

"If she won, I figured she'd be in Washington and on TV before anyone at Mirabal High knew about it."

"Oh, Jasmine." Her mother's voice crackled with misery. "I always said God was a god of mirth more than mercy. He and his angels laugh at the way we contort ourselves. Albertine, and you, Ms. Detective, I need to be alone with my family. You leave now."

I nodded and said to the principal, "Can you get me into the school? I know it's almost midnight, but I'd like to get to the computers before some wiseass decides to wipe the server."

8

Mirabal High was built like a giant E, but missing the middle prong. The computer lab was on the second floor of the far wing. When we reached the end of the long hall and turned left, we saw the light from the lab at once.

The lab door was locked, but Albertine had a master key. The

344 • LOVE & OTHER CRIMES

room was filled with rows of monitor-covered countertops; it took a moment before we saw Dexter Vamor at a machine by the windows. Marcena was standing behind him.

I raced across the room to him, shoving Marcena out of the way. I leapt onto Dexter, knocking his hand from the keyboard. He rolled back in his chair, pushing me off-balance, and reached for an ankle holster.

I lunged forward, hands around his neck, fingers digging into his larynx. He still managed to fire twice before he lost consciousness.

Black hands covered mine, pulling me away from Vamor. "Ms. W, didn't I specifically order you to keep me in the loop and not to hotdog?"

9

Marcena and I sat with Albertine Diaz in the principal's office.

"Thank you for alerting the police," Diaz said formally to Marcena. "It was a big help to have Lieutenant Rawlings see Dex actually trying to shoot us. And thank you, Vic, for figuring things out quickly enough to stop him before he erased Hana's files."

It was two days after the shoot-out in the lab. I'd spent most of the previous afternoon with the Elgar family. Verena was mourning her granddaughter Keisha's theft of Fannie Lou's work, but more than that, she was upset with herself for not seeing how her daughter, Jasmine, was hurting.

"After Ty died, I wanted to weave this cocoon around Fannie Lou, and I didn't see how I was cutting Jasmine and Keisha out. They were always here, Sunday dinner, girls playing together, going to swim lessons together, but I read the story wrong. Jasmine put Keisha in a private school and I thought she was cutting herself away from me, from us and the neighborhood. I didn't see the world of hurt she was living in."

Jasmine and her mother agreed that Keisha needed a meaningful penalty for stealing Fannie Lou's work, but no one wanted to see her publicly shamed. She was sixteen, and sixteen-year-olds act without thinking about consequences ten times a day. We didn't want a mark on her record that would add another barrier to any education or jobs she would want in a few years. When I left, they were deciding on a combination of community service— Keisha coaching neighborhood kids one afternoon a week—and curtailing of Keisha's own social life.

"And Fannie Lou is going to join Keisha in coaching," Verena said. "I'm distressed if she was boasting on herself and making Keisha feel like a lesser girl."

What I didn't understand was Dexter Vamor's role in the story, but Marcena explained that.

"He saw the video clips the girls sent in. He knew the essays were identical, but he knew Keisha had the winning presence, and he wanted a win. He wanted a job on cable and he figured if he ingratiated himself with 'the lady from London' and had a beautiful poised girl like Keisha to be the face of Chicago's South Side, he'd have a chance to make himself known internationally. So he deleted Fannie Lou's submission."

"And then Hana read Keisha's essay," I said. "She instantly recognized the language from Fannie Lou's work; she called Marcena to say she had questions about the essay, but she wanted to talk to Vamor first, I guess."

Marcena nodded. "That's how I reconstruct it, too. She confronted him, and he shot her. And then he tried to romance me. I suppose he thought he could dazzle me into not questioning his role in the essays, but I'm forty-five; when good-looking thirty-year-olds try to dazzle me, I always wonder what's really going on with them."

She looked at me with a smile half guilty, half mischievous: she would never apologize for the havoc she'd wreaked five years ago, but she wanted me to know she'd learned from it.

"And the prizes?" the principal asked. "I hope you're going to readmit Fannie Lou's essay. She may not be the most mediagenic girl in your database, but she did write the essay. She is a gifted student in a community without very many of them."

"Oh, yes." Marcena produced her brilliant public smile, five hundred watts of dazzle. "*The Edge* is going to profile the whole family. We'll fly the grandmother and the cousin out along with Fannie Lou. And I'm twisting some arms at the London Conservatory of Music: we think we'll come up with a nice package for the cousin."

I drove Marcena to the airport a few days later. I still wondered why she was in the computer lab with Vamor when Albertine Diaz and I arrived there.

"Vic, you're such a Victorian." She repeated the label in a voice light with scorn. "Just because an apple has a worm in it doesn't mean you can't enjoy the apple. You take everything in life too hard. You want everyone to be moral and well behaved, but all you get is bruises when you try to make that happen. Relax, learn to enjoy the pleasures that come your way. Life is too short, the time for rosebuds is here for an instant. Gather them while you can."

I pulled up to the International Terminal. "Maybe you're right, Marcena. I guess I'm the person following after you, trying to get the worms out of the apples so they don't choke an innocent bystander."

She leaned across the gearshift and kissed my cheek. "None of us is innocent, darling. We all carry a shadow of guilt for something. I just let the world see mine."

She grabbed her bag from the backseat and strode into the terminal without a backward glance.

Note

Marcena Love first appeared in *Fire Sale,* where she crossed a line between reporting on a major crime centered on V.I.'s old South Chicago high school and participating in it. I published "God of Mirth" as a stand-alone e-book (Morrow, 2018). I wrote it in the wake of the Parkland shooting: as distressed and disturbed as I was by that massacre, I was equally distressed by knowing how many African-American children grow up in the middle of gun violence without their trauma being recognized, let alone discussed.

About twenty years ago, I did some work with local Head Start groups under the guidance of the eminent psychiatrist Dr. Carl Bell (1947–2019). Civil war was raging in Lebanon and the former Yugoslavia when I met him; he told me that children of color in Chicago (and elsewhere in America) experience at least as much violence as children in Beirut or Sarajevo, and that like children in war zones, African-American children suffer terribly from PTSD. He studied violence, created strategies for teaching nonviolence—he said that by the age of five, inner-city children have witnessed so much violence that they are already exhibiting signs of shell shock. He tried to come up with programs for helping children and teens recover from the violence they experience.

My local synagogue (KAM Isaiah Israel) prays every Sabbath for the victims of gun violence during the preceding week in the city of Chicago. At Yom Kippur, the book of remembrance we published contained over five hundred names of the people—most of them children—we were trying to keep in mind during the 2019 calendar year.

I wrote this story with a lot of grief in my heart.

PHOTO FINISH

I

When he came into my office that July afternoon, I thought I'd met him before. It was something about his smile, sweet but aloof, as if inviting and withholding at the same time. I usually check databases before my first meeting with a new client, but whatever Hunter Davenport did hadn't made my favorite search engines yet. If I'd seen him before, it wasn't on the evening news.

"I'm glad you could meet me on short notice, Ms. Warshawski. I'm only in town a few days, and these Chicago hotel bills mount up." He had a trace of that southern drawl we northerners secretly find appealing. "They warned me summer in Chicago could make Charleston feel cool, but I refused to believe them until I got off that plane."

I shook his hand and offered him the armchair in the alcove where I meet clients. Outside, the heat was turning sidewalks into reflecting pools, but in my windowless office, all seasons and hours are alike; with air conditioning and floor lamps, it might have been midwinter.

"Charleston, South Carolina? Is that your home, Mr. Davenport?"

"I lived there when I was a teenager, but most of my adult life has been spent in Europe. I can't quite shake the accent, or a yearning for long summer afternoons when time stops and all we do is lie in the tall grass waiting for fish to rise and drinking lemonade."

I smiled. I feel nostalgia for those same endless summers, when my friends and I kept our ears cocked for the Good Humor truck while we jumped rope.

"So what brings you to Chicago when you could be in Charleston getting just as hot and visiting your old haunts in the bargain?"

He smiled again. "Since the grandmother who raised me died, there hasn't been anything to take me back. I'm looking for my father. Someone told me he'd retired to Chicago. I didn't see him in any of the phone books, so I thought I'd better get an investigator. The folks at the *Herald-Star* said you were good."

That was enterprising: an out-of-towner going straight to the dailies for advice. "When did you last see him?"

"When I was eleven. When my mother died, I guess he couldn't stand it. He left me at my grandmother's—my mother's mother—and took off. I never even got a postcard from him after that."

"And why do you want to find him now? After what, fifteen years?"

"A pretty good guess, Ms. Warshawski. I'm twenty-four. When my grandmother died, I started thinking I wanted more family. Also, well"—he played with his fingers as if embarrassed—"I wondered if he didn't have a side to his story I ought to hear. I grew up listening to my granny and my aunt—the unmarried daughter who lived with her—repeat what a bad old bag of bones my old man was. They blamed him for my mama's death. But I began to see that was impossible, so I started wondering about all the rest of what they had to say about my folks. I guess every man likes to know what kind of person his own old man was—what he's got to measure himself against, so to speak."

I'm no less human than the next woman—I couldn't resist the self-deprecating smile or the wistful yearning in his blue-gray eyes. I printed out a contract for him and told him I needed a five-hundred-dollar advance. Under the floor lamp, his helmet of ash blond hair looked like spun gold; as he leaned forward to hand me five hundreds in cash, I could almost imagine the money to be some conjurer's trick.

"I do accept checks and the usual credit cards," I said.

"I don't have a permanent address these days. Cash is easier for me."

It was odd, but not that odd: plenty of people who visit detectives don't want a paper trail. It just made me wonder.

His story boiled down to this: his father, also named Hunter Davenport, was a photographer—at least, he had been a photographer when young Hunter's mother died. Hunter Senior had been a freelance journalist in Vietnam, where my client's mother had been an army nurse. The two met, married, produced young Hunter.

"That's why I lived in Europe as a child: after the war my father covered hot spots in Africa and Asia. My mother and I lived in Paris during the school year and joined him on assignment during the summer. Then she died, in a car wreck in South Africa. It had nothing to do with whatever conflict he was covering. I don't even know where he was working—when you're a kid, you don't pay attention to that kind of thing. It was just the ordinary dumb kind of wreck she could have had in Paris or Charleston. He wasn't with her—in the car with her, I mean—but my grandmother always blamed him, said if he hadn't kept her half a world away, it never would have happened."

He stumbled through the words so quickly, I had to lean forward to make out what he was saying. He stopped abruptly. When he spoke again it was in a slow flat voice, but his knuckles showed white where he gripped his hands against his crossed legs.

"I was with her when she died. My mother was so beautiful. You never will see a woman as beautiful as her. And when she was covered with blood—it was hard. I still see her in my dreams, that way." He took a deep breath. "It must have been hard for him, for Hunter—my—my dad—because the next thing I knew, I was at school in Charleston, living with my grandmother, and I never saw him again."

"What was your mother's name? Birth name, I mean."

He'd gone away to some private world; my question jolted him back to my office. "Oh. Helen. Helen—Alder."

"And why do you think your father's in Chicago?"

"The agency. The agency where he used to sell his pictures, they told me they'd last heard from him here."

I had to work to pry more information from him: the agency was a French bureau. First he claimed not to remember the name, but when I handed the hundreds back across the table, he came up with it: Sur Place, on Boulevard Saint-Germain in Paris. No, he didn't know his father's Social Security number. Or his date of birth. He and his mother had spent so much time apart from his father that ordinary holidays and birthdays weren't times they had in common. As for where his father came from, young Hunter was similarly ignorant.

"My dad never talked to me about his childhood that I can remember. And my mother's family declared him *hors la loi*, so that—"

"Declared him ooo-la-la?"

"What? Oh, *hors la loi*—an outlaw, you know. They never talked about him."

The client was staying at the Hotel Trefoil, a tiny place on Scott Street where they unpack your luggage and hand you a hot towel when you walk in so you can wipe the day's sweat from your brow. If he could afford the Trefoil, my fee wouldn't make a dent in his loose change. I told him that I'd do what I could and that I'd get back to him in a few days. He thanked me with that tantalizing familiar smile.

"What do you do yourself, Mr. Davenport? I feel I should recognize you."

He looked startled. In fact, I thought he looked almost frightened, but in the pools of lamplight, I couldn't be certain. Anyway, a second later he was laughing.

"I don't do anything worth recording. I'm not an actor or an Internet genius that you should know me."

He left on that note, making me wonder how he afforded the Trefoil. Perhaps his Charleston grandmother had left him money. I laid the five hundreds in a circle on my desktop and ran a marking pen over them. They weren't counterfeit, but of course fairy's gold vanishes overnight. Just in case, I'd drop them at the bank on my way home.

The Internet easily found the phone number for Sur Place, which cheered me: young Davenport had given me information so unwillingly that I'd been afraid he'd manufactured the agency's name. It was nine at night in Paris; the night operator at the photo agency didn't speak English. I think he was telling me to call tomorrow, when Monsieur Duval would be in, but I wasn't 100 percent sure.

It was only two in Chicago, and Sherman Tucker, the photo editor at the *Herald-Star,* was at his desk taking calls. "Vic, darling, you've found a corpse and I get the first look at it."

"Not even close." Sherman has a passion for the old noir private eyes. He keeps hoping I'll behave like Race Williams or the Continental Op and start stumbling over bodies every time I walk out the front door. "Ever use a stringer named Hunter Davenport, or heard anything about him? He used to freelance in Africa, but someone thinks he might have moved to Chicago."

"Hunter Davenport? I never heard of the guy, but he gets more popular by the hour. You're the second person today asking for him."

"Did you refer an extremely beautiful young man to me?" I asked.

Sherman laughed. "I don't look at guys' legs, V.I. But, yeah, there was a kid in here earlier. I told him if he didn't want to take a missing person to the cops to go to you."

Sherman promised to call me if any of his staff recognized Davenport's name. I felt as though I was trailing after my own client, but I checked the city and suburban directories just to be sure. There were a lot of Davenports, but no Hunters. I frowned at my desk, then dug out the phone directory disk for the Southeast from a service I subscribe to and looked up "Alder" in Charleston, South Carolina. There weren't any. A whole bunch of Aldermans and Aldershots were listed, but no plain Alders.

The client had said his granny was dead. She didn't seem to have any living relatives besides young Hunter. No wonder he wanted to find his father.

I checked with the Department of Motor Vehicles, but Hunter Senior didn't have a driver's license. For almost any other search, I'd need a Social Security number or a place and date of birth or some such thing. Of course, if the guy really had retired to Chicago, it was possible he'd been born here. I looked with distaste at the hundred or so Davenports in the city, and the two hundred more scattered through the suburbs. As a last resort I'd start calling them to see if a cousin or brother was mooching from them, but first I'd see what I could learn from the County.

They know me in that mausoleum on Washington Street, but the warmth of my reception still depends on who's working the counter that day. I was lucky this afternoon. A middle-aged clerk who was marking time until he could take early retirement and devote himself to his homemade pie shop was on duty. I've bought desserts from him from time to time; he was willing to give me a fifteen-year stack of registers at one go.

Twenty minutes before closing, when even my friendly clerk was snarling at citizens to hurry up and finish, I found Hunter Davenport. He had been born in 1946 at Chicago Lying-In, to Mildred and Wayland Davenport (race: white; no previous live births; home address on Cottage Grove; age of parents: twenty-seven and thirty-five, respectively). If Mildred and Wayland were still alive, they were ancient, and they probably had long since moved from Cottage Grove, but at least it was a place to start.

I detoured to my bank to deposit the five hundreds. As I was boarding the L at Lake Street, I thought I saw my client's gold halo in the crowd. I jumped off the train, but by the time I'd fought past the rush hour crowd behind me, I couldn't see him. I finally decided it must have been a trick of light.

2

Wayland Davenport had died the same year as my client's mother. Poor Hunter Senior, losing his wife and his father at the same time. His mother, Mildred, was still alive, though, living in a shabby apartment complex in Lincolnwood. When I rang the bell, we began one of those tedious conversations through the intercom, where she couldn't make out what I was saying and I kept shouting into the door mike.

"I'm too old to work," she screeched.

"Your son's work," I hollered. "His photographs. We're interested in a display—an exhibit. Africa in the 1980s through American eyes."

"You'd better go away," she finally said. "I'm not buying anything."

I ground my teeth. A woman carrying two large bags of groceries came up the walk, followed by three young children. The biggest had his own small shopping bag, but the younger two had their hands free to punch each other. The woman kept muttering an ineffectual "Michael, Tania, stop it."

When she tried to balance a bag on her hip while she fumbled for her keys, I took the bags and held the door. She thanked me with the same exhausted mutter she used on her children.

"I'm visiting Mildred Davenport in 4K, but I'll be glad to carry your bags up for you first," I said brightly.

"Oh! Oh, thank you. Michael, let go of Tania's hair."

She was on four as well, but at the other end of the hall, and no, she didn't know Mildred, more than to recognize her. The kids kept her running all day, and Mildred never left her own apartment, except on Mondays, when someone from the senior center came to take her to the store or the doctor.

"Do you know if her son is staying with her?"

"Is that who that man is? I don't like the way he looks at Tania. I told my husband it wouldn't surprise me if he was a molester, out of prison, but they won't tell us who's in the building. We could be murdered here or our children abducted, and would the management care? Not any more than they did the time the people in 5A were keeping goldfish in the bathtub and let it overflow into our place. And then the cats, yowling to get out. I have complained a thousand times—Tania, stop pinching—"

I was thankful when we reached her door. I dumped the bags on the floor, in the middle of a litter of LEGOs, Beanie Babies, and half-empty cereal bowls, and fled as the children's whines rose to howls.

Before leaving my office this morning, I had written a short letter to Mildred Davenport, giving her the same story I had tried shouting through the intercom: I was a freelance journalist writing a book on Africa through American eyes and very much wanted to get hold of some of her son's photographs from the 1980s.

At the far end of the corridor, I knocked loudly on her door. After a long wait, I heard a shuffling on the other side and then movement at the peephole. I smiled in a cheery, unthreatening way.

She opened the door the width of a chain bolt. "What do you want?"

I kept smiling. "I put it in writing—I thought that might be easier than me trying to explain it through the door."

She grudgingly took the envelope from me and shut the door

again. The television was turned up so loud, I could hear it through the closed door. After about ten minutes, she came back.

"I guess you can talk to him, but he says he doesn't know what you mean. He never was in Africa."

I followed her into her living room, where a fan stirred air so heavy it fell back like soup onto my hair and blouse. A television tuned to Oprah provided the only light. Stacks of newspaper and pieces of furniture were crammed so close together that it was hard to find a place to stand.

"Hunter! This here's the lady," she shouted over Oprah in a flat nasal.

A figure stirred in one of the overstuffed armchairs. In the flashes from the screen, I'd mistaken him for a heap of towels or blankets. Mrs. Davenport muted the sound.

"Who you work for?" he said. "They have money for prints?"

"Gaudy Press. They have some money, but they don't throw it around." I looked around for a place to sit and finally perched on the arm of another chair. "They're especially interested in your work in the 1980s. When you were in Africa."

"Never was in Africa." Hunter shot a look at his mother.

"If they want to pay you for your work—" Mrs. Davenport began, but he cut her off.

"I said I never was in Africa. You don't know anything about my life away from here."

"I'm only deaf, not crazy," his mother snapped. "Why don't you see if you can make some money? Show this lady your photographs. Even if you don't have Africa, you've got plenty of others."

"You go back to Oprah, and the lady can go back to her publisher and tell them no sale." He took the control from his mother and restored the sound; a woman whose car had broken down on the Santa Ana Freeway had been rescued by an angel.

I moved close enough to him that I could see his frayed T-shirt and the stubble of graying hair on his chin. "Your son says you were in South Africa in 1986."

He curled his lip at me. "I don't have a son. That I know of."

"Helen Alder's son? That the two of you produced after you married in Vietnam?"

"Helen Alder? I never heard of a . . ." His voice trailed away, and then he said with a ferocious urgency that astounded me, "Where are you really from?"

"Could we go where we can hear each other?"

His mother watched suspiciously when he pushed himself up from his chair, but she stayed behind when he led me to the kitchen. The stuffy air was larded with stale dishwater. The window had a two-by-four nailed across it to keep it from opening. Sweat started to gather at the back of my neck.

"Who sent you to me?" His teeth showed, crooked and tobacco stained, through the stubble.

"Your son."

"I don't have any children. I never married. I never was in Africa."

"What about Vietnam?" I asked.

He shot me an angry look. "And if I say, 'Yeah, I was there,' you won't believe I didn't marry this Helen whosis."

"Try me." I wanted to keep my voice affable, but standing in the musty room was hard on my back as well as my manners.

"I was a photographer. For the old *Chicago American* before it folded. I covered the war for them from '63 to '69. Sur Place bought a lot of my shots—the French were more interested in Indochina than we were. After the paper collapsed, I signed on with them as a freelancer."

"Where were you in 1986? Here?"

He shook his head. "Europe. England. Sometimes New York."

I took a notepad from my handbag and started fanning my face with it. "When did you come back to Chicago? Do you work for Sur Place out of here?"

His face contorted into a sneer. "I haven't worked for anyone for a long time. My mother doesn't like me sponging off her, but she's paranoid about burglary, and she thinks a man around the house, even a washed-up ex-photographer, is better than living alone. Now it's your turn. And don't give me any crap about being a freelance writer."

"Okay. I'm a private investigator. A man claiming to be Hunter Davenport Junior asked me to find you." I showed him my license.

His face began to look like dull putty. "Someone was pulling your leg. I don't have a son."

"Fair, very good-looking, most people would be proud to claim him."

He began to fidget violently with the utensil drawers. "Get the guy to give you a blood sample. We'll compare DNA. If his matches mine, you're welcome to my whole portfolio. How'd you find me?"

I told him: county birth records followed by tracing Wayland Davenport through old phone books. He'd gone from Cottage Grove Avenue to Loomis, then Montrose, stair-stepping his way up the northwest side until landing at a bungalow in the suburbs in 1974. His wife had moved into this little apartment four years ago.

"So anyone could find me," he muttered.

"And is that a problem?"

He gave an unconvincing laugh. "No one wants to find me these days, so it's no problem whatsoever. Now, you've wasted your time and mine enough. Go hunt up some real mystery. Like who your client is and why he's stolen my name."

I stopped in the kitchen doorway and looked back at him. "By the way, who is Helen Alder?"

He bared his teeth, showing a broken chip on the left incisor. "The figment of your client's imagination."

I put a business card on the countertop. "Give me a call if you decide to tell me the truth about her."

As I made my way through the dim passage to the front door, someone on television was extolling a drug whose side effects included nausea, fainting, and memory loss. Over the cheerful tout, Mildred Davenport's voice rose querulously, demanding to know whether I was going to buy any of his pictures. Her son said something inaudible. The last thing I heard on my way out was her calling to him to make sure he put the chain bolt on behind me.

When I stepped back into the sticky July heat, the back of my blouse was wet all the way across my shoulders. I smelled of stale grease. I sank into my car and turned on the air conditioner. Behind me a blue Toyota was idling, the driver lying with the seat reclining so that all I could see was the newspaper over his chest, like a character in a James Bond movie.

I made a U-turn and drove as fast as I could to the expressway. I wanted to get to the Trefoil and ask my client the same questions Hunter Davenport had put to me: Who had given me those five hundred-dollar bills and why did he really want to find Hunter Davenport?

3

My client had checked into the Trefoil as Hunter Davenport, but he'd gone out early this morning and hadn't come back yet. The receptionist wouldn't tell me if young Hunter had used another name on check-in, or if he'd shown a credit card.

"Ma'am, I'm sure you must understand that I cannot possibly discuss our guests with you."

I pulled out my ID. "I'm a private investigator. Normally I don't discuss my cases any more than you discuss your guests, but when Mr. Davenport hired me he paid cash and—something I found out this morning makes me wonder whether Davenport is his name."

He shook his head. "I'm sorry, ma'am, but unless you are with the police and have legitimate grounds for an inquiry, I cannot discuss any of our guests with any outsider. Newspaper reporters have come up with such inventive ways of violating privacy that it's our ironclad rule."

"You often have celebrities here?"

"We often have guests who prize privacy. That's why they choose the Trefoil."

The Trefoil is a small boutique hotel. There wasn't any way I could hover unobtrusively in the lobby and sneak into the elevator. I wrote a note for Hunter Davenport asking him to call me as soon as he came in. When I handed it to the receptionist, I managed a look at the cubbyhole where he put the envelope: 508. It never hurts to know.

When I got to my office, my part-time assistant told me the client had called. "He said to thank you for your help, but he's decided it's a needle in a haystack and not to go on looking. The five hundred can cover your fee and expenses."

I thought my jaw might crack my sternum, it dropped so far and fast. "When did he call?"

Mary Louise looked at her notes. "At one o'clock."

It was almost two now, so he'd stopped the investigation before I'd visited the hotel. I told Mary Louise about the case.

"Finding Hunter Senior was easier than I thought it would be, actually. But the guy claims he never had a kid. He even offered to do a DNA match. That might have been a bluff, but it didn't sound like it. He knows something about Helen Alder, something that got him pretty agitated, but I don't think it had anything to do with the kid."

Helen Alder's name didn't mean any more to Mary Louise than it had to me. We talked it over for a bit until Mary Louise left to pick her foster kids up from summer camp. Before she took off, she had me fill out an expense report and time sheet—an important reason I keep her on my payroll. I had a clean profit of a hundred fifty. At least I could afford another call to Paris.

Although it was now 9:20 in Europe, Monsieur Duval was indeed in, and indeed he did speak English. Certainly he remembered 'Unter Davenport, but this was a matter most strange, that I was the second person to ask for him in one month. Could it be that Davenport's fortunes were going to change, that he might once again be going to work? If so, Sur Place would like to continue to represent him: he had done very inventive work in the past.

"Do you know where he is now?" I asked.

"We think he maybe go to Chicago, but we have no direct word from him since four years now. One woman at Sur Place, she say he always talk about Chicago when he is unhappy."

So the client had gotten the Chicago information from Sur Place. "What kind of pictures did you buy from him?"

"All kinds. But, of course, for our clients, for Paris *Match,* or the *Sun,* we want mostly the faces that are popular with their readers. The Monaco princesses now that Princess Diana is no more, or even Princess Diana's sons. Sometimes they like Lady Gaga. You know, the celebrity. But by and by 'Unter, he fall more in love with what he sees in a bottle than what he sees behind the camera, and we have to tell him good-bye."

"Did he ever shoot a woman named Helen Alder?"

"'Elen Alder? 'Elen Alder? I do not know this woman. But I will look in our files. If you have email I will let you know."

I gave him my details, not very hopefully. If Helen Alder had been a celebrity subject, I think even I would have heard of her. Her name had clearly meant something to Davenport, although it had taken a minute to register. Maybe they'd had some brief fling in Vietnam that he'd forgotten about. She'd had a kid, named him after his biological father, brought him up on the idea that she was a widow. Then the kid found out the truth and started tracking down the photographer.

It was all useless speculation. I logged onto the Web and did a search through *LifeStory* and a few other databases but didn't find any Helen Alders. I gave it up and turned my attention to other clients' problems.

4

At three the next morning, Davenport came forcibly back to mind when the phone hauled me out of sleep.

"Vic, why would an old drunk be clutching your business card when he was run over?" It was John McGonnigal, a Chicago police sergeant I used to do a lot of work with. I'd lost track of him when the department transferred him from downtown to one of the Northwest Side districts.

"John!" I sat up in bed, trying to scramble my wits together. "What old drunk?"

"Sixtyish. Five ten, five eleven, three-day growth, chip on left incisor. Ring a bell?"

Hunter Davenport. I demanded details in exchange for a name and McGonnigal grudgingly supplied them. Hunter had been barhopping, as far as the cops could make out, ending up at the Last Belt on Lincoln around 1:00 A.M. A witness said a car had driven up on the sidewalk and hit Hunter before roaring off into the night. The few onlookers out at that hour couldn't guess at the color or the make of the car, or remember the license number.

"He didn't have any ID. Just some singles wadded up in his pocket and your card. What's the story, Warshawski?"

"There is no story. Maybe he was trying to work up the nerve to invite me out for a drink. Have you talked to his mother? No, of course not: you only just learned who he was." I gave him Mildred Davenport's address. "I'll meet you there in twenty minutes."

He began a sentence with "You can leave police business—" but I hung up before he told me where.

There's a wonderful freedom in driving the city in the pre-dawn—no one else is out, and you feel as though you own the empty streets. I coasted up to Mrs. Davenport's building at the same time that McGonnigal's unmarked car arrived.

He grunted a greeting but didn't actively try to keep me from following him into the building. He had phoned Mrs. Davenport from the hospital, waking her up, confirming her nightmares about the city's dangers, but she buzzed us in. She opened her own door the width of the chain and demanded McGonnigal's ID, then caught sight of me.

"What do you know about all this, young woman? Are you with the police? Hunter told me you weren't really interested in his photographs, but he's never been mixed up with any crimes—at least not that I know of."

"Can we come in, ma'am?" McGonnigal said. "We'll wake all the neighbors if we have to talk to you through the door."

She compressed her mouth in a suspicious line but unbolted the chain. "Hunter's been like a cat on a hot brick ever since this lady came over. He's been drinking way too much for years. I warned him after Vietnam no one would keep a drunk on their payroll forever, and I was right. All those glamorous places he used to visit, all those famous people he took pictures of, didn't count for anything in the end. He had to come home to his ma and the little bit of Social Security he can claim. So when this lady said maybe someone wanted to buy some of his old pictures, I thought he should talk to her."

McGonnigal stopped her to ask me about that; I muttered that I was a go-between with a possible buyer but nothing had come of it. Before he could push me further, Mrs. Davenport interrupted.

"Yesterday, after this lady left, someone started calling on the phone and hanging up. I thought maybe it was her bothering him, but all Hunter would say was he didn't know who was on the phone.

Finally about eight o'clock tonight—last night, I should say—the fifteenth time the phone rang, he said, 'I can't take this. They're going to drive me insane.' And off he went.

"I knew he was going out to find a bar, like he always does when he's in trouble. I told him a million times all it gets you is a hangover and the trouble still there in the morning, but you can't talk to a drunk. But the calls kept coming. Someone who just said, 'Hunter, I know where you are, Hunter,' and then hung up. So the last time I yelled before he could say anything, 'He's not here. Leave me alone or I'll have the cops on you.' I should have done it then and there, but how could I know they'd follow after him in the street?"

"Who could have been harassing him?" McGonnigal demanded of me.

I shook my head bleakly, and asked Mrs. Davenport if her son had ever discussed any threats from anyone overseas.

"If he had any troubles like that, he never said anything to me about them. He lived away from home for thirty years, and he wasn't much of a letter writer at the best of times. I don't know what he got up to, all the places he visited."

"Do you think he could have a child he never told you about?" I asked.

"With a man, anything's possible. Just because he's your own boy doesn't change that." She folded her lips tightly.

McGonnigal was demanding what that was about when his cell phone rang. He grunted into the mouthpiece a few times, then turned to Mrs. Davenport.

"Does he have any insurance? It looks like they can save him, but it's going to be expensive."

"Insurance? Where would he get insurance? He wasn't even a

vet, just a war correspondent. And if they think I've got fifty thousand lying around to pay their rotten bills, they can think again."

While McGonnigal relayed the news to the hospital, I wandered into the back room, looking for evidence of Davenport's work. I found a worn black zip case under the daybed, where he seemed to keep his clothes and a few personal items. The case was stuffed with hundreds of prints.

McGonnigal came in and watched me go through them. Near the bottom of the stack, I came on a dozen views of a woman who looked so familiar that I thought I must surely know her. Tortoiseshell combs pulled a halo of ash blond hair away from her face, and her blue-gray eyes smiled at the camera with a wistful yearning. At first I thought my leap of recognition was because she looked so much like my client. But I felt sure I knew her face, and that that was why I thought I'd known him when he had come into my office.

I tried not to let McGonnigal see I'd come on anything I knew. I was zipping up the case when it fell from my hands, scattering photographs wholesale. I managed to stick a shot of the wistful woman inside my T-shirt while I was scrabbling under the daybed for the rest.

5

Sherman Tucker, the *Herald-Star*'s photo editor, wasn't happy at climbing out of bed so early in the morning, but he met me at the paper. He took one look at the print I'd borrowed and went without speaking to a cabinet, where he pulled out a thick file.

"Were you brain-dead thirteen years ago? The only person photographed more back then was Princess Di."

"I was in law school," I mumbled. "My father was dying. I didn't follow the society pages."

Sherman slapped a dozen versions of the face onto the table: Lady Helen Banidore riding to hounds in Virginia; Lady Helen bringing her infant son, Andrew, home from the hospital; opening a charity ball; leaving a courthouse in tears after her divorce; laughing on the arm of a Marine colonel at a British embassy ball.

She had been born Lady Helen Aldershot, only child of the Earl of Revere. Revere didn't have a dime, or even a shilling, to his name, so everyone agreed it was a wonderful thing when she had married one of the heirs to Banidore Tobacco in South Carolina. Happiest of all had been the paparazzi who followed her, supplying the insatiable appetites in America and France for beautiful women with titles.

Even I used to read the reports that filtered from the *National Enquirer* into *People* and the daily papers after the star-studded wedding in the Reveres' private chapel. Following the wedding, Jim Banidore and Lady Helen moved to America, dividing their time between New York, Charleston, and Paris, with the occasional trip to London. About the time the kid was born, the tabloids began screaming that Banidore hung out in leather bars when he was in New York. Old Mrs. Banidore tried suing the *Star* over a photo of Jim in an embrace with a man in a motorcycle bar, but the matter was quietly dropped a few months later.

If Lady Helen was disconsolate at her husband's behavior, she hid it well. She'd been a lively member of the international nightclub scene before her marriage; after Andrew's birth she took up with her old playmates. The divorce was messy—old Mrs. Banidore tried to claim Andrew wasn't even Jim's son, but the terms of the family trust apparently made it important for Jim to have a male child, so he swore an affidavit of paternity.

Lady Helen's alimony, estimated at a hundred thousand dollars a month, depended on her never breathing a word about her husband's extracurricular activities. If she remarried, of course, the alimony stopped, but old Mrs. Banidore also got the family lawyers to insert a clause that gave her custody of the kid if the Banidores could prove Lady Helen was sleeping with other men.

This last clause lashed the paparazzi into a competitive frenzy. They staked out her apartment on the Faubourg Saint-Honoré; they followed her skiing in the French Alps and the Canadian Rockies; they zoomed on her nude sunbathing in the Virgin Islands. When she went on safari in Kenya with Italian racer Egidio Berni as part of the group, the photographers followed in a helicopter. That was where Lady Helen died.

The *Herald-Star* hadn't paid much attention to Lady Helen, since she didn't have a natural following in Chicago, but of course they'd covered her death. I flipped through Sherman's files to read the front-page story.

Lady Helen's safari was spending a week at a luxury lodge, from which they took day or night trips to study animals. It sounded like fun: they even followed elephants on their nocturnal treks into mineral caves.

In deference to the divorce decree, Berni stayed in one suite, Lady Helen and young Andrew in another. One evening Berni and Lady Helen decided to go for a sunset drive. An enterprising photographer had bribed one of the guides to let him know if Lady Helen and Berni were ever alone; the helicopter caught up with the

Land Rover three miles from the lodge. Berni took off, hurtling the Rover across the veldt, and smashed into a rhinoceros. He and Lady Helen were killed instantly.

Some moron brought young Andrew to the crash site, and the *Herald-Star* had used a photograph of the white-faced boy kneeling by his dead mother, cradling her head on his knees.

I would have to be brain-dead not to know that the boy was my client as a child. And I'd have to be even deader not to figure Hunter Davenport for the photographer in the chopper.

"So Andrew Banidore hired me to find one of the men who drove his mother to her death. Or who he thinks drove her to her death. And then what? He lay in wait like James Bond to—"

I stood up so fast, I knocked half the photos off Sherman's table. When he squawked a protest, I was already out the door. I shouted "I'll call you" over my shoulder and ran down the hall to the street.

I'd been an idiot. James Bond. The glimpse I thought I'd had of my client on the L platform two days ago. The guy in the car behind me yesterday morning. My client had tracked me while I located Hunter Davenport. When I'd found Davenport for him, my client breathed threatening messages over the phone until he fled the apartment, then chased him to Uptown, where he ran him over.

V.I. Warshawski, ace detective. Ace imbecile.

6

The Trefoil's tiny lobby was filled with luggage and travelers. The receptionist on duty was settling bills and handing towels and keys to joggers while juggling two phones. I took a towel with a smiled thanks and slipped into the elevator behind two lean, sweat-covered men in shorts and cropped tops.

On the fifth floor I knelt in front of 508 and probed the keyhole. I was in an agony of tension—if some other guest should come out—the maid—if Andrew Banidore had left and a stranger lay in the bed. The guest doors had nice, sturdy old-fashioned locks, the kind that look impressive on the outside but have only three tumblers. In another two minutes, I was inside the room.

Lying there in bed, Andrew Banidore looked almost like his mother's twin. The white-gold hair fell away from his face, which was soft with the slackness of sleep.

"Andrew!" I called sharply from the doorway.

He stirred and turned over, but a night spent tracking his subject through Uptown had apparently left him exhausted. I went to the bed and shook him roughly.

When his wistful blue-gray eyes finally blinked open, I said, "He's not dead. Does that upset you?"

"He's not?" His voice was thick with sleep. "But I—" He woke completely and sat up, his face white. "How did you get in here? What are you talking about?"

"You were too tired when you got in to lock the door, I guess." I sat on the edge of the bed. "You've got five minutes before I call the cops. Better make good use of them."

"What are you going to tell them? How you broke into my hotel room?"

"I'm going to tell them to look for the blue Toyota that hit Hunter Davenport early this morning. If you rented it, that'll be easy, because you had to show someone a driver's license. If you stole it, it'll still have your fingerprints on it."

I went to the bureau and rifled through the documents on top. He was traveling on a British passport. He had a first-class ticket on Air France, with an open return date. He had a rental agreement with one of the big chains for a blue Toyota. His wallet held an American driver's license issued by the state of South Carolina, a variety of credit cards, and two photos of his mother.

"Put those pictures down."

I held them between my fingers, as if poised to tear them. "You can always get more. Most photographed woman in the world and all. There are a million pictures of her lying around. I just saw twenty-eight of them."

"She gave those to me. I can't get more that she gave me."

He was out of bed and across the room so fast, I just had time to slip the pictures into my shirt pocket. He tried to fight me for them, but I was dressed and he wasn't. I stood on his left foot until he stopped punching at me.

"I'll return them when you give me a few answers. You have lived in South Carolina, and your mother was killed in a car accident in Kenya. Did you happen to tell me anything else true? Is your grandmother dead? What about all those other tobacco-smoking Banidores? You really an orphan?"

He pulled on a pair of jeans and looked at me sullenly. "I hate them all. The way they talk about her, they were so happy when she died. It was as if all their dreams came true at once. The fact that Jim died of AIDS five years after I had to go live in fucking stupid Charleston—I wasn't supposed to mention that. Poor, dear Jim picked up a virus in Africa when he went out to get Andrew, they told all their friends at the country club. We should never have allowed Helen to keep the boy to begin with. Then all my he-man cousins made my life miserable claiming she was a whore and I wasn't even one of the family. As if I wanted to be related to that houseful of cretins."

"Did you kill your grandmother?"

He gave a hoarse bark of laughter. "If I'd thought of it in time. No, she died the old-fashioned way: of a stroke."

"So what made you decide to go after Davenport?"

"I always meant to. Ever since the day my mother died. Chasing her all over Europe. It was a game to him. She didn't have a life. She knew she'd lose me to those damn Banidores if she ever got caught with another man, and I was the one person she really loved. I was the only one she cared about losing.

"She was trying to protect our life together, and he—that Davenport—he was trying to destroy it. For twenty-four hours he got a taste of what that was like, how it feels when someone knows where you are and is following you. I missed him when he snuck out of that apartment building last night, but when the lady yelled he wasn't home, I found him at the bus stop. He got on a bus, and I followed the bus. He got off and went into a bar. I went in behind him. But it wasn't enough he was scared. I told him who I was, what he'd done, and he tried to tell me it was a job. Just a job. He killed my mother, he ruined my life, and he thought I should slap him on the back and say, 'Tough luck, old sport, but a man's gotta do . . .' and all that crap.

"That was when I couldn't take it anymore. I got into the car. He started to go back into the bar and I couldn't stand it. I just drove up on the sidewalk and—I should have gone straight to the airport and taken the first flight out, but my passport and ticket and everything were still here. Besides, I never thought you'd find out before I left this afternoon."

I leaned against the door and looked down at him. "You never thought. You are an extremely lucky guy: Hunter Davenport is going to live. But he has very expensive hospital bills and no insurance. You are going to pay every dime of those bills. If you don't, then I am suddenly going to find evidence that links you to that Toyota. The cursory washing they give it at the rental place—believe me, traces of Davenport's blood will be on it a long time. Do you understand?"

He nodded fractionally. "Now give me back my pictures."

"I want to hear you say it. I want to know that you understand what you've agreed to."

He shut his eyes. "I agree to pay Hunter Davenport's hospital bills. I agree to look after the man who killed my mother. I agree to live in hell the rest of my life."

I wanted to say something, something consoling, or maybe heartening: let it go, move on. But his face was so pinched with pain, I couldn't bear to look at him. I put the snapshots on his knee and let myself out.

Note

When Princess Diana died, I thought how horrible it must have been for her sons. I imagined a son who didn't have a supportive family to help him recover from the tragedy, and so he nurtured his anger against the photographer whom he felt was responsible for her death.

When I wrote this story, around 2000, the Internet was first starting to have commercial uses, but most functions that a detective now does online were still manual—like tracking Hunter Davenport through old phone directories. Cell phones were just becoming ubiquitous, but the first smartphone was still ten years away.

This story was originally published in *Mary Higgins Clark Mystery Magazine*, Spring 2001.

PUBLICITY STUNTS

I

I need a bodyguard. I was told you were good." Lisa Macauley crossed her legs and leaned back in my client chair as if expecting me to slobber in gratitude.

"If someone told you I was a good bodyguard they didn't know my operation: I never do protection."

"I'm prepared to pay you well."

"You can offer me a million dollars a day and I still won't take the job. Protection is a special skill. You need lots of people to do it right. I have a one-person operation. I'm not going to abandon my other clients to look after you."

"I'm not asking you to give up your precious clients forever, just for a few days next week while I'm doing publicity here in Chicago."

Judging by her expression, Macauley thought she was a household word, but I'd been on the run the two days since she'd made the appointment and hadn't had time to do a background check. Whatever she publicized made her rich: wealth oozed all the way from her dark cloud of carefully cut curls through the sable protecting her from the winter wind and on down to her Jimmy Choo motorcycle boots.

When I didn't say anything she added, "For my new book, of course."

"That sounds like a job for your publisher. Or your handlers."

I had vague memories of going to see Cubs star Andre Dawson when he was doing some kind of promotion at the old Marshall Field's department store. He'd been on a dais, under lights, with several heavies keeping the adoring fans away from him. No matter what Macauley wrote, she surely wasn't more at risk than a baseball hero.

She made an impatient gesture. "They always send some useless person from their publicity department. They refuse to believe my life is in danger. Of course, this is the last book I'll do with Gaudy: my new contract with Della Destra Press calls for two personal bodyguards whenever I'm on the road. But right now, while I'm promoting the new book, I need protection."

I ignored her contract woes. "Your life is in danger? What have you written that's so controversial? An attack on Kate Middleton?"

"I write crime novels. Don't you read?"

"Not crime fiction: I get enough of the real stuff walking out my door in the morning."

Macauley gave a conscious little laugh. "I thought mine might appeal to a woman detective like yourself. That's why I chose you to begin with. My heroine is a woman talk-show host who gets involved in cases through members of her listening audience. The issues she takes on are extremely controversial: abortion, rape, the Greens. In one of them she protects a man whose university appointment is attacked by the feminists on campus. Nan is nearly murdered when she uncovers the brainwashing operation the feminists are running."

"I can't believe that would put you in danger—feminist-bashing is about as controversial as apple pie these days. Sounds like your hero is a female Claude Barnett."

Barnett broadcast his attacks on the atheistic, family-destroying feminists and liberals five days a week from Global Entertainment's flagship cable stations, with round-the-clock streaming available for diehard fans. The term he'd coined for progressive women—femmunists—had become a much-loved buzzword on the radical right.

Macauley didn't like being thought derivative, even of reality. She bristled as she explained that her detective, Nan Carruthers, had a totally unique personality and slant on public affairs.

"But because she goes against all the popular positions that leftists have persuaded the media to support, I get an unbelievable amount of hate mail."

"And now someone's threatening your life?" I tried to sound more interested than hopeful.

Her eyes flashing in triumph, Macauley pulled a letter from her handbag and handed it to me. It was the product of a computer, printed on cheap white stock. In all caps it proclaimed: YOU'LL BE SORRY, BITCH, BUT BY THEN IT WILL BE TOO LATE.

"If this is a serious threat you're already too late," I said. "You should have taken it to forensics lab before you fondled it. Unless you sent it yourself as a publicity stunt?"

Genuine crimson flooded her cheeks. "How dare you? My last three books have been *Times* list leaders for eighteen weeks. I don't need this kind of publicity."

I handed the letter back. "You show it to the police?"

"They wouldn't take it seriously. They told me they could get the state's attorney to open a file, but what good would that do me?"

"Scotland Yard can identify individual laser printers based on samples of output, but most U.S. police departments don't have those resources. Did you keep the envelope?"

She took out a grimy specimen. With a magnifying glass I could make out the zip code in the postmark: Chicago, the Gold Coast. That meant only one of about a hundred thousand residents, or the quarter-million tourists who pass through the neighborhood every day, could have mailed it. I tossed it back.

"You realize this isn't a death threat—it's just a threat, and pretty vague at that. What is it you'll be sorry for?"

"If I knew that I wouldn't be hiring a detective," she snapped.

"Have you had other threats?" It was an effort to keep my voice patient.

"I had two other letters like this one, but I didn't bring them—I didn't think they'd help you any. I've started having phone calls where they just wait, or laugh in a weird way or something. Sometimes I get the feeling someone's following me."

"Any hunches who might be doing it?" I was just going through the motions—I didn't think she was at any real risk, but she seemed the kind of person who couldn't believe she wasn't at the forefront of everyone else's mind.

"I told you." She leaned forward in her intensity. "Ever since *Take Back the Night,* my fourth book, which gives a whole different look at rape crisis centers, I've been on the top of every femmunist hit list in the country."

I laughed, trying to picture some of my friends taking potshots at every person in America who hated feminists. "It sounds like a nuisance, but I don't believe your life is in as much danger as, say, the average abortion provider. But if you want a bodyguard while you're on Claude Barnett's show I can recommend a couple of places. Just remember, though, that even the Secret Service couldn't protect JFK from a determined sniper."

"I suppose if I'd been some whiny feminist you'd take this more seriously. It's because of my politics you won't take the job."

"If you were a whiny feminist I'd probably tell you not to cry over this because there's a lot worse on the way. But since you're a whiny authoritarian there's not much I can do for you. I'll give you some advice for free, though: if you cry about it on the air you'll only invite a whole lot more of this kind of attention."

I didn't think contemporary clothes lent themselves to flouncing from rooms, but Ms. Macauley certainly flounced out of mine. I wrote a brief summary of our meeting in my appointments log, then put her out of my mind until the next night, when I was having dinner with a friend who devours crime fiction. Sal Barthele was astounded that I hadn't heard of Lisa Macauley.

"You ever read anything besides the sports pages and the financial section, Warshawski? That girl is hot. They say her contract with Della Destra is worth twelve million, and even though she appeals to the guys with shiny armbands and goose steps, she can write."

After that I didn't think of Macauley at all: a case for a small suburban school district whose pension money had been turned into derivatives was taking all my energy. But a week later the writer returned forcibly to mind.

"You're in trouble now, Warshawski," Murray Ryerson said when I picked up the phone late Thursday night.

"Hi, Murray: good to hear from you, too." Murray used to be an investigative reporter until Global Entertainment eviscerated his newspaper. Now he does specials on their cable news show. He's a one-time lover, sometime rival, occasional pain in the butt, and even, now and then, a good friend.

"Why'd you tangle with Lisa Macauley? She's Chicago's most important artiste, now that Oprah has decamped."

"She come yammering to you with some tale of injustice? She wanted a bodyguard and I told her I didn't do that kind of work."

"Oh, Warshawski, you must have sounded ornery when you turned her down. She is not a happy camper: she got Claude Barnett all excited about how you won't work for anyone who doesn't agree with your politics. He dug up your involvement with the old abortion underground and has been blasting away at you the last two days as the worst kind of murdering femmunist. A wonderful woman came to you, trembling and scared for her life, and you turned her away just because she's against abortion. He says you investigate the politics of all your potential clients and won't take anyone who's given money to a Christian or a Republican cause and he's urging people to boycott you."

"Kind of people who listen to Claude need an investigator to find their brains. He isn't likely to hurt me."

Murray dropped his bantering tone. "He carries more weight than you, or even I, want to think. You should do some damage control."

I felt my stomach muscles tighten: I live close to the edge of financial ruin much of the time. If I lost three or four key accounts, I'd be dead.

"You think I should apply for a broadcast license and blast back? Or just have my picture taken coming out of the headquarters of the National Rifle Association?"

"You need a new-millennium operation, Warshawski—a staff, including a publicist. You need to have someone going around town with stories about all the tough cases you've cracked in the last few years, showing how wonderful you are. Make your social media accounts more active. On account of I like hot-tempered Italian gals I might run a piece myself if you'd buy me dinner."

"What's a new-millennium operation—one where your self-promotion matters more than what kind of job you do? Come to think of it, do you have a publicist, Murray?"

The long pause at the other end told its own tale: Murray had definitely joined the new millennium. I looked in the mirror after he hung up, searching for scales or some other visible sign of turning into a dinosaur. In the absence of those, I'd hang on to my little one-woman shop as long as possible.

I logged onto Global Entertainment and searched for Claude Barnett's stream. After a few minutes from his high-end sponsors, Claude's rich folksy baritone rolled through my speakers like molasses from a giant barrel.

"Yeah, folks, the femmunists are at it again. The Iron Curtain went down in Russia so they want to put it up here in America. You think like they think or—phht!—off you go to the Gulag.

"We've got one of those femmunists right here in Chicago. Private investigator. You know, in the old stories they used to call them private dicks. Kind of makes you wonder what this gal is missing in her life that she turned to that kind of work. Started out as a baby killer back in the days when she was at the Red University on the South Side of Chicago and grew up to be a dick. Well, it takes all kinds, they say, but do we need this kind?

"We got an important writer here in Chicago. I know a lot of you read the books this courageous woman writes. And because she's willing to take a stand, she gets death threats. So she goes to this leftist snowflake dick, this hermaphrodite dick, who won't help her out. 'Cause Lisa Macauley has the guts to tell women the truth about rape and abortion, and this chick-dick, this V.I. Warshawski, can't take it.

"By the way, you ought to check out Lisa's new book. *Slaybells Ring*. A great story which takes her fast-talking talk-show host Nan Carruthers into the world of the ACLU and the bashing of Christmas. We carry it right here in our bookstore. If you call in now Sheri will ship it out to you right away. Order online, and it will be in your hands tomorrow. Maybe if this Warshawski read it, she'd have a change of heart, but a gal like her, you gotta wonder if she has a heart to begin with."

He went on for thirty minutes by the clock, making an easy segue from me to the right's perennial favorite, Hillary. If I was a devil, she was the Princess of Darkness.

When he finished, I sat in my darkening office, staring at nothing. I felt ill from the bile Barnett had poured out in his molassied voice, but I was furious with Lisa Macauley. She had set me up, pure and simple. Come to see me with a spurious problem, just so she and Barnett could start trashing me on the air. But why?

2

Murray was right: Barnett carried more weight than I wanted to believe. He kept on at me for days, not always as the centerpiece, but often sending a few snide barbs my way. The story went viral pretty fast. Between Barnett and the Net, Macauley got a load of free publicity; her sales skyrocketed. Which made me wonder again if she'd typed up that threatening note herself.

At the same time, my name getting sprinkled with mud did start having an effect on my own business: two new clients backed out midstream, and one of my old regulars phoned to say his company didn't need any work for me right now. No, they weren't going to cancel my contract, but they thought, in his picturesque corpo-speak, "we'd go into a holding pattern for the time being."

I called my lawyer to see what my options were; he advised me to let snarling dogs bite until they got it out of their system. "You don't have the money to take on Claude Barnett, Vic, and even if you won a slander suit against him, you'd lose while the case dragged on."

On Sunday I meekly called Murray and asked if he'd be willing to repeat the deal he'd offered me earlier. After a two-hundred-dollar dinner at the Filigree he did a five-minute story at the end of his own cable show, recounting some of my great successes. This succeeded in diverting some of Barnett's attention from me to Murray—my so-called stooge. Of course he wasn't going to slander Murray on the air—Barnett could tell lies about a mere mortal like me, but not about someone with a big media operation to pay his legal fees.

I found myself trying to plan the total humiliation of both Barnett and Macauley. Let it go, I would tell myself as I turned restlessly in the middle of the night: this is what he wants, to control my head. Turn it off. But I couldn't follow this most excellent advice.

I also did a little investigation into Macauley's life. I called a friend of mine at Channel 13, where Macauley had once worked, to get the station's take on her. My friend Beth Blacksin told me Macauley moved to Chicago after college hoping to break into broadcast news. After skulking on the sidelines of the industry for five or six years she'd written her first Nan Carruthers book.

Ironically enough, the women's movement, creating new roles for women in fiction as well as life, had fueled Macauley's literary success. When her second novel became a bestseller, she divorced the man she married when they were both University of Wisconsin journalism students and began positioning herself as a celebrity. She was famous in book circles for her insistence on personal security: opinion was divided as to whether it had started as a publicity stunt, or if she really did garner a lot of hate mail.

I found a lot of people who didn't like her—some because of her relentless self-promotion, some because of her politics, and some because they resented her success. As Sal had told me, Macauley was minting money now. Not only Claude, but the *Wall Street Journal,* the *National Review,* and all the other conservative outlets hailed her as a welcome antidote to writers like Marcia Muller or Denise Mina.

But despite my digging I couldn't find any real dirt on Macauley. Nothing I could use to embarrass her into silence. To make matters worse, someone at Channel 13 told her I'd been poking around asking questions about her. Whether by chance or design, she swept into Corona's one night when I was there with Sal. Sal and I were both enthusiastic fans of Belle Fontaine, the jazz singer who was Corona's Wednesday night headliner.

Lisa arrived near the end of the first set. She'd apparently found an agency willing to guard her body—she was the center of a boisterous crowd that included a couple of big men with bulges near their armpits. She flung her sable across a chair at a table near ours.

At first I assumed her arrival was just an unhappy coincidence. She didn't seem to notice me but called loudly for champagne, asking for the most expensive bottle on the menu. A couple at a neighboring table angrily shushed her. This prompted Lisa to start yelling out toasts to some of the people at her table: her fabulous publicist, her awesome attorney, and her extraordinary bodyguards, "Rover" and "Prince." The sullen-faced men didn't join in the raucous cheers at their nicknames, but they didn't erupt, either.

We couldn't hear the end of "Little Lies" above Lisa's clamor, but Belle took a break at that point. Sal ordered another drink and started to fill me in on family news: her lover had just landed a role in a sitcom that would take her out to the West Coast for the winter, and Sal was debating hiring a manager for her own bar, the Golden Glow, so she could join Becca. She was just describing—in humorous detail—Becca's first meeting with the producer when Lisa spoke loudly enough for everyone in the room to hear.

"I'm so glad you boys were willing to help me out. I can't believe how chicken some of the detectives in this town are. Easy to be big and bold in an abortion clinic, but they run and hide from someone their own size." She turned deliberately in her chair, faked an elaborate surprise at the sight of me, and continued at the same bellowing pitch, "Oh, V.I. Warshawski! I hope you don't take it personally."

"I don't expect Chanel Number Five from the sewer," I called back heartily.

The couple who'd tried to quiet Lisa down during the singing laughed at this. The star twitched, then got to her feet, champagne glass in hand, and came over to me.

"I hear you've been stalking me, Warshawski. I could sue you for harassment."

I smiled. "Sugar, I've been trying to find out why a big successful writer like you had to invent some hate mail just to have an excuse to slander me. You want to take me to court I'll be real, real happy to sort out your lies in public."

"In court or anywhere else I'll make you look as stupid as you do right now." Lisa tossed her champagne into my face; a camera flashed just as the drink hit me.

Fury blinded me more than the champagne. I knocked over a chair as I leaped up to throttle her, but Sal got an arm around my waist and pulled me down. Behind Macauley, Prince and Rover got to their feet, ready to move: Lisa had clearly staged the whole event to give them an excuse for beating me up—and to make me look out of control.

Queenie, who owns the Corona, was at my side with some towels. "Galen! I want these people out of here now. And I think some cute person's been taking pictures. Ms. Macauley, you owe me three hundred dollars for that Dom Pérignon you threw around."

Prince and Rover thought they were going to take on Queenie's bouncer, but Galen had broken up bigger fights than they could muster. He managed to lift them both and slam their heads together, then to snatch the fabulous publicist's bag as she was trying to sprint out the door. Galen took out her phone, erased the photos, and handed the bag back to her with a smile and an insulting bow. The attorney, prompted by Galen, handed over three bills, and the whole party left to loud applause from the audience.

Queenie and Sal had grown up together, which may be why I got Gold Coast treatment that night, but not even her private reserve Veuve Clicquot could take the bad taste from my mouth. If I'd beaten up Macauley I'd have looked like the brute she and Barnett were labeling me; but taking a faceful of champagne sitting down left me looking—and feeling—helpless.

"You're not going to do anything stupid, are you, Vic?" Sal said as she dropped me off around two in the morning. "'Cause if you are, I'm babysitting you, girlfriend."

"No. I'm not going to do anything rash, if that's what you mean. But I'm going to nail that prize bitch, one way or another."

Twenty-four hours later Lisa Macauley was dead. One day after that I was in jail.

3

All I knew about Lisa's murder was what I'd read in the papers before the cops came for me: her personal trainer had discovered her body when he arrived Friday morning for their usual workout. She had been beaten to death in what looked like a bloody battle, which is why the state's attorney finally let me go—they couldn't find the marks on me they were looking for, nor any blood under my fingernails. And they couldn't find any evidence in my home or office.

They kept insisting, though, that I had gone to her apartment late Thursday night. They asked me about it all night long on Friday without telling me why they were so sure. When Freeman Carter, my lawyer, finally sprang me Saturday afternoon, he forced them to tell him what they had. The doorman was claiming he had admitted me to Lisa's apartment just before midnight on Thursday.

Freeman taxed me with it on the ride home. "The way she was carrying on, it would have been like you to demand a face-to-face with her, Vic. Don't hold out on me—I can't defend you if you were there and won't tell me about it."

"I wasn't there," I said flatly. "I am not prone to blackouts or hallucinations: there is no way I could have gone there and forgotten it. I was blamelessly watching the University of Kansas men pound Duke on national television. I even have a witness: my golden retriever shared a pizza with me. Her testimony: she threw up cheese sauce on my bed Friday morning."

Freeman ignored that. "Sal told me about the dust-up at Corona's. Anyway, Stacey Cleveland, Macauley's publicist, had already bared all to the police. You're the only person they can locate who had reason to be killing mad with her."

"Then they're not looking, are they? Someone either pretended to be me or else bribed the doorman to tell the cops I was there. Get me the doorman's name and I'll sort out which it was."

"I can't do that, Vic: you're in enough trouble without suborning the state's key witness."

"You're supposed to be on my side," I cried. "You want to go into court with evidence or not?"

"*I'll* talk to the doorman, Vic: you go take a bath—jail doesn't smell very good on you."

I followed Freeman's advice only because I was too tired to do anything else. I slept the clock around, waking just before noon on Sunday.

In the morning I had forty-seven messages from reporters from around the world, including Japan, where Macauley's books also were bestsellers. When I started outside to get the Sunday papers I found a camera crew parked in front of the building. I retreated, fetched my coat and an overnight bag, and went out the back way. My car was parked right in front of the camera van, so I walked the three miles to my office.

When the Pulteney Building turned condo last April I'd moved my business to a warehouse on the edge of Wicker Park, near the corner of Milwaukee Avenue and North. Fringe galleries and night spots compete with liquor stores and palm readers for air here, and there are a lot of vacant lots, but it was ten minutes—by car, bus, or L—from the heart of the financial district, where most of my business lies.

I had twice my old space at two-thirds the rent. Since I'd had to refurnish—from Dumpsters and auctions—I'd put in a daybed behind a partition: I could camp out here for a few days until media interest in me cooled.

I bought the Sunday papers from one of the liquor stores on my walk. The *Sun-Times* concentrated on Macauley's career, including a touching history of her childhood in the resort town of Rhinelander, Wisconsin. She'd been the only child of older parents. Her father, Joseph, had died last year at the age of eighty, but her mother, Louise, still lived in the house where Lisa had grown up. The paper showed a frame bungalow with a porch swing and a minute garden, as well as a tearful Louise Macauley in front of Lisa's doll collection. ("I've kept the room the way it looked when she left for college," the caption read.)

Her mother never wanted her going off to the University of Wisconsin. "Even though we raised her with the right values and sent her to church schools, Madison is a terrible place. She wouldn't listen to us, though, and now look what's happened."

The *Tribune* had a discreet sidebar on Lisa's recent contretemps with me. In the *Herald-Star,* Murray published the name of the doorman who had admitted "someone claiming to be V.I. Warshawski" to Macauley's building. It was Reggie Whitman. He'd been the doorman since the building went up in 1978, was a grandfather, a church deacon, coached a basketball team at the Henry Horner homes, and was generally so virtuous that truth radiated from him like a beacon.

Murray also had talked with Lisa's ex-husband, Brian Gerstein, an assistant producer for one of the local network news stations. He was appropriately grief-stricken at his ex-wife's murder. The picture supplied by Gerstein's publicist showed a man in his mid-forties with a TV smile but anxious eyes.

I called Beth Blacksin, the reporter at Channel 13 who'd filled me in on what little I'd learned about Lisa Macauley before her death.

"Vic! Where are you? We've got a camera crew lurking outside your front door hoping to talk to you!"

"I know, babycakes. And talk to me you shall, as soon as I find out who set me up to take the fall for Lisa Macauley's death. So give me some information now and it shall return to you like those famous loaves of bread."

Beth wanted to dicker, but the last two weeks had case-hardened my temper. She finally agreed to talk with the promise of a reward in the indefinite future.

Brian Gerstein had once worked at Channel 13, just as he had for every other news station in town. "He's a loser, Vic. I'm not surprised Lisa dumped him when she started to get successful. He's the kind of guy who would sit around dripping into his coffee because you were out-earning him, moaning, trying to get you to feel sorry for him. People hire him because he's a good editor, but then they give him the shove because he gets the whole newsroom terminally depressed."

"You told me last week they met up at UW when they were students there. Where did they go next?"

Beth had to consult her files, but she came back on the line in a few minutes with more details. Gerstein came from a small Long Island town. He met Lisa when they were both Wisconsin juniors, campaigning for W's first election in 2000. They'd married three years later, just before moving to Chicago. Politics and TV kept them together for another three years after that.

Brian rented an apartment in Rogers Park on the far north side of the city.

"And that's typical of him," Beth added as she gave me his address. "He won't own a home since they split up: he can't afford it, his life was ruined, and he doesn't feel like housekeeping, I've heard a dozen different whiny reasons from him. Not that everyone has to own, but you don't have to rent a run-down apartment in gangbanger territory when you work for the networks, either."

"So he could have been peevish enough to kill Lisa?"

"You're assuming he swathed himself in skirts and furs and told Reggie Whitman he was V.I. Warshawski? It would take more— more gumption than he's got to engineer something like that. It's not a bad theory, though: maybe we'll float it on the four o'clock news. Give us something different to talk about than all the other guys. Stay in touch, Vic. I'm willing to believe you're innocent, but it'd make a better story if you'd killed her."

"Thanks, Blacksin." I laughed as I hung up: her enthusiasm was without malice.

I took the L up to Rogers Park, the slow Sunday milk run. Despite Beth's criticism, it's an interesting part of town. Some blocks you do see dopers hanging out, some streets have depressing amounts of garbage in the yards, but most of the area harks back to the Chicago of my childhood: tidy brick two-flats, hordes of immigrants in the parks speaking every known language and, along with them, delis and coffee shops for every cuisine.

Gerstein lived on one of the quiet side streets. He was home, as I'd hoped: staking out an apartment without a car would have been miserable work on a cold day. He even let me in without too much fuss. I told him I was a detective and showed him my license, but he didn't seem to recognize my name—he must not have been editing the programs dealing with his ex-wife's murder. Or he'd been so stricken he'd edited them without registering anything.

He certainly exuded misery as he escorted me up the stairs. Whether it was grief or guilt for Lisa, or just the chronic depression Beth attributed to him, he moved as though on the verge of falling over. He was a little taller than I was, but slim. Swathed in a coat and shawls he might have looked like a woman to the night doorman.

Gerstein's building was clean and well maintained, but his own apartment was sparely furnished, as though he expected to move on at any second. The only pictures on the walls were a couple of framed photographs—one of himself and Lisa with W, and the other with a man I didn't recognize. He had no drapes or plants or anything else to bring a bit of color to the room, and when he invited me to sit, he pulled a metal folding chair from a closet for me.

"I always relied on Lisa to fix things up," he said. "She has so much vivacity and such good taste. Without her I can't seem to figure out how to do it."

"I thought you'd been divorced for years." I tossed my coat onto the card table in the middle of the room.

"Yes, but I've only been living here nine months. She let me keep our old condo, but last summer I couldn't make the payments. She said she'd come around to help me fix this up, only she's so busy. . . ." His voice trailed off.

I wondered how he ever sold himself to his various employers—I found myself wanting to shake him out like a pillow and plump him up. "So you and Lisa stayed in touch?"

"Sort of. She was too busy to call much, but she'd talk to me sometimes when I phoned."

"So you didn't have any hard feelings about your divorce?"

"Oh, I did. I never wanted to split up—it was all her idea. I kept hoping, but now, you know, it's too late."

"I suppose a woman as successful as Lisa met a lot of men."

"Yes, yes she certainly did." His voice was filled with admiration, not hate.

I was beginning to agree with Beth, that Gerstein couldn't possibly have killed Lisa. What really puzzled me was what had ever attracted her to him in the first place, but the person who could figure out the hows and whys of attraction would put Dear Amy out of business overnight.

I went through the motions with him—did he get a share in her royalties?—yes, on the first book, because she'd written that while they were still together. When she wanted a divorce his lawyer told him he could probably get a judgment entitling him to 50 percent of her proceeds, even in the future, but he loved Lisa, he wanted her to come back to him, he wasn't interested in being vindictive. Did he inherit under Lisa's will? He didn't think so, I'd have to ask her attorney. Did he know who her residuary legatee was? Some conservative foundations they both admired.

I got up to go. "Who do you think killed your wife, ex-wife?"

"I thought they'd arrested someone, that dick Claude Barnett says was harassing her."

"You know Barnett? Personally, I mean?" All I wanted was to divert him from thinking about me—even in his depression he might have remembered hearing my name on the air—but he surprised me.

"Yeah. That is, Lisa does. Did. We went to a media convention together right after we moved here. Barnett was the keynote speaker. She got all excited, said she'd known him growing up, but his name was something different then. After that she saw him every now and then. She got him to take his picture with us a couple of years later, at another convention in Sun Valley."

He jerked his head toward the wall where the photographs

hung. I went over to look at them. I was vaguely aware of Barnett's face: he was considered so influential in the nation's swing right-ward that his picture kept popping up in newsmagazines. A man of about fifty, he was lean and well groomed.

He was usually smiling with affable superiority. In Sun Valley he must have eaten something that disagreed with him. Lisa was smiling gaily, happy to be with the media darling. Brian was hold-ing himself upright and looking close to jovial. Although Claude had an arm around Lisa, he looked as though thumbscrews had been stuffed under his nails to get him into the photo.

"What name had Lisa known him by as a child?" I asked.

"Oh, she was mistaken about that. Once she got to see him up close she realized it was only a superficial resemblance. But Bar-nett took a shine to her—most people did, she was so vivacious—and gave her a lot of support in her career. He was the first big booster of her Nan Carruthers novels."

"He doesn't look very happy to be with her here, does he? Can I borrow it? It's a very good one of Lisa, and I'd like to use it in my inquiries."

Brian said in a dreary voice that he thought Lisa's publicist would have much better ones, but he was easy to persuade—or bully, to call my approach by its real name. I left with the photo carefully draped in a dish towel, and a written promise to return it as soon as possible.

I trotted to the Jarvis L stop, using the public phone there to call airlines. I found one that not only sent planes from O'Hare to Rhinelander, Wisconsin, but also had a flight leaving in two hours. The state's attorney had told me not to leave the jurisdiction. Just in case they'd put a stop on me at the airport, I booked a flight under Sestieri, my mother's maiden name, and embarked on the tedious L journey back to the Loop and out to the airport.

4

L isa's new book, *Slaybells Ring,* was stacked high at the airport bookstores. The black enamel cover with an embossed spray of bells in silver drew the eye. At the third stand I passed I finally gave in and bought a copy.

The flight was a long puddle-jumper, making stops in Milwaukee and Wausau on its way north. By the time we reached Rhinelander I was approaching the denouement, where the head of the American Civil Liberties Union was revealed as a major baddie. He had fired one woman staffer for threatening a sexual harassment suit, fired a second for surreptitiously listening to Lisa's heroine, Nan Carruthers, on her headphones at work.

The two women banded together to expose their ex-boss's reason for opposing a crèche at city hall: he secretly owned a company that was trying to put the crèche's manufacturer out of business. The women gave the information to Nan Carruthers, who promptly made all the information public.

The book had a three-hankie ending at midnight mass, where Nan joined the employees—now triumphantly reinstated (thanks to the enforcement of the Civil Rights Act of 1964 by the EEOC and the ACLU, but Macauley hadn't thought that worth mentioning)—in kneeling in front of the public crèche.

I finished the book around one in the morning in the Rhine-lander Holiday Inn. The best-written part treated a subplot between Nan and the man who gave her career its first important boost—the pastor of the heroine's childhood church, who had become a successful televangelist.

When Nan was a child he had photographed her and other children in his Sunday school class engaged in forced sex with one another and with him. Since he held a threat of awful reprisals over their heads, they never told their parents. However, when Nan started her broadcast career she persuaded him to plug her program on his Thursday night "Circle of the Saved," using blackmail to get him to do so. At the end, as she looks at the baby Jesus in the manger, she wonders what Mary would have done—forgiven the pastor or exposed him? Certainly not collaborated with him to further her own career. The book ended on that troubled note. I went to sleep with more respect for Macauley's craft than I had expected.

In the morning I found Mrs. Joseph Macauley's address in the local phone book and went off to see her. Although now in her mid-seventies, she carried herself well. She didn't greet me warmly, but she accepted without demur my identification of myself as a detective trying to find Lisa's murderer. Chicago apparently was so convinced that I was the guilty party they hadn't bothered to send anyone up to interview her.

"I got tired of all those Chicago reporters bothering me, but if you're a detective I guess I can answer your questions. What'd you want to know? I can tell you all about Lisa's childhood, but we didn't see so much of her once she moved off to Madison. We weren't too happy about some of the friends she was making. Not that we have anything against Jews personally, but we didn't want our only child marrying one and getting involved in all those dirty money deals. Of course we were happy he had the right kind of politics, but we weren't sorry when she left Brian, even though our church frowns on divorce."

I let her talk unguided for a time before pulling out the picture of Claude Barnett. "This is someone Lisa said she knew as a child. Do you recognize him?"

Mrs. Macauley took the photo from me. "Do you think I'm not in possession of my faculties? That's Claude Barnett. He certainly never lived around here."

She snorted and started to hand the picture back, then took it to study more closely. "She knew I never liked to see her in pants, so she generally wore a skirt when she came up here. But she looks cute in that outfit, real cute. You know, I guess I can see where she might have confused him with Carl Bader. Although Carl was dark-haired and didn't have a mustache, there is a little something around the forehead."

"And who was Carl Bader?"

"Oh, that's ancient history. He left town and we never heard anything more about him."

All I could get her to say was that he'd been connected to their church and she never did believe half the gossip some of the members engaged in.

"That Mrs. Hoffer always overindulged her children, let them say anything and get away with it. We brought Lisa up to show proper respect for people in authority. Cleaned her mouth out with soap and whipped her so hard she didn't sit for a week the one time she tried taking part in some of that trashy talk."

More she wouldn't say, so I took the picture with me to the

library and looked up old copies of the local newspaper. In *Slaybells Ring*, Nan Carruthers was eight when the pastor molested her, so I checked 1985 through 1987 for stories about Bader and anyone named Hoffer. All I found was a little blurb saying Bader had left the Full Bible Christian Church in 1988 to join a television ministry in Tulsa, and that he'd left so suddenly the church didn't have time to throw him a going-away party.

I spent a weary afternoon trying to find Mrs. Hoffer. There were twenty-seven Hoffers in the Rhinelander phone book; six were members of the Full Bible Christian Church. The church secretary was pleasant and helpful, but it wasn't until late in the day that Mrs. Matthew Hoffer told me the woman I wanted, Mrs. Barnabas Hoffer, had quit the church over the episode about her daughter.

"Caused a lot of hard feeling in the church. Some people believed the children and left. Others figured it was just mischief, children who like to make themselves look interesting. That Lisa Macauley was one. I'm sorry she got herself killed down in Chicago, but in a way I'm not surprised—seemed like she was always sort of daring you to smack her, the stories she made up and the way she put herself forward.

"Not that Louise Macauley spared the rod, mind you, but sometimes I think you can beat a child too much for its own good. Anyway, once people saw little Lisa joining in with Katie Hoffer in accusing the pastor no one took the story seriously. No one except Gertie—Katie's mom, I mean. She still bears a grudge against all of us who stood by Pastor Bader."

Finally, at nine o'clock, I was sitting on a horsehair settee in Gertrude Hoffer's living room, looking at a cracked color Polaroid of two unhappy children. I had to take Mrs. Hoffer's word that they were Katie and Lisa—their faces were indistinct. Time had fuzzed the picture, but you could still tell the girls were embracing each other naked.

"I found it when I was doing his laundry. Pastor Bader wasn't married, so all us church ladies took it in turn to look after his domestic wants. Usually he was right there to put his clothes away, but this one time he was out and I was arranging his underwear for him and found this whole stack of pictures. I couldn't believe it at first, and then when I came on Katie's face—well—I snatched it up and ran out of there.

"At first I thought it was some wickedness the children dreamed up, and that he had photographed them to show us, show the parents what they got up to. That was what he told my husband when Mr. Hoffer went to talk to him about it. It took me a long time to see that a child wouldn't figure out something like that on her own, but I never could get any of the other parents to pay me any mind. And that Louise Macauley, she just started baking pies for Pastor Bader every night of the week, whipped poor little Lisa for telling me what he made her and Katie get up to. It's a judgment on her, it really is, her daughter getting herself killed like that."

5

It was hard for me to find someone in the Chicago Police Department willing to try to connect Claude Barnett with Carl Bader. Once they'd done that, though, the story unraveled pretty fast. Lisa had recognized him in Sun Valley and put the bite on him—not for money, but for career advancement, just as her heroine did to her own old pastor in *Slaybells Ring.*

No one would ever be able to find out for sure, but the emotional torment Lisa gave Nan Carruthers in her book must have paralleled Lisa's own misery. She was a success, she'd forced her old tormentor to make her a success, but it must have galled her—as it did her heroine—to pretend to admire him, to sit in on his show, and to know what lay behind his flourishing career.

When Barnett read *Slaybells,* he probably began to worry that Lisa wouldn't be able to keep his secret to herself much longer. The police did find evidence of the threatening letters in his private study. The state argued that Barnett sent Lisa the threatening letters, then persuaded her to hire me to protect her.

At that point he didn't have anything special against me, but I was a woman. He figured if he could start enough public conflict between a woman detective and Lisa, he'd be able to fool the night man, Reggie Whitman, into believing he was sending a woman up to Lisa's apartment on the fatal night. It was only later that he'd learned about my progressive politics—that was just icing on his cake, to be able to denounce me on his show.

Of course, not all this came out right away—some of it didn't emerge until the trial. That was when I also learned that Reggie Whitman, besides being practically a saint, had badly failing vision. On a cold night any man could have bundled himself up in a heavy coat and hat and claimed to be a woman without Whitman noticing.

Between Murray and Beth Blacksin, I got a lot of public vindication. Sal and Queenie took me to dinner with Belle Fontaine to celebrate on the day the guilty verdict came in. We were all disappointed that they only slapped him with second-degree murder. But what left me gasping for air was a public opinion poll that came out the next afternoon. Even though other examples of his child-molesting behavior had come to light during the trial, his listeners believed he was innocent of all charges.

"The femmunists made it all up trying to discredit him," one woman explained that afternoon on the air. "And then they got the *New York Times* to print their lies."

Not even Queenie's reserve Veuve Clicquot could wipe that bitter taste out of my mouth.

Note

I wrote "Publicity Stunts" for *Women on the Case,* Marty Greenburg, ed. (Delacorte Press, 1996). In the original version, V.I. is using old media, newspapers, and radio. I haven't updated technology and media for most of the stories in this collection, but this one depends so heavily on the use of mass media that I changed radio to streaming—it felt clumsy to leave it in the original. I kept the old newspapers, though—nostalgia for print, I guess.

For readers worried about Mitch and Peppy, I didn't include them because their cave would have weighed down the story, but they were happily ensconced in a doggy spa.

HEARTBREAK HOUSE

Natasha's hair, as sleek and black as a raven's wing, framed the delicate oval of her face. Raoul thought she had never looked more desirable than now, her dark, doe-like eyes filled with tears and a longing beyond tears.

"It's no good, darling," she whispered, summoning a valiant smile. "Papa has lost all his money. I must go to India with the Crawfords to mind their children."

"Darling—for you to be a nanny—how utterly absurd. And in that climate. You must not!" His square, manly face suffused with color, betraying the strength of his feeling.

"You haven't even mentioned marriage," Natasha whispered, looking at the bracelets on her slender wrists, wondering if they, too, must be sold, along with Mama's diamonds.

Raoul flushed more deeply. "We're engaged. Even if our families don't know about it. But how can I marry you now, when I have no prospects and your papa cannot give you a dowry."

Amy looked up. "Wonderful, Roxanne. Your strongest effort yet. Do Raoul and Natasha get married in the end?"

"No, no." Roxanne took the manuscript back. "They're just the first generation. Natasha marries a planter, not that she can ever give her heart to him, and Raoul dies of blackwater fever in the jungle during the Boer War, with Natasha's name on his *writhen* lips. It's their grandchildren who finally get together. That's the significance of the last page."

She turned the manuscript over and read aloud to Amy: "*Natalie had never met Granny Natasha, but she recognized the face smiling at the head of the bed as she embraced Ralph. It seemed to say 'Good speed and god bless,' and even, in the brief glimpse she caught before surrendering herself to love, to wink.*"

"Yes, yes, I see," Amy agreed, wondering if there were another person in New York—in the world—who could use *writhen* with Roxanne's sincere intensity. "Very much in the spirit of Isabel Allende or Laura Esquivel."

Roxanne looked haughtily at her editor. She didn't know the names and didn't care to learn them. If Amy thought the star of Gaudy Press needed to copy someone, it was time that Lila Trumbull, Roxanne's agent, paid a visit to Gaudy.

Amy, an expert on Roxanne Craybourne's own doe-like glances, leaned forward. "All the South American writers who've been winning Nobel Prizes lately have ghosts haunting their work. I thought it was a nice touch, to show the *New York Times* and some of these other snobs in the most delicate way imaginable that you are fully aware of contemporary literary conventions, but you only choose to use them when you can enhance them."

Roxanne smiled. Amy really was quite nice. She'd proved it the weekend she'd stayed at the Taos house, after all. It was terrible to be so suspicious of everyone that you couldn't trust their lightest comments. But then, when she thought how badly Kenny had betrayed her. . . .

Amy, watching the shift from complacency to tragedy on her star's face, wondered what nerve-storm she now had to deflect. "Is everything all right, Roxanne?" she asked in a gentle, caring voice that would have astounded her own children and grandchildren.

Roxanne gave a little sniff, brushing the hint of a tear from her left eye. "I was thinking of Kenny, and how badly he treated me. And then to see it written up in the *Star* and the *Sun*. It's too much to suffer tragedy, without having it plastered around the supermarkets where all one's friends see it and badger one forever. Not to mention Mother's insufferable mah-jongg club."

"Kenny? What—did his embezzling habits not die at the end of his parole?" Amy was startled out of maternal concern into her normal sardonic speech. She cursed herself as soon as the words were out, but Roxanne, in as full a dramatic flight as one of her own heroines, hadn't noticed.

"I thought he was trying." She fluttered tapered, manicured fingers, muscular from the weight of the rings they held up. "Mother kept telling me he was just taking advantage, but it's the kind of thing she's always saying about my boyfriends, ever since high school, jealous because she never had half as many when she was young. And when he hit me the first time and said he was *truly* sorry, of course I believed him. Anyone would have. But when he walked off with a million in bearer bonds it was just too much. What else could I do? And then, well, you know I had to spend *months* in the hospital."

Amy did know. There had been dreadful late-night meetings at

Gaudy Press over the news that Roxanne Craybourne might have suffered permanent brain damage when Kenny Coleman beat her up for the last time. Even Roxanne, on checking out of the rehabilitation clinic where she'd spent two months after leaving the hospital, had decided she couldn't forgive Kenny that. She divorced him, changed her security system, and moved the twenty-four-year-old gardener who'd brought her flowers every day into the master suite.

And then, in eleven weeks, gone on to write the thrilling tale of Natasha, the heiress victimized by her papa's trusted henchman, who embezzled all his money. "Poured white-hot from her molten pen" was the copy Gaudy would run in the national ad campaign.

"And I'm terrified that she'll marry that damned gardener next," Amy told her boss the next morning. "First it was the dreadful surgeon who slept with his women patients, then Kenny, and now some gardener who needs a green card."

Clay Rossiter grinned. "Send her a wedding present. She thrives on that kind of situation."

"I'm the one who has to hold her hand through all these trials," Amy snapped. "She doesn't thrive: she trembles on the verge of a nervous breakdown."

"But Amy, sweetie, don't you see—that's what makes her such a phenomenal success. She's the helpless waif who crops up in *A Clean Wound, Embarrassment of Riches,* and the rest. She believes in the agonies of all those idiotic Glendas and Corinnes and—who did you say the latest was—Natasha? Did you persuade her she couldn't call it *Passage to India?*"

"It was tough," Amy said. "Of course she'd never heard of E. M. Forster—I finally had to show her the video of *Passage to*

India before she listened to me. And even then she only agreed to a title change when I persuaded her that Forster's estate would make money from her because his fans would buy the video thinking it was her story. And no, I haven't got a clue whether he's got an estate or if it would get royalties, and don't go talking to Lila Trumbull about it either, for pity's sake. We're calling Natasha's misery *Broken Covenant*. Oh, by the way, *A Clean Wound* hit the paperback list at number two. We're printing another five hundred thousand."

Rossiter smiled. "Just keep feeding her herbal tea. Send her roses. Let her know we're her best friends. See if you can engender some kind of vicious streak in the gardener, assuming he hasn't got one already."

"*You* do that," Amy said, getting to her feet. "I've got a meeting with one of our few real writers—Gary Blanchard has done a beautiful book, a kind of modern-day quest set in the Dakotas. It'll sell around eight thousand, ten if we're lucky. *Broken Covenant* should make it possible to give him an advance."

After Amy left, Clay went back to the email he'd received from Jambon et Cie PLC, his corporate masters in Brussels. They were very disappointed in Gaudy's third-quarter performance. It's true they'd made a profit, thanks to the strong showing of *Embarrassment of Riches* in hardcover, but Gaudy needed several more bankable stars. They were too dependent on Roxanne Craybourne—if they lost her, they'd be dribbling along with the nickel-and-dime stuff, the so-called literary writers, which Jambon were doing their best to discard. If Clay Rossiter didn't want to be looking for a new job in six months, Jambon expected a marketing plan and sales numbers to show the list was acquiring market flexibility.

Clay curled his lip. Eighteen pages of numbers followed, a demented outburst of someone's spreadsheet program. Title by title Brussels had gone through Gaudy's list, with projections of sales based on changing the number of copies in BuySmart, the amount of bus-side advertising, the weight of paper used in dust jackets, the number of trips each sales rep made to key accounts. And Clay was expected—ordered, really—to give a written response to all these projections by the end of the month.

"The curse of modern business is not tight capital, bad management, low productivity, or poor education, but the personal computer," he snarled.

His secretary poked her head through the door. "Did you say something, Clay?"

"Yes. Idiotic boys—and girls—who've never held a book think they can run the book industry from three thousand miles away because they have a microchip that lets them conjure up scenarios. If they'd ever ridden a truck from a warehouse into BuySmart they'd know you can't even tell how many copies the store took, let alone—oh, well. What's the use. Send a note down to Amy that she cannot give her new literary pet—what's his name? Gary Blanchard?—more than twenty thousand. If he wants to walk, let him. If I see Farrar or Knopf on the spine when the book comes out it will not make me weep with frustration."

Isabella trembled in his arms. "I must not. You know I must not. Your mama, if she saw me—"

Her raven hair, enhancing the milky purity of her skin, cascaded over his shoulders as Albion pulled her to him more tightly. "She will learn to love you as I do, my beautiful Mexican flower. Ah, how could I ever have thought I was in love before?"

Albion Whittley thought distastefully of all the spoiled debutantes he'd squired around New York City. He wasn't just Albion Whittley—there was that damned IV after his name, meaning his parents expected him to marry someone in their set. How could he expect them to believe that the gardener's daughter stood head and shoulders above all the Bennington girls he'd had to date? The purity of her heart, the nobility of her impulses—every penny she earned going back to Guadalupe to her crippled grandmother.

"Albion, darling, are you enjoying your little holiday? Isabella, I left my gloves on my dressing table. Fetch them while my son and I have a talk."

Mrs. Albion Whittley the Third had appeared on the terrace. Her tinkling laugh and light sarcastic manner made both young people blush. Albion dropped Isabella's hand as though it had turned to molten lava. The girl fled inside the mansion. . . .

"Beautiful," Amy gushed, marveling at her own acting ability. "They triumph over every obstacle in the end? Or is it like Natasha, only able to experience happiness through her granddaughter?"

Roxanne looked reproachful. "I never tell the same story twice. My readers wouldn't stand for it. Albion joins the CIA to prove his manliness to Mama. He's sent on a secret mission to Central America, where he has to take on a drug lord. When he's wounded, Isabella finds him in the jungle and nurses him back to health, but the drug lord is smitten by her beauty. Since she knows Albion's mother is implacable, she agrees to become the drug lord's mistress. This leads her to a jet-setting career in Brazil and Spain, and she meets Mrs. Whittley as an equal in Majorca. In the end the CIA kills the drug lord, and Albion, who's never forgotten her, rescues her from the fortress where she's been incarcerated."

"Wonderful," Amy said. "Only I don't think we can call it *The Trail of Broken Hearts.*"

She tried explaining how disrespectful this might seem to the American Indian community, but gave up when her star's eyes flashed fury.

"Everyone knows how good I am to the Indians who live on my estate in Taos. I'm not having them wreck my book because of some hundred-year-old battle they can't forget. And after the way Gerardo treated me—he was half Indian, and always bragging about it—I think they owe me some consideration for a change."

"It's the libraries," Amy said hastily, trying to remember who Gerardo was: the gardener, she guessed, who'd brought Roxanne flowers every day. "Libraries can be *so* ignorant. We don't want your book shelved with Indian literature, do we? Your loyal fans will want to see it prominently displayed with new fiction."

They agreed in the end on *Fool's Gold,* with a Central American pyramid to be shown in jagged pieces around a single rose. Roxanne settled her jacket around her shoulders and held out her cup for more tea. She wasn't sure she even wanted a Central American pyramid. Wouldn't it always remind her of the misery she'd felt when Gerardo betrayed her? Her mother had warned her, but then Mother was positively lying in wait to watch her misery.

Amy, alert to the quiver in Roxanne's chin, asked if the cover decision troubled her. "We'll get Peter to do a series of layouts. You know we're not tied to what we decide today."

Roxanne held out a hand. Amy tried hard, but she wasn't sensitive—she wasn't an artist, after all—she lived in the world of sales and bottom lines.

"This whole discussion overwhelms me with memories of Gerardo. People said he only wanted me for my money. And to get a green card. But it's not impossible for love to flourish between a man of twenty-four and a woman my age. Just think of Cher. And despite all those ridiculous exercise videos she isn't any better looking than I am."

That much was true. Adolescent passion kept Roxanne young. Her own skin could indeed be described as milky, her dark eyes lustrous, childlike, confiding. Her auburn hair was perhaps hand-tinted to keep its youthful shades of color, but if you didn't know she was fifty-one you'd assume the rich browns and reds were natural.

"When I found him in bed with my maid I believed Gerardo, that she was homesick and he was comforting her. My mother ridiculed me, but how can you possibly live so cynically and ever be happy?"

Roxanne held her hands out in mute appeal—two poignant doves, Amy thought, murmuring, "Yes, indeed."

"But then, the night I got back from Cannes, I found them together at the swimming pool. He wouldn't come to Cannes with me—he said he shouldn't leave the country until his immigration status was straightened out, so I raced home a day early just to be with him, but then even I had to realize—and he'd paid for her abortion, with money I'd given him."

"You poor child," Amy said, patting her hand. "You're far too trusting."

Roxanne lifted her doe-like eyes in mute gratitude. Amy was so warm, a true friend, unlike the hangers-on who only wanted to sponge from her success.

"Someone in Santa Fe suggested I talk to a psychiatrist. As if I were sick!"

"How dreadful," Amy sounded shocked. "And yet, the right psychiatrist—a sympathetic woman, perhaps—could listen to you impartially. Unlike your mother or your friends, who are always judging you and scolding you."

"Is that what psychiatrists do?" Roxanne opened her eyes wide. "Listen?"

"The good ones do," Amy said.

"YOU DID WHAT?" Clay Rossiter screamed. "*You're* the one who needs a psychiatrist. We can't have her getting over her neuroses. They're what drive her books. Look, fifteen weeks after finding Raoul in bed with her maid she produces a bestseller for us. We can do an initial run of a million nine. That's our paychecks for the entire year, Amy."

"Raoul was the hero of *Broken Covenant.* Gerardo was her gardener. You're not the one who has to feed her tea and bolster her after the cad has been found out. Not to mention take her to Daniel and listen to the storm of passion while it's at gale force."

Clay bared his teeth at her. "That's what we pay you to do, Amy. You're the goddam star's goddam editor. She likes you. We even had to write it into her last contract that she will only work with you."

"Don't lose sleep over it. The chances are against Roxanne

entering therapy. She's more likely to pick some New Age guru and have a deep mystical experience with him." Amy got up. "You know Gary Blanchard signed with Ticknor and Fields? I'm really annoyed, Clay. We could have kept him for twenty-five thousand: he's very humble in his needs, and it makes me sick to lose a talented writer."

"He's humble because he knows no one wants to read artistic work. Let Ticknor and Fields have him. They don't have Jambon et Cie breathing down their necks." Clay picked up his latest printout from Brussels and waved it at her.

Amy skimmed it. Jambon was disappointed that Clay had rejected all of their previous marketing proposals but pleased he had let Gary Blanchard go. All of the scenarios they had run on Quattro showed that every dollar spent on advertising would lose them thirty cents on revenue from Blanchard's work. They definitely did not want anyone on the Gaudy list who sold fewer than thirty-eight thousand in hardcover.

"This isn't publishing," she said, tossing it back at him. "They ought to go into breakfast cereal. It's more suited to their mentality."

"Yes, Amy, but they own us. So unless you want to look for a job right before Christmas, don't go signing any more literary lights. We can't afford them."

> "I dreamed I went to the airport to catch my flight to Paris, but they wouldn't let me in first class. They said I was dirty and badly dressed, and I had to fly coach. But all the coach seats were taken, so I had to go by Greyhound, and the bus got lost and ended up in this dreary farmhouse in the middle of Kansas."

Dr. Frohlich nodded, fingertips together. "What does Kansas make you think of?"

Clarissa thought this was a funny question: Why hadn't he asked about first-class travel? But she said, "My mother grew up on a farm in Kansas. They didn't have indoor plumbing, and she had to wash all the bedsheets in a tub by hand."

"Do you suppose that's why she gets so angry when you wear expensive clothes and jewelry?" Dr. Frohlich said.

"Oh!" Clarissa put a hand to her mouth. "I thought she would be grateful to me for buying her a luxury condo, but instead, she's angry all the time."

Amy choked. "Roxanne. Dear. Where's the story?"

"It's here. In front of you. Have you forgotten how to read?"

"But your readers expect passion, romance. Nothing happens. The doctor doesn't even fall in love with Clarissa."

"Well, he does of course, but he keeps it to himself." Roxanne picked up the manuscript and thumbed through it. She began reading aloud, clicking her rings against the chair arm for emphasis.

Clarissa put her hand trustingly in the older man's. "You don't know how much this means to me, doctor. To finally find someone who understands my life."

Dr. Frohlich felt his flesh stir. His professional calm had never been pierced by any of his patients before, but this gamine-like waif, abused by father, constantly criticized by mother, so in need of trust and guidance, was different.

He longed to be able to say, "My dear, I wish you would

not think of me as your doctor, but your dearest friend as well. I long for nothing more than to protect you from the blasts of the stormy world beyond these walls." But if he spoke he would lose her trust forever. A psychiatrist must never violate the precious boundary between patient and doctor.

Roxanne dropped the pages with a thump, as though that settled the point.

"Well, why can't he marry her?" Amy asked.

"Amy, you didn't read it, did you? He's already got a wife, only she's in an institution for the criminally insane. But his compassion is so great he can't bring himself to divorce her. Clarissa realizes that she's been leading a shallow life, expecting fame and love and material rewards, but when she sees how self-sacrificing Dr. Frohlich is, she follows his example. She becomes a nun and spends the rest of her life working with a leper colony."

Amy blinked. She didn't think leper colonies still existed, but that was a minor point. "It seems a little downbeat for your readers, Roxanne. I wonder if—"

"Don't wonder at me, Amy," Roxanne snapped, her luminous eyes flashing magnificently. "Dr. Reindorf says happy endings are difficult to find."

Dr. Reindorf was the psychiatrist Roxanne had been consulting; she had dedicated the book to him and assured Amy he was *thrilled* to be part of her literary and psychological evolution.

"Dr. Reindorf says if my readers keep expecting every book to be a panacea they'll be just as bad off as me, expecting every man I fall in love with to solve all my problems."

"I WARNED YOU," Clay hissed. "Send her off to the fucking shrinks and what happens? We get cheap psychology about her readers and a book no one will buy. The woman can't write, for Christ sake. If she loses her adolescent fantasy about true love she loses her audience."

"Maybe Dr. Reindorf will betray her as badly as Gerardo and Kenny, and that surgeon, her first husband, who gave us *A Clean Wound.*"

"We can't take that chance," Clay said. "You've got to do something."

"I'm sixty," Amy said. "I can take early retirement. You're the one who's worried about it. You do something. Get the publicity department to plant a story in the *National Enquirer* that Roxanne is getting therapy from a child molester."

She meant it as a joke, but Clay thought it was worth an effort. His publicity staff turned him down.

"We can't plant stories about our own writers. Publishing is a community of gossips. Someone will know, they'll leak it to someone else who hates you, and the next thing you know, Roxanne will be at Harper's and you'll be eating wiener-water soup."

Clay began to lose sleep. *Final Analysis,* done in silver with a suggestive couch on the cover, came well out of the gate, but on-line reviews began killing it before the second printing was ready. It jumped onto the *Times* list in third place but stayed there only a week before plummeting to nineteenth. After two weeks, *Final Analysis* fell off the list into the black hole of overstock and remainders.

The emails from Brussels were hot enough to scorch the veneer from Clay Rossiter's desktop, while Roxanne's agent, Lila

Trumbull, called daily to blame Clay for not marketing the book properly.

"But you can't market long dull dreams and their interpretation," Clay howled to his secretary. "As I told Amy."

Clay fired Amy, to relieve his feelings, then had to rehire her the next morning: Roxanne had an editor clause in her contract. She could leave Gaudy if Amy did.

"Only if she's going to keep turning out cheap psychology it won't matter. Pretty soon even Harlequin won't touch her. And, by the way, we won't be able to afford you. How long has she been seeing this damned shrink?"

"About nine months. And the last time she was in New York she only stayed overnight so as not to miss a session. So it doesn't seem to be following the course of her usual infatuations."

"He's not in New York? Where is he?"

"Santa Fe. This isn't the only town with psychiatrists in it, Clay."

"Yeah, they're like rats: wherever you find a human population, there they'll be, eating the garbage," Clay grumbled. "Maybe he can fall off a mesa."

When Amy left, he stared at the clock. It was eleven in New York. Nine A.M. in New Mexico. He got up abruptly and took his coat from behind the door.

"I have the flu," he told his secretary. "If some moron calls from Brussels, tell him I'm running a high fever and can't talk."

"You look healthy to me," she said.

"It's the hectic flush of fever."

He was out of the office before she could chide him further. He flagged a cab, then changed his mind. The cops were forever questioning cabdrivers. He took the long slow bus ride to Queens.

At LaGuardia he found a man who looked like one of his self-important young Belgian masters, with a laptop, a garment bag, and his sports jacket slung over his arm. It was pathetically simple to remove his driver's license and a credit card and to buy a ticket to Albuquerque. On the long flight to Albuquerque, Clay went through his seat-mate's jacket pockets when the man got up to use the bathroom. According to his driver's license, the man's home was in New Mexico. He wouldn't miss his license until after Clay mailed it back to him, with cash for the price of the rental, of course.

Hey-ho for a life of crime, he grinned to himself at the car rental counter. If the Belgians fired him, he'd become an airline pickpocket.

The rest of his mission turned out to be just as simple. He called Dr. Reindorf and told him the truth, that he was Roxanne's publisher, that they were all worried about her, and could he have a word in confidence. Someplace quiet, remote, where they wouldn't run the risk of Roxanne seeing Clay and feeling spied upon. Reindorf suggested a mesa with a view of Santa Fe below it when he'd finished seeing patients for the day.

Clay made the red-eye back to New York with an hour to spare. The next morning Amy stuck her head around his door. She started to ask him something but decided he really did have the flu, his eyes were so puffy. It wasn't until later in the day that Roxanne called her, distraught at Reindorf's death.

"She somehow ended up going to the morgue to look at the body. Don't ask me why," Amy told Clay's secretary, since Clay had gone home sick again. "It had been run over by a car several times before being thrown from the mesa. The cops hauled her ex-gardener in for questioning but they don't seem to have any suspects."

"The news should revive Clay," his secretary said.

Ancilla's hands fluttered at her sides like captive birds. "You don't understand, Karl. Papa is dead. His work—I never valued it properly, but I must try to carry it on."

"But, darling girl, it's too heavy a burden for you. It's just not a suitable job for a woman."

"Ah, if you knew what I felt, when I saw him—had to identify his body after the jackals had been at it—no burden could be too big for me now."

Karl felt pride stir within him. He had loved Ancilla when she had been a beautiful, willful girl, the toast of Vienna. But now, prepared to assume a woman's role in life—to shoulder a load most men would turn from—the spoiled child lines dropped from her cherry lips, giving her the mouth of a woman, firm, ripe, desirable.

"I love it," Clay said. "I'm ecstatic. And you're calling it *Life's Work?* You got her to change it from *An Unsuitable Job for a Woman?* Good going. It's been only seventeen weeks since that shrink died and she's already cured. We ought to be able to print a million, a million-five, easy. I'll text Brussels. We'll go out to celebrate."

"I'd rather celebrate right here." Amy shut his office door. "We have a chance to sign a really brilliant new writer. Her name is Lisa Hazen, and she's written an extraordinary novel about life in western Kansas during the 1960s. She's going to be the next Willa Cather."

"No, Amy. Hispanic experience is good. Indian experience is outstanding; African is possible. But rural Kansas is of no interest to anyone these days except you. I'm certainly not going to pitch it to Brussels."

Amy leaned over the desk. "Clay, Lila Trumbull called me seventeen weeks ago. The day after you went home sick with the flu."

"She's always calling. How can you know what day it was?"

"Because that was when Roxanne's shrink's body was found." Amy smiled and spoke softly, as if to Roxanne herself. "Lila thought she saw you on the Albuquerque flight the day before. She was in first class and thought it was funny you were flying coach. She says she tried to talk to you but you didn't hear her."

Clay shifted in his chair. When he spoke his voice came out in a croak.

"I couldn't have been there. I was home with the flu."

"That's what I told her, Clay. You were home sick—she must have been mistaken. And that's what I'll tell anyone else who asks. . . . I'll call Lisa Hazen's agent and tell her fifty thousand, okay?"

Clay stared at her glassily, like a stuffed owl. "Sure, Amy. You do that."

Amy stood up. "Oh—and, Clay, in case you're thinking how good I'd look at the bottom of a mesa—or under a Seventh Avenue train—I hope you remember Roxanne's contract. She's made it clear a dozen different ways that she won't work with you."

Clay's secretary came down to Amy's office a few minutes later. "Can you talk to old Mr. Jambon in Brussels? Clay's gone home sick again. I hope there isn't anything serious wrong with him."

Amy smiled. "He's fine. He just got a little overexcited this morning about Roxanne's new book."

Note

I wrote "Heartbreak House" for an anthology called *Murder for Love,* ed. Otto Penzler (Dell, 1996). I had enormous fun creating over-the-top scenarios for a series of romance novels, and even more fun imagining the inner workings of the Gaudy Press. Whenever I need a publishing company in my work, I use Gaudy. They publish Murray Ryerson's biography of Boom-Boom Warshawski in *Brush Back,* and in this collection they publish Lisa Macauley's books in the story "Publicity Stunts."

I wrote "Heartbreak House" in 1996, when publishing was beginning to change in ways that completely altered the industry. Big conglomerates began acquiring publishing houses, and often the parent company might know next to nothing about the book business. In Gaudy's case, they've been bought by Jambon et Cie—i.e., Ham and Company, in Brussels.

Although Amazon existed in 1996, they were a fringe player. The sales behemoths of that era were the big-box stores, as well as the big chains, of which Barnes & Noble was the largest. Again, for all the books that I write, when I need a big-box store I turn to By-Smart, a company I created for *Fire Sale.* (Their motto: "Be Smart, By-Smart." I worked in advertising and sales promotion for thirteen years, and every now and then I like to flex those old muscles.)

Hailed by P. D. James as the "most remarkable" of modern crime writers, **SARA PARETSKY** is the *New York Times* best-selling author of twenty-two novels, including the renowned V.I. Warshawski series. She is one of only four living writers to have received both the Grand Master Award from the Mystery Writers of America and the Cartier Diamond Dagger from the Crime Writers Association of Great Britain. She lives in Chicago.

SARA PARETSKY'S V.I. WARSHAWSKI COLLECTION

KILLING ORDERS

From *New York Times* bestselling author Sara Paretsky comes another electrifying novel of suspense in her beloved V.I. Warshawski series…

They say blood is thicker than water. Private eye V.I. Warshawski has her doubts, especially when it comes to the bad blood between her and her great-aunt Rosa. But when the old lady reaches out, V.I. answers the call.

FALLOUT

Accompanied by her dog, V.I. tracks her quarry through a university town, across fields where missile silos once flourished—and into a past riven by long-simmering racial tensions, a past that holds the key to the crimes of the present.

Exciting and provocative, fiercely intelligent and witty, *Fallout* is reading at its most enjoyable and powerful.

SHELL GAME

Winner of the Sue Grafton Memorial Award!

A *Boston Globe* Best Book of 2018!

Acclaimed detective V.I. Warshawski tackles a pair of perplexing cases involving those closest to her in this compelling and timely adventure that centers on some of the most divisive and pressing issues of our time.

DEAD LAND

Chicago's legendary detective V.I. Warshawski knows her city's rotten underbelly better than most, but she's unable to avoid it when her goddaughter drags her into a fight over lakefront land use, in this propulsive novel from *New York Times* bestseller Sara Paretsky.

This electrifying story pushes V.I. close to the breaking point as she uncovers a terrifying conspiracy stretching from Chicago's parks to a cover-up of the dark chapters in America's meddling in South American politics.

LOVE & OTHER CRIMES

New York Times bestselling author Sara Parestky is the master of twisting suspense and propulsive plot. In this collection, Paretsky showcases her extraordinary talents with fourteen short stories, eight of which feature the indomitable detective. In their ranks is one brand-new V.I. story! This is an essential omnibus for lovers of crime and bone-chilling suspense.